THE ORIGINS OF
TRADE UNION POWER

THE ORIGINS
OF TRADE
UNION POWER

BY

Henry Phelps Brown

CLARENDON PRESS · OXFORD

Oxford University Press, Walton Street, Oxford OX2 6DP

London New York Toronto
Delhi Bombay Calcutta Madras Karachi
Kuala Lumpur Singapore Hong Kong Tokyo
Nairobi Dar es Salaam Cape Town
Melbourne Auckland

and associated companies in
Beirut Berlin Ibadan Mexico City Nicosia

Oxford is a trade mark of Oxford University Press

Published in the United States
by Oxford University Press, New York

First published 1983 ✓
Reprinted 1985

British Library Cataloguing in Publication Data
Brown, Henry Phelps
The origins of trade union power.
1. Trade unions—History
I. Title
331.88   HD6475.A2
ISBN 0-19-877115-0

Library of Congress Cataloging in Publication Data
Brown, Henry Phelps, Sir, 1906–
The origins of trade union power.
Bibliography: p.
Includes index.
1. Trade-unions—Great Britain—Political activity—
History.   2. Labor policy—Great Britain—History.
3. Trade-unions—Political activity.   4. Labor policy.
I. Title.
HD6667.B76   1983   322'.2'0941   83–1920
ISBN 0-19-877115-0

Printed in Great Britain by
Antony Rowe Ltd,
Chippenham

ACKNOWLEDGEMENTS

THIS work has been greatly helped by the support of two Foundations. The award of a Research Fellowship by the Leverhulme Trust Fund, and of a grant by the Houblon–Norman Fund of the Bank of England, enabled me to enjoy the research assistance of Dr Jane Morgan and Mrs Joan Hayes. The materials which these very able colleagues assembled were invaluable, and I wish to record also how much I owe to the stimulus they both brought me through their lively interest in the work.

Chapter XII, on trade unionism in the USA, benefited greatly from the comments of two American specialists in the field, Dr H. M. Douty, formerly of the US Department of Labor, and Professor Lloyd Ulman of the University of California at Berkeley. I am fortunate to have been able to submit my draft to such authorities. It had earlier profited by discussion with Mr Peter Cappelli of Nuffield College, Oxford.

Professor George S. Bain of the University of Warwick was most generous in providing me with works from his own library as sources for Chapter XIII on Canadian trade unionism, and in reading and commenting upon a draft of that chapter.

Chapter XIV, on Australian trade unionism, was read in draft by Professor Keith Hancock of the Flinders University of South Australia, and by the Hon. J. E. Isaac, Deputy President of the Australian Conciliation and Arbitration Commission. Again I have to record my good fortune in being able to submit my work to two experts in the field, and express my gratitude for the improvements that their comments enabled me to make.

Dr Terence Rodgers of the Bath College of Higher Education has kindly allowed me to draw on his researches into Sir Allan Smith. These have made a notable contribution in bringing out Sir Allan's significance.

The outstanding helpfulness of Dr Kenneth O. Morgan of The Queen's College, Oxford has placed me under a special obligation. With Dr Jane Morgan he has read a draft of the whole work and commented on it in detail throughout. He has saved me from many errors, and made suggestions for improvement of which I have availed myself freely. Thanks to his vigilance and learning, my final text is altogether better than the draft on which he worked with such care.

In fairness to the scholars whose help I have acknowledged, I must ask the reader to bear in mind that the decisions on the final text have been my own. I have not always accepted the advice of the commentators, and they must not be identified with anything I have said or failed to say.

These acknowledgements would be sadly incomplete without an expression of my indebtedness to the constant efficiency of my secretary, Mrs Victoria Banbury.

May 1982   HENRY PHELPS BROWN

CONTENTS

FIGURE

TABLE

INTRODUCTION: THE PRESENT IMPACT AND A HISTORICAL APPROACH

THE power of British trade unions has never been more manifest than in the hour of the British predicament. It appears very differently according to the standpoint of the observer. To those who are concerned with economic recovery and development, the trade unions appear as a factor in past retardation, and an obstacle to present endeavours to raise productivity. In the struggle against inflation, they have stood out as composing a body endowed with its own authority, willing to negotiate with government, but failing agreement, able to break through any line on pay that the Government tries to hold. There have followed denunciations of their monopoly power, and of the threat to the constitution manifest in their ability to defy the authority of government. 'In the last ten years', a former Permanent Secretary of the Department of Employment wrote in 1980, 'three successive Prime Ministers have been prevented by the industrial and political power of the unions from pursuing policies they declared essential in the national interest. All lost the elections which followed the defeat of their policies.'[1]

Yet the unions contain half the employees of the country. In recent years their membership has extended widely among the white-collared, even among the professional occupations, where not long ago trade unionism would have been unthinkable. Their power has been achieved by no deliberate strategy. They have grown out of the body of our society. If so many people in so many walks of life have joined them, that is because they meet needs that are felt widely and often deeply. The power that they have come to wield has been acquired in the course of a historical development, in which the systematic pressure of economic and social forces has been punctuated by the contingency of events. The study of this process helps us towards the understanding of present trade union power that is needed for the guidance of policy towards it.

The object of this work is therefore to examine some of the critical factors and historical turning-points in the process by which British trade unions attained their present position in the economy and polity. This historical approach will be reinforced by comparisons with the trade unionism of some other countries.

I

The power of organized labour to resist cost-reducing changes has been reckoned a major cause of the British predicament. A number of close comparisons have shown that the output per head of British workers is markedly lower than that of their opposite numbers in European industry. But this output per head depends on much more than the worker himself: for one thing, it varies with the amount and efficiency of the equipment working with him. Thus Christopher Saunders found that the value added per person engaged in engineering in 1970–2 was more than half as great again in both Germany and France as in Great Britain;[2] but this could not all be put down to the persons whose tally is divided into the output. There is also capital to be considered. Estimates available for the capital in the German engineering industry indicate that it was substantially greater than the British capital, but not in proportion to the much greater German output, so that output per unit of capital was much higher in Germany. One reason for this will have been that most of the German equipment had been installed more recently. And more than capital: the specific contribution of labour to performance has to be disentangled from many confluent factors, which react upon one another. 'Economic performance', Saunders concludes, 'depends less on the volume of resources available than on the effectiveness with which these resources – manpower, management, capital equipment, technology – are in fact used.'[3]

Special interest therefore attaches to one study that has analysed the sources of difference in productivity, and separated the contribution of labour from that of some other factors. This is a study by C. F. Pratten[4] of 100 international manufacturing companies.

On the face of the record, productivity appears relatively low in the British plants of these companies: in the North American plants output per employee-hour was higher by 56 per cent, in the German by 35 per cent, in the French by 28 per cent. But though the comparison was always between plants making similar products by similar processes, these plants might be of different size, age, and design; they might be more or less fully utilized; and they might have long or short production runs. When allowance was made for such factors as these, what was left of the differences in output per employee-hour was properly attributable to labour – to the relative incidence of strikes, restrictive practices, and manning quotas, and to differences in personal efficiency. Output per employee-hour now appears as higher by 12 or 13 per cent in the North American plants than in the British, by 19 per cent in the German plants, and by 10 per cent in the French. These are much lower figures than the gross figures found when every sort of influence is taken into account – as here at first, and earlier by

Saunders – but they are still formidable for a country that must export to survive.

Managers in a position to compare industrial relations in Great Britain with those in other countries in which their corporation operates have been keenly aware that they encounter special difficulties here. Sir Terence Beckett, when managing director of Ford (UK), spoke of the frustration of 'working with a trade union movement which is different in character from that in almost any other country. The trade union movement with which we deal is much more fragmented here than elsewhere.' In addition, the movement

has the debilitating and costly tradition of leaving the honouring of agreements to the discretion of individual members rather than establishing some form of control over them, to the general and long-term advantage of the members. In short, on this issue the unions don't deliver. The result is a less predictable situation than in other countries and it gives a greater opportunity for dissidents to ignore the interests of the majority and pursue sectional interests.[5]

This raises the question of stoppages, and their effect on productivity. Reports of the working time lost through industrial disputes in various countries indicate, so far as they are comparable, that the United Kingdom has been among neither those most nor those least affected in recent years. But the cost of stoppages has extended beyond the working days actually lost to the constraint on managers by the threat of the strike, particularly the unofficial local strike that may be called without notice at any time. The effect on productivity may be great where no stoppage occurs at all, because the likelihood of conflict has seemed so great that managers have not braced themselves to bring in cost-saving changes.

These resistances have checked investment, especially of the kind that would make labour redundant. But not only have they resisted the raising of productivity directly: by keeping up their pressure for higher pay in a market environment that has not allowed firms to cover rising costs by equally rising prices, they have helped to squeeze profits and cut down the funds available for investment. The rate of profit in British industrial and commercial companies was 10 per cent or more (making allowance for inflation) through most of the 1960s, but it was falling, and by the end of the 1970s it was below 5 per cent; investment meanwhile was reduced to a third of what it had been.[6] The share of the labourers in the harvest was being raised at the expense of the seed corn.

Some measure of the extent to which productivity has been held down by restrictive practices has been provided by the willingness of employers to buy those practices out. 'Productivity bargaining' began with the agreement reached in the Fawley refineries in July 1960. It was widely adopted in the plant bargaining that was now spreading. Its essence was that trade unionists agreed to changes in working practices such as they had formerly defended obdurately in return for rises in pay. Demarcation rules requiring certain tasks, however simple, to be performed exclusively by members of a particular craft; make-work rules requiring, for example, that a craftsman be accompanied by a mate; limitations on output – restrictions of these kinds had been developed to avoid flooding the market with a certain kind of skill, and generally to safeguard men's jobs. After years of full employment the men were prepared to trade these now dispensable safeguards for higher hourly rates. Management calculated that the restrictions raised labour costs so much that a substantial rise in rates was not too much to pay in order to get rid of them.

Alternatively, and subsequently, some employers have welcomed the changed balance of supply and demand in the labour market during the 1970s as an opportunity to reduce overmanning and remove restrictive practices. Though the Government's policy of fiscal and monetary restraint has made life hard for them, they approve it as the necessary condition for putting through the changes in the use of labour needed to raise British productivity to international levels. 'Industry has been forced by the discipline of the market place', a number of leading industrialists stated in a letter to *The Times*, 'to tackle slack working arrangements which have been encouraged by many trade union leaders, in a permissive climate of inflationary full employment and connived at by some managements for fear of risking industrial disruption.'[7]

2

Inflation in recent years has afflicted all Western countries in some degree, and both the increase in the size of British pay claims from 1968–9 onwards and the militancy with which they were pressed were part of an international movement. The British trade unions, moreover, gave their loyal support to policies of wage restraint brought in by Labour Governments, notably in 1948–50 and 1975–7; to that end their leaders bore much internal stress. But the structure of British trade unions and pay negotiation, and the prevailing attitude of the negotiators on the union side, both tend to quicken the rate at which pay in money is pushed up once the inflationary spiral is in motion. The disturbance of relativities by the uncoordinated agreements of different groups settling at different rates, and the disputes about differentials between unions representing different grades of worker, promote claims that chase one another upwards. The 'adversary' approach to industrial relations, and insistence on the autonomy of the union in 'free collective bargaining', mean that each group claims to be judge in its own cause, to reject any form of arbitrament or joint allocation, and to back its own claim by its own clout.

In 1968 the insistent propensity to push up money earnings began to hamper the economy in another way. That unemployment had risen over the half-million mark the year before might have been taken as a phase of the four-year cycle, but this time hardly any recovery followed. Instead in 1970 there was some further rise, and all through 1971 a steep one, until unemployment was higher than ever before in normal times since the war, and nearing the million mark. The familiar remedy of an expansion of demand was applied in full measure in the next Budget, with a prompt effect on employment. But there was an effect also on the balance of payments; and manual workers' earnings continued to rise at the annual rate of 13 per cent. The Conservative Government had taken office in 1970 committed against incomes policy, and had begun by dismantling the Prices and Incomes Board left by its predecessor: now it imposed a price freeze for six months, and set up its own Board to regulate pay under the norms of the ensuing phases.

President Nixon had made a similar U-turn in the United States the year before. In February 1971 he had reported to Congress that he did not intend to impose wage and price controls: in the following August he ordered a ninety days' freeze of pay and prices, to be followed by a phase of restraint under the surveillance of a Pay Board and a Price Commission. The similar steps had been taken for similar reasons. In the old cycle, cost-inflationary pressure used to fall as unemployment rose, but now the rise of unemployment was being accompanied by an unchecked upsurge of pay. Governments desirous of reducing unemployment could no longer simply expand demand, for a large part of the expansion would simply be absorbed by higher labour costs, and would serve only as fuel for inflation.

We can see now that these events marked a turning-point in economic history. The rise in unemployment of the preceding years was to prove no cyclical and temporary set-back. Instead, the rise of productivity was checked in the long term. Output per employee ceased to rise in 1973. At the same time the force of cost inflation was intensified. Thus 'stagflation' appeared. The rise of costs was heightened first by the upward trend of the prices of primary products in world markets, in 1972, and then by the traumatic lifting of the price of oil in 1973.

Meanwhile the British Government twice tried to stop the Mineworkers pushing through pay rises that it deemed contrary to the national interest: in both struggles the union won. When in the autumn of 1971 the National Coal Board offered the Mineworkers far less than the big rises they were claiming, the Mineworkers took the offensive by imposing a ban on overtime and holding a ballot that approved a strike which began in January 1972. They not only stopped all the pits, but maintained twenty-four-hour pickets throughout the country to stop the movement of coal wherever stocks were held. The Government declared a state of emergency; there were power cuts and black-outs; in February most industry was put on a two- or three-day week. A Court of Inquiry was now set up, and was looked to for recommended rises much greater than the last improved offer of the Coal Board. It provided them: the Mineworkers would not accept them until they had been to Downing Street and won yet more from the Coal Board there.

In the autumn of 1973 the story was repeated of the Coal Board offering far less than the rises claimed by the Mineworkers; but this time the Prime Minister was joined with the negotiations from an early stage, and what the Coal Board had offered was all that was permissible under the statutory incomes policy now in force. It was the upholding of this policy that was now at stake. By a majority of four-fifths the miners voted for a strike. Forthwith the Prime Minister called a general election. By a narrow margin he lost it. The minority government that now took office let it be known that a settlement might be reached outside the limits of incomes policy. It was so reached, and miners' pay was raised by some 25 per cent. The restraints of incomes policy were allowed to lapse when they reached their statutory term in July, and within 1974 earnings of employees as a whole rose as the miners' had done, by 25 per cent.

That explosion was alarming. The Labour Government had no wish to embrangle itself in wage control, but it was threatened not only with a runaway inflation at home but with a collapse of our balance of international payments. The TUC accepted the reality of the threat, and joined in social contracts that held the rise of pay down very effectively through the rounds of 1975–6 and 1976–7. But the second round was carried through only under rising tension between a Government that was forced to take up a loan from the International Monetary Fund on that Fund's terms, and trade unionists who saw the loss of their own purchasing power more clearly than the crisis of the economy at large, and resented increasingly the tying of their hands. The TUC in October 1977 voted a return to free collective bargaining. For one more round the Government held on course, though now without a social contract. The guideline of 10 per cent that it laid down for 1977–8 was soon breached by Ford's wage-earners and by the miners. Most significantly, in the public sector it was breached by a strike of firemen – not long ago it would have been unthinkable for them to strike and put lives at risk; but now they said that the responsibility was the Government's. In 1978–9, reacting against the 15 per cent rise in earnings that had actually come about, and trying to ensure that its measures of reflation would not be all mopped up in higher pay, the Government aimed at 5 per cent. Not for one moment would trade unionists abide by that. They swept it away in the 'winter of discontent', in which the salient events were a road transport strike with aggressive use of secondary picketing, and widespread strikes of manual workers in the public services, especially affecting schools, cemeteries, and hospitals.

These events of 1974–9 were transacted in part under an uneasy alliance between a Labour Government and the TUC, but in part as an outright conflict between the imperatives of national policy designed to check cost inflation and reduce unemployment on the side of government, and the traditional reactions of trade unionists against reductions of their real incomes and restrictions on their freedom to take industrial action in self-defence. Mr Callaghan as Prime Minister was well aware of the clash of principle. In 1976 he warned the Labour Party Conference that government could no longer spend its way out of a recession as governments had done in past years.

Each time we did this the twin evils of unemployment and inflation have hit hardest those least able to stand them. Not those with the strongest bargaining power, no, it has not hit those. It has hit the other poor, the old, the sick. We have struggled, as a party, to try to maintain their standards, and indeed to improve them, against the strength of the free collective bargaining power we have seen exerted as some people have tried to maintain their standards against this economic policy.[8]

Thus stagflation became manifest as the dominant problem of the 1970s. Production became stagnant, and even receded. Unemployment rose to rates not reached since the inter-war years, and to even higher absolute numbers. But there was no deficiency of monetary demand. The flow of spending had risen, and continued to rise; but it was matched, and continued to be matched, by the rise of costs. By the rise of labour costs it was more than matched. But the Government could not reduce unemployment by increasing investment and thereby the demand for labour, for the additional outlay would be taken up not in paying for more jobs at existing rates but for existing jobs at higher rates. Stagflation was being perpetuated by free collective bargaining and union power.

3

The extent of that power had already been signalized by the unions' rebuff of the endeavours of government to make them change their ways. Two such attempts had been made, one to check the unofficial strike, the other to provide a framework of law within which unfair industrial practices might be distinguished from fair. In both cases the Government was worsted. In the second, the trade unions defied not only the administration but the Crown in Parliament.

The first encounter was in 1969. In the previous year the Donovan Commission had reported 'that the prevalence of unofficial strikes, and their tendency (outside coalmining) to increase, have such serious economic implications that measures to deal with them are urgently necessary'.[9] This led the Labour Prime Minister and his Secretary of State for Employment to propose a procedure of general application that provided for the resumption of work during a 'conciliation pause' within which a settlement might be attempted. The Secretary of State would be empowered to issue an Order requiring the strikers to resume normal working for the twenty-eight days of this pause, and if they did not, they might be fined by an Industrial Board. It was further proposed that the Secretary of State should be empowered to issue Orders to terminate disputes between unions by laying down lines of demarcation, and to require a union to ballot its members before calling a strike; and it appeared that Orders of both these kinds might be enforced by the Industrial Board fining recalcitrant unions. The prospect of these fines – 'the penal clauses', as they were called – aroused a fierce opposition among trade unionists that came to be shared by a large number of Labour MPs and a substantial part of the Cabinet. In a day of critical negotiation with the leaders of the TUC the Prime Minister found himself obliged to withdraw the objectionable proposals in their entirety.

The succeeding Government proposed a much more comprehensive legal framework of industrial relations, and this was set up by the Industrial Relations Act of 1971. This Act distinguished a number of 'unfair industrial practices' and created an Industrial Court with jurisdiction over them. An employer, for instance, who suffered an unofficial strike, might go to the Court to seek an injunction against its leaders – an order, it might be, to refrain from picketing the workplace. These leaders no longer enjoyed the immunity from actions for damages that hitherto covered all those taking part in a 'trade dispute': henceforward that immunity attached only to trade unions registered under the Act and to persons duly authorized to act on their behalf. The provision for this registration was important: the Act conferred considerable benefits on unions, but only on those that had registered under it, and registration was conditional upon the rule book meeting certain requirements that the Act laid down. At a number of other points the Act brought the authority and sanctions of the law to bear upon the informal current course of industrial relations – thus to organize a strike to secure the dismissal of a non-unionist was made an 'unfair industrial practice'; or again, where an agreed procedure was lacking or there had been continued disputes, the Industrial Court was empowered to promulgate a recommended procedure and make it binding on the parties.

From its first view of the proposals so enacted the Council of the Trades Union Congress denounced them as 'a major attack on the rights of work-people and the trade union movement'. Its objection was not to this or that clause merely, but to the very idea of the Bill. When the Bill became law it set out to stultify it by ignoring it. It published a Handbook advising member unions how to avoid its incidence. It instructed them not to register under it, and in the end Congress expelled the twenty unions, mostly small, that did register. The unions tried also to ignore the Industrial Court. When this Court imposed swingeing fines on the two biggest unions for contempt, the fines were collected by sequestration of the union's assets. But its impact on current practices was brought home more vividly and in the eyes of many more alarmingly when it sent individual trade unionists to gaol. Twice it found that some dockers were guilty of an 'unfair industrial practice' in picketing inland depots, and enjoined them to desist; when they ignored the injunction it ordered them to be committed to prison. On the first occasion, the Official Solicitor appeared in the Court of Appeal before the men had actually been imprisoned, to argue successfully for the lifting of the order for lack of sufficient evidence that the injunction had been broken. On the second occasion, five dockers were actually imprisoned, but on the morning of the fifth day after the committal order the House of Lords in giving judgement in another case held that shop stewards were to be treated as agents of their union: the prisoners included shop stewards of the Transport and General Workers' Union, and on the afternoon of the same day the Official Solicitor applied to the Industrial Relations Court for the release of all five, and secured it. The ability of the Industrial Relations Court to enforce its orders had been challenged conspicuously and successfully; it even seemed that the Government had felt obliged to paralyse the arm of its own law. When a Labour Government took office in 1974 it repealed the Act forthwith. In its place, a new law retained and strengthened the protection the Act had given the employee against unfair dismissal, and added clauses establishing the immunities of striking unions and the rights of pickets.

Meanwhile battle had been joined between the Government and the miners. We have seen how they engaged twice over wages. The first struggle, in 1972, was notable for the miners' use of flying pickets and mass pickets, not only to stop the movement of coal but also to prevent oil-burning power stations receiving deliveries of oil. The second, early in 1974, was virtually submitted to the judgement of the electorate, as the major issue on which the Government went to the country; and as the Government lost the election the miners were held by some to have brought it down. The considerations in the voters' minds must have been complex; something turned on the timing of the election; the margin was in any case narrow; but in the face of the origin of the election and its outcome for the miners, this was the most conspicuous demonstration and endorsement of trade union power ever yet achieved.

The Conservative Government that took office in 1979 imposed cash limits on the nationalized industries. To keep within the limits on the coal industry while maintaining its investment programme, early in 1981 its Chairman proposed to close twenty-three pits. The protest of the miners' union was backed by the threat of an official strike; without waiting for this to be called 30,000 miners, mainly in South Wales, came out unofficially. In a major conflict the miners might have drawn on the support of the railwaymen and the steel workers under a new triple alliance. The Prime Minister who had recently declined to call in the union and the Coal Board to a meeting with ministers now concurred in a meeting between them and the Secretary of State for Energy in which it was agreed that the closure notices should be withdrawn and the Government would, in effect, reconsider the cash limit. On this John Biffin, the Secretary of State for Trade, observed that the Government had given in to industrial muscle, and added

I think the Government were very wise . . . to decide that this was not the area where they would put at risk their authority. I think that what we have seen demonstrated over the last week is something which we have long known in this country, and that is the capacity of certain sections of organized labour to exercise an extraparliamentary authority which is, if you like, almost baronial.[10]

4

A position that to outsiders seems a usurpation is held by many trade unionists to be entirely constitutional. Supported by the philosophy of pluralism, they regard themselves as an estate of the realm. They form such an estate, they would say, not merely in being entitled to a measure of self-government within defined bounds, and to the representation of their members' interests over against government: much more, in matters of basic concern to those members they really deny the right of any overarching authority of government altogether. Whatever the political colour of the administration of the day, the TUC will deal with it as one high contracting party with another. It will bargain with it. This was made clear by Len Murray in his Granada TV Lecture on 'The Democratic Bargain' in May 1980.[11] 'Effective government', he said, 'rests on acknowledging the pluralistic basis of our democracy.' 'Trade unions regard the state as a federal system.' In relation to Government they 'see their role as bargaining, as offering their co-operation – on agreed terms'.

Now it is true that Mr Murray began by speaking of bargaining as a creative process, a way of reaching consensus, and 'industrial democracy in action'; but this is to imply the acceptance of a common purpose. That is very different from the striking of a bargain between two parties each seeking its self-interest, and backing its quest with its bargaining power. Bargaining implies entering into an agreement to act in a certain way only when that has been made worth your while by what you get from the other side. It also implies using your power to inflict loss on the other side – or on associates, and the surrounding community – so long as it withholds assent to the terms you demand.

When that power is used in the name of trade unionism to resist the Government the question is raised whether the country is governable; and this, not only among the political opponents of Labour. A veteran Fabian and political scientist, Professor William Robson, writing before the Heath Government went down in its clash with the miners in 1974, declared that 'the most important domestic issue in British politics is whether the trade unions can ultimately defeat or destroy the policies of *any* government. The outcome of this conflict, which is ultimately based on the confrontation of political authority by industrial power, is by no means clear.'[12]

A poll conducted by Opinion Research and Communications in January 1980 put the question: 'Some people feel that British trade unions have too much power and show too little responsibility. Do you think this is true or not true?'[13] Seventy-eight per cent of all respondents, and even 56 per cent of active trade union members, thought it was true.

If bargaining were only the process of working out the mutual accommodation and understanding that Len Murray depicted, this response would be strange. But bargaining at every level has actually carried with it the possible exertion of trade union power to disrupt, to inflict hardship, to coerce individuals, and to obstruct the changes vital to an endangered economy. That has been seen and felt, up and down the country, even by those who had no choice but to take part in trade union action themselves. But the activists have not been constrained by any code or countervailing power, save for the transient effects of depression.

So runs the indictment. But 'I do not know the method', said Burke, 'of drawing up an indictment against an whole people.' The trade unionists of the United Kingdom at the present time amount to nearly half its whole working population. Man for man, and woman for woman, they are not less altruistic, reasonable, and public-spirited than their fellow citizens. If they seem often enough to be disaffected and bloody-minded, they are of the same stock as their parents who with high morale bore the blitz and formed the armed forces of the Second World War. Their propensities are often inimical to economic progress, but those are long-standing characteristics of the British people at large. Nor are they alone in combining to shelter themselves from competition and to profit from monopoly power. A hundred years ago the great economist W. S. Jevons observed, in the Preface to his work on *The State in Relation to Labour*, 'One result that clearly emerges from a calm review is that all classes of society are trades unionists at heart, and differ chiefly in the boldness, ability and secrecy with which they push their respective interests.'[14] In one issue of *The Times* a few years ago there appeared both a letter from Professor Friedrich von Hayek speaking of 'trade union leaders who owe their power to the very privileges which the law has granted them but which must be revoked', and the report that 'four leading telephone cable manufacturers who recently ran a price ring for more than ten years are to pay back £9m to the Post Office'.[15] The President of the National Graphical Association told the conference of his union in 1980, 'If we have a bad law, and there have been many in the past and we may be facing more, we have no alternative but to break it.'[16] We ask, by what right does he set the interests of his union above the law? But intense attachment to professional interest, and loyalty among brethren of the craft, produces the same refusal to comply among journalists. When the House of Lords decided that Granada Television must name the source within the British Steel Corporation from whom it obtained a document, *The Times* stated a reasoned case to show why this decision was mistaken and harmful: this justified the stand it took – 'we would not give our sources if we were in the same position as Granada.'[17] The difficulty arose because the Law Lords 'have little understanding of the way society operates in reality. Their personal detachment from society – except for the society of the law – has led to their divorce from the realities of the democratic system.'[18] Change that to the industrial system and industrial relations, and you have exactly what trade unionists would say of judge-made law, and of law made by Parliament in so far as it was lawyer-contrived. Their justification of their non-compliance could equally be that the law had been made in ignorance of the realities to which it was meant to apply.

It is also to be remembered that even when, judged by the rise of wages, trade unionists have been pressing forward relentlessly, their reactions have been largely defensive. They have been claiming rises to keep up with the cost of living, or to restore differentials between grades, or relativities with other occupations with which close comparison was customary. Even the miners, whose break-out was the most conspicuous, were only moving back towards the place in the league table from which they had come down during the years of the great contraction of their industry. In another sense the basic purpose of a union is and remains defensive: its purpose is to remedy the weakness, inherent in modern conditions of production, in the position of the isolated worker over against the employer. The larger the unit of employment, the more necessary the defence of the interests of those farthest from the centres of decision-taking. But even in small units, where contacts are closer, not all managers are considerate, humane, or even efficient. Restrictive practices, again, are a spontaneous and collective form of protection – as tariffs have been a form of protection obtained by employers: because the law has protected man's livelihood where this depended on the ownership of physical property but not, until recently, recognized any property in jobs, the trade unionist has done what he could to fill the gap.

This he has done wherever wage-earners have formed a numerous group, living solely by hiring themselves to an employer, with little prospect of doing anything else throughout their lives. Trade unionism, including those of its practices that are anti-social and counter-productive, responds spontaneously and naturally to the situation of the permanent wage-earner. The impulse to combination and restriction rises as that type of worker becomes numerous. Already at the opening of the eighteenth century – to take one example – the journeyman weavers of the West of England had tried to make good the pre-entry closed shop. In their employers' petition to Parliament in 1706 the journeymen were alleged to have demanded that no master should take any apprentice unless he was enrolled in their books, or employ any journeyman unless he was already a union member. It was further alleged that when they struck they terrorized blacklegs. The instance comes from C. R. Dobson's instructive work *Masters and Journeymen: a Prehistory of Industrial Relations 1717–1800*.[19] The evidence this work provides of manifold trade union activities – and of the interventions, mediatory as well as repressive, of the public authorities – is so full, and so striking in its continuity with the present day, that the term Prehistory in the title seems hardly appropriate. Where we find employment in the modern sense, the past becomes contemporary: despite all the differences of intervening centuries, wage-earners naturally react in the same way to the same predicaments.

Not only do some of the essentials of employment remain the same for the worker: the present attitudes of trade unionists have often been received by transmission from earlier times. Behind the leaders of today are the gaunt pioneers, the tenacious tireless organizers, the brave spokesmen putting their own jobs at the risk of the blacklist. There were fiery men whose patience gave out quickly and who turned to violence. There were studious, patient men, self-taught; and men whose unionism was sustained by deep religious faith. Among the rank and file there were the many thousands, men and women alike, who would hold out with grim unswerving loyalty through week after hungry week of strike or lockout. To many a trade unionist in the past, be he national figure or nameless, must be ascribed the virtues of courage, and self-sacrifice, and devotion to the common good.

In the very different world of today these forerunners are remembered. There are traditions in the regions still of the protagonists in the great struggles of the past. As thoughtful trade unionists look back on the rise of their unions, they see the working people on the march under their own leaders and their own banners. In a country whose social evolution has been exceptionally continuous, to say that the procedures and attitudes of today are the legacy of history is more than a platitude. There are implications for practical policy, for in more than one way the past of trade unionism is a living past. The workings of contemporary trade unionism cannot be examined, and operated upon, as if they had come off the drawing board. We can enter into the present problem of trade union power only when we have set it in the light of history.

5

History has many qualities to stir the imagination and grip the attention, but when we follow the historical approach to a present problem we expect insights from it. We had better speak of these rather than of the lessons of history. That there are lessons in some sense is agreed: history would not be a subject of serious study otherwise. But the lessons are not yielded as directives. Those of us, whether within trade unionism or without, who are concerned about its present place and functions in the economy, and who inquire how it has attained them, will not come by any instructional manual showing us how to set about repairs. On the other hand those who attempt to reform institutions without knowledge of their historical background are likely to make mistakes that those with that knowledge will avoid. What sort of guidance is it, then, that the knowledge instils? There are in fact several ways in which it informs the judgement without providing any specific prescription.

One of these derives from the fact that though history never repeats itself in the sense that a whole situation reappears, there are many common elements between past and present. Bygone affairs were not transacted on another planet: the motives, reactions, and propensities displayed in them are the same as those in play around us now. By studying them we enlarge and sharpen our knowledge of them. Chess players can improve their game by working through games of the masters, even though they themselves never encounter in their own later games any particular situation that they studied: what they will be retaining is the way in which the masters have dealt with possibilities, offensive or defensive. The clinical skill of the physician has been ascribed to the analysis of past experience subconsciously recalled: in his diagnosis of the case before him, he brings to bear his observations of cases studied in the past, though none of these may have closely resembled the one before him, and none may be explicitly present to his mind. The analytic historian who asks why past events followed the course they did is, like the clinician, analysing the influence and interplay of certain factors. These factors – not least human nature – are constantly present in human affairs. His understanding of the present will be increased by his view of them as they appear in the past.

If this holds of affairs at large, whatever the contemporary problems to be tackled, the case is stronger still within any one department of affairs such as trade unionism. For here the extent of recurrence and continuity is much greater than on the broad national front. The isolated wage-earner's sense of weakness in the wage-bargain; the tendency of men of the same craft to club together; the circumstances in which negotiations break down; the intensity with which men will defend the differential for their skill – time has brought changes in this field, but they are small in comparison with the core of identity, in attitude and propensity. Those who have not learned how long British miners sometimes held out without strike pay may misconceive the motives for striking, and underestimate the sacrifices that trade unionists will make when they are standing on an issue, as they see it, of principle. Economists unenlightened by history have fallen into the trap of supposing that trade unionists conduct their bargaining as a way of maximizing their gains.

Mention of the miners puts us in mind of another way closely associated with the diagnostic in which history yields insight. We know much more about an acquaintance as we learn his past history. His present behaviour is more significant if we know how it came about – if a man has a limp, did he have this from infancy, or was it a war wound? Insight and empathy depend very much on what we know of how people have come to be what they are. What is true of people holds also of institutions like trade unions. Our assessment of trade union power as it exists today will depend on our understanding of how it has been attained. Did it come about as the natural outcome of economic, social, and political development, or by the deliberate intent of trade union leaders, or according to the preponderant purpose of the community, or as the unforseen consequence of the actions taken by wage-earners in self-defence?

There is another way in which the past makes the present intelligible. It enables us to understand attitudes that are incongruous with the needs of the present day, for it shows how they have been inherited and preserved. We encounter the living past, the power of myth. A movement such as trade unionism has been until recently needs the unifying and galvanizing force of tradition. A 'group memory' is more than a figure of speech: events of the far past instil attitudes which institutions pass on to successive generations of entrants, who come to behave as if those events had happened to them. Their perception of the world about them is historically conditioned.

There is also this cautionary effect of studying history. Whatever the practical problems that we are tackling, we learn from history that human affairs proceed by accumulation of the contingent. We have to accept that contemporary trade unionism, no less than that of the past, is set in history, and changes in it will come about only under the complex unpredictable sway of historical forces. Among these will be the actions of those who pursue a conscious policy, and they may well be able to move unionism in the direction they seek; but there will be no solutions with the neatness of abstract systems.

6

The historical approach is supported here by a comparative study of trade unionism in the USA, Canada, and Australia. Comparative studies sharpen the definition of our view of our own country, both when they reveal similarities and when they throw up differences.

The similarities of institutions like trade unions make a powerful impression by their spontaneity. Anyone who looks back to the antecedent of the trade union in the gilds must equally be struck by the closeness of the similarity between its manifestations in very different times and places. The Dublin masons in the sixteenth century and the Porters' Gild of Peking in the twentieth are both active in preventing interlopers from entering their trade.[20] The masons of Aberdeen, the carpenters of Peking, and the craftsmen in the Panch of Ahmedabad, all use the same ways of deciding what rate to maintain and how to maintain it.[21] The seventeenth-century Japanese gilds called Kumiai maintained apprenticeship and enforced the closed shop like any European gild.[22] These propensities to combination, appearing in similar, sometimes almost identical regulations and institutions in widely separated times and places, cannot have been imported and copied from one another. That they grew up independently indicates that they – and their counterparts in the trade union – spring from drives that are basic to human nature. Some of the effects of those drives may be harmful, but they express needs that cannot simply be thwarted. In returning to British trade unionism after some study of the trade unionism in other countries, we can see even more clearly than by the light of the historical approach how natural, in the strict sense of that word, trade unionism is.

But we can do more than this: we can begin to distinguish the active from the passive factors in the setting within which it has developed. This we can do with the help of the differences that appear in the other countries. When we find American trade unions developing mainly the contract with the single corporation or plant we have to re-examine the considerations that show how much British unions and employers gained from industry-wide bargaining: what were the actual differences between the two economies, or societies, that set their negotiations on different courses? That the British trade unions should have promoted the Labour Party after Taff Vale seems so natural that only the facts need recounting: but when we find that the Canadian trade unions failed to launch a Labour Party, for all their legal disabilities, and the American trade unions never attempted it, we are made to think again about the necessary conditions for the British development. If the Australian trade unions, founded in the British traditions, for the most part accepted – indeed demanded – compulsory arbitration at the end of the nineteenth century, are we satisfied with the account given for the British unionists' withdrawal from commitments to arbitration by that time? Formally, one can say that the comparative method offers the student of human affairs some compensation for his inability to carry out controlled experiments. In these experiments, all the factors that bear on the outcome are held constant save one: the observed changes in the outcome can then be ascribed to those in the varied factor. When we compare trade unionism in countries with as much in common as those just named there is no question of 'holding all factors constant save one' – of the British and Australian settings, for instance, being exactly or even substantially alike in all respects save that one which caused the difference of attitude towards arbitration. Yet the similarities are extensive enough for the differences to be instructive. When we say that, we are implying in more formal language that many factors being common to the two countries can be eliminated as possible causes of what is specific to one or other of them. This does prove to help us greatly in our search for those causes. We come back to the study of our own affairs with fresh questions in mind: as the traveller returning from residence abroad notices things at home he never saw before.

Notes

[1] Denis Barnes and Eileen Reid, *Governments and Trade Unions* (London, 1980), p. x.

[2] This was after the figures of value added in national currencies had been converted to common units by applying 'purchasing power' exchange rates for machinery (C. Saunders, *Engineering in Britain, West Germany and France: some statistical comparisons* (Sussex European Research Centre, 1978), pp. 14–15).

[3] C. Saunders, *Engineering*, p. 87.

[4] C. F. Pratten, *Labour Productivity Differentials within International Companies* (University of Cambridge, Dept. of Applied Economics, Occasional Papers No. 50, Cambridge University Press, 1976).

[5] At an American Chamber of Commerce lunch, *The Financial Times*, 17 Jan. 1979.

[6] *Pay 1981/82* (Confederation of British Industry, Oct. 1981 (7)), Chart 17.

[7] *The Times*, 26 Nov. 1981.

[8] Labour Party Conference proceedings, 28 Sept. 1976.

[9] Royal Commission on Trade Unions and Employers' Associations. Report (Cmnd. 3623, June 1968, HMSO, London), para. 415.

[10] *The Times*, 23 Feb. 1981.

[11] Delivered in Guildhall, London, on 23 May 1980. The quotations that follow are from pp. 81, 84 and 80 of *The Role of the Trade Unions* (London, 1980).

[12] W. A. Robson, 'The Constraints on British Government', *Political Quarterly*, 44, 1973, 119.

[13] *The Times*, 21 Jan. 1980.

[14] London, 1882.

[15] *The Times*, 13 June 1978.

[16] Ibid., 23 June 1980.

[17] Ibid., 6 Aug. 1980, editorial, 'We shall keep our word'.

[18] Ibid., 31 July 1980, editorial, 'A charter for wrongdoing'.

[19] London, 1980. The reference is to p. 20.

[20] J. J. Webb, *The Guilds of Dublin* (London, 1929), pp. 112–13; J. S. Burgess, *The Guilds of Peking* (Columbia University Press, 1928), p. 80.

[21] K. D. Buckley, *Trade Unionism in Aberdeen 1878 to 1900* (Edinburgh, 1955); J. S. Burgess, *The Guilds of Peking*, p. 93; E. Washburn Hopkins, *India Old and New* (New York, 1901).

[22] Yosoburo Takekoshi, *The Economic Aspects of the History of the Civilization of Japan* (London, 1930), vol. III, ch. LXXVII.

I

THE VICTORIAN ACCEPTANCE OF THE TRADE UNION

THE history of British trade unionism is sometimes narrated as a struggle against oppression, and there are instances enough of conflicts long drawn out, of harsh reaction on the one side and fortitude in affliction on the other, to bear out that interpretation. Yet what is also remarkable is the extent to which the unions gained acceptance and approval in the course of the nineteenth century, and became integrated in the economic and political structure of the country. This came about, on the side of government and the employers, through a recognition that the trade unions of the day were not capable of obstructing the economy, and on the whole played a helpful part in it. Their advocates could show how responsibly they conducted their business, and what useful functions they performed for their members. Monopoly power might be implicit in combinations, but those of manual workers were observed to be subject to such effective constraints that though they could soften the impact of market forces they could not resist them. In the experience of Victorian employers it was the most skilled, responsible, and steady workmen who took the lead in the unions, and unionism had an uplifting influence on the weaker brethren. Industrial relations were found to be at their best when strongly organized unions entered into voluntary negotiations with stable associations of employers.

This perception of trade unionism was to have two consequences of profound importance for the development of the United Kingdom in the twentieth century. By convincing a majority of parliamentary opinion irrespective of party that the trade unions had a function to perform that was invaluable to their members and useful to the economy, they enforced the conclusion that if the common law were inimical to the unions, then a cavity must be hacked in it within which they might function. By promoting the acceptance of the trade unions as part of the structure of society, it ensured that when manual workers came increasingly to look for social and economic reform they found ready to their hands a labour movement in the form of the trade unions that was sited and aligned to work for change from within, not to batter the walls from without. In this second consequence may lie a reason why revolutionary, communist, and Marxian parties have never taken hold in the United Kingdom.

But the perception of trade unionism that took these effects is remote from our view of the unions today. It was even very different from any assessment that would have been freshly formed of the unions as they actually were by the time Parliament came to take its most drastic action upon their legal position. The conviction that their legal immunities must be affirmed by statute, which was to reach its fullest application in the Trade Disputes Act of 1906, was founded on a view of the trade unions that by then had ceased to correspond with the facts. It is therefore worth pausing here to look a little more closely into how that view was formed.

I

The inability of the unions to resist market forces had been a fact of experience. As communications improved, and the numbers seeking work continually rose, the potential of competition increasingly limited the power of any group to exact a higher price for its services. Technical change was always liable to bypass any toll-gate held by a union. When Parliament came in 1871 to face the question of whether to legitimize or outlaw the increasing number of trade unions, the unions of the day were probably less able to obstruct the economy by the exertion of monopoly power than their predecessors the trade clubs had been in the narrower channels of the early century. The wool-combers were a case in point. Adam Smith had remarked on their monopoly power in his *Wealth of Nations*, in 1776:

Half a dozen woolcombers, perhaps, are necessary to keep a thousand spinners and weavers at work. By combining not to take apprentices they can not only engross the employment but reduce the whole manufacture into a slavery to themselves, and thus raise the price of their labour much above what is due to the nature of their work.[1]

For long the trade club of the wool-combers stood astride the Yorkshire worsted industry, prescribing wage-rates, limiting the number of apprentices, and enforcing its demands by strikes. But then came mechanization.

Down to 1825–32 [Clapham has recorded] no comb machine had been a real success; but the beginnings of machinery helped in the rout of the Yorkshire combers after their great strike of 1825. For another twenty years the machine was to hang over them; it fell and crushed their union to powder in the late forties. Thereafter, for more than half a century, few trades were so ill-provided with trade union machinery as wool-combing.[2]

From the 1870s onwards the Cambridge economist Alfred Marshall made the world of labour his special concern, and he was moved to ask why the bricklayers of his day did not proceed to get 'an enormous rise' by pressing their own demands independently, for such a rise in their own pay would still make only a small proportionate increase in the whole cost of a building.[3] He found the reason lay in the restraints that the market laid on them. Though unlike many other trade unionists they were sheltered from foreign competition, they could not main-tain a monopolistic price for their labour unless they could stop non-members within the country from taking up bricklaying. They would also have to be assured that the other building trades did not follow suit and push their wages up too, so as to raise the whole cost of building to a prohibitive height. But neither of these conditions was likely to be satisfied. Some years later, about 1880, the masons pressed their demands so hard by striking that builders would not accept penalty clauses for failure to complete by a given date in contracts that contained much stonework; architects then devised patterns of brick-work in lieu of masonry. 'Perhaps another generation will elapse', Marshall wrote later, 'before the number of skilled masons in England is as large as it would have been if their union had shown more moderation in 1880.'[4]

If the trade unions did not appear able in practice to exploit monopoly power, neither were they credited with much bargaining power. The rise – and fall – of wages was seen still to depend on the market forces of supply and demand, even in the presence of strong trade unions. The minority report of the Royal Commission of 1867–9 was actually able to cite evidence showing that some of the most powerful trade unions had done little to press wage claims.

The engineers embrace the great body of workmen in the trade and have a reserve fund which at one period amounted to nearly £150,000. . . . But the wages of their trade have hardly been raised for 25 years except by the voluntary act of the masters. . . . The union since the year 1852 has engaged in no general strike and has expended but a trifling portion of its funds (about 6 per cent) in disputes about wages. . . . The shipwright's union is one of the most powerful and embraces almost the whole body of workmen; yet wages are regulated to this day by the old scale of 1825 and have hardly risen since that date . . . The operative printers have long had completely organized societies, embracing almost the entire trade; yet we learn from a member of the Master Printers Association of London that there has been absolutely no rise in wages of compositors from 1810 to 1866.[5]

When Parliament came to consider legislation consequent upon the reports from the Royal Commission, an influential declaration in

favour of legalizing the unions was made by Thomas Brassey, the son
of the great railway contractor. He was guarded initially in his assessment of the trade union's effects.

So far as their action had been brought to bear upon trade he regarded it . . .
as essentially illiberal, anti-social and not conducive to the general advantage
of society. Upon the other hand he believed that the power of trade unions
had been greatly exaggerated; nor did he think they had rendered that service
to the working man in procuring an increase of the rate of wages which some
of those whose guidance they followed could lead them to suppose, or that
their agitation and organization could influence the rate of wages in a sense
unfavourable to the interests of the masters to an extent to which some
alarmists thought possible. . . . It was argued that because wages had been
advanced in some cases at the request of the trade unions, therefore trade
unions were the cause of the increase of wages. It was, however, to the
operation of the laws of supply and demand, rather than the action of trade
unions, that the increase of wages ought to be attributed.[6]

In fact the trade unions learned the practical wisdom of being guided in
the timing and amount of their claims for rises, or the strength of their
resistance to the employer's demands for reductions, by what came to
be called 'commercial considerations' – that is, the current and prospective state of the industry, and the phase (as we see it now, looking
back) of the eight-year cycle. Wage-rates were most likely to be raised
in the rising phase of the cycle, and to be reduced in the falling phase,
though not by as much as they had previously risen. A protracted
stoppage caused great hardship, even when strike pay was issued, and
would not be deliberately entered into on a calculus only of immediate
returns.

A further restraining influence on the exertion of union bargaining
power lay in the general atmosphere of a customary structure of
differentials between grades, and relativities between industries. This
was implicitly accepted as a guide to reasonable settlements.

If we look closer at the pre-war arrangements for adjusting relations [Henry
Clay said, looking back in 1927], it becomes clear why so few disputes led to
stoppages. In a sentence, the parties to the negotiations never had to face the
problem as it presents itself to analytical study; all they had to do was to make
slight modifications and adjustments in a system of rates and conditions,
which was generally accepted . . . If we seek an explanation of those wage
standards, we can find it only by an historical investigation; but, however and
wherever established, they were stable compared with the prices of commodities, they tended to move together and to preserve stable ratios between
them, and they may fairly be said to have constituted a system.[7]

For these reasons the trade unions of the Victorian era commended
themselves, at least negatively, in that they were found to have little or
no power to deflect or obstruct the working of market forces – to push

up wages at the expense of the profits of the employer, or the international competitiveness of British industry. In 1892 Alfred Marshall summed up a cautious assessment by saying that 'the power of Unions to raise general wages by direct means is never great; it is never sufficient to contend successfully with the general economic forces of the age, when their drift is against a rise in wages.'[8]

2

But the trade unions also commended themselves positively. They not only performed a useful function for their own members by providing various forms of social insurance, but they stood out as attracting the most skilled and responsible workmen, and exerting a steadying and uplifting influence on their members generally. Lyon Playfair, the great technologist (as we should say today) remarked on this incidentally in the course of an address 'On Industrial Competition and Commercial Freedom' in 1888. 'What class of workmen produce cheap things?' he asked. 'They are the men of technical skill and trained intelligence who seek more education for themselves and their children . . . They are men who, by combination, have raised their position and shortened their hours of labour.'[9] The implication for the employer was not only that trade unionists were to be respected because they were personally among the most skilful and intelligent of his employees, but that the labour which received the full trade union rate was not dear, because it was highly productive. This was all the more so, because the unions actually strengthened the character and improved the performance of their members. On this consideration, so unfamiliar at the present day, the Victorians laid stress. Alfred Marshall concluded that 'the power of Unions to sustain high wages depends chiefly on the influence they exert on the character of the workers themselves.' He instanced what unionism had done to give 'a new spirit and a trust in and care for one another' to the London dockers, 'once among the most miserable, and the dearest workers in the country'.

Though there is no longer room [he continued] for Unionism to render services of this order to skilled workmen, there is still much that it can do even for them. Unions all can, and most of them in fact do, exercise an elevating influence by punishing any member who conducts himself badly, or who is frequently out of employment from excessive drinking.[10]

The same approval of the uplifting influence of the unions, and in particular their stress on temperance, was expressed in one of the two reports brought in by the Royal Commission on the Relations of Labour and Capital set up in Canada in 1889. Trade unions, this report said, 'inculcate a spirit of self-control, of independence and of self-reliance . . . and are earnest promoters of temperance principles among the working class'. In an Appendix it added that 'where organisation has made much progress the moral standing of the people is also high. No one can become a member who is not sober.'[11]

The attitudes of the employers were various. We shall deal with them in the chapter devoted to employers' organizations. Some employers were implacably opposed to unionism. Some big employers – notably most of the railway companies – refused to recognize unions. On occasions, some employers united to fight and break a union. But the drive to resist was never sufficiently widespread or powerful to overcome the obstacles to combination inherent in the dispersion of small firms and the individualism of their proprietors. No national employers' movement of any consequence developed against the unions. In the 1890s some employers found themselves caught between increased foreign competition and the heightened militancy of the unions; but until then, and those sectors apart, most employers who had unions to deal with had been able to work out a tolerable way of getting on with them. Eminent spokesmen of the employers there were who would claim more than that, who would agree with Alfred Marshall that though unionism brought liability to the occasional major strike, that prospect was still preferable to the continually harassing stoppages of the guerrilla warfare that must ensue otherwise. 'There is no doubt' Sir Benjamin Browne, a spokesman of the iron and steel and coal industries of the North East told the Royal Commission on Trade Disputes, 'that they [the trade unions] stop far more disputes than they make and I am a great upholder of trade unions.'[12] By the turn of the century there was already a long experience of negotiation in a variety of forms, and where that was established the union appeared as no less indispensable than its existence was intelligible. At a time when institutions were on so much smaller a scale than now, and more relations were face to face, many an employer would have seen the union as a natural enough development among men with whose working lives he was closely acquainted. In any case the development was inevitable. As Thomas Brassey said, in the speech already quoted;

As to trade unions, the guilds of the Middle Ages were their forerunners and taking into account the great changes which had since been brought about – the substitution of machinery for manual labour and the concentration of workmen in great industrial centres – the formation of combinations with the view to carrying out objects in which they felt interested was he thought but the natural result of what had occurred. It was further worthy of notice that no law, however severe, had succeeded in putting a stop to such combinations, and that the severity of the enactments against them had simply had the effect of causing proceedings to be secret which it was for the general advantage should be public.'[13]

The integration of the trade union in Victorian industrial society was thus made easier by the absence of any consolidation of the employers as a hostile force.

The judgement of members of the two Houses of Parliament, and the society with which they mingled, will have been influenced by the findings of the two Royal Commissions that examined the trade unions during the reign of Victoria – the one in 1867–9, the other in 1891–4. Each was set up because of manifestations disturbing to the public awareness: the earlier one arose out of criminal assaults on blacklegs in Sheffield and Manchester, that of the 1890s out of the sense of a new animus and purpose stirring the world of labour that had been signalized in the great London dockers' strike of 1889. But the effect of both reports was to establish the main body of trade unions as useful components of the social and economic structure. The union spokesmen examined by the earlier Commission were evidently outstanding for their personal respectability, and distinguished by the prudent conduct of their unions' affairs. The Minority Report of 1869 concluded:

It does not appear to be borne out by the evidence, that the disposition to strike on the part of workmen is in itself the creation of unionism, or that the disposition increases in proportion to the strength of the union. It appears in fact that the relation of the unions to strikes is rather the converse, and that many unions are hastily formed when the spirit of demanding a rise is rife; but that the effect of the stabilised societies is to diminish the frequency and certainly the disorder of strikes and to guarantee a regularity of wages and hours rather than to engage in constant endeavours to improve them. . . . It appears that the strongest, richest and most extended of all the unions are to be found in those trades in which the wages and the hours of labour show the greatest permanence, and in which on the whole the fewest disputes occur.[14]

The Report of 1894 concluded, largely on the evidence of leading employers, that industrial relations were at their best when strongly organized trade unions met stable employers' associations in voluntary negotiations. The leaders of a strong union, it was true, might some-times bring it out on strike when its members would not have moved of themselves; and when powerful organizations on both sides did become involved in a conflict, it was often protracted. But the alternative was worse – in the absence of well-established unions there would be 'continual local bickerings, stoppages of work, and petty conflicts'. A study of industrial relations on the Tyne in the 1880s remarked on 'a growing consensus of opinion that the legal recognition of trades unions has run side by side with the disuse of illegal practices, and that the growth of organization is almost coincident with increasing willingness to listen to reasonable argument.'[15]

Of themselves, then, institutions had been shaping aright. Public

policy should welcome the continuing extension of voluntary organization on both sides of industry.

This judgement went beyond any verdict that found in favour of the
trade union simply as a means of benefit to its members, for it held in
effect that the union should be enabled to exercise its functions as a
useful and indeed indispensable part of industrial organization. To
those contemporaries whose sympathies went out directly to the great
mass of the working population, leading laborious lives at standards of
living that though rising were still narrow, with few safeguards against
misfortune, the case for the trade unions would be made out if they
could be shown to have improved the lot of their members, without
having imposed evident and equivalent losses on others. It was in this
way that Sidney and Beatrice Webb envisaged the unions in their two
great works, the *History of Trade Unionism* (1894) and *Industrial
Democracy* (1898), which are landmarks in the history of the labour
movement. But these immensely weighty, scholarly, and persuasive
volumes must also, by their careful and assiduous argument, have
conveyed the impression that the unions they surveyed formed an
essential part of any system of rational social administration, such as
was dear to the authors' hearts.

Meanwhile there had been an integration of trade unionism within
the body politic as well as economic. The parliamentary activity of the
TUC and the rise of Labour as a political party will be considered in
Chapter IV. Here we may remark on the entry of trade unionists
personally into positions of an elevation not previously accessible to
manual workers. The first two be be elected to the House of Commons
were Alexander Macdonald and Thomas Burt of the miners, who
entered the House in 1874. In 1881 a trade union leader was made a
factory sub-inspector, and four more were appointed by 1886. The
leader of the stonemasons, Henry Broadhurst, was the first trade
unionist to hold office in government when he became Under-
Secretary in the Home Department in Gladstone's administration of
1886. While he was in that office six union officials were appointed as
Justices of the Peace. Thomas Burt was Parliamentary Secretary to the
Board of Trade in Gladstone's last administration, in 1892.

The memoirs of these accepted leaders of Victorian unionism reveal
them as deeply deferential. John Burns has left an account of how the
'old' unionists appeared in the eyes of the 'new' at the Congress of
1890:

Physically the 'old' unionists were much bigger men than the 'new', and that,
no doubt, is due to the greater intensity of toil during the last twenty or thirty
years. . . . The 'old' delegates differed from the 'new' not only physically but
in dress. A great number of them looked like respectable city gentlemen; wore
very good coats, large watch-chains and high hats – and in many cases were of

such splendid build and proportions that they presented an aldermanic, not to say a magisterial form and dignity.[16]

The touch of caricature brings out the assimilation.

3

Yet there was one respect in which even the old unionism remained intrusive and discordant. From the acceptance with which trade unionism had come to be received, the law courts had stood out. Between the common law and the power of combination there was a basic conflict: the common law protected the rights of the individual, which combinations inherently overrode or impaired. Even when unions had been freed from all taint of criminality, they still found that they could not take what to them were normal and necessary actions without inflicting damages on others to whom the courts would give redress. If the common law continued to be upheld and applied, the unions would be prevented from performing their accepted functions. In three or four ways the inherent opposition between the cohesive propensities of combination and the individualist and liberal presumptions of the common law came to a head at the turn of the century. The next two chapters consider how the issues were resolved, and reflect on the outcome.

[1] Adam Smith, *Wealth of Nations*, Bk. I, ch. x, pt. II.
[2] J. H. Clapham, *An Economic History of Modern Britain*, vol. I (Cambridge, 1926), Bk. I. ch. v, p. 206.
[3] J. K. Whitaker (ed.), *The Early Economic Writings of Alfred Marshall*, vol. 2 (London, 1975), p. 346.
[4] Alfred Marshall, *Industry and Trade* (London, 1919), Bk. III, i. 4, p. 409.
[5] Parl. Papers, 1868–9, vol. XXXI, p. 270.
[6] Parl. Debates 1869, vol. CXCVII, 1358.
[7] Henry Clay, *The Problem of Industrial Relations* (London, 1929), pp. 12, 13.
[8] Alfred Marshall, *Elements of the Economics of Industry* (London, 1892), Bk. VI, ch. XIII, p. 19.
[9] The extract is from *Memoirs and Correspondence of Lyon Playfair*, ed. Wemyss Reid (London, 1899), p. 370.
[10] Marshall, *Elements*, Bk. VI, ch. XIII, pp. 16–17.
[11] Greg Kealey, *Canada Investigates Industrialism* (University of Toronto Press, 1973), pp. 36, 54.
[12] Report of the Royal Commission on Trade Disputes and Trade Combinations, 1906: Evidence, Parl. Papers 1906, vol. LVI, Q.2780.
[13] Parl. Debates 1869, vol. CXCVII, 1357.
[14] Parl. Papers 1868–9. XXXI. [4123], p. xxxv.
[15] L. L. Price, *Industrial Peace* (London, 1887), p. 6.
[16] *A Speech by John Burns on the Liverpool Congress* (London, 1890), quoted here from R. W. Postgate, *The Builders' History* (London, 1923), p. 343.

II

THE TRADE UNION AS A COMBINATION, AND THE PRINCIPLES OF THE COMMON LAW

I

ANY combination conflicts by its very nature with the endeavour of the common law to preserve the freedom of the individual. Without taking any unlawful action its members may bring a crushing pressure to bear upon another person. Each may do what would be of small account if he did it alone: he may refuse to sell below a certain price, he may withdraw his custom or his supplies from a certain trader, he may leave a certain job. But when a number of persons combine to take such action in concert, their monopoly, boycott, or strike can inflict great, perhaps ruinous losses on others.

This potential of combination led a Lord Chief Justice of the eighteenth century, Lord Mansfield, to declare that a trade union (as we should call it today) and a price ring were both criminal conspiracies, inherently and without their members taking any unlawful action.

Persons in possession of any articles of trade [he said] may sell them at such prices as they individually may please, but if they confederate and agree not to sell them under certain prices, it is conspiracy; so every man may work at what price he pleases, but a combination not to work under certain prices is an indictable offence.[1]

In a more restricted but still very wide form this reaction of the common law survived until the 1870s. The courts by that time differed from Lord Mansfield in that they held that men were free to agree together not to work for less than certain rates, and to withhold their own labour in concert if those rates were not forthcoming; but if they went beyond this, and tried to secure the withdrawal of other men working for lower rates, they were seen as passing over from the legitimate pursuit of their own interests to an indictable conspiracy to inflict injury. Any trade union activity in the way of recruiting or picketing might be treated as interference and obstruction; to threaten a strike might be coercion and molestation. But in 1869 the Royal

Commission on Trade Unions reported that 'the effect of the doctrine of conspiracy ... ought not to continue'. In 1875 Disraeli's Government enacted that 'an agreement or combination by two or more persons to do or procure to be done any act in contemplation or furtherance of a trade dispute ... shall not be indictable as a conspiracy if such act committed by one person would not be punishable as a crime.'[2] That was final. Since then there has been no question of the normal function of the trade union, the concentration of action to defend and advance common terms and conditions of employment, being impeded by the criminal law in time of peace. In wartime, it is true, striking was made an offence under the law. It is also true that if pickets overstepped a certain line in their endeavours to persuade they could be prosecuted for intimidation. But these exceptions apart, trade unionists by acting in combination could inflict injury on others and obstruct them in the course of their business without criminal taint, provided that their actions were not individually of a criminal kind, and that they were taken – 'the golden formula' – 'in contemplation or furtherance of a trade dispute'.

2

The Act of 1875 has been seen as the affirmation of democratic values in place of the narrower outlook of judges whose social background made them insensitive to the needs that trade unions were meeting, and hostile to the wage-earners' assertion of their claims. But over and above any such difference of attitudes there was a basic divergence between the principles of the common law and the realities of industrial life. The common law, Sir Otto Kahn-Freund has pointed out, 'knows nothing of a balance of collective forces. It is (and this is its strength and its weakness) inspired by the belief in the equality (real or fictitious) of individuals, it operates between individuals and not otherwise.'[3] On the one hand, it is concerned to protect the individual in his freedom to conduct his own affairs in his own way, without obstruction, molestation, or injury by others. It sees the employer as an individual, and is not able to distinguish between one small employer among a hundred such, each hiring one or two workmen, and the great employer providing their sole locally available source of livelihood for hundreds of workers. It sees only the contract of employment between the individual workman and the employer, and is not able to find a status for the combination of workmen that negotiates a collective agreement, or a place for the terms of the agreement itself.

From this incongruity between the presumptions of the common law and the circumstances of actual labour markets a number of difficulties arose when issues of industrial relations came before the courts.

First, there was the conflict already noticed between the formation of trade unions to defend the economic liberties of their members, and the prima-facie assumption of the common law that a combination was tainted with conspiracy. This conflict arose in the world of the old-style craftsmen: indeed one can see how individuals would turn to unionism even in what was initially a freely competitive labour market. For in the assertion of each person's right to exert his labour as he deems best, there is a contradiction: what one person chooses to do may be impeded and even rendered impossible by what someone else chooses to do. Free competition that gives openings to the enterprising exposes all persons to jostling and disturbance. Working life has been made tolerable in practice only because there have been few labour markets in which competition has been really free: there have been barriers to competition in the form of customary attachments and costs of movement, and producers could follow a traditional way of life within the shelter of those barriers. But from 1760 onwards the rapidly rising labour force flowed over them, and revolutionary improvements in transport began to break them down. The craftsman who wanted to take a pride in his work and sell his highly finished products at substantial prices was harassed by the competition of interlopers who would drive the prices of his kind of product down, and force him to lower his standards. The invention of machines threatened to deprive him of his livelihood altogether. His reaction was to form unions to try to save his independence. Combination appeared as a defence of individualism. Thus one way in which the trade union arose was as an endeavour to maintain men's common law right to do what they would with their own labour, as they had been accustomed to do. But the union once set up would be viewed by the common law as a conspiracy.

A second difficulty raised by the incongruity between the presumptions of the common law and the facts of the labour market lies in the size of the unit of employment. The big employer, it has been said, is 'a monopoly in himself'. Not many employers, it is true, have been in a position to impose terms on a captive labour force. Applicants have often had access to a number of potential employers. There have been times of labour scarcity when employers have actively competed for labour. At times and places where labour was weak, it was often sheltered by the rule of custom. But as firms grew larger, and fluctuations of trade brought on changes in pay from year to year, many workers found their rates of pay being set unilaterally, take it or leave it, by the employer. Whatever their possibilities of moving in the longer term, in the foreseeable future their livelihood depended on their keeping their present jobs. Inherent in their employer's position was a form of economic power. They joined in a union to attain counter-vailing power. The sole buyer of labour then had to come to terms with a sole seller: monopsony was met by monopoly. But it is in the nature of the common law, as it 'operates between individuals' that the workers' monopoly being achieved by combination is overt as the employer's is not, and the attention of the law is drawn to it.

It is drawn necessarily. Though the workers' purpose was defensive, the power of combinations is always potentially oppressive. Herein lies a third source of difficulty, namely in the conflict between the inherent reaction of the common law against the abuse of power of combination, and the scope that trade unionists need if their union is to be effective, indeed even be allowed to exist. After the Act of 1875 the exertion of power in a trade dispute could no longer be treated as a criminal conspiracy, but in several cases in the 1890s and 1900s the courts held that it might constitute a civil conspiracy. In what circum-stances might this be held? Some commentators see the judges' decisions as based only on the injury which in their view the action taken would cause to the public interest. Others have found the basis not in the injury inflicted by the action but in the predominant purpose of the actors – was this to protect their own interests or to injure another, by way (it might be) of spite, revenge, or punishment? In either case the focus was upon injury going beyond the immediate parties to a trade dispute, and the most likely occasion was the secon-dary boycott or the sympathetic strike. What was new in the law was that the courts treated such civil conspiracy as a tort, and allowed parties who suffered injury thereby to sue the conspirators individually for damages. Alternatively the plaintiffs might seek an injunction against the conspirators, requiring them to cease and desist from the action complained of. Failure to comply with this injunction would constitute contempt of court, for which the penalty was imprison-ment: so that the distinction between the civil and the criminal law in its application to trade disputes became blurred in the last resort. But since action would lie only against the impecunious individual mem-bers or officials of a trade union, an employer would have little prospect in practice of recovering damages, or even his costs. The chief use of resort to the courts would have been to obtain injunctions. But now a change in procedure made it possible to recover damages from the funds of the trade unions themselves. Hitherto the trade union like any other unincorporated association could not be sued, simply because it had no legal personality: if any action were entered against it, then just as if an action were entered against a village cricket club, it could simply apply to have its name struck out. But now the courts decided that the procedure by which unincorporated bodies could sue and be sued through a 'representative action' could be applied to trade unions, and that a trade union could sue and be sued in its registered name. In any case the view was coming to be widely held that trade unions were by now so like corporations in their functions and capacities that they should be allowed to acquire the rights, and must thereby assume the responsibilities, of corporate personality.

The great jurist F. W. Maitland showed how hard it had become to hold that corporations could exist only where they had been specifically created by enactment, when the Companies Act of 1862 had long since 'placed corporate form and legal personality within easy reach of "any lawful purpose"'. 'It seems seriously questionable,' he went on to observe, 'whether a permanently organized group, for example a trade union, which had property held for it by trustees, should be suffered to escape liability for what would generally be called "its" unlawful acts and commands by the technical plea that it had no existence in the eye of the law"'.[4]

Some months after Maitland wrote these words, Mr Justice Farwell did entertain an action not against certain officers of a trade union but against the trade union itself: in a famous decision, in September 1900, he granted the Taff Vale Railway Company an injunction against the Society of Railway Servants. It is true that he stood on a doctrine of virtual enactment. 'The legislature,' he declared, 'in giving a trade union the capacity to own property and the capacity to act by agents has, without incorporating it, given it two of the essential qualities of a corporation; essential, I mean, in respect of liability for tort.'[5] His judgement was reversed by the Court of Appeal, but restored in a momentous decision by the House of Lords in July 1901. The litigious manager of the Taff Vale Railway could then come back to the charge with an action for damages against the Railway Servants 'for having conspired to induce the workmen of (the) company to break their contracts, and also for having conspired to interfere with the traffic of the company by picketing and other unlawful means'. The union had to pay £23,000 in damages and costs.

The decision of the House of Lords in this Taff Vale Case was at once recognized as momentous by alert trade unionists. Its menace was made manifest to all when the inflation of damages on the Railway Servants followed. The torts of civil conspiracy and procuring breach of contract were now powerfully sanctioned by the possibility of proceeding not against the individual members or officials who took the wrongful action but against their union, and recovering damages from it that could easily cripple it. Few firms did so proceed. There was no employers' offensive, no concerted action, nor any spontaneous move to take advantage of the new law. When the Denby and Cadeby Main Collieries sought £125,000 in damages from the Yorkshire

Miners' Association, the Court of Appeal held in 1905 that the union was not responsible for the acts of its branches and of its officers which in this case were *ultra vires*.[6] But one outstanding case there was in 1903. The miners of South Wales had their customary 'stop days': when the spot price of coal fell they would stay away from the pits for a day to reduce supplies and support the price, and they believed that this was in the employers' interest as well as their own. But when the Glamorgan Coal Company sued the Miners' Federation, the House of Lords found in 1905 that

to conspire to procure persons to break contracts is manifestly unlawful; that there was no legal justification in the fact that the defendants had no malice against the plaintiffs, and honestly believed that keeping up the prices of coal would benefit employers as well as workmen; and that the defendants were liable in damages for their unlawful acts.[7]

The possibility, indeed the likelihood of such judgements helps to explain why so few cases were taken to court: the trade unions were lying low. Some strikes did still occur, but it was perilous for a trade union to engage deliberately in any major struggle. The right to strike, intact in principle, was nullified in practice. It is true that if a strike took place without any breach of contract by any striker, or persuasion of any blackleg to stay away after he had been engaged, or any other wrongful act on the part of any union member or official, then the firm from which the labour was withdrawn would have no grounds for action against the union, however great the loss they suffered. But what trade union with a host of members in many different places could rely on those conditions being observed? It appeared that soon after the Royal Commission on Labour had established the merits of voluntary negotiations with strong unions, the courts had made it impossible for those unions to function.

3

It was not only their liability to be sued under the Taff Vale judgement, but certain previous judgements which gave plentiful grounds for suing them, that troubled the unions. The right of peaceful picketing that had been thought secured by the Act of 1875 was affirmed in the text of that Act only as an authorization to attend 'to obtain or communicate information': it was now held that this did not authorize persuasion. One judge observed that the effect was that 'You cannot make a strike effective without doing more than what is lawful.' Ever since 1853 it had been a tort to procure a breach of contract: the courts now began to award damages against trade union officers who brought their members out on strike when these members would be leaving their work in breach of their own contracts of service. When the courts developed the law of civil conspiracy it inhibited secondary action. By this law, combinations were held illegal if their objects were something other than the advancement of their members' interests. When members of a union combined to withdraw their labour from their own employer so long as they could not reach agreement with him about their wage, the stoppage might injure him, but their object clearly was to advance their own interests by obtaining a better wage. Suppose, however, that the dispute is not about wages but about his dismissal of a worker, as they allege, for union activity; and suppose the union threatens to call out the staff of one of that employer's customers, unless the customer ceases to deal with that employer – then has not the effective object of the trade unionists moved from the protection of their own interests to the punishment of the employer? In that case they are liable for civil conspiracy.

There were thus four legal constraints on the unions in what they had thought to be the exercise of their functions. All four were judge-made. They concerned picketing, procuring breach of contract, civil conspiracy and, to top them all, the liability of the union itself to be sued. It was generally agreed that the law of unionism was in confusion.

Members of Parliament were put under pressure to have the position clarified by legislation. The House of Commons debated the issue first in 1902, when Richard Bell of the Railway Servants – the appellants in the Taff Vale case – pleaded that the unions be returned to the position in which they had been placed by the Acts of 1871 and 1875. When David Shackleton of the cotton weavers and the TUC Parliamentary Committee proposed a Bill the next year, 1903, it contained a clause that would give immunity from actions except in respect of wrongful acts performed 'with the directly expressed sanction and authority of the rules' of the trade union. But the Speaker required that this clause be dropped as inconsistent with the title of the Bill, and the Bill as introduced dealt only with the law of picketing and civil conspiracy. The dropped clause is believed to have been adopted on the advice of the Liberal lawyers Asquith and Haldane, and to have satisfied the trade union leaders at the time.[8]

But then came the news of the swingeing damages exacted from the Railway Servants: the mood of Congress hardened, and it required that the law provide complete immunity. In the debate of 1903 the Government undertook to set up a Royal Commission. In each of the next two years a private member's Bill was brought in again, this time with three clauses, to deal with Taff Vale as well as Shackleton's two issues. There was widespread support for these Bills that bespoke widespread pressure from constitutents – in the second reading debate in 1904 the Member for Oldham, Winston Churchill, said that though he had not previously been greatly concerned with these matters, the interests of his constituents forced him to pay the closest attention to the debate.[9] The Bills of 1904 and 1905 both passed their second reading, and the latter also went through Standing Committee. Asquith had been right in saying when the issue first came before the House that it was not a party matter.

The support given to the Bills was based on three arguments. The first was a consideration or inducement rather than strictly an argument: many speakers, including those who opposed the Bill, began with a tribute to what trade unions had achieved, especially in promoting industrial peace. Thanks to them, it was said, industrial relations had improved immeasurably in the last thirty years. Second, there was the fact that to reverse the Taff Vale judgement was not to take a leap in the dark or to confer a novel privilege, but simply to return the trade unions to the position they had held under the law for many years before – and held it without complaint being made of their abusing it. Third, especial weight was laid on the contention that Parliament in its wisdom in 1871 and 1875 had decided deliberately that trade unions should not be incorporated, and – in effect – it was not for the Law Lords to assume a superior wisdom now. In the 1904 debate Sir Robert Reid, who as Lord Loreburn was to become Lord Chancellor in the Liberal Governments of 1905–11, declared that after long consideration Parliament decided in 1871 not to confer the full status of incorporation on trade unions: 'The anomalous position of 1871 was created of set purpose for a good reason.' He was not going to criticize the Law Lords who made the 1901 decision, but their interpretation was clearly against the intention of Parliament.[10] This does more than justice to the Parliaments of the 1870s, which hardly raised the issue of incorporation in its relevant form, but were concerned with it as it affected the friendly society functions of trade unions: the question was whether the unions should be given the right to sue their members and be sued by them. Their 'trade aspect' was another matter. But the belief was strong that Parliament at this time had foreseen the Taff Vale issue and decided it.

From 1902 onwards the Government was under rising pressure to take action. It was loath to do so. Some employers certainly wanted the law to be left as it then stood. The evidence of employers to the Royal Commission was to be practically unanimous in finding that since the Taff Vale judgement 'strikes have been less frequent, that in the conduct of trade disputes there has been less violence and intimidation, and that the disputes themselves have been easier to settle.'[11] Many Members of Parliament, on the other hand, were under pressure to reverse the judgement from constituents more numerous than the employers. But the Government were deterred by the misgivings of their lawyers. Some objected on principle to the conferment of legal privileges on any section of the community. Those others who did think it necessary to undo the consequences of Taff Vale were uncertain or divided about how to do it. The Government did not give a passage to the private members' Bills, and launched no Bill of its own, on the plea that it must await the report of the Royal Commission. This was long deferred. Before it appeared the new Liberal administration under Campbell-Bannerman had taken office and gained a sweeping victory in a general election.

In the election campaign candidates had been pressed to pledge themselves to the reform of trade union law. This stood high on the agenda of the new Parliament. Haldane, then Secretary of State for War, related later:

The importance of the question we in the Cabinet knew well. The Attorney-General and the Solicitor-General, Lawson Walton and Robson, had studied it; I had been the leading counsel of the trade union in the Taff Vale case, and Asquith had devoted much thought to it. But we considered it too violent a proposition to say that a trade union should under no circumstances be capable of being sued in tort. We therefore prepared a Bill which sought to restrict the technical operation of the law of agency, so that a distant trade union in a different part of the kingdom which had nothing whatever to do with the dispute might be able to feel secure about its benefit funds, leaving those who had actually behaved illegally to bear the brunt of having done so.[12]

The majority of the Royal Commission were of the same mind. They included Sidney Webb, the great historian and apologist of the trade unions.

That vast and powerful institutions [the majority held] should be permanently licensed to apply the funds they possess to do wrong to others, and by that wrong inflict upon them damage perhaps to the amount of many thousand pounds, and yet not be liable to make redress out of those funds would be a state of things opposed to the very idea of law and order and justice.[13]

The need was rather to tackle the law of agency in which the unions were entangled. What was wrong was not that the duly appointed executive bodies of trade unions should be held responsible for the consequence of wrongful actions performed with the authority of the union, but that the members' painfully accumulated funds were at the mercy of the consequences of some rash step taken, it might well be without the knowledge of any union officer, by any one of scores of thousands of members scattered across the country.

So when the Attorney-General introduced the Government's Bill, he argued that it would be wholly anomalous to enable trade unions to inflict great damages while holding them immune from claims for redress: this would be 'a privilege for the proletariat ... a sort of benefit of clergy to trade unions'.[14] Instead, his Bill provided that trade unions might appoint executive committees for the conduct of disputes, and be held responsible only for actions authorized by those committees; they would be held free of liability for the actions of a member or agent that the executive repudiated as soon as they were brought to its notice. The Bill was given its second reading.

Two days later, on 30 March 1906, the House proceeded to the second reading of a Labour Bill – the same as had passed its second reading and gone through Committee a year before; and this provided complete immunity from actions at tort. 'It became plain,' Haldane recounted, 'notwithstanding the arguments we brought forward, that it was going to be carried against the Government by a huge majority.'[15] To the professional instincts of the lawyers those arguments seemed overwhelming. As Sir Edward Carson was to say later in debate, to legislate for immunity would amount to enacting that 'as regards tortious or wrongful acts committed by trade unions, all the laws of the realm, whether statute or common, are hereby repealed': it would affirm that 'the King can do no wrong; neither can a trade union'.[16] But most Members were prepared to accept that anomaly. The pledges they had given during the election were supported by the arguments from past experience and the intentions of the Parliaments of the 1870s. Now that the terms of the Government's Bill were before them there was added an argument from simplicity. The Bill was complicated. Even though it would also remove the threat of action for civil conspiracy, its main clause did not preclude the possibility of a union that engaged in a strike being subject to an action for damages – and therefore to the injunction. Who could tell what avenue of attack legal ingenuity would open up next? The law of agency, said the Member who introduced the Labour Bill, was judge-made law: 'it was useless for all practical purposes as a means to enable them to escape from one set of legal difficulties, to invite them to take another equally dangerous and to a considerable extent an unknown path, amidst legal subtleties.'[17] Keir Hardie said that they did not want barbed wire to fortify their position, they wanted to be put beyond the range of the enemy's guns.

The Prime Minister became aware that the House was not going to vote with the Government. His own sympathies were with the argument from simplicity. In a big Cabinet, without secretary or agenda, the issue may never have been argued out, but left to the lawyers among the Ministers. What the Prime Minister did now was to put the helm hard over and turn across the bows of his hapless

Attorney-General. In a short speech he paid tribute to the contribution the trade unions had made to good industrial relations, repeated the argument that the judge-made law in this case had been 'expressly disavowed by Parliament', and continued 'I have voted for this Bill two or three times in the past, I always vote for the second reading of a Bill with the understood reservation of details, which are to be considered afterwards . . . Shall I repeat that vote today? (Cries of 'Yes'). I do not see any reason under the sun why I should not.'[18]

The details that he purported to reserve were in the method to be used to free the trade union from liability – to restrict agency, or confer outright immunity. In fact this was the main issue; but he had cast the die. The lawyers maintained their resistance for some time in the Cabinet. Asquith in particular reserved to the end his view 'that the simplest and most practical way of dealing with the matter was to alter the law of agency in its application to trade unions',[19] but when it came to a vote he and the other lawyers in the Cabinet fell in with the Prime Minister's wish for the clean sweep. In the Committee of the House on 3 August the Government adopted the clause conferring outright immunity.

The Trade Disputes Act of 1906 accordingly declared that a trade union could not be sued 'in respect of any tortious act alleged to have been committed by or on behalf of the trade union'.[20] The immunity was as complete as that. It was not even limited to acts committed in a trade dispute.

Has the legislature, [asked Lord Macnaghten when giving judgement in the Taff Vale case] authorized the creation of numerous bodies of men capable of owning great wealth and of acting by agents with absolutely no responsibility for the wrongs they may do to other persons by the use of that wealth and the employment of those agents? In my opinion, Parliament has done nothing of the kind. I cannot find anything in the Acts of 1871 and 1876, or either of them, from beginning to end, to warrant or suggest such a notion.[21]

But this is what the legislature had done now.

And more than this. Though the immunity from actions at tort relieved the right to strike from the threat that any breach of a contract of employment might be sued, the decisions that entangled strike action with civil conspiracy had also to be dealt with. If all that had been done was to give the unions relief from the liability to be sued that Taff Vale had imposed, particular union members and officers who engaged in strike action might still be pursued in the courts on the ground of civil conspiracy, and be subject to injunctions. This possibility was removed by Section 1 of the Act, which declared that 'an act done in pursuance of an agreement or combination by two or more persons shall, if done in contemplation or furtherance of a trade dispute, not be actionable unless the act, if done without any such agreement or combination, would be actionable.' Thus the Act of 1906 invoked 'the golden formula' to set strike action outside the scope of civil conspiracy, as the Act of 1875 had devised it to set strike action outside the scope of criminal conspiracy.

The Act also dealt with the two other issues that had been raised by the courts towards the end of the nineteenth century. The trade union officer who called members out on strike was protected against action for inducing breach of contract by Section 3, which stated that 'an act done by a person in contemplation or furtherance of a trade dispute shall not be actionable on the ground only that it induces some other person to break a contract of employment.' Section 2 of the Act now affirmed that it was lawful for pickets in any number to attend – always 'in contemplation or furtherance of a trade dispute' – at a house or works, 'if they so attend merely for the purpose of peacefully obtaining or communicating information, or of peacefully persuading any person to work or abstain from working'. This implemented the recommendation of the majority of the Royal Commission of 1906, that 'watching and besetting' be legalized. The majority had recommended this despite their finding

that watching and besetting for the purpose of peacefully persuading is really a contradiction in terms. The truth is that picketing – when it consists of watching or besetting the house etc. however conducted – is always and of necessity in the nature of an annoyance to the person picketed. As such it must savour of compulsion, and it cannot be doubted that it is because it is found to compel that trade unions systematically resort to it.[22]

The dissenting Commissioner, the South Wales coal magnate Sir William Lewis, pointed out that the employers who gave evidence from all branches of industry were unanimous in saying that there was no such thing as peaceful picketing. 'I have always thought that the matter of peaceful picketing is a matter of absolute hypocrisy', Edward Carson declared in the House.[23] 'Peaceful persuasion is no use to a trade union.' But it was now legalized; and the police and the bench were left to draw the line between it and intimidation.

Notes

[1] In R. *v.* Eccles, Hawkins, *Pleas of the Crown*, vol. i, p. 348 (1772 ed.). Quoted here from A. L. Haslam, *The Law relating to Trade Combinations* (1931), p. 15.

[2] Conspiracy and Protection of Property Act, 1875, s.3.

[3] O. Kahn-Freund, *Labour and The Law* (2nd ed., London, 1977), p. 1.

[4] Introduction to Otto Gierke, *Political Theories of the Middle Ages* (Cambridge, 1900), p. xxxviii.

[5] Quoted here from H. A. Clegg, A. Fox, and A. F. Thompson, *A History of British Trade Unions since 1889*, vol. I (London, 1964), p. 314.

[6] *The Labour Gazette*, March 1904, p. 71; June 1905, p. 185; May 1906, p. 154.

[7] Ibid., Sept. 1903, p. 244; May 1905, p. 152.

[8] H. A. Clegg *et al.*, *History of British Trade Unions*, pp. 322–3.

[9] Parl. Debates, 1904, vol. 133, 998.

[10] Ibid., 981–2.

[11] Report of the Royal Commission on Trade Disputes and Trade Combinations, 1906 Parl. Papers 1906, vol. LVI, cd.2825): Majority Report, para 39.

[12] Richard Burdon Haldane, *An Autobiography* (London, 1929), pp. 211–12.

[13] Royal Commission on Trade Disputes and Trade Combinations, 1906, Majority Report, p. 8.

[14] Parl. Debates 1906, vol. 154, 1306–07.

[15] Ibid.

[16] Parl. Debates 1906, vol. 162, 1733.

[17] Parl. Debates 1906, vol. 155, 22–8.

[18] Ibid., 51–4.

[19] Parl. Debates 1906, vol. 162, 1713.

[20] Trade Disputes Act, 1906; 6 Edw. VII, c. 47, 4 (i).

[21] Taff Vale Railway Co. v. Amalgamated Society of Railway Servants, A.C. (1901), 436; per Lord MacNaghten.

[22] Royal Commission on Trade Disputes and Trade Combinations, 1906: Majority Report, Art. 48.

[23] Parl. Debates 1906, vol. 154, 1320–8.

III

REFLECTIONS ON THE SETTLEMENT OF 1906

I

THE Trade Disputes Act of 1906 marked the British acceptance of what came to be known as voluntarism. One of the strongest arguments for the conferment of complete immunity had been that it would only restore the state of affairs that had obtained without complaint of abuse for many years before the Taff Vale judgement; and this agreed with the finding of the Royal Commission on Labour in 1891–4 that industrial relations were best conducted between strong organizations meeting by mutual consent to arrive at agreements whose observance depended on good faith. Both these assessments rested on a view of the trade unions as they had been observed in the years after their legitimization in the 1870s. If to enable industrial relations to proceed by bargaining, understanding, and consent, the trade unions must be endowed with an exceptional privilege – let us not draw back, the argument ran, for they have shown that they can be trusted with it. The Prime Minister, Sir Henry Campbell-Bannerman, put the case very directly in the crucial speech that announced his intention of voting for the second reading of the Labour Bill that would confer complete immunity from actions at tort. He looked back to the trade union legislation that he had witnessed as a young Member of Parliament in the 1870s. Those Acts, he said,

had a most beneficent effect. They gave life and strength to trade unions, very much to the alarm of a great body of opinion in the country, which had contracted a habit of looking upon these Associations with dread and suspicion. That prejudice still lingers in some quarters; but the great mass of opinion in the country recognise fully now the beneficent nature of trade union organisations, and recognise also the great services that those organis-ations have done in the prevention of conflict and the promotion of harmony between labour and capital. I believe myself that all the best employers – I almost hope I might say, all the good employers – in the country welcome anything which gives freedom and power to associations of so useful and beneficent a character as these. That is a great revolution in the attitude of public feeling. And that is a revolution which we are bound to take into account today.[1]

In the same way the former Prime Minister, A. J. Balfour, leading now for the Opposition, observed that

there is no party . . . who does not recognize to the full all that trade unions have done, the gap which they have filled in the social organisation and the impossibility of carrying on organised labour except by an institution formed upon their model . . . Undoubtedly trade disputes in this country have been carried on with a wisdom and a moderation on both sides which cannot be paralleled in any other industrial community.[2]

Yet we remarked at the outset that by the time that the legal status of the trade unions was being decided on that view of their place in the community, the character of their members and their own potential impact had changed greatly. There were three ways in which these changes had come about.

2

One had been signalized by the strike of the London dockers in 1889. What had impressed the public then was that a body of men previously regarded as inherently uncouth and disorderly should have shown themselves capable of discipline and organization, and brought forth leadership from their own ranks, so as to sustain an orderly strike through six weeks to its successful conclusion. They were the advance guard of a movement among the unskilled labourers of the cities at large, and among the semi-skilled who worked alongside the craftsmen in industry but were excluded from their societies. Hitherto, however much these people had needed unions, they had not proved capable of maintaining unions for themselves, and with rare exceptions outsiders had not come in to administer unions for them; but now the general elementary education first made available in the 1870s was taking its effect. Of the whole population of London in 1891, it was estimated, rather less than a quarter had passed through an efficient school, but by 1901 the proportion was more than a half, by 1911 more than three-quarters.[3] Literacy brought access to ideas. Some of the leaders of the New Unionism were animated by a will to change the order of society and a rejection of the authority of the employer very different from the conformity and deference of the leaders of the older unions. The members of these unions too were becoming more militant. Among skilled and unskilled alike, the currents of trade unionism and socialism mingled. A growing conviction that the established order in industry was not only unjust but inefficient arose also from the severity of the depressions in each decade from the 1870s onwards. The British economy was losing its industrial ascendancy; its staple manufactures which had dominated the markets of the world were losing ground to foreign competitors, and it was failing to develop the new industries as they did. The depressions went deeper in the United Kingdom than in those other industrial countries, and lasted longer. They brought severe unemployment. In absolute numbers this increased in successive depressions, and it became increasingly resented; it intensified what contemporaries noted as 'the spirit of unrest'.

3

The upsurge of the New Unionism spent its force, and there followed a time of reaction. But a permanent change had been revealed not only in the animus of manual workers but in the potential coverage of their unions, especially in transport. This was the more important because of the power which this factor of wide coverage had enabled the miners to wield in 1893: for the first time in British history the Government itself had been drawn in to get a settlement in an industrial dispute. Here lay the second source of change in the impact of the unions.

A divide had been crossed in 1889 when a number of the miners' local associations that hitherto had been dealing with the coal-owners separately, district by district, came together to form the Miners' Federation, and agreed that if one district were locked out by the owners demanding a reduction of wages, a conference might approve a stoppage throughout the Federation. This covered so great a part of the supply to the home market that its stoppage would mean before long the halting of industry, of railways and the supplies of food they carried everywhere, as well as the exhaustion of the stocks of domestic fuel. It was this that threatened in 1893, when the owners moved to bring basic wages down, the Miners' Federation would take no cut at all, and a lock-out began at the end of July. As autumn drew on into winter, factories were being put on short time or stopped altogether, and households lacked fuel for heating and cooking. The President of the Board of Trade attempted conciliation, but in a conference lasting more than two days he failed. He had acted in this as in previous disputes with the approval and blessing of his colleagues in the Government, but any such intervention, the Prime Minister, Mr Gladstone, pointed out, 'could not be said to be on the part of Her Majesty's Government in an official sense, because in an official sense Her Majesty's Government had no right to intervene'.[4] Earlier in that year, 1893, he had declined to intervene in a protracted and bitter conflict involving the dockers and seamen of Hull, even by allowing the House of Commons to discuss a proposal for ending it, on the ground that for the House to intervene without some definite prospect of success would arouse expectations without the House being able to fulfil them, and this 'would amount to a public mischief'.[5] But the port of Hull could be at a standstill without the whole country being strangled: it was otherwise in mid-November, when the pits in the Miners' Federation area had been stopped for more than three months. At any rate, within less than two weeks of the breakdown of the President's conference the Prime Minister himself wrote to the parties suggesting that they meet again under the chairmanship of his Foreign Secretary. True, he probably did not move until soundings had shown that agreement could at last be reached, as in fact it was at the first session, but it was widely felt that the Government had entered upon an unprecedented and dubious type of commitment: its reason for doing so was the newly revealed power of trade unionists to withhold an essential supply on the national scale.

By 1906 it was apparent that what the miners had done in 1893 might be within the reach of the railwaymen and other transport workers. Trade unionists possessed of this power were able to bring a pressure to bear on the employers much greater than that exerted by the mere stoppage of the employers' undertakings: they could also inflict great hardship on the community – in modern parlance, they could cause widespread disruption – and this would bring in the Government to achieve a settlement in the only immediately practicable way, namely, by inducing the employers to concede terms acceptable to the unionists. But more than that: the unions concerned would realize that they were now possessed of a power that would secure them direct access to governments, and a sanction with which to back demands on government that might go beyond any issue they had with their own employers. The trade union that the advocates of the Act of 1906 wished to set free to exert its bargaining power had been envisaged as using that power only against employers; but before long trade unions were to threaten to use it against the Government too.

4

The third change that had come about in the trade union world concerned the relations between trade unionists and management at the place of work. The very introduction of the term 'management' indicates one source of the change. A manager used to be merely a deputy of the employer, or an executive charged with certain departmental duties: but towards the end of the nineteenth century a distinct managerial function began to be discerned, with its own professional principles applicable to all manner of industries. This was specially so in the United States, from which spread notions of 'scientific management'. At the same time, also from the United States, there came new types of automatic machinery which, once they were set up, could turn out work of a form and precision that used to be attainable only by the skill of the craftsman's hand. They could also turn it out more rapidly, and – even more disturbing – they could be operated by unapprenticed men after brief training. The craftsman's skill was a costly acquisition that he had paid for by long years of apprenticeship, but part of its reward had always been the virtual autonomy it gave him, so long as it was indispensable, in the way his work was arranged and carried out. This used to be taken for granted. But now it was being broken in upon by the new type of manager, who changed layouts and the allocation of tasks, removed problem-solving from the shop-floor to the drawing-office, and tried to bring in new incentive methods of wage-payment, with work study, even the stop-watch; all this together with the coming of the new automatics into the machine shops. The craftsman reacted strongly to maintain his customary way of working; but from the managers' point of view what had once been accepted as in the nature of things now appeared as 'restrictive practices'. In engineering a major struggle ensued for the control of the workshop, between the craft unions which were seeking to uphold custom and practice, and the employers who were asserting the right of management to manage. In 1897–8 the employers, forming and rapidly extending an industry-wide association, fought out and won a protracted dispute with the unions on this issue. The terms of settlement gave them the right to introduce in their workshops any condition of labour under which any members of the unions had been working when the dispute began. That seemed comprehensive and – after so exhausting a conflict – final: but in fact the struggle had only begun. The trade union as a contestant with management for the control of the work-place was attaining a significance that had found no place in the Victorian acceptance of the union.

This was because union custom and practice were now coming under attack as obstacles not merely to the introduction of up-to-date methods and machinery but to the very survival of British firms under mounting competitive pressure. Contemporaries were keenly aware that Great Britain had ceased to be 'the workshop of the world'. 'This is the crisis of our industry', the economist Alfred Marshall wrote during the engineering dispute of 1897–8. 'For the last 20 years we have indeed been still progressing; but we have been retrograding relatively to the Americans and to the nations of central Europe (not France, I think) and to Eastern lands.'[6]

In Belgium, Germany, Bohemia, Hungary and Japan [Marshall also wrote] crowds of men are learning to manage machines which a few years ago required high skill, but which have now been so improved that they will do excellent work in the hands of a mere 'ploughman'. This tends of course to open out new kinds of mechanical work that require high skill: but England cannot keep much of that work, unless she is also able to grow with the age in the application of the more abundant lower skill to suitable work. . . . Unless the A.S.E.[7] bona fide concedes to the employers the right to put a single man to work an easy machine, or even two or more of them, the progress upwards of the English working classes . . . will, I believe, receive a lasting check.[8]

The leader of the engineering employers in the great dispute, Col. Henry Dyer, described the powerful impression made on him by a visit to the Pittsburgh steelworks. After a great battle (into the bloody course of which he did not enter) these works had done away with trade unionism. A highly efficient management was now free to manage. It was delivering rails to Calcutta at the same price as English producers could sell rails in England.

The majority of the men employed had come to the works during the strike as unskilled men, and had been educated to perform the duties required of them, with the result that the output had been increased two-thirds ... The [English] federated engineering employers are determined to obtain the free-dom to manage their own affairs which has proved to be so beneficial to the American manufacturers as to enable them to compete successfully in what was formerly an English monopoly.[9]

It was alleged, and certainly believed by as careful an observer as Marshall, that the New Unionism that had taken its rise in 1889 was more insistent than the old on upholding restrictive practices, especially when those were regarded as protective of employment. That 'make-work' practices were enforced and even extended in reaction to the heavy unemployment in the cyclical depressions from the 1870s onwards does seem likely. In this, as in the desire to maintain the craftsman's autonomy, the action of the trade unionists is wholly intelligible. But the conflict in which it engaged them raised the question of the power of the trade union to obstruct economic change on which depended the ability of the British people to maintain and advance their standard of living in an increasingly competitive world. This consideration had not entered into the more static and parochial view within which the Victorian acceptance of the trade union had been formed.

5

In these ways the actual state of the unions in 1906, and their potential impact on polity and economy, had become substantially different from those of the unionism envisaged by those who took the decision to set the unions outside the law. The type of union that had gained approval accepted the existing order in industry and society, whereas many unionists of 1906 rejected it as unfair and denied the legitimacy of profit. The approved unions operated locally by region or trade, and it was with employers that they negotiated: the Government in considering how it should formulate the law concerning the unions did not think of their coming into conflict with itself. But in one instance the unions had already shown their power to hold up a vital supply throughout most of the country, and before long their spokesmen would be coming direct to Downing Street. Rules upheld by unionists at the place of work had been passed over as custom and practice that formed no part of the active policy or function of the typical union; but when these rules came into conflict with technical innovation and managerial authority they were revealed as basic to the purposes of trade unionism.

Are we to conclude, then, that the fateful decision of 1906 was taken on a view of trade unions that was out of date, and underestimated alike their actual power and the will of their members to use it? Was it by projecting the image of a deferential yesterday that the friends of the unions sheltered the turbulent present day? Was a far-reaching legal immunity restored to the unions on the assumption that they could be regarded as informal clubs, at a time when already they really needed legal regulation as among the most powerful corporate bodies in the land? There is an evident case for answering 'yes' to all these questions. But a proper answer to the last question calls for an examination of the possibilities open in 1906.

One of these is the course actually taken. It is not to be dismissed as having been forced as a U-turn on the Government simply by political pressure. The case for it is that it was the course passionately desired by the trade unionists themselves; they felt it to be vital to the continued functioning of their unions. Hitherto in this discussion we have looked at those unions from the outside, from the point of view of the observer who is concerned with economic progress and orderly governance but has never found himself in a position where he himself depended on his trade union for the protection of his livelihood. But from the earliest days of their working lives, harsh experience had taught many trade unionists the lesson of that dependence. They felt, moreover, with reason, that they, the working people, had erected their unions by themselves. Governments and lawgivers had not helped the wage-earner to raise himself: if they, especially the law courts of late, had intervened, it had been to try to put the unions down. The trade unionists were in any case the underdogs in society. They were as often confronted by employers with demands for reductions in wages as they were themselves able to negotiate a modest rise. It was essential for them, and the barest justice, that they should not have to keep up the unequal struggle with their hands tied by the law. The right to strike was conceded, even by their adversaries, but the formal right was empty without immunity from action for damages caused by the strike: if the simplest, surest way of conferring this was to ban all actions at tort against trade unions, such an immunity, far from being an anomalous privilege, only levelled the scales of economic justice.

The strength of this case varies with the circumstances to which it is applied. It is strong where the unionists are weak, and struggling only to vary terms otherwise dictated. It fails increasingly of application as unions grow in power and in their ability to enforce their demands not only by withdrawing labour from the employer but by imposing losses on third parties and disrupting the life of the community. But it is a basic problem of the place of trade unionism in society that those who view the union from within can genuinely and passionately perceive it so differently from those who view it from without. Policy towards trade unionism must take this into account. There are limits beyond which that policy cannot go without the consent of the trade unionists themselves.

It was for this reason that one alternative course that actually had its advocates at the time among the trade unions themselves was not in fact practicable. Year after year the leader of the dockers, trying to hold his union together in the reaction that followed the rise of the New Unionism, moved at the TUC a resolution in favour of compulsory arbitration. The leader of the railwaymen, seeking in vain to obtain negotiating rights from the railway companies, as an MP brought in a private member's Bill providing that railwaymen's wages should be fixed by a court to which either party might take the other. Interest in compulsory arbitration was stimulated by the example of New Zealand and Australia. By an Act of 1896 New Zealand had outlawed strike and lock-out, and set up a special court of arbitration, presided over by a judge with the status of a judge of the Supreme Court, to make awards in those cases where the parties could not reach agreement by themselves. This was without precedent. It seemed a step of great potential significance. New Zealand became celebrated as 'the land without strikes'. Western Australia and New South Wales soon followed its example, which is believed also to have prompted a project for compulsory arbitration drawn up by the French socialist Minister Millerand. The widest extension came in 1904, when an act of the new Commonwealth of Australia outlawed strike and lock-out in all disputes within the jurisdiction of the Commonwealth, and set up a Court to make awards that would bind the disputants. Here it seemed, in the words of an early President of the Court, was 'a new province for law and order'.

Compulsory arbitration also appealed strongly in principle to Sidney Webb as a philosophic exponent of trade unionism. When he signed the Majority Report of the Royal Commission set up after Taff Vale, he appended a Memorandum in which he wrote:

I cannot accept the assumption underlying the report that a system of organised struggles betwen employers and workmen, leading inevitably now and again to strikes and lock-outs – though it is, from the standpoint of the community as a whole, an improvement on individual bargaining – represents the only method, or even a desirable method, by which to settle the conditions of employment. A strike or a lock-out – which is not only lawful, but under existing circumstances, as a measure of legitimate defence against economic aggression, may be sometimes even laudable – necessarily involves so much dislocation of industry; so much individual suffering; so much injury to third parties, and so much national loss, that it cannot, in my opinion, be accepted as the normal way of settling an intractable dispute. . . . I cannot believe that a civilised community will permanently continue to abandon the adjustment of industrial disputes – and incidentally the regulation of the conditions of life of the mass of its people – to what is, in reality, the arbitrament of private war. A more excellent way is, I believe, pointed out in the experimental legislation of the past decade in New Zealand and Australia. We have in the factory, mines, shops and sanitary legislation of the United Kingdom, long adopted the principle of securing, by law, the socially necessary minimum, as regards some of the conditions of employment for certain classes of labour. The various industrial conciliation and arbitration laws of New Zealand and Australia carry the principle a step further, so as to include all the conditions of employment and practically all classes of labour. Such a system appears to offer, to the general satisfaction of employers and employed, both a guarantee against conditions of employment that are demonstrably injurious to the community as a whole, and an effective remedy for industrial war.[10]

Within two or three years the example of Australia in a cognate matter was in fact going to embolden the British Government to commit itself (through a Bill brought in by Winston Churchill) to the statutory regulation of minimum wages – this at first only in a very limited area and tentative way, it is true; but the principle was to be accepted. What, then, of that other Australian example, and the reasonable case of the intellectuals like Sidney Webb, and the plea by the unions of the unskilled workers? They were of no account. In the debate about how the law on strikes should be settled after Taff Vale none of the participants proposed to escape the legal perplexities by simply outlawing the strike and substituting compulsory arbitration. In 1906 the TUC voted down the resolution in favour of compulsory arbitration for the eighth successive year. Only weak unions wanted it. The members of the strong unions would not have it at any price.

It had been amid union weakness that compulsory arbitration had taken hold overseas. The New Zealand Act had been entitled 'an Act to encourage the formation of industrial unions' – which would be able from the first to take employers to the Court, when without the Court the employers could have disregarded them with impunity. In Australia compulsory arbitration was instituted and gained accept-

ance after trade unionism had suffered crushing defeats during a
depression of great severity. For the Australian wage-earner it meant in
practice the ability to gain an acceptable rate, legally enforceable upon
the employer, without the cost of building up organizations and
sustaining the conflicts needed to secure recognition and negotiate
advances from reluctant employers. But where unions were already
strongly organized, and had secured recognition and negotiating
rights, compulsory arbitration threatened their members with a loss of
their personal freedom to accept or reject the terms on which they
would work. To work under compulsory arbitration is in principle to
be required to work on terms that are laid down and changed from
time to time by an external authority. It may be in the common interest
that we should each and all of us subordinate ourselves in this way. It
may well be that the earnings of any one group that did proceed in this
way would rise as much over the years as they would do through the
tussles of bargaining, and without the cost of the tussles. But the
Boards of Conciliation and Arbitration that were working well in a
number of regions of industry in Victorian times broke down because
the union members felt that settlements were being made over their
heads and simply handed out to them. Where union members have
taken part in struggles over particular terms, where they have felt that
they have personally accepted a settlement be it even when they have
been beaten, there they will not readily give up the final word on terms
to a third party. Sidney Webb had stated the case for compulsory
arbitration to impose the 'socially necessary minimum' where trade
unionism was weak or lacking. He did not consider how it could be
imposed to stop 'industrial war' where strong trade unions were out
for more than the minimum, or the rank and file were implacably
opposed to cuts.

6

So compulsory arbitration, for all its being talked of, was not a
practicable alternative course in 1906. Yet two other courses there
were that would have provided a more ordered legal or procedural
setting for union activity. One course was for the legislators, the other
for the employers.

The first course follows from the observation that the much disputed immunity clause was not after all an essential part of the Trade
Disputes Act, 1906: all the shelter that the trade unions needed in
practice from actions at tort was given them by the other clauses of that
Act. 'It was the policy of the 1906 Act', Sir Otto Kahn-Freund wrote,
'to create a "catalogue" of economic torts which would not give rise to
liability if committed in contemplation or furtherance of a trade
dispute.'[11]

With the advantage of hindsight' [he went on to observe] one can say that it would have made little difference if (the immunity from all actions at tort) had been left out of the 1906 Act. What mattered were the immunities from certain kinds of conduct in contemplation or furtherance of a trade dispute. If those acting for a union were covered by one of those immunities, the union could not – even without the union privilege – have been vicariously liable for their acts.[12]

An alternative course open to Parliament, then, instead of conferring 'the union privilege' of complete immunity from all actions at tort, was 'to create a "catalogue"' of practices on which it would confer immunity specifically.

The case against this, and for providing the complete immunity, is the case for simplicity and certainty – for freedom from the embranglements of litigation and the unforseeable developments of case law. This was the argument that Asquith used to justify his vote for complete immunity, against his own better judgement: 'there was less risk of actual legislation on disputed questions going to courts of law,' he said, 'passing from one stage of appeal to another, and involving loss of temper, money and time, by adopting the perfectly simple and common-sense method embodied in the alternative clause.'[13]

But there is another side to the question. It was natural for trade clubs to operate informally in mid-Victorian times; but in providing immunity for the trade unions of its day the Parliament of 1906 was doing much more than restoring the old state of affairs. This was so partly because the trade unions were now bigger, and the damages they could inflict for which the sufferer was denied redress were greater. It was so also because the question had now been explicitly posed whether the basic principle of civil law – that the property of wrongdoers shall be liable to compensate those who suffer by their wrongdoing – should not apply to trade unionists as to everyone else; and when Parliament answered that it should not, the effect must have been to deepen the impression that there was a basic opposition between trade unionism and the law, such that if trade unions were to be able to perform their functions, they must be free of legal regulation. The tradition was strengthened that the law was inherently oppressive to trade unionists. But more than this again: in choosing the clean sweep rather than the '"catalogue" of economic torts which would not give rise to liability', Parliament decided that, uniquely among all our institutions and procedures, trade unions and industrial relations should be exempt from regulation by law. So long as the basic principle of complete immunity stood on the statute books, Parliament had denied itself the possibility of distinguishing between different actions by the trade union, according to the balance between the union's need of those actions in order to fulfil its functions, and the damages they inflicted on others. It had denied itself also the possibility of adapting regulations to new practices and problems as they emerged. It would not be able to draw up and maintain a code that distinguished between permissible and impermissible practices, and provided immunity to the permissible with sanctions against the others.

Three practices may be instanced and reviewed in this connection. One is the secondary strike or boycott, in which the employees of the customer or supplier of a firm with which unionists are in dispute are called out, though these employees have no dispute with their own employer. Another is the sympathetic strike: here again the strikers have no dispute with their own employer, but their action is distinguished from the secondary strike because it does not directly increase the economic pressure on the original dispute, but only increases the publicity given to it, or adds to the disruption imposed on the public and the Government. The third practice is the withdrawal of labour by reason of a dispute – typically a demarcation dispute – between two groups of workers. With consideration of the first two practices is bound up that of picketing. Disraeli's Act of 1875 had listed and forbidden various forms of violent, threatening, and vexatious picketing. The Act of 1906 had explicitly legalized picketing with the object of peaceful persuasion. But evidently not only the way in which the pickets behaved, but the circumstances in which they could lawfully be posted at all, were matters that Parliament might regulate. These practices can be variously regulated by law. The starting-point is the principle that the basic right to strike can be upheld only if the trade union is able by striking to inflict losses on the employer and, inevitably, on those who deal with the employer as suppliers or customers, and in some measure on the surrounding community. But the question how far the trade union needs to be able to support its case by taking action to inflict losses on those with whom it is not in dispute is an open one. It had been raised by the decisions of the courts on civil conspiracy, in so far as they distinguished the predominant purpose of protecting the strikers' own interests from that of inflicting injury on another party, a distinction which can be attempted only when that other party is extraneous, and not directly engaged in negotiation with the strikers. The same distinction in the area of application of strike action appears if we cease to distinguish purposes but ask how far trade unionists whose sole purpose is to defend and advance their own interests are entitled to inflict injury on third parties, and procure such infliction by others. Section 98 of the Industrial Relations Act, 1971, made it an 'unfair industrial practice' to take strike action against an extraneous party not involved in a dispute with the purpose of making that party break a contract with a party to the dispute. That Act failed entirely of effect, and was repealed, but the issue would not go away, and the Employment Act of 1980 came back to the charge with a distinction between immediate customers and suppliers of parties of the dispute, against whom action might continue to be taken, and others, truly extraneous, against whom action was banned.

There was, then, a legal alternative to the settlement of 1906, and one to which we have been groping painfully of late. Indeed one might withdraw the term 'settlement': what was done then was too simple and sweeping – it placed the trade unions outside the law altogether in respect of civil proceedings, and this was tolerable only so long as they remained voluntarily within a certain boundary of strike action. The alternative, open at the time in principle, was to have drawn the boundary by statute. Within it the unions would have enjoyed all the shelter of the actual settlement of 1906. In any action they took outside it they would have been exposed to the civil law relating to combinations of whatever form. The intensity of trade union opposition to later proposals for such regulation does not show that if it had been adopted in 1906 they would have found their bargaining power much reduced by it.

7

The other alternative course in 1906 was open not to Parliament but to the employers. For the most part the employers had actually shown themselves satisfied with things as they were; or rather, they did not wish for the intervention of the law in their dealings with their own workers locally, and they were not organized to develop policy on this or any other issue at the national level. Particular employers were adamantly opposed to unionism among their own employers, but when Lord Lansdowne came to explain why the Unionist Peers would not oppose the legislation of 1906, he gave as one of his reasons 'the fact that throughout the discussions on the Bill the employers of labour in Parliament did not, as far as I know, raise a little finger to arrest its progress'.[14] We have seen how many employers in engineering saw in the impact of new equipment and methods upon the traditional practices of the craft unions an issue of such magnitude that they formed a broad association and sustained a long struggle with the unions in 1897–8. But this was exceptional. For the most part the employers exercised little influence on union structure and function, by reaction or initiative, locally or at the national level. The rising membership and more militant attitude of the trade unionists from the turn of the century onwards brought forth no employers' counterpoise to the TUC. It was otherwise at this time in Sweden. The employers there, apprised of the growing strength of the unions in 1902 by a general strike that was a demonstration for the extension of the suffrage, proceeded to form their national organization. In 1909 they were enable to defeat the unions in a great struggle about wages – a general strike that fairly soon collapsed, followed by a long-drawn-out stoppage in engineering. By the end of 1911 the membership of the unions had been halved. The unions learned their lesson. They had begun as British trade unions had begun, growing up in various forms, some as craft, some as industrial, some as general unions. Now they set to work to regroup this congeries into a small number of unions of which each would be the sole union in a given industry, and these would all be committed to accept the direction of the council of their national organization. The task took them a quarter of a century, and was never entirely completed, but it provided a structure which was capable of entering into agreements at the national level with the corresponding organization of employers, agreements on matters both procedural and substantive, with the assurance that these would be observed down the line. Many factors entered into this ability of the Swedish trade unions to negotiate a 'central framework agreement', but one essential was the strength of the employers' organizations, both historically and currently. Generally, trade unions cannot be more orderly than the employers give them the chance to be.

We have then to ask how the development of British trade unionism would have been affected if it too had encountered in the early 1900s employers' associations that were strongly developed both by industry and at the national level. Against the increased strength of immediate resistance to union claims may be set pressures exerted towards a more efficient unionism in the longer run. The authority of union officials would have been strengthened when employers' associations would not permit any departure from agreed terms. In face of strong employers' associations concerned to negotiate realistic agreements, union members would have had an inducement to amalgamate or transfer membership so as to form industrial unions, or adopt joint negotiating arrangements. At the national level, advances in industrial relations could have been proposed, negotiated with the employers, and promulgated throughout the area of membership.

We have surveyed what we have called alternative courses. In one sense, it is true, these alternatives were not open. The resort to arbitration could not have been made compulsory, because the stronger unions did not like it. Had anyone proposed the distinction between fair and unfair practices, it could not have been enacted, because trade unionists who wanted the clean sweep commanded too many votes. Employers were not putting the trade unions under pressure to improve their organization, because the employers themselves had little concern or capacity to organize for purposes of industrial relations. But one cannot say that the obstacles here were inherent in the nature of the task being attempted by the trade unions, or in the type of British institutions, or the character of the British people. What could not actually have come about in 1906, taking all things as they were, was still possible on the supposition of only minor and credible changes in the situation. Consideration of the alternative courses then serves to remind us that there is nothing inevitable or authoritative about the actual course of development: the present state of industrial relations, trade union law, or trade union structure is not established as natural or necessary by the mere fact of their having evolved in the way they have. We are reminded of the continuing possibility of change.

Notes

1 Parl. Debates 1906, vol. 154, 52.
2 Parl. Debates 1906, vol. 155, 1531.
3 H. Llewellyn Smith, *New Survey of London Life and Labour*, vol. I (London, 1930), ch. VIII, Table II.
4 Parl. Debates 1893, vol. xi, 1744.
5 Ibid., 1743.
6 Letter dated 5 Dec. 1897 to Edward Caird, Master of Balliol, in A. C. Pigou (ed.), *Memorials of Alfred Marshall* (London, 1925) p. 399.
7 Amalgamated Society of Engineers.
8 Letter dated 22 Oct. 1897, in A. C. Pigou (ed.), *Memorials*, p. 388.
9 Letter to *The Times*, 7 Sept. 1897.
10 Report of Royal Commission on Trade Disputes and Trade Combinations, 1906: Memorandum by Sidney Webb, p. 18.
11 Sir Otto Kahn-Freund, *Labour and the Law*, 2nd ed. (London, 1977), p. 258.
12 Ibid., p. 275.
13 Parl. Debates 1906, vol. 162, 1713.
14 parl. Debates 1906, vol. 166, 703.

IV

THE TRADE UNIONS AND THE LABOUR PARTY

I

THE British trade unions have gained greatly from their close partnership with the Labour Party. Since 1906 this has constantly provided Members of Parliament to defend trade union interests and keep the issues of special interest to trade unionists before the House. When Labour has been in office it has legislated to remedy unwelcome rulings of the courts, repeal obnoxious enactments, or extend the scope of trade union action. We are not concerned here with the pursuit by Labour Governments of social and economic policies that were approved of by trade union leaders, and may in some instances have been prompted by them. The actions that concern us are only those in which the Labour Party has served to throw off restrictions upon trade union power, or assert that power over its opponents in the field.

We have seen that the pressure of trade unionists in the constituencies was likely to have been enough to ensure that Campbell-Bannerman's Government in 1906 adopted a more radical remedy for the Taff Vale judgement than its own lawyers' Bill; but it was on the second reading of the Labour Bill that the Prime Minister made his crucial speech, and eventually it was the proposal in that Bill that provided the most contentious provision of the Trade Disputes Act. In the closely balanced House after the elections of 1910 the Labour members lacked bargaining power against a government that they dared not bring down; but they pressed for legislation to lift the ban on the use of trade union funds for political purposes that the Law Lords had imposed in Osborne's case, they were highly critical of the Government's first Bill, and in the Act of 1913 they obtained a measure which, though they liked it little at the time, made the trade unions the copious fount of funds for their Party. The first Labour Governments, in 1923–4 and 1929–31, were minority administrations. The second of these followed upon the Trade Disputes and Trade Unions Act of 1927 which the unions bitterly resented. This Act's outlawing of the sympathetic strike directed against the Government – as in the General

Strike – was a denial of their right to solidarity in a dispute where the Government took the side of the employers. More particularly they resented as spiteful and damaging the clause that by substituting 'contracting in' for 'contracting out' was to cut back severely the trade union contribution to the Labour Party. But a minority administration could not touch the Act.

It was otherwise when Labour was returned with a thumping majority in 1945: out went the Act then, in Labour's first year. Very promptly also the trade unions achieved their ultimate and annihilating victory over employers long distinguished for their obduracy, when the coal-mines and the railways were nationalized.

When Labour came back to office in 1964 and 1974 the services that the Party could render to the unions were demonstrated repeatedly. In 1964 the Law Lords had ruled, in Rookes v. Barnard, that the immunity from actions at tort that trade unionists enjoyed under the Trade Disputes Act of 1906 did not extend to the tort of intimidation by threatening a breach of contract. By the Trade Disputes Act of 1968 the Labour Government provided that it should so extend. A first charge upon the Government of 1974 was to repeal the Conservatives' Industrial Relations Act of 1971; but this Act for the first time had provided a remedy against unfair dismissal, and that was retained in the Government's new Act. This was part of a whole code developed at this time to protect the employee and strengthen the hand of the negotiator, from the Redundancy Payments Act of 1965 through the Employment Protection Act of 1975 and the Trade Unions and Labour Relations (Amendment) Act of 1976. The Acts of 1974 and 1976 dealt among other things with the closed shop. Though it was the Conservatives who had contributed the Contracts of Employment Act of 1972, and some elements that Labour retained from the rejected Act of 1971, the protection of the unions and the leverage put in the hands of negotiators were due to the Labour Party in office. It had been made clear, too, that so long as that party could expect its recurrent term of office, the trade unions could snap their fingers at legislation or judicial decisions that they found restrictive: for the next Labour Government would legislate to repeal or reverse them. When the Conservative Government called in 1981 for comments on proposals for reducing trade union immunities, the Engineering Employers' Federation rejected all thoroughgoing measures on the ground that they would simply be repealed by the next Labour Government. The Federation stated in its evidence,[1]

Unions will not willingly acquiesce in any significant reduction in their immunities, and under the British political system it is virtually certain that immunities taken away by a government of one complexion will be at least restored by another government more sympathetic to the cause of union power. There is no merit therefore in initiating this kind of debilitating struggle in industry merely to make use of a temporary political advantage.

The advantages which the trade unions enjoy in this way from their link with the Labour Party appear forcibly on an international comparison. The link seems natural here: but sweep the horizon – which countries show any counterpart to it? At the one pole, in Scandinavia, especially in Sweden, we see a close relation between the unions and social democracy. At the other pole, or rather, over that broad range of countries whose trade unionism and politics are more fissured than ours, there can be no one link between unions and party. More significant is the diversity among countries comparable with ourselves. In the international comparisons made later in this work we find familiar features in Australia, but the United States and Canada present striking contrasts: in the one, unions that abstained of set purpose from integrating themselves with any one political party; in the other, unions that have made more than one attempt to launch a Labour Party without as yet drawing out a national Labour vote. Evidently the British link is distinctive. We cannot take it for granted. The question arises, how it came about.

The answer traditionally given by the unions themselves is simple: it is they who launched the Party, manned it in its early days, and at all times have financed it. On the face of the record this is so. It was indeed the TUC that convened the meeting which in 1900 set up the Labour Representation Committee, out of which the Labour Party arose. If not many unions were ready to commit themselves to common action at first, the Law Lords' judgement in the Taff Vale case brought a great change in the use the unions had for the Committee, and transformed its destinies. The accession of more and more trade unions gave the Committee the resources to put a substantial number of independent Labour candidates in the field at the 1906 election. Of the 29 then elected, 23 were trade unionists; and twelve years later, of the 57 Labour MPs elected in 1918, 48 had been sponsored by trade unions. Near the outset, in 1903, a conference of the Labour Representation Committee had taken the momentous decision that unions should no longer confine themselves to supporting their own parliamentary candidates, but should contribute to a common fund. On their affiliated membership of 700,000 they would pay a penny a head a year, which would yield £3,000. By 1978, the unions were contributing £1.50 m out of the total £1.67 m income of the Labour Party. In addition, they were making contributions locally where they sponsored candidates, and putting up campaign funds for general elections.

2

But this short statement of facts lies on the surface of complex contingencies and hazardous advances. Only with hindsight do we know that it was a Labour Party capable of achieving a majority at Westminster that was being launched by the Labour Representation Committee. The trade unions in any case were only participants in a convergence of interests and ideas. So far as history may be schematized, we can say that there were three stages. In the first, trade unionists felt the need to have their own spokesmen in Parliament, but could put them forward only with the agreement of the Liberal Party in the constituencies. In the second, a strong drive for independent Labour representation, obtaining much trade union support through the Labour Representation Committee, led to the formation of the Labour Party in 1906; but it made little headway, and in 1914 it had little prospect of expanding at the expense of the Liberal Party. The war changed that radically: the third stage comprises 1914–22, and sees the achievement of a Labour vote as a substantial proportion of the national electorate.

The first stage opens as far back as the time of the Reform Act of 1867. At first the practical issue was only the effective use of the vote now given to many urban wage-earners: they must make it a condition of their supporting a candidate that he should endorse measures in the interests of 'the industrious classes'. A radical in the Liberal Party was most likely to do this, but there could also be a sympathetic Tory. What now made some leading trade unionists feel that they must send some of their own sort, working men, to speak for them in Parliament, was the undermining of the legal status of the unions. In 1867 the Court of Queen's Bench held that a trade union could not proceed under the Friendly Societies Act to protect its funds because its objects being in restraint of trade rendered it an illegal organization – a judgement whose implication for the status of trade unions went far beyond its immediate effect. Meanwhile an outbreak of crime that, rightly or wrongly, was linked with trade unionism in Sheffield, had led to the appointment of a Royal Commission on Trade Unions, and Parliament was expected to legislate on its Report. This state of legal insecurity caused the London Working Men's Association, a committee of trade unionists formed to agitate for reform, to turn to direct representation. It put a number of trade unionists forward as candidates in the election of 1868, but all failed. Then came a second legal blow. Gladstone's Government accompanied an Act which finally relieved the trade unions from the taint of criminal conspiracy with a separate Act, the Criminal Law Amendment Act, which laid such restrictions on striking, especially on picketing, as to cripple the unions in practice.

This time a Labour Representation League took up the challenge. Prominent in this association of trade unionists were the members of the Junta, the group of national officers of the New Model unions who recently had been so successful in securing a tolerable verdict from the Royal Commission. The League threw itself into the 1874 election, with the repeal of the Criminal Law Amendment Act as a main aim. Two of its candidates, Thomas Burt of the Northumberland Miners and Alexander Macdonald of the Scottish Miners, were elected – we have seen that these were the first trade unionists to sit in Parliament. There followed a great victory. In 1875 Disraeli's Government gave the unions all they had been asking for: relief from the taint of criminal conspiracy; repeal of the Criminal Law Amendment Act, with a new and fair law of picketing in its place; and instead of the old Master and Servant Act based on subordination, an Employers and Workmen Act based on contract.

It might have been expected that the political exertion which had produced so great an effect in its first campaign would have gone on from strength to strength. Nothing of the sort happened. The Labour Representation League died away. The TUC, which from its formation in 1863 had been adopting motions in favour of Labour representation, for years did nothing practical to that end. There were two obstacles. The first was money. Even after the Corrupt Practices Act of 1883, which greatly reduced the costs to which candidates were liable in practice, elections were expensive. As the deep depression of the 1870s cut into union membership, and the recurrence of heavy unemployment in the mid-80s drew on the funds of the surviving unions, few unions except the miners' were disposed to finance an election and pay an allowance to a successful candidate. Still less were unions willing to pay their own members' money away into a common fund for the support of candidates from other unions: at the Trades Union Congress of 1891 a proposal to set up a parliamentary fund by a levy of a penny per member was defeated by a vote of more than two to one. The second obstacle was the presence of the Liberal Party already entrenched in the constituencies. To run an independent Labour candidate, it was held, was only to split the vote against the Tory and let him in: the only practicable course was to get the trade unionists' man adopted by the local Liberal caucus. When at long last the TUC moved on from an annual resolution on the return of working men to Parliament, and set up a body which in 1887 hived off as the Labour Electoral Association, this set out, working through the trades councils in many parts of the country, for the most part to gain the co-operation of the local Liberals. It became a large body, with 750,000 members in its affiliated unions and trades councils in 1890. Six years later it had ceased to exist. In two general elections meanwhile it had achieved nothing except to support those Liberal–Labour candidates whom the local Liberal caucuses would have been willing to endorse in any case.

It was as Lib–Labs that trade unionists were making their way into Parliament. They were financed by their own unions. They accepted the policies of the radical wing of the Liberal Party, and were devoted to the leadership of Gladstone. If they stood for certain objects of special interest to Labour, they were at pains to deny that theirs was a class interest: they held that they could watch over the interests of the constituencies at large just as well as a Member from one of the other parties. In the House they sat as Liberal Members, but met as an informal group to discuss Labour questions. Of the first two to enter in 1874, Burt had stood as Radical-Labour but was not opposed by the Liberals; Macdonald stood as a Liberal. In 1880 they were joined by Broadhurst, who was to become a junior minister under Gladstone. In 1885 came a substantial increase: eleven in all were returned, six of them miners. In the four general elections in 1886–1900 the number varied, rising to fourteen in 1892 and falling to nine in 1900.

3

The keynote of the second stage was independence. In the 1890s some trade unionists throughout the country were becoming impatient with what the Lib–Lab members were getting done and could be expected to do. They saw no prospect of making any substantial progress through the existing channels of representation with the measures that working people needed – the eight-hour day; restriction of overtime and piece-work; prohibition of child labour; old-age pensions, and maintenance for those now dependent on the relieving officer or the workhouse, and paid work for the unemployed. Only independent Labour members could pursue those aims without constraint. What could be achieved by a compact minority was being shown by the Irish members.

It was independence above all for which Keir Hardie stood. As a miners' agent he had not been effective. In the TUC he had been a rebel. His socialism was vague and romantic. What he cared for passionately was that working men should enter Parliament able to speak out for the bitter wrongs and the deep longings of their fellow workers, without cramping commitments to any party. In 1893 he presided over a conference that brought delegates together from the independent labour organizations and socialist societies that had been growing up in recent years especially in the North of England, and in the West Riding most of all; there were delegates also from some trades councils, and from the Social Democratic Federation and the Fabians. This conference set up the Independent Labour Party. The candidates whom it would support must pledge themselves if returned to act in the House as members of that Party 'in advancing the interests of Labour irrespective of the convenience of any political party'; they must sit in opposition 'no matter which party be in power'.[2] In fact the ILP candidates were singularly unsuccessful in the next two general elections; but in the constituencies the movement was advanced by the devotion of its adherents.

The significance of the setting up of the Labour Representation Committee in 1900 was that it yoked a number of trade unions with the ILP in the cause of independent representation, with the approval of the TUC. There was much in the programme of the ILP to put off the old guard of the TUC – the 'taxation, to extinction, of unearned income', and the nationalization of the means of production (including the land), distribution, and exchange. This was directly antipathetic to those leading trade unionists who were Liberals. Others there were who held that politics of all colours like religion should be kept out of trade unionism because it was divisive. In 1895 the TUC had altered its rules so as to exclude delegates from trades councils, who were apt to take a political and socialist line. But then the outlook of the TUC changed. Its leading members seem to have become increasingly alarmed by the reaction of the Engineering Employers in the great dispute of 1897–8, with the foreboding that this presaged a general intention of British employers to copy American attacks on trade unions; and by legal decisions affecting the law of civil conspiracy and picketing which seemed to be progressively diminishing the right to strike. Before the TUC met in 1899 the leaders of the ILP knew that the TUC was going to join forces with them. The resolution that the TUC adopted at its meeting instructed

the Parliamentary Committee to invite the co-operation of all the cooperative, socialistic, trade union, and other working organisations to jointly co-operate on lines mutually agreed upon, in convening a special congress of representatives from such of the above-named organisations as may be willing to take part to devise ways and means for securing the return of an increased number of labour members to the next Parliament.

The resolution came up from the Doncaster Branch of the Railway Servants, but Keir Hardie and Ramsay MacDonald in the ILP may well have known what was going on.[3]

If it was the rising tension of the times that brought the TUC in, it was able to come in only because of Keir Hardie's policy for the ILP. Hardie had consistently played down all doctrinal commitments that would put the trade unionists off: provided he could get an independent group of MPs acting together in the House on issues as they arose, he did not want to insist on their subscribing to any articles of faith. In the same way, when the Labour Representation Committee began to act and the contributions of the trade unions were pooled for the support of candidates at large, Ramsay MacDonald as Secretary of the Committee had to walk delicately. This he was well qualified to do. He was himself a leading ILP'er and socialist, but his socialism was of an evolutionary and parliamentary type that allowed him to direct his energies upon practical measures which were within the purview of the radical wing of the Liberals, and provided some common ground with the Lib-Lab trade unionists.

Eighteen months after the Labour Representation Committee was set up, the Law Lords pronounced their Taff Vale judgement. It was this that brought a substantial number of trade unions in to the support of a national Labour Party. It would be natural to suppose that the TUC would then have regarded the nascent party as a counter-attack it had itself mounted against legal oppression. In later years, it is true, it has claimed that it had conveniently hived politics off. At the Congress of 1904 resolutions concerning the Labour Representation Committee were ruled out of order because they purported 'to endorse or amend the constitution of an independent and outside body'. This body, moreover, so far from serving as an instrument of the TUC, began to appear as a rival. At least when the Labour Party was formed with its strength in the House of 1906, a problem of 'overlapping' in parliamentary business arose. Henderson was anxious to avoid 'separate action', but the Parliamentary Committee of the TUC insisted on going its own way: in 1908 its Secretary even expressed himself in Congress as 'thanking the Labour Party most heartily for the support it had given the Parliamentary Committee for their work in Parliament'.[4] The Parliamentary Committee had its reason for standing apart. It had to be prepared to work with the Government of the day, whatever its political colour; it did not want to be identified with a party which must be in opposition – and, as it must have seemed in those days, perpetual opposition. Henderson, on the other hand, was a trade unionist in origin and feeling as well as a leader in the House, and his view was that the TUC and the Party were 'two sides of one movement'.

That view became more difficult to uphold because the prospects of the Party did not brighten after 1906. The immediate difficulty was the frequent unwillingness of local Liberal associations to adopt trade unionists as candidates. But this would not have held Labour up if these candidates could have dispensed with Liberal support: the needed organization could have been created if the response of voters to an independent Labour candidature had been there. But the Labour Party had little to offer as yet that would outdo the New Liberalism of Lloyd George and Winston Churchill – trade boards fixing minimum

wages; old age pensions, health and unemployment insurance; with a
People's Budget, taxation of land values, and an assault on the House
of Lords. The appeal of the Labour Party could have been greater only
if working men had been really stirred by the prospect of realizing a
socialist society, but few of them had been. Class consciousness was
powerful but it was subtle in its gradations and zones: there was no one
working class whose self-awareness would throw a massive vote
behind its champions in the class conflict. Nor does the industrial strife
of the time uniformly denote political alignment. The claim of the
trade union at the place of work was distinct from the appeal of the
Labour Party in a general election. The miners who engaged in a great
struggle that brought a national crisis about in 1912 were many of
them Liberal voters. South Wales in those years was torn by strife, with
troops patrolling the Rhondda, and young syndicalists drafting 'The
Miners' Next Step': but, Kenneth Morgan says, 'in every case in 1910
and later, where there was a direct, head-on clash between Liberals
and Labour at the polls, Labour came off second best . . . Political
labour did not yet menace the Liberal ascendancy in Wales to any
decisive extent.'[5] 'The present Labour representation in Parliament',
Philip Snowden wrote in 1913, 'is there mainly by the good will of the
Liberals, and it will disappear when that good will is turned to resentment.'[6]

Thus in 1914 the answers to two questions remained doubtful –
whether a Labour Party independent of the Liberals would develop
into a substantial national party; and if it did so, what its relations
would be with the TUC.

4

The first of those questions was to be answered definitively in the next
eight years. We have said that those years 1914–22 formed the third
stage in the emergence of the Labour Party. From the regional, limited,
and uncertain electoral support of 1910–14 the Party rose by 1922 to a
high proportion of the national vote, so that it displaced the Liberals as
the party of government alternative to the Conservatives. This proportion, moreover, it maintained fully, save for one dip in 1931, through
the inter-war years, until a further lift at the end of the Second World
War raised it to a yet higher if more irregular plateau. Labour received
29 per cent of the votes cast in the election of 1922. The proportion
rose in each of the three subsequent elections, to reach 37 per cent in
1929. After the set-back in 1931, when the Party itself was split, it
recovered to rather more than 37 per cent again in 1935. In 1945 it was
nearly 48 per cent. But these shares of the total vote depend on how
many candidates of all sorts are put forward. More significant of the

emergence out of the war years of, as it seems, an extraordinarily fully formed, settled and solid Labour vote, are the figures that David Butler has calculated of the average vote per candidate. Some of these are set out in Table 1. They mark a transformation.

TABLE 1

Average Vote per Candidate of each
Party in General Elections, 1922–45.

	Con %	Lib %	Lab %
1922	48.6	38.4	40.0
1923	42.6	37.8	41.0
1924	51.9	30.9	38.2
1929	39.4	27.7	39.3
1931	67.4		33.0
1935	54.8	23.9	40.3
1945	40.1	18.6	50.4

Source: D. E. Butler, *Electoral System in Britain Since 1918* (2nd ed., Oxford, 1963), Table 22, p. 173.

It was due to several great changes originating in the war years. There was first the experience of full employment. The standing of the individual worker over against the foreman was transformed; manual workers generally were assured by their scarcity of an unaccustomed independence; and the earnings of many of them rose relatively to those of the middle classes, especially after these had borne hitherto unheard of rates of tax. The Whitley Committee, appointed to probe the causes of the industrial unrest of 1916, found them in the lack of recognition of the workers' manhood, and their right to be informed and consulted within industry no less than they were as citizens. Full employment made for confidence in asserting such claims as these. They sprang from attitudes that inherently distinguished the Labour Party supporter from the radical Liberal. Those attitudes were strengthened by the idealism, looking towards post-war reconstruction, that bore up broad sectors of the community. When in the end those hopes were dashed down, the post-war boom was followed in 1921–2 by severe depression, and the Government's policy of cuts ended all expectations of a brave new world, the revulsion of feeling strengthened support for the party that alone offered a basic change in the system that permitted such vicissitudes, disillusionment, and suffering.

Full employment had made most difference of all to the unskilled workers in the towns. It was in the election of 1918 that most of them were able to vote for the first time. They were numerous, making up about 30 per cent of the urban labour force. At the best of times they had been under-employed, many of them in casual work – a state of affairs that is hard to envisage today, because during the War it was removed permanently; the advance of education meanwhile, and the better provision for unemployment after the War, prevented it returning. Down to the war it was among the disabilities of these unskilled workers that the rules of registration worked in practice to deprive them of the vote. Unlike many skilled workers, and the miners and textile workers, they had no traditional attachment to existing parties. It is likely that they – and those of their womenfolk who got the vote at the same time – would have been drawn from the first to the Labour candidate.

A third great change that came about during the War was the break-up of the Liberal Party. It had seemed not long before that Labour could advance its candidatures only through postern gates held by the Liberal Party; and now the Liberal walls had crumbled. More important than the collapse of constituency organization was the loss of faith by the Liberal following. The trumpet gave an uncertain sound. The reputation of Asquith was tarnished as a leader in war, of Lloyd George as a leader in peace. The writing of hypothetical history is as impossible as it is alluring. We cannot tell whether, if the War had not split the Liberals, many of their supporters who actually transferred to Labour would have stayed with them indefinitely; or whether the working out of the vein of Liberal reforms, and the growing education, political awareness, and readiness to assert claims among the manual workers, would in any case have ensured the displacement of the Liberal Party by Labour. But we can be sure that the break-up of the Liberal Party brought it about that this displacement was effected more rapidly and completely.

5

The second undecided question of 1914, the relations between a Labour Party once established and the TUC, has received no final answer. In 1931 and 1969 it brought Cabinet crises. Each of these sprang from the conflict between two principles. On the one hand was the view that the TUC and the Party were 'two sides of the same movement', so that when the Party formed the Government, there should be consultation on policy between the leaders of the two sides, and the Government should at least not adopt measures that were repugnant to the TUC. On the other hand it was held that the Party having come into office by reason of its representation in a democratically elected Parliament was exclusively responsible for preserving and advancing the national interest as the Government understood that to be; and no particular interest group should claim a special link with and consideration from the Government, still less a veto on its proposals. In the crisis of 1931 it was Arthur Henderson who stood foremost for the unity of the movement, and led the withdrawal from the Cabinet of Ministers who followed the TUC in rejecting cuts in social benefits deemed necessary for the defence of sterling. The crisis of 1969 arose from the opposition of the TUC to proposals for dealing with the unofficial strike by new procedures backed with a measure of compulsion. It is discussed in Chapter X of this work, which notes that what made the Cabinet finally abandon the proposals was the intimation that they would not get enough support among Labour members to carry them in the House.

In these two cases of collision, the issues were either public fiscal and social policy, albeit with a special bearing on the unemployed, or the introduction of new dispute procedures, backed by some compulsory powers. In such fields it was not clear how far the party in office must accede to the wishes of the trade unions. The relations between the unions and the Parliamentary Party remain under constant discussion and review in the constitution of the Party and the procedure for the formation of the Party programme. But one matter of great importance to the trade unions has never been in doubt: at the outset of this chapter we saw that whenever the unions have wanted legislation to repeal Conservative Acts, reverse decisions of the courts, or increase their effectiveness in bargaining, the Labour Party in office has provided it.

Notes

[1] *The Times*, 25 June 1981. See also the letter from Anthony Frodsham, Director General of the Engineering Employers' Federation, ibid, 8 July 1981.

[2] A. W. Humphrey, *A History of Labour Representation* (London, 1912), p. 135.

[3] See David Marquand, *Ramsay MacDonald* (London, 1977], p. 66–7.

[4] TUC Report, 1908, p. 114. Quoted here from Ross M. Martin, *TUC: The Growth of a Pressure Group 1868–1976* (Oxford, 1980), p. 116.

[5] Kenneth O. Morgan, *Rebirth of a Nation: Wales 1880–1980* (Oxford, 1981), p. 145.

[6] *Labour Leader*, 16 May 1911, quoted here from Roy Douglas, 'Labour in Decline, 1910–14', in K. D. Brown (ed.), *Essays in Anti-Labour History* (London, 1974), p. 125.

V

THE TRADE UNIONS OVER AGAINST
THE GOVERNMENT

IT was only with the relations between workers and their employers in view that Parliament in 1906 had restored the immunities of the trade unions in the exercise of their power. Yet we have seen that already a union's power to cut off vital supplies had involved the Government in a dispute; and though that involvement had as yet been only a way of successful peace-making, the prospect was apparent of a clash between the requirements of a Government responsible for the maintenance of vital supplies, and the terms acceptable to the trade unionists concerned. In fact, the Act of 1906 was followed by twenty years of strain and conflict between the authority of the Government and the desire of the trade unionists to use their newly formed and strongest weapon in defence of their vital interests. The present chapter considers these relations down to the end of the General Strike of 1926, except that the special issues raised by the Government's intervention into industrial relations in the two Great Wars are dealt with separately in Chapter VI. The resistance of the trade unions to the attempt to regulate them by the Industrial Relations Act, 1971, is discussed in Chapter XI.

I

The trade unions whose vigour pulsed so high around 1890, and whose extension had attained among the miners the power to bring the Government in to end the stoppage of 1893, were soon to undergo ten years of reaction and repulse. From 1895 until near the end of 1905 the administration was unionist, and for all the tradition of Disraeli there was a great difference in practice between the remoteness from the unions of ministries led by Salisbury or Balfour, and the accessibility of Gladstone's colleagues. But the unionists escaped any head-on collision, and even any involvement in a major dispute, for the unions were hamstrung: we have seen how decisions in the courts limited their activities in various ways and led up to the Taff Vale decision, which put in jeopardy the whole funds of any union that engaged in a strike. The Unionist Governments were not confronted with any challenge to their authority by the unions, or any crisis of the economy requiring them to intervene. In engineering, the dispute of 1897–8 was greater in extent and duration than any previous stoppage in any industry, but it did not hold up essential national supplies. Wage-earnings fell more than might have been expected in the depression that followed the boom during the Boer War.[1] Real wage-earnings were no higher in 1905 than they had been twelve years before.

For the unions the overwhelming victory of the Liberals in the election of February 1906 was a release from bondage. The Ministers were more kindly disposed towards them personally, even though the lawyers had their reservations about the complete reversal of Taff Vale. Sympathies and outlook apart, Liberal members were very conscious of pressures in the constituencies. With the sure prospect of release from Taff Vale before them, the unions took the initiative promptly, and pushed wages up sharply. This was the rebound from the ten years of repulse, and the first fruits of the Lib–Lab alliance.

But when the following year the railwaymen moved to break down the rigid resistance of the Companies to trade unionism, they raised an issue that was soon to be unmistakably one not of alliance but of confrontation between unions and government. At first, it is true, the Government seemed to be involved only as a conciliator, and one whose influence would in practice be brought to bear mainly on the employers, to induce them to offer terms acceptable to their workers. The workers in their tens and hundreds of thousands cannot be forced to go to work on terms they reject, under whatever auspices those terms have been awarded. But the employers are sensitive to pressure. They find it harder to stand between the public and a settlement that the public needs greatly. Unlike their workers they are subject to effective coercion by law, because they are far fewer, and because what is to be enforced is not the work they shall perform for given terms, but the terms on which they shall pay for given work. These terms, moreover, concern only one factor of production – though that often the most important – in their businesses; and changes in cost are always arising from various sources, over against possible changes in price, so that there is by no means the direct relation between the terms of the workers' employment and the profit of the business in which they work that there is between those terms and the workers' own incomes.

For all these reasons it might seem that for the unions to involve the Government was invariably to gain an ally. It was when the coal-owners had been brought in to give up, at least for the time being, the claim for a reduction in wages which the miners had been resisting, that Gladstone's Government had got a return to work in 1893. It was by pressure on the employers that the Liberal Government after 1906 twice averted the disruption of the whole economy by a strike of the one other union that had the power at that time to stop a vital service – the Railway Servants. This union was pressing for recognition; the railway companies, except the North Eastern, were refusing on principle to grant it. In 1907 they rejected three successive requests for a meeting with the officers of the union, and the members voted for a strike. Under threat of special legislation, Lloyd George forced on the railway directors a scheme of conciliation boards that gave union officers a foot inside the door, and the strike was averted. In 1911 the railwaymen did strike, suddenly: a spontaneous stoppage in Liverpool roused railwaymen throughout the country, and the executive of their union gave the companies twenty-four hours in which to grant full recognition. But Lloyd George got the railwaymen back to work after only two days: he urged the national interest in the then critical state of international relations after Agadir to make the directors give way, and for the first time depute some of their number to meet the union officers.

So far the disputes had had two limiting conditions: the union members had been prepared to settle for terms that the Government had been able to obtain from or was prepared to enforce upon the employers; and the union had not made deliberate use of the political power inherent in its ability to threaten economic catastrophe. These conditions were now to be removed.

The absence of the first condition harassed the Liberal Government as it endeavoured to settle the coal strike that was threatening to bring industry to a halt in the spring of 1912. The Miners' Federation was claiming a national minimum wage of 5s. a day for men and 2s. for boys. Most of the coal-owners accepted the principle of a minimum, but how it should be applied was a different matter: they held that the districts differed far too much for any single national figure to be practicable, and they wanted the amount to be negotiated, district by district. They also required safeguards to ensure that the minimum would be secured only to those who did a fair day's work. The Prime Minister with three members of his Cabinet met the parties and pleaded with the miners to accept these district negotiations: but they would have nothing less than the single national 'five and two'. What was the Government to do? Taking the strikers together with those who were laid off for lack of fuel, there were reckoned to be two million out of work, and each day that the strike went on the numbers grew. The Government was prepared to impose a settlement on the coal-owners by legislation, and the principle of a statutory minimum wage had already been admitted in the Trade Boards Act of 1909, but to fix the wage in shillings and pence by Act of Parliament was a very different matter. In any case there was great force in the argument that a single minimum could be too low for the high-paying fields yet so high as to put the jobs of miners in the poorer fields at risk. The Government had met a long-standing demand of the Miners' Federation by the Eight Hours Act, also of 1909, but this uniform regulation of the whole industry had caused great disturbances in its application to the variety of local conditions. The Bill that now became law on the eighth day after it was brought in gave the miners only so much as the Government believed they could demand in their own interest. It followed the Trade Boards Act in not itself fixing wages but setting up joint boards to do this from time to time. It avoided the difficulties into which the Eight Hours Act had run by providing separate boards district by district. In both these respects it disappointed the Miners' Federation.

What then would happen if the miners said 'This is not good enough', and the strike went on? The appalling possibility had been faced in the Commons, in the debate on the motion giving leave to introduce the Bill. The Prime Minister hinted, in that event, at Parliament's being 'hereafter . . . compelled to take other and different measures to defend against paralysis and starvation the industries and the people of this country',[2] but he did not go farther. It was left to Bonar Law for the Opposition, in his survey of alternative policies, to indicate one way in which Government might intervene directly to get a resumption of work:

the Government should say to both parties 'That is the way the strike must end'; and to secure that result they would have been bound to put all possible pressure on the masters to open the pits, and all possible pressure on the men to induce them to go back to the pits. . . . Anyone who has considered the subject knows perfectly well the kind of pressure that has been used in other countries, and which is the only possible kind of pressure, if such a course were taken.[3]

He may well have been thinking of what Clemenceau and Briand had been doing to put down strikes in France. Often troops were sent in, and clashes and bloodshed followed: as many as 40,000 troops were drafted into the Pas de Calais when a miners' strike there was suppressed in 1906. The arrest of leaders was common. The toll of the strikes of 1907–8 is given as 104 years of prison sentences, twenty killed, and more than 600 injured.[4] When in 1910 a strike on the Nord railway began to spread to other lines, the Council of Ministers placed the railwaymen of the Nord under military mobilization for twenty-one days, and Briand had the strike committee arrested. Lloyd George equally may have had these measures in mind when he asked Bonar

Law what it was he really meant by saying he would bring pressure to bear upon the parties.

Did he mean that he would imprison the miners' leaders? Did he mean that he would imprison the masters if they refused to open their mines? Did he mean that he would take possession of these mines in the interest of the State, if the masters refused to work them on these terms? Did he mean that he would sequester the unions' funds? Did he mean that he would prosecute men because they refused to work?[5]

Clearly the Government understood its powerlessness, if the miners refused to settle for what was granted and assured to them in the Act, and yet the game was to continue to be played under British rules. No one knew what in fact the miners would do. The Act was a victory for the miners of Scotland and South Wales, but it only gave the English miners statutory backing for what many of them could have obtained from their own employers by direct negotiation. Perhaps the Government had its plans for action to maintain essential supplies if the miners decided to continue the strike, but as they balloted the spectre of famine hung over the land. In a poll of 445,000, there was a majority of 43,000 for staying out. But the districts were divided: in particular, the biggest district of all, South Wales, where funds had been run down by a struggle the year before, had voted by two to one for going back to work. The Miners' Executive decided that as a two-thirds majority had been held necessary for calling the strike, so it was necessary for continuing it, and Conference agreed. The strike ended, says the historian of the miners, 'with great dissatisfaction among the pitmen, who felt that the Government had cheated them of an assured victory'.[6] If they had stayed out, would the Government have had to come back to the House with another Bill, giving them their national minimum of 'five and two'? Or, with summer coming on, would the economy have managed somehow to scrape along, without utter famine of essentials in any one locality, until the miners themselves were exhausted by hunger, and perhaps borne down by the dis-approval of the community they were making suffer by their rejection of the not unreasonable terms Parliament had given them?

The Second Reading debate on the Coal Mines Bill had brought out the dual aspect of this manifestation of trade union power over against the community, over against government – the menace and aggression it signified to those whose own standing was distant from the miners, the defensive and limited purpose which was all that those with more understanding of them ascribed to it. Leading for the Conservatives, A. J. Balfour had characterized the magnitude and abuse of trade union power in terms that some commentators may have thought they were coining freshly sixty years later.

We see the spectacle [he said], the new, the strange, and the portentous spectacle of a single organisation, acting within its legal powers, practically threatening to paralyse, and in a large measure actually paralysing, the whole of the trade and manufacturers of a community which lives by trade and manufactures. The power they have got, if used to the utmost, is, under our existing law, almost limitless, and there is no appearance that the leaders of the movement desire to temper the use of their legal powers with any consideration of policy or of mercy. Can anybody quote from history in respect of any of the classes on whom are visited, and often justly visited, the indignation of the historical commentator, a parallel case? Has any feudal baron ever exercised his powers in the manner which the leaders of this great trade union are now using theirs? . . . is there any American Trust which at any period of its history has used or misused the powers given it by the law to the detriment of private individuals and general trade to the extent which we have seen and are now seeing in this country?[7]

But the Prime Minister presented the other aspect of trade union power when he spoke later in the debate. The miners' leaders, he said – and he had spent long hours with them – might not have

pursued a wise or prudent or considerate course; but I do say that to compare the action which they have taken to the action of purely selfish people who exploit and blackmail firms or persons for their own particular purpose is not a just or fair comparison. I can tell the Rt Hon. Gentleman that this claim . . . is a claim for a reasonable minimum wage for underground workers.[8]

2

This dual aspect of trade union power is a key to some critical passages of our political history from 1912 onwards. Trade unionists concerned with the terms and conditions of their employment, and using the withdrawal of their labour in the usual way as a sanction in their bargaining with their employers, had extended their organization so as to be able to stop virtually the whole of an essential industry. Thereby they threatened to dislocate the economy and inflict hardship if not disaster on the community generally, and this brought the Government in with a powerful concern to secure a settlement. It had been no part of the deliberate plans of the unionists to do this, but experience showed that the influence of government was exerted on the employers to obtain terms acceptable to the trade unionists. There were some who took the inference. If the union control of essential services could be given wider coverage, the threat to halt them would be so formidable that it would surely never have to be put into effect: the Government would have to bring the employers round.

This was a major consideration in the agreement to confer with a view to joint action that was reached in 1914–15 between the Miners'

Federation, the National Union of Railwaymen, and the National Transport Workers' Federation. This was the Triple Alliance, so called, but the alliance was a loose one. The most active element of joint action envisaged was that the three unions should present their separate claims at the same time. There was no provision for the calling out of unions on strike in support of one of the three involved in a dispute, nor could such provision easily be made when each union could call a strike only by following a procedure laid down in its own constitution. But what was expected was that the very threat of joint action coming about would be enough to ensure that it did not have to be taken. 'If they [the railwaymen] agreed upon a national strike,' a leader of the General Labourers said to a conference of the National Transport Workers' Federation in June 1914, 'it would mean that the whole of the transport workers and the miners would become involved. If that were so then there would be no need for a railway strike.'[9]

On one view, a new and major factor had arisen not in industrial relations only but, a much graver matter, in the constitution: for here was a vast combination armed with the power to bend the Government to its will, under threat of the total disruption of the economy. One of the first actions of the Triple Alliance had been to send a deputation to the Prime Minister, in the midst of the war, to demand among other things the restoration of trade union practices when the war ended. *The Times* wrote: 'This body of trade unionists is formally attempting to supersede the constitutional government, and to frighten the appointed Ministers of the Crown into doing their will.'[10] The deputation was in fact received courteously and given some of the assurances it sought. That might be explained by the need to conciliate organized labour in the interest of the war effort, but it may well also mark the evident if paradoxical innocence of unconstitutional intent among the trade unionists themselves. It is true that one member of the deputation, Bob Smillie the miners' leader, had declared on the eve of the interview that 'if an evasive answer is given by the Prime Minister trade unionists will have something to say. Governments that were not amenable to reason were amenable to force.' But this was a blast on the trumpet. The spokesmen of the Alliance would have seen themselves as following in the footsteps of the Parliamentary Committee of the TUC, whose function it was to represent to Ministers the resolutions that Congress adopted year by year; and if their own representations were implicitly supported by their formidable power to blockade the economy, they still would have seen themselves only as holding in reserve the traditional and sole means of self-defence of the working man.

None the less, the War had been raising the standing of the trade union leaders over against government, and giving them an enhanced sense of the power they wielded in the land. When in March 1915 the leaders of certain trade unions concerned with the production of munitions had been called in to meet the Chancellor of the Exchequer and the President of the Board of Trade, and after three days of debate had signed what was in effect a treaty with the Government, a land-mark had been set up. By this Treasury Agreement, as it was called, the trade union leaders agreed, during the War, to give up the strike and go to arbitration instead; and to relax practices restrictive of output. In return the Government promised to limit the profits of firms in which the practices were relaxed, and to secure the restoration of those practices after the War. The employers concerned had made some progress in their own negotiations on these matters before the confer-ence at the Treasury, but the Government did not call them in to this conference nor forewarn them of its proposals: it recognized that the power lay with the unions, and dealt with them realistically as 'high contracting parties'. Only then could it proceed to enact a statutory code for the production of munitions as it did by the first Munitions of War Act.

As the war went on, moreover, the Government of the day depended increasingly on the support of trade union officers and leaders, both in all detail of local and industrial administration, and at the national level, where the Labour MPs who became Ministers were all trade unionists. In Asquith's coalition of 1915, Arthur Henderson of the Iron-moulders – who had led the unions in reaching the Treasury Agreement – became President of the Board of Education, and William Brace of the South Wales Miners and G. H. Roberts of the Typo-graphical Society were given junior office. When a Ministry of Pen-sions was set up in 1916, George Barnes of the Engineers was appoin-ted to lead it – the same George Barnes who had led the Engineers in the great struggle of 1897–8. Lloyd George on forming his Coalition made Henderson one of the members of his inner War Cabinet; John Hodge of the Steel Smelters became the first Minister of Labour; Barnes remained at the Ministry of Pensions; among the junior Ministers Brace and Roberts were joined by James Parker of the General Workers.

What is here relevant [the Webbs observed] is that these Trade Union officials were selected, in the main, not on personal grounds, but because they repre-sented the Trade Union Movement. They accepted ministerial office with the approval, and they relinquished ministerial office at the request of the National Conference of the Labour Party, in which the Trade Unions exercised the predominant influence.[11]

The Webbs were partial witnesses, but they were recording an unmistakable contemporary impression when at the same time they observed a

revolutionary transformation of the social and political standing of the official representatives of the Trade Union world – a transformation which has been immensely accelerated by the Great War. We may, in fact, not unfairly say that Trade Unionism has, in 1920, won its recognition by Parliament and the Government, by law and by custom, as a separate element in the community, entitled to distinct recognition as part of the social machinery of the State, its members being thus allowed to give – like the clergy in Convocation – not only their votes as citizens, but also their concurrence as an order or estate.[12]

The power of the unions over against governments had indeed been transformed in a short span of years. In politics those years had been dominated by Lloyd George. From his settlement of the railway dispute of 1907 onwards, he had also been the dominating figure in industrial relations. It would be natural to attribute much of the higher standing of the unions over against governments to his spontaneous feeling for the workers, his radicalism, and especially his darting tactical sense, and the realism in negotiation that showed him how pressure could be put on the employers, whereas the trade unionists could be got back to work only on terms acceptable to them. It is true, his personal influence did tell in this way, sometimes at the expense of established procedures that would have given less scope for the exertion of power. Yet if he accepted and endorsed the advancement of the unions, he did not himself initiate or promote it.

What it did spring from was, first, the growth of the unions themselves. Between 1906 and 1914 the membership of British trade unions had almost doubled; between 1914 and 1920 it doubled again. Most of the increase in the earlier period had come during the intense and widespread conflicts of 1911–14. The aspirations aroused, the thinking quickened, and the militancy stirred at that time, count for a second factor in the growth of trade union power. But this was part of an international movement: even more in numbers than in the United Kingdom, and no less in militancy, trade unions were thrusting up at this time in other countries – in France, Germany, Sweden, and the United States.[13] So simultaneous a common manifestation cannot have been due to transmission from one country to the other, even though some international currents are apparent. It must rather be attributed to the working populations of the different countries, the United Kingdom among them, having reached at this time a certain level of industrialization, urbanization, and education that promotes militant and massive trade unionism wherever it occurs. When we put the United Kingdom in its international setting, the growth of trade union power at this time appears as part of the development of western capitalism.

But then came a distinct experience, that of full employment during the First World War. There had been local shortages of particular kinds of labour before, in the most active years of the trade cycle, but never labour shortages so universal and sustained as these. They carried bargaining power down to the shop-floor, and gave initiative and independence to groups whose dependence used to be on national leadership. This was a third factor. It meant that the power of the trade unions to be reckoned with was pervasive – in the administration of the war effort there must be effective agreement not only at the national level but with local officials and with shop stewards. The source of this power was the value put upon the head of the individual worker by his sheer scarcity during the War and the boom that followed it. With the breaking of the boom this source was lost, and unemployment began to exert its pressure from the other side; but if trade unionists' actions had perforce to become restrained, their conception of their own due place in the industrial and political structure had been raised permanently.

3

The impetus with which the unions came out of the War soon brought them into collision with the Government. When this provided for the ending of its wartime financial control of the mines, the miners entered a demand for the maintenance of a national wage that was tantamount, as the Government saw it, to an insistence on the continuance of control. If the miners were on strike or were locked out, they would expect to bring the Triple Alliance into action. Part of the Government's response was to pass an Emergency Powers Act, in June 1920, under which it could requisition vehicles, goods, and premises, and send in troops, in any emergency threatening to deprive the community or a substantial proportion of it of the essentials of life. From the trade union point of view, this enabled the Government to frame a strike-breaking organization. But Lloyd George would do his utmost to negotiate his way through; and when a number of his proposals were all rejected by the miners, it was still not clear how much their partners in the Triple Alliance were disposed to stand out with them. The proposals the miners had rejected had included one for arbitration: but the railwaymen had accepted arbitration earlier that year, the dockers had accepted a Court of Inquiry, and it seemed to them hard to be asked to bear all the hardships of a strike because the miners differed. J. H. Thomas for the railwaymen particularly objected to being asked in effect to commit his union to the outcome of negotiations from which he was excluded. So in October 1920 the miners came out on strike alone. But meanwhile a groundswell rose among the railwaymen. When the miners had been out for five days, a

Special Delegate Conference of the Railwaymen decided to call its members out. The impact on Lloyd George was decisive. He offered new talks immediately, and the negotiations that followed led to a settlement.

Though the settlement had been reached more readily because the miners were not wholeheartedly behind their claim, Lloyd George's change of stance remained as a clear demonstration of the potential power of the Alliance; and the miners may have thought their position impregnable the following year, 1921, when a week after they were locked out their two partners in the Alliance issued strike orders to take effect in only four days' time. The Government had handed the mines back to the owners, the boom had broken, and the owners were proposing to revert from the wartime national rates to the old district negotiations, and to open with big cuts. It was above all the breaking up of the national negotiation to which the miners objected, and their partners in the Alliance found common cause in resisting an attack on industry-wide bargaining. Their support will have been the more readily given also because the miners were clearly on the defensive now. On the other hand, unemployment was mounting, prices and wages were coming down all around: those who were pledged to make great sacrifices on behalf of the miners became alarmed at their obdurate refusal to compromise. This was the harder to bear, when the Miners' own executive was known to be divided on it. While negotiations went on the strike orders had been put back, to take effect at 10 p.m. on a Friday. On the Thursday evening the Miners' secretary, speaking to a meeting of MPs in the House of Commons, is said to have allowed the possible acceptability of district negotiations as a temporary form of settlement. Lloyd George was informed, and in the small hours of Friday he wrote to the Miners inviting them to consider it in renewed discussions: they refused. The partners in the Alliance asked the Miners to change their minds, and accept the invitation: they refused. Thereupon the partners decided to withdraw their strike notices. That day – Friday 15 April 1921 – went down to history as Black Friday. It was the end of the Triple Alliance.

But it was by no means the end of the belief in the overwhelming pressure that unions could exert by acting together. In 1924 the London tramwaymen, trying to make good the cuts they had suffered not long before, came out on strike in support of a wage claim, and the busmen – themselves more highly paid – came out in sympathy. This complete stoppage of surface transport had a powerful impact on the people of London, and on the Labour Government that was now in office. The Prime Minister, Ramsay MacDonald, wrote to Ernest Bevin as leader of the Transport and General Workers to warn him that any extension of the strike was 'bound to bring in the Government'.[14] Bevin replied by a letter in which, as Alan Bullock has said, 'the General Secretary of the TGWU addressed the Prime Minister as if he were negotiating with an equal power';[15] and on the same day announced that the three railway unions had agreed to call out the Underground. The next day the Cabinet approved a draft proclamation of a state of emergency, and set in motion a number of measures to enable London to carry on, such as the protection of any services still running, the recruitment of special constables, and the use of naval ratings in the power stations of the Underground lines. At the same time the Government promised to bring in a Bill to reorganize the public transport of London, which a Court of Inquiry appointed at the outset of the stoppage had held to be the necessary condition for higher wages. The TUC General Council and the National Executive of the Labour Party joined in condemning the Government's use of the Emergency Powers Act which the Coalition Government had passed in 1920: instead they demanded that the Government should nationalize London transport and subsidize it to enable higher wages to be paid. But the prospect of the Bill, together with an improved offer from the employers, led to the calling off of the Underground strike, and to a settlement accepted by the tramwaymen.

4

The tramwaymen's dispute was seen as a demonstration of the power of the sympathetic strike. The leaders of the TUC hardly needed this reminder in what was now their mood of militancy in defence. After Black Friday the direction of the combined forces of the unions, where that was necessary, devolved upon them for the first time. Down to 1921 in all industrial matters the trade unions had dealt with the Government individually. Though the TUC had been represented in the discussions that led to the Treasury Agreement on munitions production in 1915, so had been thirty-three different unions, and the TUC had not signed the agreement. When the railwaymen or the miners were in conflict amounting to a national emergency, the TUC did not intervene. But when the Triple Alliance had gone, how should mutual support and solidarity among the unions be organized and directed except by the TUC? In 1920 it had adopted a new constitution: the Parliamentary Committee had been replaced by a General Council empowered to 'keep a watch on all industrial movements and . . . attempt, where possible, to co-ordinate industrial action'. Bevin, though he was not to join the General Council himself until 1925, had taken a leading part in planning and promoting it. His leadership and bearing had just shown his confidence in the force he wielded and in his justification for wielding it. A number of members of the General

Council must have shared his attitude. They saw Black Friday as a gratuitous failure of nerve whose very shamefulness placed them under an obligation to be resolute the next time. They would undertake the concerted strike only in defence: striking was too costly, painful, and risky an affair for workers to come out when they had no dispute with their own employers, unless they saw their fellow workers under a major attack. The issue would be purely industrial, a question of wages and hours; those joining in would only be engaging in a sympathetic strike; their action raised no constitutional issue. True, they meant to put pressure on the Government, in a way that lay outside the channels of parliamentary democracy: but the aim was still only to get the Government to bestir itself, to involve itself in the original dispute, and use its powers to get a settlement on terms the workers could accept. Experience, moreover, had given reason to believe that the mere threat of concerted action would be enough to rouse the Government and bring home to it the strength of the workers' case. Partly because of this expectation, but also because the role of directing action at the national level was new to the members of the General Council, they gave extraordinarily little thought to the development of their new commitment and role.

In 1925 they plunged into it. When the market for coal contracted sharply, and the miners called for support in their resistance to the owners' demands for lower wages and longer hours, the General Council called on trade unionists to place themselves 'without qualification and unreservedly at the disposal of the Miners' Federation'.[16] It can have had no doubt of its stance. The sense that they were all in this together was the deeper because 1925 looked like being a repetition of 1921, when the breaking of the miners' stand against wage-cuts was followed by successive cuts in other industries. But the General Council had no plan. All it did was to appoint a Special Committee to work together with the Miners. This Committee looked at ways of imposing an embargo on the movement of coal. It soon appeared that the embargo would in practice extend to a strike throughout the old Triple Alliance, and that there was a powerful groundswell of support for it — the harshness of the coal-owners' terms had seen to that.

The aim of the Government, under Baldwin, had been to stand aside and let the coal-owners and the Miners reach their own settlement: but both were obdurate in their refusal to compromise. The coal-owners gave notices that expired on 31 July. Just three weeks before that the Government intervened for the first time when it used its good offices to try to bring the two sides together. When that failed it appointed a Court of Inquiry which the Miners boycotted. On 27 July the Special Committee of the General Council visited the Prime Minister, and probably raised the possibility of a subsidy to the industry to enable the coal-owners' notices to be suspended while an inquiry into the industry was conducted: we know at least that the Cabinet discussed a subsidy the next day, when the threat of the stoppage was brought before it for the first time. On the evening of Wednesday 29 July the Special Committee saw the Prime Minister again: it appears that they now made it clear that in default of a subsidy they would send out notices for a coal embargo. The following morning the Prime Minister and his Chancellor of the Exchequer, Winston Churchill, worked out plans for a subsidy. Meanwhile a conference of union executives sat all day in the Central Hall at Westminster, and it approved the embargo. The Prime Minister met the Miners again, and proposed an inquiry into ways of improving the industry, but the Miners demanded a subsidy as a condition of continuing work while the inquiry went on. The Prime Minister ruled it out at the time; but faced with that impasse, in the evening the Cabinet decided by a majority 'that as between a national strike and the payment of assistance to the mining industry, the latter course was the less disadvantageous'.[17] The fateful decision was announced the next day, Friday the 31st. Forthwith it was dubbed Red Friday.

It was Red in that it was a reversal of Black Friday. Before Black Friday, Lloyd George has been rather willing than otherwise to take on a strike by the Triple Alliance. 'I think we had better have a strike', he said to Thomas Jones. 'Let them kick their heels for a week or a fortnight. It will help the moderates against the extremists.' And again, 'I believe you can prick the bubble. These men have always had the idea they can strangle the community.'[18] He could say this because of the extent of the preparations that the Government had made against such a stoppage. But, said Thomas Jones, the succeeding administrations allowed the organization under the Supply and Transport Committee to run down, so that on Red Friday the Government was caught out.[19]

In the eyes of many observers, the redness of that day was of a deep and threatening hue because it had seen economic power being wielded outside Parliament in order to overturn the judgement of a democratically responsible executive. Ramsay MacDonald, who two years before had been Prime Minister in the first Labour Government, declared that

it has handed over the appearance of victory to the very forces that sane, well-considered, thoroughly well examined Socialism feels to be probably its greatest enemy. The Tory Government, in . . . the methods it adopted to bring this temporary settlement into being, has sided with the wildest Bolshevik, if not in words, certainly in fact and in substance.[20]

But in the eyes of the trade unionists that day had not been intended to be Red at all, either politically or constitutionally.

When the Bill for the subsidy came to be debated in the House of Commons, it was really common ground that the Government had yielded to a threat. To most Conservatives it seemed a threat to the constitution. While Baldwin put the case for a subsidy to avoid the loss and suffering that a great stoppage would cause, a case that would justify a subsidy to avert any major strike or lock-out, the members behind him are said to have sat dissatisfied and silent: they came to life only when at the last he spoke of the menace to democracy the Government had felt when it had found itself confronted 'by a great alliance of trade unions who had the power and the will to inflict enormous and irreparable damage on their country'.[21] Winston Churchill too noted

a growing disposition among the great trade union authorities of the country to use the exceptional immunities which trade unions possess under the law, not for the purpose of ordinary trade objects, but in the pursuit of far-reaching political and economic aims. It is, obviously, impossible for a Parliament, elected as we are upon what is virtually a universal suffrage, to allow its authority to be disputed by any section or organisation however respectable or however powerful. We have heard in this Debate of an attempt to hold up the whole community, of the threat of cutting off the vital supply services. The use of such a threat as a political weapon, which has been more and more apparent in recent years, is a grave fact which will require the profound and continuous attention of the House of Commons.'[22]

But J. R. Clynes from the General and Municipal Workers put the actual intent of the trade unionists with the candour of a clear conscience, and showed how unaware they had been, within their own intense and narrow perspective, of their own constitutional involvement.

I was present [he said] as representing a large trade union during the whole of the time of the two great conferences which have considered this matter . . . and I can assure the Prime Minister that he is completely in the wrong in reaching his conclusion that this movement was not wholly and solely a movement in defence of wage standards. The speeches delivered by those who addressed those gatherings were expressed in terms indicating a deep sense of responsibility . . . The reason why those conferences took place was that in the other trades the men working on the railways, the general workers employed in transport services and so on, felt that the wage standards of the miners must be maintained lest their own wages would later on be forced down . . . May I point out that in this instance the workers were not the attacking party? They simply put their backs to the wall, as men who were called upon to act on the defensive.[23]

Such was indeed the intent of the rank and file. That of the leaders of the TUC went beyond it, though still without meaning to usurp the functions of government. They were working in the tradition of the

Parliamentary Committee, the immediate predecessor of the General Council as the top body of the Congress, which had customary access to Ministers in order to urge on them measures that lay within the ambit and power of government but particularly concerned trade unionists. This, it seemed, was all that the Special Committee of the General Council had been doing now: it had urged the Government to grant a subsidy that would enable the mines to carry on with the existing wages and hours while a fresh inquiry into the industry in all its aspects was conducted. True, it backed this plea by the threat of blocking vital supplies and services, and for the Government this made a basic difference of principle; but it did not seem to do so to the trade union leaders. Here they may have been misled by their own experience. When in 1920 it seemed that the United Kingdom might become involved in the defence of Poland against Russia, a Council of Action was formed from the Labour Party and the trade unions, and a deputation whose spokesman was Ernest Bevin told the Prime Minister, Lloyd George, that they were opposed not merely to military intervention, but to any form of help to those at war with Russia. Three days later a conference including 700 trade union delegates called on the Council of Action to ensure that British forces would not be used against Russia, and empowered it 'to call for any and every form of withdrawal of labour which circumstances may require.'[24] Meanwhile discussions between the Council of Action and the Prime Minister continued. Bevin's biographer has termed them 'negotiations'[25] and the Prime Minister seems to have raised no question of constitutionality. In fact, given the state of public opinion generally, he was most unlikely to have undertaken a military intervention, even without any Council of Action. But it might well appear that the industrial power of the trade unions had been mobilized effectively to ensure that the foreign policy of the Government did not conflict with a basic article of faith of the labour movement; and that this had been accepted as a natural development.

It is unlikely too that the trade union leaders would have seen more clearly what it really was that they were about in 1926, if they had not expected the walls of Jericho to fall once again at the blast of their trumpet. Lloyd George had given way at once when the railwaymen threatened to come out in support of the miners in 1920; some thought he had given way again over Poland; even Black Friday had been interpreted as the missing of an open goal. And when on Red Friday the Government was instigated to take the desired action, in the eyes of the leaders of the TUC that was all there was to it.

But there was much more to it in the oratory of some speakers on each side. After Red Friday, too, the Government could no more submit to a renewed threat of a general strike than after Black Friday the trade union leaders could fail to make the threat good if it was challenged.

The subsidy would end on 30 April 1926. A collision between Government and TUC was inevitable then unless the inquiry that was sitting under Lord Samuel provided a basis of negotiation between the miners and the coal-owners, or the Government was prepared to impose a scheme of reorganization on the coal industry by legislation, as Asquith's Government had done in 1912. It must have been for such outcomes as these that the trade union leaders were hoping, for between Red Friday and the following April, though the Government was preparing against a general strike, the General Council did nothing. At the Congress in September 1925 a proposal to empower the General Council to levy unions and call them out in a common cause was opposed by the big unions and defeated; a plan that Ernest Bevin had been promoting among the former members of the Triple Alliance, to provide a more specific and binding commitment to joint action, continued to be held up by the members' regard for their autonomy. When the report of the Samuel Committee appeared, in March 1926, the TUC seized on it as providing a basis for negotiation between the parties.

But that was not how the parties themselves saw it. The TUC was to find itself forced into a stance and an action that it had not planned either to enter or avoid. Because the recommendations of the Samuel Report included a wage-cut, the Miners would have none of it. The coal-owners would not negotiate unless the Miners agreed beforehand to accept cuts, and they issued notices under which work could continue on 1 May only on severely worsened terms. That closed one path to settlement for the TUC, and it strengthened the bond of loyalty by which they were attached to the Miners, for all their misgivings over the Miners' obstinacy. There remained the other path, marked out by the Report's proposals for reorganization. That too was really closed on 14 April, when the Special Committee of the TUC called on the Prime Minister and he refused to take up any scheme for reorganization as a government measure. The TUC continued to press reorganization on the Government. At the eleventh and more than the eleventh hour, when the lights were already out in No. 10 Downing Street, Ernest Bevin was still at work next door, roughing out a plan. If Bevin had had more influence in the Council – he had joined it only in the preceding October – and if, a much greater if, Baldwin and his party in the Cabinet and the House had been willing to legislate for the industry and impose reorganization, then there might have been no General Strike. But as it was, the Miners and the coal-owners being intransigent to the last, and the TUC being committed to a broad sympathetic strike in support of the miners, and the Government having barred the path along which the TUC had hoped to approach a settlement within the industry – when the miners came out the TUC was bound to honour its commitment.

But to what effect? When the walls fell at the sound of its trumpet, it had not asked what sort of siege artillery the trumpet would make if the walls did not fall. Looking back on the General Strike afterwards, spokesmen of the General Council blamed the Government for having made a political and constitutional issue out of what was only a sympathetic strike in support of the miners. But an ambiguity lurked in that exculpatory use of the term 'sympathetic strike'. The weight of the sympathetic strike was to bear not on the miners' employers but on the Government. To the Government, moreover, it was bound to present itself as a form of intimidation, as a threat to disrupt the economy and inflict hardship on the community unless the Government did as it was told. But suppose the Government did not give in, and the strike took place? A complete general strike would be self-destructive: the people of a country would be depriving themselves of food and water, heat and light. A strike of wide coverage that left essential supplies and services intact would inflict much inconvenience and deprivation indiscriminately on the community at large, including trade unionists and their families, with a loss of income largely but not wholly concentrated on the strikers. If the Government did not decide that it must assume responsibility for removing these hardships by reaching a settlement with the leadership concerned, it would leave the public to bear them in the knowledge of which groups were inflicting them. Would the public then bring great pressure to bear upon the Government, to relieve them of their hardship by reaching a settlement with the strikers? If the strike were widespread, then a great part of its victims would be suffering from self-inflicted wounds, for they would be the strikers themselves and their households. If the strike were of narrower coverage, the strikers would be at a disadvantage with their neighbours in that they would be acting not in defence of their own livelihoods, which generally arouses sympathy, but in a sense gratuitously, and as if they were seizing hostages. When in 1893 and 1912 a stoppage of the mines threatened a standstill of much of industry, the concern of the miners was with their own wages: the public would have felt the need for a settlement acceptable to the miners, and the Government responsive to that feeling was drawn in to help find one. But if a strike is begun as a means of putting pressure on the Government, the hardships it causes, instead of being a secondary consequence, become the chosen means to its end. Those who have to bear those hardships are unlikely to do so with sympathy, or to respond by calling on the Government to accede to the strikers' demands. They, and the Government, are more likely to say to the strikers, 'You started this: you can stop it'.

Nor is the general strike a form of pressure that builds up as the days go by. On the contrary, if it does not achieve its purpose by its immediate psychological impact as an immense demonstration of resentment or concerted purpose, its continuance appears at best as wearisome and wasteful, at worst as protracted blackmail. There is also the question of the willingness of the strikers to stay out, when striking means substantial sacrifices and carries real risks for them, the issue is one that does not concern their own jobs and earnings at all closely, and in any case they see no progress being made on it. At the end of the first week of the General Strike, on Sunday 9 May, the General Secretary of the TUC, Walter Citrine, wrote in his diary

We can hold out for three or four weeks at the longest. I do not think it possible to continue longer than that. Even the most ardent advocates of the General Strike have usually reasoned in terms of a few hours' or days' stoppage at the most. The silent power of labour has always been visualised as being capable of enforcing a speedy decision. I have never heard anyone previous to this event who has contemplated a General Strike lasting even a fortnight; and this strike is complicated by a number of other considerations. Many of the men are running heavy risks. The railwaymen and electricians have struck in defiance of severe legal penalties. [Railwaymen were also subject to penalties for breach of contract, and loss of superannuation.] Can we afford to risk complete defeat? I do not mean defeat in the sense of our movement never being able to recover, but to risk the disintegration that may follow rapidly from a return to work in certain sections. The logical thing is to make the best conditions while our members are solid. We must retreat, if we have to retreat under compulsion, as an army and not as a rabble.[26]

The General Council virtually decided to call the strike off on Tuesday the 11th. It made its decision known to the Government at noon on Wednesday the 12th. During a meeting on the Tuesday morning Citrine had noted that 'the men are as firm as a rock. What then can be the cause of apprehension?' It was the knowledge that 'once the strike has reached its highest point . . . then we shall have dribblings back to work here and there, and possibly large desertions.'[27] At the decisive meeting on the Tuesday evening that apprehension was already realized. 'Reports had come in that men were trickling back, and we knew that if that continued it would not be long before they were streaming to work.'[28]

In this particular case, moreover, there was no prospect of negotiation. Lord Samuel had come back from abroad to give what help he could, but he could see no way by which the industry could carry on, even through an interim period of reorganization, without a subsidy or a cut in labour costs. There was no possibility of the Government renewing the subsidy. The obstinacy of the miners precluded all discussion of costs. If it were not for that, the TUC would have had a basis of negotiation: had it been able to offer an acceptance of cuts *ad interim* if the Government would legislate for reorganization of the industry, the Government could not have refused outright. But as it was, the TUC had only been able to threaten: renew the subsidy or else ... And the threat having failed, it could only withdraw unconditionally.

In the year after the General Strike the Government legislated to make striking illegal if it was like that strike. An Act of 1927 declared that any strike was illegal if it had any object other than or in addition to the furtherance of a trade dispute within the trade or industry in which the strikers were engaged, and was designed or calculated to coerce the Government either directly or by inflicting hardship upon the community.[29] This provision was never invoked in any prosecution before the Act was repealed by the incoming Labour Government in 1946. But in any situation to which it was applicable it would in any case have been ineffective: strikers who were capable of coercing the Government could hardly have been deterred by the threat of being proceeded against in courts of summary jurisdiction. But in fact the occasion never arose, nor since the Act was repealed have trade unions threatened a government with strikes in order to force it into a course of action that they desired it to initiate. What they have seen as their self-defence is another matter: they have pitted their economic power against the Government when they have felt that it was constraining them unfairly, whether by its legislation or its incomes policy. That is a story to which we shall come later.

Notes

[1] E. H. Phelps Brown and M. H. Browne, *A Century of Pay* (London, 1968). Fig. 11 and p. 100; Appendix 3, Table for UK, 1860–1913.

[2] Parl. Debates 1912, vol. XXXV, 1733.

[3] Ibid., 1741.

[4] E. Dolléans, *Histoire du mouvement ouvrier*, vol. 2 (Paris, 1946), p. 145.

[5] Ibid., 1779.

[6] R. Page Arnot, *The Miners: a History of the Miners' Federation of Great Britain*, vol. II (from 1910 onwards), (London 1953), p. 110.

[7] Parl. Debates 1912, vol. XXXV, 2078–9.

[8] Ibid., 2090–1.

[9] Quoted here from G. A. Phillips, 'The Triple Alliance in 1914', *Economic History Review*, 24, 1, 1971, 67.

[10] *The Times*, 3 Aug. 1916.

[11] S. and B. Webb, *The History of Trade Unionism* (London, 1920 ed.), pp. 645–6.

[12] *History of Trade Unionism*, p. 635.

[13] Phelps Brown and Browne, *A Century of Pay*, Table 9, p. 94.

[14] David Marquand, *Ramsay MacDonald* (London, 1977), p. 318.

[15] Alan Bullock, *The Life and Times of Ernest Bevin*, vol. I (London, 1960), p. 241.

[16] G. A. Phillips, *The General Strike* (London, 1976), ch. III, n. 27. The present narrative relies closely on the detailed account of events in this work.

[17] Ibid., p. 61.

[18] Keith Middlemas (ed.), *Thomas Jones, Whitehall Diary*, vol. I. 1916–1925 (London, 1969), pp. 146, 148.

[19] Ibid., p. 152.

[20] In a lecture to an ILP summer school. Quoted here from David Marquand, *Ramsay MacDonald* (London, 1977), p. 424.

[21] Parl. Debates 1924–25, vol. 187, 1591.

[22] Ibid, 1689–90.

[23] Ibid., pp. 1674–5.

[24] Alan Bullock, *Ernest Bevin*, vol. I, pp. 135–42.

[25] Ibid., p. 138.

[26] Lord Citrine, *Men and Work: an Autobiography* (London, 1964), pp. 188–9.

[27] Ibid., p. 196.

[28] Ibid., p. 204.

[29] Trade Disputes and Trade Unions Act, 1927; 17 & 18 George V, ch. 22, 1 (1).

VI

THE BAN ON STRIKE AND LOCK-OUT IN THE TWO GREAT WARS

TWICE in times of national emergency the British Government has imposed a general ban on strike and lock-out. This was in time of war, but the ban imposed during the Second World War was maintained through six subsequent years of peace. The ban implied compulsory arbitration. For all the exceptional circumstances of those times we may be able to learn something from this experience about the applicability of an arbitration system to British trade unionism.

I

Mention has already been made of the Treasury Conference in which leading members of the Government and trade union leaders worked out in March 1915 a code for the conduct of industrial relations during the War. This provided that there should be no interruption of the output of munitions by strike or lock-out, and if the parties to a dispute could not reach agreement between themselves they must submit to arbitration. But the undertaking entered into by union leaders could not and did not forthwith commit their members up and down the country. As the cost of living rose, strikes broke out. The Government thereupon judged it advisable to give the agreement statutory backing by a Munitions of War Act which made it an offence to take part in a stoppage in any of the industries scheduled in the Act, and provided that other industries might be brought under the Act by Royal Proclamation. The miners had been omitted from the schedule in virtue of an undertaking given by their leaders that they would settle all disputes directly with the owners, or failing that, accept the finding of an independent chairman. But when the South Wales miners, seeing the mounting profits of the owners, claimed a war bonus, and the owners refused it, the miners rejected arbitration. The Board of Trade then drew up proposals which were accepted by the Miners' Executive and, under pressure, by the owners; but a conference of delegates from the lodges resolved 'that we do not accept anything less than our original proposals, and that we stop the collieries on Thursday next until these demands are conceded'. The Munitions of War Act had come into force just ten days before. A Royal Proclamation was now issued, bringing the South Wales collieries under the Act, and on the Tuesday before the fateful Thursday posters went up throughout the valleys announcing this and making it clear that to strike would be a punishable offence. The Miners' Executive advised the men to return to work pending a settlement. On a card vote the delegates decided by a majority of nearly two to one to stand by their decision to strike. On the Thursday 200,000 miners struck. On the following Monday the Minister of Munitions, Lloyd George, went down to Cardiff by special train, and gave the miners the essentials of their demands.

That was in August 1915. A month later all the shipwrights in the Fairfield yard on the Clyde struck, the grievance being the manner in which two of their number had been dismissed. Of the strikers seventeen deemed to be ring-leaders were brought before one of the Tribunals set up under the Munitions of War Act; they were fined and given twenty-one days to pay. Meanwhile the strikers went back to work. When the day to pay came, most of the accused paid, though apparently not out of their own pockets; but three refused and were sent to prison. That trade unionists had been sent to prison for striking caused such an outcry on the Clyde that the Government hastily sent down a Commission of Inquiry under Lord Balfour of Burleigh. But its interim report did not satisfy the local leaders, who sent a telegram to the Minister of Munitions in the name of 97,500 workers on the Clyde, calling for the release of the three shipwrights within three days under the threat of a general stoppage. They were called to London to meet the Minister and the Secretary of State for Scotland, and when they had been persuaded to withdraw their threat it was suggested to them that somebody might be willing to pay the three men's fines. Somebody did, the men were released, and the affair was over. It was necessary to deny persistent reports that the Government itself had paid the fines.

These trials of the strength of the ban on strikes, coming within the first two months of its promulgation, might have been thought to have shown its weakness, its fatuity even. An official historian of labour administration during the war, Humbert Wolfe, remarked of the South Wales case that 'it was demonstrated that if a sufficiently large body of men were determined to break the law, they could do so with impunity, as long as public opinion was not strongly against them.'[1]

One can go farther than that, for the Act proved ineffective against the determined opposition even of small groups. In January 1916, for example, after a sit-in strike about the dismissal of a shop steward in the gun-mounting works of Beardmore's on the Clyde, twenty-eight men were fined by a Munitions Tribunal. The Ministry of Munitions offered to remit their fines if they would only express their regret. This they refused to do. They never paid their fines; no endeavour was made to collect them, still less to imprison the contumacious men. Nor did the Act serve to prevent the number of days lost through disputes from rising. When strikes went on in 1917 and greatly increased in 1918 no attempt was made to bring them under the Act. The biggest engineering strike of the war, in the spring of 1917, was settled by a conference in which the Minister of Munitions met not only the national officers of the Amalgamated Society of Engineers but the unofficial strike committee, two of whose demands were effectively conceded. In November of the same year a strike at Coventry about the differential for skill and the recognition of shop stewards was settled after a long conference in which General Smuts took part on behalf of the War Cabinet.

Striking in wartime, it is true, might be a political offence. Under the Defence of the Realm Regulations six members of the Clyde Workers' Committee were deported from the Clyde in March 1915, and warrants were issued for the arrest of some of the leaders of the engineering strike in the spring of 1917. A strike at Coventry in July 1918 was terminated when Winston Churchill as Minister of Munitions caused a proclamation to be issued under the Military Service Act by which the strikers would have been called to the colours if they had not returned to work by the appointed day. But strikers were not prosecuted as a means of compelling them to continue working while submitting their dispute to arbitration.

In these ways it might appear that the attempt to enforce resort to arbitration by legal sanctions against stoppages showed itself to be inherently impracticable. But we must not let the instances of the undoubted breakdown of the Munitions of War Act of 1915 and its successors blind us to the wide area over which they were effective. The Tribunals established under them issued some 8,000 awards of which almost all were accepted without a stoppage. As late as September 1918, when a long-drawn-out dispute between the Co-operative Wholesale Society and the Amalgamated Union of Co-operative Employees began to threaten food supplies, it was found sufficient to bring the dispute under the Acts by Proclamation and refer it to arbitration. It was arguable, moreover, that the original Act never had a fair trial before Lloyd George bypassed it at Cardiff, and served notice – as it was thought – on any group powerful enough to gain direct access to him that they too could ignore it. The trade union leaders in the Treasury Conference had entered into commitments on behalf of their members, whose full meaning the members needed time to grasp. No immediate and complete departure from customary ways could be expected: patience was needed, and willingness to tolerate some transgression of the law meanwhile, in trust that its message would come home in time and attitudes be changed. Such seems to have been the faith of the great conciliator and arbitrator of the day, Sir George Askwith: the Act of 1915, he believed, could have been administered, if only those who flouted it had not been positively rewarded.

Probably there were many workers for whom the thought that the strike was outlawed, and arbitration specially provided as an alternative, would have tilted the balance against striking. But there can have been few trade unionists who would have seen in the Acts a categorical prohibition of striking, either on the moral ground that they ought to obey the law whatever it was, or on the pragmatic ground that they did not want to be punished for breaking it. Their sense of the moral propriety of the right to strike, and the strength of feeling that was usually aroused before a strike would be contemplated, went too deep for that. Measures of even forcible repression against politically motivated obstruction of the war effort they could understand and largely accept, but not a measure that required them to surrender a vital right of self-defence in purely industrial matters that concerned them deeply as workmen at their place of work. That right had been painfully won, and the lesson of the struggle was that the law was inherently inimical to the rights of trade unionists, which could be safeguarded only by setting industrial relations outside the law. It was a lesson that was not to be unlearned all in a day.

In all this the trade unions as such were only indirectly concerned. The Munitions of War Acts made no mention of them. Their national officers generally supported the Treasury Agreement, and did their best to avoid or terminate stoppages. But in the last resort they had no authority over a group of their members determined to strike and willing to do so without strike pay: the threat of expulsion could hardly be made good if the ground of action were one that the membership generally would regard as legitimate, or, if those concerned were likely to move into a rival union, or form a breakaway union. That a ban on strikes in favour of arbitration cannot be made effective through acceptance by the national executives of British trade unions, however wholehearted, was made clear in 1915–18. It was likewise made clear that a legal ban on striking could not in practice be enforced on any substantial number of strikers – say a hundred or more – who were determined to defy it, especially if they were supported by the local community.

2

But the ban was imposed again during the Second World War. In July 1940, at a desperate hour between Dunkirk and the Battle of Britain, there was issued the Conditions of Employment and National Arbitration Order. This made much the same provision for industrial relations during the war as the Treasury Agreement had made in its day. Its ban on strikes and lock-outs was accompanied by the setting up of a National Arbitration Tribunal, and backed by penal sanctions. It is significant that the inclusion of those sanctions was endorsed by the new Minister of Labour, Ernest Bevin, a trade union leader with a deep awareness of the outlook of the manual worker. He did not expect or intend that the sanctions would be applied, or need to be applied, at all widely, and the question of their power to quell any strong or general resistance would not have arisen in his mind. The ban had been adopted, like the other provisions of the same Order, for the conduct of industrial relations during the War, only after consultation with the representatives of employers and trade unions at the national level. Like other laws it depended for its effectiveness on voluntary acceptance by the great majority of citizens; but given this, like other laws it must also be provided with pains and penalties to bring the minority who might choose to transgress it into line with the compliant majority.

It was in the light of this conception of its function that the Order was applied by the Ministry of Labour. It had to deal with a great increase in the number of strikes, but they were almost all short, and confined to single firms or localities. They were usually settled by direct negotiations on the spot, with the Ministry continuing to provide its services of conciliation and arbitration. It did also prosecute under the Order, but sparingly, and far from persistently. There were thirty-eight prosecutions in all in England and Wales, and in fourteen of them the number of accused exceeded a hundred; but there were only four prosecutions after 1943, even though the number of working days lost through disputes doubled the next year. In Scotland it was the same: there had been more prosecutions there initially, seventy-one in all, but nearly half of these were in coal-mining, and strikes there became so numerous that in 1944 the Lord Advocate practically ceased to prosecute. The one strike or series of strikes that was of wide extension was not dealt with under the Order at all: when in 1941 some 6,000 engineering apprentices throughout the Clyde and Lancashire came out, the Minister of Labour decided that those of them who were of military age should be instructed to report for medical examination, and that ended the stoppages. The inference is clear that the Ministry regarded the Order as having the force of a joint declaration of intent by trade unionists, employers, and Government, supported by sanctions that would serve to remind the occasional careless or contumacious deviant of its seriousness; but that the Ministry became increasingly chary of attempting even this use of sanctions as time went on.

The only case of really large numbers being prosecuted, and of trade unionists being sent to prison, was not initiated by the Ministry. This is the famous Betteshanger case. In December 1941 miners at the Betteshanger Colliery in Kent rejected an arbitration award of allowances for a difficult seam, and the work of the 1,620 men at the colliery stopped. The Permanent Secretary of the Ministry of Labour at that time, Sir Harold Emmerson, has since described the attitude of his Ministry – and no doubt of his Minister, Ernest Bevin – in terms that must have echoed the thoughts of Sir George Askwith as he reflected on the strike of the South Wales miners in his day.

Under the National Arbitration Order [he wrote] the strike was illegal and to make matters worse it was backed by local union officials. In the Ministry of Labour we felt that the great value of the Order lay in its moral effect. Any quick resort to prosecution could only weaken its authority, we might possibly lose union support, and the work of the Chief Executive Commissioner and his staff would be made more difficult. But in coal-mining the Mines Department decided on action under the Order and we were only their agents when it came to legal action. The Secretary for Mines, who was himself a former miners' leader decided on prosecution, and he had Cabinet backing. Reluctantly we set the machinery of the law in motion.[2]

It was decided to deal only with the 1,050 underground workers, but that meant finding Justices of the Peace to sign 1,050 summonses in duplicate, and extra police to serve them on the accused in person. Had the accused pleaded 'Not Guilty', the proceedings must have lasted for many months, but the Miners' Union agreed that they should all plead guilty, and accept a decision on a few cases as applying to them all. Most of them were fined £1; but the three local union officials were sent to prison, one for two months, the other two each for one month, all with hard labour. That came as a shock, and there was a threat of sympathetic strikes.

But the real trouble [Sir Harold Emmerson has recorded] was that the only men who could call off the strike were now in gaol. The Secretary for Mines went down to Kent to see them accompanied by Mr Ebby Edwards, then the National President of the Miners' Union. Negotiations were reopened and five days after the hearing an agreement was signed, in prison, between the colliery management and the Kent Miners' Union. Apart from some face-saving words, it gave the men what they wanted. Then the Secretary for Mines took a deputation to the Home Secretary asking for the immediate release of the three local officials. The men would not start work until their leaders were free. After eleven days in prison they were released. The mine reopened.[3]

Only nine of the men fined had paid. The colliery company offered to pay on behalf of the men, but the Ministry of Labour strongly advised it not to. The magistrates' clerk wanted to know whether he should issue the warrants he had made out committing to prison the more than a thousand miners – all now back at work – who had not paid their fines. Bevin's advice was that the fines should not be rescinded but the warrants should not be issued.

This affair demonstrated, if demonstration were needed, the physical impossibility of applying penal sanctions against a large number of strikers who were determined to resist them, and supported in their resistance by the local community of workers. It also showed the likely consequences of proceeding solely against certain of the strikers' leaders or imposing discriminatory penalties upon them: the strike would have gone on, and might well have spread to other pits, as long as the three union officials were in gaol. This difficulty precipitated the withdrawal of the Order in the end, though only six years after the War. In the autumn of 1950 the Labour Attorney-General prosecuted one man from each of ten gas-works that had gone on strike in London. In the first months of 1951 he prosecuted seven leaders of striking Liverpool dockers who had come to London to call the London dockers out. A main consideration in the decision to prosecute in the first case was the inconvenience being inflicted on the public, and in the second the belief that the accused were politically motivated and more concerned to break the hold of the trade union officers over their members than to raise a substantive issue of wages. But trade unionists who had no sympathy for the actions that the Attorney-General was trying to check saw in his procedure the dangerous principle of discrimination and victimization. The dilemma remained: large numbers could not be prosecuted in practice, small numbers – unless the dispute were trivial – could be obtained only by a selection of the accused that would be widely resented and resisted. But as long as the law remained the law, it could not just be disregarded; or be applied only to the weak and willing and never to the powerful and recalcitrant. These considerations, brought to a head by the prosecutions of 1950–1, led in 1951 to the withdrawal of Order 1305 in so far as it outlawed strike and lock-out.

But if the law could be ignored by strikers whose numbers, cohesion, and logistic position gave them sufficient power, did the outlawing of strike and lock-out do anything but bring the law into contempt? Is there any reason to believe that there would have been one working day more lost through disputes if in July 1940 the leaders of the employers and trade unionists had simply joined with the Government in a declaration of the principle actually embodied in the Order, and this had been made known throughout the land as a National Covenant, binding in honour and patriotic duty only? Evidently Ernest Bevin did find reason to believe that there would have been. It may be that he thought it only fair to the majority who would observe the rules voluntarily to provide sanctions against the few who would be irresponsible and selfish. Though sanctions would be effective only if they were needed rarely, the main line could be held only if the occasional break-out were checked.

We do know that at a time of great stress Bevin did appeal to penal sanctions again, though this in a special case. In March 1944, the miners were striking over the terms of a new agreement – after Scotland and South Wales had struck for a time, 120,000 Yorkshire miners came out and stayed out. It was at this time too that the engineering apprentices were striking. Part of Bevin's response was to obtain the agreement of the representatives of trade unions and employers in the Joint Consultative Committee to a new Defence Regulation, 1AA. This made it an indictable offence to 'instigate or incite any other person to take part in, or otherwise act in furtherance of, any stoppage among persons engaged in the performance of essential services'. The penalties might be as much as a fine of £500, or five years' penal servitude, or both. By the same Order in Council[4] 'Defence Regulation 1A – which prohibited acts calculated to prevent or interfere with persons carrying on essential services – was amended so as to make peaceful picketing illegal.'[5] But no one was prosecuted under Regulation 1AA. Four Trotskyites who were prosecuted for fomenting the apprentices' strike were actually indicted under the Trade Disputes Act of 1927.[6] In the nature of things, we are told, it was hard to obtain evidence of incitement; in any case the dissident group did not try to start an outbreak, but waited till one occurred and then fanned the flames. Why, then, did Bevin invoke fresh penal sanctions? He did so, probably, in the first place, because at a time when his policy of leadership by consensus was under challenge from rising unrest, and this was just when the mounting of the invasion of Europe made uninterrupted industrial output more vital than ever, he felt it essential to reaffirm the powers of coercion that he kept in reserve. But more, he was convinced to the point of obsession that the unrest did not arise from the overt issues in dispute but was the work of insidious political agitators. It was to repel this intrusive bacillus that he formulated Regulation 1AA. We cannot infer from this any stiffening of his judgement on the place of compulsion in industrial disputes proper.

That judgement evidently had come to be that sanctions were useless against major movements; but this did not mean that they might as well never have been provided. He may have seen the prospect simply of being brought into court and publicly charged with (in effect) obstructing the war effort as a real deterrent, irrespective of what penalties the court might inflict. Mining and engineering were not everything: he may have seen attitudes in much else of the field of employment as amenable to this constraint, at least in time of war. The Order gave influence and authority to the officers of the Ministry in their approach to local disputes.

We cannot tell how the balance of these considerations falls out in practice by comparing the actual record of disputes in the years covered by the Order with what the record would have been under some other regime. But the experience of those years does warn us against taking up either of two opposed positions. One of these is that arbitration can be made compulsory by Act of Parliament. The other is that no restraint on striking and no inducements to accept arbitration can take effect over against employees' use of their bargaining power. In the middle ground between these positions, much depends on the attitudes and traditions of employees.

Notes

[1] Humbert Wolfe, *Labour Supply and Regulation* (Oxford, Clarendon Press, 1923), p. 127.

[2] Royal Commission on Trade Unions and Employers' Associations 1965–1968: Report (Cmnd. 3623, June 1968), Appendix 6, para 2.

[3] Ibid., para. 6.

[4] S. R. & O. 1944, No. 461.

[5] H. M. D. Parker, *Manpower, a Study of Wartime Policy and Administration* (London, 1957), p. 470.

[6] Alan Bullock, *The Life and Times of Ernest Bevin*, Vol. II (London, 1967), p. 302, n. 2.

VII

EMPLOYERS' ORGANIZATIONS

I

EMPLOYERS can influence the development of trade unionism in various ways. If they counter-attack the first unions vigorously, they will force them to organize more closely and over a wider front. If they are ready to accept union officers as spokesmen of their own work-people, they will tacitly endorse whatever pattern of union loyalties the work-people adopt. The politics as well as the industrial tactics of the trade unionists will be influenced by the employers' stance: uncompromising resistance is likely to stimulate left-wing socialism or syndicalism; readiness to negotiate is more conducive to a democratic labour movement. The bargaining area may be affected by either side, but the employers' impact will be powerful when their unwillingness to unite obliges the unions to negotiate with each of them separately, or – the other way about – when an association of theirs insists on a common settlement. Firms concerned to maintain 'fair prices' will work for industry-wide bargaining because it 'puts a floor under competition'. The direction of his labour force was always a concern of the employer. As this concern becomes specialized, it is from the employer's side that procedures – for processing grievances, or conducting negotiations – are likely to be developed, as a part of the administrative function of management. Within the firm, much depends on the employer's need to exert an active control over the work of the labour force. His workers always have to be subject to discipline in respect of time-keeping, regular attendance, and orderly behaviour. They must always be given incentives for effort, or deterrents against slackness. These elements inherent in employment will of themselves call forth a kind of unionism within the workshop, and the employer's methods and responses will go some way to determine the kind of industrial relations that result. Even more when firms come under the pressure of competition, managers are driven to make changes in working methods, or require standards of performance, that conflict with custom. Equally at a time of technical change in the industry, firms that will not be left behind must break up long-standing arrangements for the allocation of labour. At these times practices which have been long accepted become the objects of contention, defended by labour as protective, attacked by employers as restrictive. In the present century procedures and institutions have been developed for industrial relations within the firm. The employers have had their share of initiative in this, particularly in the development of grievance procedure and joint consultation.

These considerations make it surprising that we hear so little about employers and their associations, in comparison with the trade unions. But there are reasons for this. One is the ease of informal association among the employers of the same trade in a close-packed locality. Adam Smith called the pained attention of his readers to this in the *Wealth of Nations* in 1776.

We rarely hear, it has been said, of the combinations of masters, though frequently of those workmen. But whoever imagines, upon this account, that masters rarely combine, is as ignorant of the world as of the subject. Masters are always and everywhere in a sort of tacit, but constant and uniform, combination, not to raise the wages of labour above their actual rate. To violate this combination is everywhere a most unpopular action, and a sort of reproach to a master among his neighbours and equals.[1]

More than a hundred years later Alfred Marshall observed the same sort of tacit combination, sanctioned by neighbourly disapproval of the deviant, among the farmers of Cambridgeshire. Where associations have been more positive and active they have still escaped notice because the employers being few in number have been able to make contact with one another and meet as need arose: they could be quite capable of co-ordinated action without maintaining any office or staff. This was under the limitation that the action could only be intermittent and confined to one locality. But associations that did have constitutions and permanence still kept their heads down: the very fact of their existence made them suspect of fixing prices, restricting output, or otherwise making life comfortable for themselves at the expense of the consumer. Adam Smith again, though revered as the philosopher of private enterprise, voiced the general suspicion of its inherently restrictive propensities. 'People of the same trade', he wrote, 'seldom meet together even for merriment and diversion, but the conversation ends in a conspiracy against the public, or on some contrivance to raise prices.'[2]

But British employers had a particular reason for not standing forth and making their presence known: they did not feel the country was with them. Down to the last quarter of the nineteenth century, the accepted values of society had remained those of a landowning aristocracy. With some local exceptions, the men of enterprise had not been admired by their neighbours as pinnacles of the qualities and achievements to which all aspired. Nor were the employers united by common wrongs to right or objects to pursue. Trade unionism is a movement, with internal conflicts enough, but still one movement, because of deep-going attitudes, purposes, and traditions held in common. There has been no employers' movement. Trade unionists were long accustomed to address each other as Brothers: not so the employers. Ever since the TUC was founded in 1868 the trade unions have had an organization to protect and advance their interests at the national level. Intermittently from the eighteenth century onwards some employers were found to support bodies intended to bring political pressure to bear when legislation concerning industry or industrial relations impended. Between the 1880s and 1914 more than one such body was active in stirring up public opinion against trade unions and lobbying at Westminster. But only since the First World War have employers generally had organizations whose coverage and standing over against government began to match those of the TUC. When these were set up, moreover, they provided no political counterpart to the TUC, no such presence at Westminster or publicity in Fleet Street.

These considerations make the thinness of the records understandable. It does not mean that there can have been no underlying activity. Employers and their associations may actually have taken powerful effect on the development of trade unionism. Let us see.

2

In the early days of industry the individual employers differed from one another as men always do: some were harsh and grasping in their treatment of their workers, some kindly and paternal. But they had this in common – that they lived near by. In the early nineteenth century, Kenneth Morgan tells us, 'most Welsh pits had been small in scale. The majority of coalowners then had been Welshmen, often nonconformist, who lived locally and enjoyed a close, paternalistic relationship with their workers. Often they would attend the same chapels or patronize the same local *eisteddfoddau*.'[3] George Clark of the Dowlais Ironworks told the Royal Commission of 1867:

My own men are like my children and I should as soon think of refusing to listen to my own children as of refusing to listen to any man who came from the works to talk to me on any matter because I think it of equal importance that my men and I should be on good terms as that I should be on good terms with my own family.[4]

Keir Hardie looked back to the same setting in the West of Scotland coalfield. 'In the past,' he told the Royal Commission in 1891, '. . . there was a personal relationship between the mine-owner who owned one pit and his workmen, he knew them all.'[5] These instances from mining illustrate a general characteristic. Feared or beloved, the employers were neighbours. Their work-people knew about them personally, and their family affairs; and many of the employers' families themselves fully shared the outlook and interests that characterized the neighbourhood, and often differentiated it from other places not far away.

Sometimes the effect was to defer the growth of trade unionism. There might be deputations of work-people to the employer to ask for a rise; the notice he gave of a cut might be met by a strike; but there was no continuing organization. But when unions were formed and wielded their bargaining power, the reactions of the employers were various.

On the one hand there were employers whose reaction was sharply hostile. Men who were building their own businesses up were impatient of restraints. They were pioneers and risk-takers: they saw no reason why those who had not shared their pangs and efforts should claim a share in their reward when that at last accrued. By reasons of their very success in expanding their businesses they were likely to have a cash-flow problem and be vulnerable to a strike. Temperamentally, they were unsympathetic to those who wanted to argue and bargain, instead of taking their jackets off and getting stuck in. But more than that, for one's own workmen to combine to present their demands long appeared as a form of insubordination. The problem of negotiation was entangled with that of discipline. The maintenance of discipline in a labour force unaccustomed to steady effort during regular hours was a major problem in the early days of the factory system; how to provide the incentives and deterrants that will keep up the worker's effort has remained a major concern of management. To allow the workers to gang up to resist the employer in one matter threatened the extension of resistance to him in others, until he was no longer master in his own house. Trade unionism raised another difficulty there: though the employer might be willing to discuss their grievances with his own work-people, he resented a trade union officer – an outsider – coming between them and him. For these reasons the unquestioning reaction of some employers to the appearance of a union in their trade was to join with fellow employers in order to break it. The master bookbinders of London failed in such an attempt in 1839. The master printers of Edinburgh succeeded in 1846–7. The Master Tailors' Association, formed after a strike in 1866, crushed the union in the following year.

But there were also employers who were prepared to negotiate. Given the concentration of an industry in a district, it was likely that the workers in the different firms would be moved to press for a rise together; and when trade was bad the employers were under a common pressure to cut wages, against a general resistance. The employers, or a committee appointed by them, would then meet the men's leaders – it might be at an inn – to reach a settlement.

The associations that acted in these ways, to break unions or negotiate with them, were sometimes formed *ad hoc*, and sometimes existed already for other purposes. These other purposes might include the maintenance of benevolent and mutual insurance funds – the small masters' counterpart in the building trade of the friendly benefits of the craft societies. Some associations were concerned with parliamentary business: the Ironmasters, for example, kept an eye on railway bills. Some associations, again, drew up lists of wages, and of prices, though they hardly seem to have attempted to impose either on their members. The President of the Glasgow Master Builders told the Royal Commission of 1867 that the objects of the association included 'in particular fixing the rate of wages to be paid', and that a member who did not abide by the fixed wage rate was fined £5.[6] But the fine was not heavy, and the instance is exceptional. As the same witness himself observed later, 'The men have the power of controlling each other: a power that the masters have not.'[7] It was commonly held, moreover, that what wages each employer paid was a matter solely between him and his own work-people: only when there was a movement for a general change did the association come in. The drawing up of a list of wages therefore only provided guidelines for the members of an association. It was part of that general purpose which may be called the exchange of information. A sense of what they could gain from this, and from mutual support when need arose, drew employers together, and outweighed the secretiveness and competitiveness that separated them.

It was only some employers who were affected in this way; and often enough those who were so affected associated only intermittently. A trade union having negotiated an agreement might return in two years' time to renew the negotiation, only to find that the employers' organization had completely disappeared. In what ensues we shall bring together some information about associations that were brought to notice as comparatively well established. But this would be to give a misleading impression were it taken as a typical account of employers in general. What is more typical of them down to the First World War is their reluctance to combine.

Many associations were formed only in reaction to the impact of unionism: or it was that impact which brought latent combination into

action. The Royal Commission of 1867 was given a number of
instances. The Clyde Master Shipbuilders formed an association in
anticipation of a strike in 1866. The Midland Association of Flint
Glass Manufacturers was set up in 1858 after two or three months of a
strike which was then turned into a general lock-out. The Royal
Commission of 1891–4 was told by spokesmen of a trade union, the
West Riding Power Loom Weavers, that when their union was
founded in 1881 and pressed for a uniform wage-rate throughout the
district, the previously unorganized employers were moved to form
their own association, and at once became the stronger. Where an
employers' association existed already it might react to trade union
pressure by widening its membership. After the formation of the
Amalgamated Society of Engineers in 1851 the unionists' demands on
workshop matters which the employers felt should be within their own
sole control led them to set up a Central Association – the first
employers' association in the industry to extend beyond a district. The
London Master Builders formed the Central Association to deal with
the strike of 1859.

The associations formed with this combative purpose used various
weapons. When some members' works were struck the association
circulated the names of the strikers to ensure that other members
would not engage them. This was regarded as perfectly fair in a
stand-up fight, and was distinguished from the blacklisting of leading
trade unionists with a view to barring them from employment at all
times. The employers' spokesmen agreed that the blacklist was inde-
fensible, and were at pains to deny that their associations ever made
use of it; but trade union witnesses were convinced that they did.
Alternative methods of checking union membership were the dis-
charge note, which an applicant for employment would be required to
produce to show that he left his last employer in good standing; and
the declaration that men were required to make, or the document they
were required to sign, on being engaged or on returning to work after a
strike or lock-out, by which they abjured union membership. When a
stoppage was in progress, the employers' association might help a
member from its strike fund: in particular, it might subsidize the
importation of blacklegs from a distance. The Royal Commission of
1867 was told how blacklegs had been brought into North Country
coal-mines from Cornwall, Scotland, and Cumberland.

Almost all the evidence to that Commission shows the employers'
associations of the time as dealing with the unions mostly by way of
occasional collision. There is some evidence of settled relations
between them, but it is slight. On the Thames the shipbuilders were
still observing a book of rates that had been drawn up in 1825. The
General Builders' Association of Birmingham, though it would not

touch wages, did negotiate with the unions over a set of rules which they had proposed. There was mention of arbitration – one association required its members when in dispute to have offered arbitration to their workers before they could claim support from it; another said that advising members on arbitration was one of its functions. But generally the associations did not maintain stable relations simply because they were not stable themselves. Sometimes they were formed to meet a crisis, and broke up once that was over. The thought of the members may well have been that they had turned out like a voluntary fire brigade, and would always do so again in the hour of need, but meanwhile an association would simply have no agenda. They were the more likely to think and act in this way if organization on the trade union side also was spasmodic. Henry Briggs told the Royal Commission of 1867 about the great strike in the collieries of the West Riding in 1844,

There was no real West Riding Masters' Association at that time, but they met when there was any special action taken on the part of the men, or when it was thought necessary to have a reduction or an advance in the price of coals. There was not any strict association of the masters, and not any strict association among the miners; the unions were got up just to resist any reduction or maintain any advance almost at a few days' notice.[8]

George Clark of Dowlais (already quoted) reported of the South Wales Ironmasters' Association, of which he had been President for ten or eleven years, that it used to meet every fifteen months or so to consider

whether the state of trade does or does not justify an alteration in the rate of wages; but it has not worked particularly well, and of late we have not met, and whether we shall meet again I know not; but that we do very little business may be best proved by the fact that there is no paid officer.[9]

Whether or not the employers' association had some permanence of organization in the 1860s, it was in the dealings between each employer and his own work-people that wages were seen as being fixed. These dealings, moreover, were properly the employer's own affair. No outsider, not a fellow employer any more than a trade union official, had a right to intervene, or interpose his ruling. But if unreasonable claims were made upon an employer, a common interest drew other employers to help him make a stand. From time to time, moreover, the union side would claim a general rise, or the employers themselves would try to impose a general cut. The resultant collision would align the two sides throughout most of a district. The settlement might be worked out between representatives of the two sides, and that would be a beginning of multi-employer negotiation; but if the struggle ended with the outright victory of one side or the other, the terms on which work was resumed might still be left to be arrived at in each firm.

3

A quarter of a century later the prospect was very different. The Royal Commission on Labour in 1891–4 found itself concerned not only with trade unions but with the procedures and institutions of industrial relations. There were still employers, the railway companies notably, who refused to deal with trade unions. Employers fighting unionism used the same weapons as before – the sacking of unionists, the blacklist, the document, the importation of blacklegs. But in many sectors and districts of industry an ongoing relation had been worked out between employers' associations and the officers of the trade unions organizing the workers concerned. The employers' association, usually covering one district of a trade, was now more likely to be a permanent organization. Its representatives would meet under standing arrangements with trade union officials to negotiate agreements that would be accepted as binding throughout the works of the members of the association. Whether or not this negotiating body met regularly, it constituted an institution in itself. It provided a far more stable and constructive relation than the intermittent collisions and settlements of the 1860s. The majority of the Royal Commission found in it the most practicable way of conducting industrial relations. It worked best, they said, when organization was strong on both sides.

This development can be ascribed in part to the change in economic climate from 1873. The boom of that year was the climax of the most rapid economic growth in the century. The years of the two trade cycles that followed, down to the end of the 1880s, became known as the Great Depression. Unemployment was very high in the slumps. Though standards of living rose for those in work because the cost of living fell, money wages were no higher in 1888 than they had been in 1873. This state of the labour market discouraged militancy. Forward movements in which the rank and file assert themselves with confidence are fostered by a high level of demand for labour, and encouraged by the success of the first claims. The Great Depression extinguished militancy of that kind. It singled out for survival the well-organized union of higher-grade workmen, led by cautious men of limited aims. Whatever the members of the union might still be doing to uphold custom in the shops against the employer's desire to change, the officials themselves sought agreement from the employers' association only on common terms on which the employers could negotiate without impairing their prerogatives. Here were a type of union and a way of working with unionism that the employers could accept.

But the employers also contributed to this development by their own initiative. Some among them, as early as the 1850s, had thought that they would reach agreement more readily if instead of scrambling into a meeting with the union when an issue arose they set up a permanent joint board. Many other employers at the time would reject any such arrangement out of hand simply because it would mean recognizing the trade unions, or accepting arbitration and letting an outsider fix the wages they were to pay. Outside the building trades the craft unions kept to their accustomed ways. But in a number of trades elsewhere, the clash between the rising bargaining power of the trade unions and the market forces fluctuating sharply in the course of the trade cycles of the 1850s and 1860s led to protracted disputes. A less costly way of reaching a settlement had attractions to both sides. The Joint Board which was widely accepted as a model was that set up in 1860 in the hosiery trade of Nottingham. In 1864 a County Court judge brought the Wolverhampton builders into a board. In 1869 an ironmaster set up a board for the iron and steel trade of the North of England. In Boards of Conciliation, or Conciliation and Arbitration, such as these an equal number of employers and trade union officials would sit together, to negotiate across the table; but – it was hoped and sometimes found – they would also grow used to sitting together *around* the table, as a common council for the industry in their district. When they appointed a standing committee to deal with grievances, they found it effective in preventing stoppages. They had an independent chairman: his task was to bring the two sides together, and failing that he might have a casting vote, or the decision might be submitted to his arbitration, or to an outside arbitrator. For a time these arrangements worked well; but then difficulties multiplied. The greatest of these was that in the great depressions of the 1870s and 1880s the Boards were called on to mediate severe wage cuts. When wage rises were the order of the day, union members had been willing enough to delegate authority to delegates sitting round the table with the employers, and even to leave the fixing of the exact amount with an arbitrator; but to take a deep cut asked too much of their trust in their own officers and loyalty to the system.

The heyday, then, of the Board of Conciliation and Arbitration did not extend beyond the 1880s. But this was only a particular form of provision for meetings between representatives of an employer's association and trade union officers, which continued to extend.

4

This account of employers' associations in the later nineteenth century, though slight, has still brought out some ways in which they impinged on trade unionism. One strong influence they exerted passively. Whatever the attempts of some employers to stamp unionism out at its first appearance, whatever the continuing unwillingness of some employers to recognize unions, over a wide range of industry employers had come to accept unions as natural and inevitable. Not a few employers saw strong unions as positively desirable. But, reluctantly or willingly, employers took the unions as they found them. They did not force regrouping upon them, by the strength of their counter-attack or by insistence on certain negotiating procedures. The patchwork quilt of trade union structure was left undisturbed.

This was made possible by the employers' acceptance of an agenda and area of collective bargaining that gave the unions negotiating rights over wages and hours throughout a district but did not regulate the immediate relations of management and worker within the firm. Here most employers remained authoritarian, within the limits set by custom and practice. All employers in any case were concerned day by day with the problems of the discipline and motivation of a hired labour force. The anxiety that trade unions aroused at their first appearance was not just that they would push up wages but that they would resist the employer's authority within the firm. But then came the discovery that the employer's prerogative of fixing wage-rates could be given up without the prerogatives of management within the firm being given up too. The employers granted the trade unions recognition on the tacit condition that it be only for a restricted agenda of negotiation at the district level. The trade unions for their part did not have to provide their own internal organization, or adjust their relations one with another, as they would have had to do if they were to have negotiated what would now be called a works agreement or plant contract.

5

This settlement depended on certain conditions. It was easier to reach and maintain where firms were not under great pressure of competition. Many manufacturers had been sheltered from international competition by the technical lead which industry had held. They did compete with one another in the home market, but according to accepted rules of the game. Employers of that kind could take a more accommodating view of trade unions than those whose selling prices were held down by forces beyond their own control. The shipowners were subject to fierce competition in freight rates: when the New Unionism began to organize the seamen, and even the ships' officers, in 1890, the shipowners formed the Shipping Federation that broke the union. In the years down to 1914 the directors of the railways, except

the London and North Eastern, stood out by their refusal in principle
to recognize the unions and negotiate with union officials: but in those
years they were caught between the rising costs of coal, rails, and
timber, and the effective holding down of their charges by an Act of
Parliament in 1894. The employers who opposed trade unions may
have differed from those who accepted it more in their circumstances
than in their sympathies. But the settlement blessed by the Royal
Commission of 1891–4 also required that the trade union leadership
should have limited aims and that the rank and file should be content
with them, and particularly that they should not try to restrict the
accepted scope of the prerogatives of management at the place of
work.

In both these respects of competitive pressure and trade union
attitudes a great change was coming about in the last fifteen years or so
of the century. The ground was shifting under the feet of the Commis-
sioners. Industry after industry was being made aware that it had lost
its technical lead over the foreigner. Competition from American and
German manufacturers bore down increasingly on markets not only
overseas but at home. The competitive pressure that had prevented
industrial relations in some industries from developing along the
recommended lines of the Royal Commission bore down on more
industries now, forcing employers to watch every penny of costs and
denying them the possibility of letting the customer pay for an
accommodation with labour. At the same time, from the other side,
employers were troubled by a changed attitude of labour. The New
Unionism was not only a movement of the semi-skilled and unskilled,
typified by the London dockers' strike of 1889: it also conveyed a
change of mood among the craftsmen, an increased determination to
defend their customary practices and assert their control of the workshop. In part this marked a rise of militancy; in part it was a defensive
reaction against the breaking down of the craftsman's autonomy by
the introduction, particularly in the engineering shops, of new automatic equipment, and new methods of work allocation and wage
payment, most of them of American origin.

These innovations attempted by management were linked with a
major change in the structure of industry. The size of the concern was
growing. The family firm was yielding to the multi-plant corporation.
The private owner was giving place to the professional manager. This
last was a type of employer more concerned than his predecessors with
efficiency – a word which itself began to gain currency at this time. It
did so in discussions where it stood as the condition for survival under
foreign competition. The salaried manager stood in no paternal relation to the work-people, and had less sympathy for their attachment to
traditional practices.

These forces that pressed upon industrial relations from both sides made employers develop their associations or use their existing associations aggressively. In 1894 the employers' federation in the boot and shoe industry was moved by an 'American Invasion' – Chicago boots underselling them in their home market because of better productive methods – to demand from the union not only a two years' standstill on wages, but 'a free hand for employers over machinery and the organization of production, and the abandonment by workers of all restriction of output.'[10] This demand the Federation enforced by a lock-out; its members used the threat of the withdrawal of orders to force reluctant firms to lock their own workers out too. But the most notable instance was the formation of an industry-wide employers' association in engineering in 1897. Its leader, Colonel Dyer, managing director of the great combination of Armstrong and Whitworth, in Newcastle and Manchester, was determined to break down the endeavours of the Amalgamated Society of Engineers to uphold customary working practices and control the way in which work was allocated. In pursuance of that determination Colonel Dyer himself led a movement which extended an existing association from the North East, Scotland, and Belfast to organize employers in the industry throughout the country. The employers then seized the opportunity of a claim for the eight-hour day raised by the unions in London to impose a general lock-out.

The struggle that followed impressed itself on the country at the time by its length, its intensity, and the area it covered. Looking back on it we see it as a landmark in two respects. In both it marked the employers' initiative.

It was a landmark, first, because it extended collective bargaining in a major industry from the district to the national level. During the dispute the number of firms in the employers' federation rose from 180 to 702. In the settlement of this dispute there was no bargaining about wages and hours, only an agreement that changes in rates might be negotiated in the districts; but that the greater part of a widely dispersed industry, and a labour force organized by many trade unions, had been brought into one settlement was remarkable. 'Other industries, old and new, took note.'[11]

But the second feature making the struggle of 1897–8 a landmark was that it was basically about workshop control: the settlement – again on the employers' initiative – provided for the first time a procedure to regulate relations at the place of work. Paradoxically, the same impulse as extended the bargaining area to cover the whole industry took the concern of bargaining down into the workshop. The negotiations between employers' associations and trade unions that the Royal Commission had commended had bypassed the workshop:

that remained a private arena, in which the employer exercised the prerogatives of management, and the workers maintained custom and practice, according to some tacit understanding, or the local balance of power. It might suit either party to the negotiations that settled wages and hours in common to act as if affairs in the arena could be left to look after themselves. But now tensions in the engineering shops had risen too high. The craftsmen complained of new equipment and methods of management that degraded them; employers complained of the men being infected by the aggressive spirit of the New Unionism. The issue on which the federated employers stood was their freedom to manage. On wages they would accept arbitration, but on the manning of machine tools, freedom to apply piece-work, and the right to take on apprentices without limitation, they would fight. When at last the terms of settlement were agreed they provided the desired assurance against the obstruction of the executive arm of management. But appended to them were the *Provisions for Avoiding Disputes*. For the first time these provided a procedure by which a dispute arising at the place of work, and affecting it might be only one person in the first instance, might be taken up, and pursued if necessary between the trade union and the employers' association to the national level; no stoppage was permissible meanwhile, 'but work shall proceed under the current conditions'[12] – a clause, familiar later as the *status quo* requirement, that was to give continual difficulty. But the essential was that the procedure of multi-employer collective negotiation had been carried down, on the employers' initiative, into the face-to-face relations within the firm. The terms of settlement, Oliver Clarke tells us, 'in particular the provisions for avoiding disputes, were widely copied.'[13]

6

As we see it now, the drive of the engineering employers was for higher productivity when that was needed basically at a turning point of our national fortunes. It was through higher productivity won through new methods that other countries were beginning to wrest our markets from us. When Alfred Marshall was visiting a large engineering works in Bohemia in 1891, the manager said

'Look at that lad. A few months ago he was working in the country for 5s. a week. I now pay him 12s. and he is looking after three semi-automatic machines. In your country none but skilled engineers are allowed to work those machines, though no skill is needed for it: and each engineer is compelled to confine his attention to one machine.'[14]

It was because of observations like these that Marshall followed the struggle of 1897 'with an interest amounting to excitement.' Not long since he had endorsed trade unionism as salutary in its influence on individuals, and a stabilising if minor influence on the economy. But now trade unionists were animated by a new spirit, and the environment had changed too, to make the exertion of their power harmful to the community and to themselves. When he wrote the letter already quoted (p. 46) he saw the real issue as transcending the immediate matters in dispute: it lay entirely in the question whether England is to be free to avail herself of the new resources of production. . . . I have often said that trade unions are a greater glory to England than her wealth. But I thought then of trade unions in which the minority, who wanted to compel others to put as little work as possible into the hour, were overruled. Latterly they have, I fear, completely dominated the Engineers' Union. I want these people to be beaten at all costs: the complete destruction of Unionism would be as heavy a price as it is possible to conceive: but I think not too high a price. If bricklayers' unions could have been completely destroyed twenty years ago, I believe bricklayers would now be as well off and more self-respecting than they are: and cottages would be 10 or 20 per cent larger all round.[15]

Eighty years and more later, the issue is still with us. Then was not a great opportunity missed at the turn of the century? Did not British employers fail at that time to carry out a function with which they were charged in the common interest, and break down the resistance to the raising of productivity? What ailed them? It was held that if they closed their ranks they were always stronger than the unions. When in 1901 a series of articles in *The Times* attributed the increasingly poor showing of British over against American and German industry to the enforcement of restrictive practices by trade unionists, the manager of the *Manchester Guardian* commented

If we have been passed in the race of industrial efficiency by America, which I take to be a proved fact in more industries than one, the trade unions are not to blame. For one thing their power is absurdly exaggerated, and more so by the weak employer than by one who is capable. The strongest trade union in Great Britain, the Amalgamated Society of Engineers, went down before the combination of masters who were contending for a point of efficiency. Whenever the newspapers of this country care to combine in earnest to secure the more efficient working of Linotype machines . . . not all the efforts of the Typographical Association nor the London Society of Compositors can stand in the way. Nor would they struggle against it. The difficulty in this matter is to induce employers to see their common interest. In America, where Unionism is more powerful but more aggressive than here, the employers as a class have been taught to combine more readily on emergency, they aim more at securing efficiency of Labour and less at low money wages, and above all they will make any sacrifice to secure the real control of their own enterprises.

On the contrary, in England the employers in comparison are apt to attach too much importance to low money wages, they are lazy in resisting small encroachments on their liberty which may later on become a dangerous interference, and they are much slower to swallow individual jealousies for a common purpose. But then we have not the same level of ability to draw upon for our employing class here as in the newer country.[16]

Dibblee could only surmise the employers' potential power: what is certain is that they did not choose to exert it. Some firms brought actions for damages after Taff Vale, but very few. We have seen how the absence of employers' opposition in Parliament to the conferment of complete immunity at tort by the legislation of 1906 impressed itself upon the Tory peers. That Trade Disputes Act once having been passed, and the immunity having been automatically conferred upon the employers' association as a trade union no less than upon an association of employees, employers could unite to lock out every member of a union that had attacked any one of their number, and maintain the lock-out until resistance was broken: and thanks to the Act the union members whose families they may have reduced to starvation would have no remedy at law. But the British employers did not do this.

It is true that not all employers were so inert as Dibblee suggested. We have seen how some of them attacked the first appearances of trade unionism. Relations with the old-style craft unions were one thing when stable trading allowed customary practices to continue, and quite another when competition forced managers to disturb them. Relations changed again in the 1880s and 1890s when deferential attitudes on the trade unionists' side were displaced by militancy. There might be no formal association of employers simply because none was necessary: the employers concerned were always in touch with one another, and when a dispute arose, the conciliator G. R. Askwith told the Royal Commission of 1906, they could put up a fund within hours if need be.[17] Employers often met strikes by bringing in blacklegs, and when strife on the picket line ensued the pickets were taken to court: many trade union witnesses before the Royal Commission of 1891–4 spoke of their own convictions.

None the less, on an international comparison, the British employers do appear as passive in their relation with the unions, less aggressive individually than American employers, less willing to combine for defence and attack than employers in both continents. There are deterrents to combination for employers in all countries, especially the inequality of their resources, and their competitive attitude towards one another: but these did not prevent employers in Sweden, Germany, and the United States from combining to attack trade unions. To account for the comparative unwillingness of British employers to act in that way we must look for factors peculiar to the UK.

One such factor was the dominance of the family business. Capital for manufacturing business was not provided by investment banks, and even after the coming of general limited liability in 1862 little was provided by the shareholder at large; firms founded by men of enterprise grew by ploughing back their profits, and remained within the possession of the founder's family. This limited their growth, and thereby increased the number of firms in an industry: the very number of firms was itself often an obstacle to association. But more, family ownership fostered an inward-looking attitude, which to a business man's normal reserve in dealing with competitors added a jealous pride of proprietorship. The later generations of ownership, again, might be content to follow the settled ways of management handed down to them, and these left undisturbed the no less traditional practices of the trade unions.

But this factor of the family business only carries us part of the way. Already when the Royal Commission reported in 1894 that 'employers frequently seem to combine rather unwillingly'[18] amalgamations were going on, the size of the firm was growing, and the professional manager was appearing increasingly among the foremost employers. Over against the New Unionism was the New Management. Why did not a more detached and calculating capacity for combination arise out of this harder pressed and more professional setting? Why again, as it appears, are British employers still reluctant to combine? In 1979 the Director General of the Confederation of British Industry wrote to his members, 'You cannot expect employer unity here, as you can in Germany for instance. Businessmen in the UK are highly competitive. It goes against their natural instinct to come together.'[19]

Part of the explanation may lie in that heritage of attitudes which is called national character. The term may pass provided that we understand it in no narrowly genetic sense, and allow for the marked differences of outlook of employers in different regions and industries. With these qualifications in mind, we might say on an international comparison that British behaviour has been characterized by a dislike of regulation but an avoidance of conflict. There have been some fighting trades, and there the employers would not combine with their competitors. Elsewhere they did also compete, but according to the rules of the game, and the canon of live and let live. They would associate as occasion required, but without long-term commitment; the binding rules of the cartel were not for them, nor those of the employers' association as a fighting force – strike funds were little used and soon lapsed. Trade unionists were the employers' own work-people: though their demands had to be resisted when they went too far, every effort should be made to reach a fair settlement without conflict.

But this attitude depended on a comfortable environment. It could have been maintained only because a large part of British industry had been sheltered from foreign competition by its technical lead. As that lead was lost, employers who found themselves dependent on increasingly competitive markets were not so conciliatory towards the unions. Between the early 1890s and 1914 the harder trading conditions imposed by increased foreign competition over against increased trade union pressure resulted in an extension and energizing of employers' associations.

That they still launched no offensive in the German or Swedish way may be explained by a second suggestion about the employers' outlook. Dibblee was telling employers that they had only to act with unity and determination in order to break a given resistance down. Employers might not dispute his contention, yet be quite unmoved by it: they would feel in their bones that they might win the battle but lose the war. They were opposed by unions whose strength lay not in their funds but in the dogged tenacity and solidarity of their members. The Engineering Employers in 1897–8 found themselves engaged not simply in dislodging the unions from this or that position, but in combating a whole culture, a heritage of attitudes. The craftsmen maintained a ceaseless pervasive pressure, a molecular bombardment of management. It came about in the nature of these men, and despite agreements about the prerogatives of management entered into at the national level. After the national settlement, 'encroachments' went on in the shops.

Local branches and district committees who for years had been struggling against piece-work, for stricter overtime limitation, for maximum proportions of apprentices, for the right of craftsmen to man machines, for the union shop, could not suddenly stop the struggle. Where they offended, the Federation would ask the union to bring them into line, which they did when they could.[20]

In 1907 the whole national agreement had to be revised, to remove 'asperities'. But the men who were keeping up a spontaneous and ingrained resistance were the men with whom managers were working day by day, on whose goodwill they depended for output. They were the men, moreover, with whom they wished to live in relations of mutual respect. National character enters again here: though held by foreign observers to be more divided by class than neighbouring democracies, the British seem to be less stiffly hierarchical, less prone to give an authoritarian form to executive relations, more concerned that functional relations should be good personal relations. This has been widely seen as raising the quality of working life at the cost of productivity. Action by management to raise productivity by removing restrictive practices would be felt by the workers as deeply wounding. Many managers were sufficiently identified with their workers to shrink from that.

7

The First World War brought a further stimulus to employers' organization. All industry, whether or not it was directly at work on munitions, had to deal with government and its controls of materials and manpower. Some leading businessmen were themselves drawn into wartime administration. They saw the great powers that government could exert to organize production, especially under the direction of a Minister such as Lloyd George. In exerting those powers government dealt readily and directly with representatives of the trade unions at the national level. But the employers' associations had no such standing with the Government – not even the engineering employers had been a party to the Treasury Agreement of March 1915, though this committed employers to certain present and future actions. In the wartime administration of industry the Government used individual employers in large numbers, as it did not use trade union officials. But at the national level the employers had no representative body like the TUC.

Some attempts had been made to establish national organizations before the War. They were stimulated by the heightened tension of the 1890s, the reopening of the issues of labour law, and the increase in social legislation. The Liberty and Property Defence League, founded in 1882, gained the adherence of many employers' associations as the militancy of the New Unionism changed the climate of industrial relations. The League even enlisted the support ultimately of Sir Benjamin Browne, the industrialist of the North-East who had been distinguished for his advocacy and practice of good relations with the unions, attained through mutual respect and understanding. But as its title indicated, the League was there to propagate doctrine: it attracted the zealous or the aggrieved, but did not offer representation for all purposes to firms of all sorts. Shortly after its foundation it secured the rejection of an amendment to the Employers' Liability Bill of 1893 that would have put a stop to contracting out – though this practice was in fact abolished soon afterwards, by the Act of 1897. It issued a pamphlet, *The Case against Picketing*, in 1897, and this was believed to have stiffened the attitude of magistrates, and even to have influenced the courts' interpretation of 'watching and besetting' in Lyons v.

Wilkins (1899) and Charnock v. Court (1899). After the great struggle in the engineering industry in 1897–8 it joined with the Free Labour Protection Association that Colonel Dyer, the engineering employers' leader, had formed, to set up an Employers' Parliamentary Council. This was intended to keep a watch on legislation, and secure a hearing for employers more commensurate with that of which the TUC was assured. It survived to sponsor some amendments in the House of Lords to what became the fundamental Trade Disputes Act of 1906. Its spokesman, the Earl of Wemyss, then described it as composed of representatives of the Central Associations of shipping, building, iron, printing, cotton, and a number of minor industries, but he did not name engineering, or mining, or the railways. The Council seems to have depended very much on his personal exertions, and he was already eighty-eight years of age. His amendments were lost, and we hear no more of the Council afterwards. It seems to have had even less substance than the National Federation of Associated Employers of Labour which had been formed to resist the legislation on unions in the 1870s, and which likewise disappeared after the Government's Bill was passed in 1875. The TUC had an agenda of parliamentary business and government policy that it was concerned to raise year by year: unemployment, hours of work, safety, the minimum wage, pensions, and more besides. But the employers as a whole seem to have had too little concern with Parliamentary business or the intentions of government to keep a national headquarters in being. In the First World War the impact of government on business changed that position radically. Hence the foundation of the Federation of British Industry (FBI) in 1916.

That foundation was also promoted by a change in the type and role of the employer. In earlier times when most firms were smaller it was natural to identify the employer with ownership, and over against labour to set simply capital. The function of management was not distinguished. But as firms grew larger it became apparent that there was a task of organization and administration to be performed that had its own professional requirements. These could not be met solely by technical qualifications; they were imposed in much the same form in firms of quite different technical processes. But they might be met by men of administrative experience gained in various fields – as by Colonel Dyer, for instance, who after a distinguished career in the administration of ordnance factories became the managing director of Armstrong-Whitworth; or Sir Vincent Caillard, a soldier who was for twenty-five years President of the Council of Administration of the Ottoman Public Debt, and subsequently became financial director of Vickers. From the 1890s onwards, moreover, a stream of new thinking about methods of management was flowing in from the United States.

Cartoons in *Punch* might still represent the employer as the glossy, frock-coated capitalist; but a type of manager was being detached from ownership, and the role of management separated from that of the technical expert. Men of this type, in this role, found that they shared a common approach to the task of organizing wartime production. Their impulse was to carry the same approach on to the problems of reconstruction after the war.

The FBI had begun by including industrial relations in its agenda. It published its commentary on the reports of the Whitley Committee that investigated the causes of industrial unrest during the War, and it accepted the Committee's recommendations for improving relations by setting up joint industrial councils. In February 1919 it resolved to 'take immediate action in conjunction if possible with the Engineering Employers' Federation and the National Organisations representing labour with a view to summoning a joint conference of employers and employed for the formation of proposals for dealing with the present grave conditions of industrial unrest.'[21] Early in April a great National Industrial Conference did assemble, on the invitation of the Government. But the FBI failed to present itself there as the body mainly representative of the employers.

The man who did stand out as their spokesman, was the Director of the Engineering Employers' Federation, Sir Allan Smith. He had served in the offices of the Federation for the past thirty years. During the War he had been vastly active and influential in the administration of munitions, from his negotiation of the Shell and Fuses agreement with the trade unions onwards. He had been a member of the Whitley Committee with its ready ear for the claims of labour at the place of work, and had signed the first report that recommended the setting up of a Joint Industrial Council in each industry, with district joint councils and works committees. It was now on his motion, as amended by the Labour leader, Arthur Henderson, and by Lloyd George, that the National Industrial Conference set up a Joint Committee of thirty employers and thirty trade unionists, to consider present problems and make recommendations. He became chairman of the employers' panel. The Joint Committee's recommendations were far-reaching. There should be a permanent National Industrial Council; a statutory forty-eight hour week and a national minimum wage; machinery for avoiding disputes in each industry; and measures against unemployment, including organized short time and restrictions on overtime. The Committee outlined the form of actual legislation on hours and wages, by which the desired limits might be applied to the variety of working practice. On behalf of the government, Lloyd George accepted the Committee's report.

Meanwhile the demonstrated lack of a body to represent employers nationally in industrial relations led Sir Allan Smith to provide one, by gathering a National Council of Employers' Organizations (NCEO) around his own Engineering Employers' Federation. This body was at once recognized by the Government as representing the employers in all labour questions. A first issue of policy before it – in practice, before Sir Allan Smith and his Engineering Employers, whose influence was preponderant – was whether and how to pursue the proposal for a permanent National Industrial Council. When Lloyd George accepted this among the other proposals of the Joint Committee, the expectation arose that the Government really meant to act on the cry of 'home rule for industry', and place industrial policy in the hands of the Council. The employers – not least those in engineering – who were still chafing under the close control exercised by government during the War, would have had their reason for welcoming this change, and if it also gave recognition to the greatly enhanced status of the trade unions at the national level, the employers would still sooner deal directly with the unions there than have the unions sway the policy of government. But to legislate for maximum hours and minimum wages was a different matter, even though the limits were wide, and the proposed hours were flexible. The Government was in no hurry to prepare legislation that the House of Commons would not stomach. The Conference that it had convened in April 1919 had served its purpose in averting a crisis. The acute phase, arising out of the stress and suffering of the War, a phase at once of ardent idealism and menacing strife, had passed by: the state of the economy, the mood of the people, the preoccupations of the Government, had all changed. But Sir Allan Smith continued to demand the legislation on hours and wages as the indispensable prerequisite to the setting up of the National Industrial Council. That legislation was part of the agreement which he had, in effect, negotiated within the Joint Committee; the TUC had made it clear that without it they would not collaborate in setting up the Council. But when in June 1920 the Government did prepare a Bill that would enable it to ratify the forty-eight-hour Convention of the International Labour Organization, Sir Allen Smith said that this was different from the legislation proposed by the Joint Committee, whose work he now regarded as at an end.

There thus emerged from the hopes and endeavours of the period of reconstruction only this one by-product for the organization of employers at the national level, the NCEO, which removed labour questions from what for the preceding three years had been the all-embracing concern of the FBI. Until 1934 the NCEO was to be dominated by the strange and strong personality of Sir Allan Smith.[22]

By origin he was a Glasgow lawyer. There met in him a dour Scots rectitude, an insistence on the formal delimitation of rights and func-

tions, and that determination to uphold the prerogatives of management which particularly marked the engineering employers. Because in
all he did he was intensely aware of what was the right path, and held
himself unswervingly to it, he was inflexible and autocratic. One
glacial glance from him repelled the overtures of humanity. The
employers who had to work with him found him in the end an
unbearable colleague. Yet given his stand on the prerogatives of
management he was genuinely anxious to arrive at an understanding
with the unions, he did advocate joint consultation both, through the
Whitley Committee, at the place of work and, through the National
Industrial Conference, at the national level. When he entered the
House of Commons after the War, moreover, and became Chairman
of the Industrial Group of MPs, he addressed himself to the economic
problems of the day, unemployment above all, with independence,
courage, and persistence in pressing constructive proposals.

This Industrial Group was a manifestation of the stimulus that the
War had given to the interest of employers in national economic
policy, and their sense that they had a distinctive contribution to make
to its administration. The very notion of national economic policy was
new – the notion that government should take the responsibility for
directing the development of the economy. It was new, too, that
businessmen should welcome and even demand the intervention of the
Government. But the war had demonstrated their ability to carry
through great tasks of reorganization in collaboration with the
machinery of government. Lloyd George had welcomed them and
their way of working. The end of the War would confront the country
with severe tasks of reconstruction at home and the recovery of
markets abroad: these were tasks that businessmen could carry
through far better than politicians of the old school. In 1916 a number
of employers founded the British Commonwealth Union to secure
representation in Parliament 'on national questions relating to
industry and commerce', and it secured the return of eighteen members
in the election of 1918. With other members who belonged to an FBI
Committee, they made up an Industrial Group of about sixty. When
Sir Allan Smith was returned in a by-election at the end of 1919, he was
soon elected Chairman of the Group.[23]

In the popular parlance of the day these were 'the men of push and
go'. Two industrialists, Sir Eric Geddes and Lord Weir, played a
prominent part in the Coalition Government, but the Group remained
backbenchers. Before long what concerned them most was
unemployment. In the last quarter of 1920 a recession set in of a great
rapidity, in the world market and at home, and Allan Smith's efforts
were directed insistently henceforward towards pressing the
Government to support industry and help it gain export markets. In

this he disregarded party lines. In December 1920 he joined Arthur Henderson, as spokesman for the joint committee of the TUC and the Labour Party, in proposing to the Cabinet that a levy of a penny in the pound be imposed on employers and employees alike, for a state fund to supplement unemployment benefit.[24] In February 1923 he voted for the Labour amendment to the Address, because it called for more effective action to revive industry and get unemployment down. Later in the same year the Industrial Group submitted to Baldwin as President of the Board of Trade detailed proposals for particular investment projects, in pursuance of 'a policy for employment rather than an unemployment policy'.[25] Baldwin demurred, Smith published the correspondence, which gave great offence. But this was only one incident in the campaign he had waged ever since he entered the House against the inertia of the Ministers concerned with industry and employment. Nor did he spare the Foreign Office, which he required to be staffed for and devoted to the promotion of British exports. Changes in that direction were made half a century later.

Being a free trader, he lost his seat in the general election that brought the first Labour Government into office at the end of 1923, and we hear no more after that of the Industrial Group that he had led. He had come into head-on collision with Baldwin, in two ways. In matters of national economic policy, and the possibility of promoting reconstruction and employment by state-assisted projects of investment, he stressed the gravity of the problem and the scope for speedy action, whereas Baldwin had no sense of urgency and disliked intervention. In matters of industrial relations, Smith presented a rigid front to the trade unionists on the manager's right to manage, and he had held the Engineering Employers on that line through the lock-out of 1922; his willingness to co-operate once that division of functions was accepted, and his deep concern for unemployment, could not overcome the harsh and cold impression made by that steely insistence. But Baldwin was bland and amiable; he grasped no nettles and drew no hard lines; he stood for peace among men of goodwill. It was to Baldwin that the day belonged.

Looking back, we can say that this was a misfortune for the British economy and the British worker. Smith faced the need for the reconstruction and modernization of much of industry that had been imposed by foreign competition since the end of the nineteenth century and intensified by the War. He saw also, in his own blinkered way, the need for managers to be able to implement changes in the interests of efficiency, and for British workers, in a competitive world, not to rob themselves of employment and higher standards of living through their adherence to restrictive practices and insistence on overmanning. The Industrial Group arose out of the mingled euphoria and apprehension of some businessmen during the War – this sense of what management in conjunction with government could achieve in the way of organiz-ation and development, mingled with their awareness of how much there was to be done. There was a boldness in their thinking, a new conception both of planning in industry and of the relations between industry and government. Problems that we are still wrestling with today were diagnosed and prescribed for pertinently then.

But after five years it was all at an end. The businessmen who entered politics found that they had another and an arduous trade to learn. The 'men of push and go' were identified with the Coalition Government and especially its leader, Lloyd George, and their influ-ence waned with his. Allan Smith himself was a wretched speaker, and singularly lacking in the power to exert personal influence. The impetus that the war had given died away.

After 1923, under the continued domination of Allan Smith, the NCEO made no constructive contribution to industrial relations. His own attitude towards the setting up of a National Industrial Council, Eric Wigham has suggested, became changed through the identifica-tion of the TUC with the Labour Party and its commitment to nation-alization, and through the experience of the General Strike in 1926.[26] At any rate, when a new effort was made to bring trade unionists and employers together to consider industrial policy at the national level, the response of the NCEO was muted.

8

The new initiative came from the General Secretary of the TUC, Walter Citrine. After the General Strike he took thought how he might restore the position of the trade unions, by drawing on the goodwill towards them which he knew had existed and continued to exist among many industrialists personally.

At first, [he wrote later] I felt it was hopeless to approach the two main employer organisations. The FBI on one side was regarded by us all as a body dwelling on lofty industrial heights and dictating policy to their member employers. I know now how exaggerated an assumption this was. The NCEO on the other hand struck me as being as belligerent and uncompromising as any of our trade unions. I saw little hope of a constructive result coming from any approach to them. Yet something must be done to develop contacts whereby the problem facing industry, not only in the sphere of labour relations but in the much wider economic sense could be discussed.[27]

He had a fresh and bold conception of the aims that the trade unions should pursue in confronting those wider economic problems:

It is conceivable, but in the last degree unlikely, that the unions may wish to do nothing to make the existing system more efficient because their aim is to hasten its breakdown. Alternatively, the unions may say their aim should be to keep up the defensive struggle for the maintenance of existing standards and to improve them as opportunity offers, but to accept no responsibility at all for any effort that can be made to improve the organisation of industry on the present basis of private ownership. A third possibility is that the unions should actively participate in a concerted effort to raise industry to its highest efficiency by developing the most scientific methods of production, eliminating waste and harmful restrictions, removing causes of friction and avoidable conflict, and promoting the largest possible output so as to provide a rising standard of life and continuously improving conditions of employment.[28]

It was in pursuit of this third aim that Citrine inserted in the President's address to the TUC of 1927 a passage suggesting joint central discussions with the FBI and NCEO. He had become more imaginative than the organized employers. There was no response at all from the FBI. The NCEO issued a statement saying that industrial problems were best discussed industry by industry.

But a very different response came from the head of Imperial Chemicals, Sir Alfred Mond. On his personal invitation a number of forward-looking industrialists gathered to meet a delegation from the TUC for the discussion of a wide agenda of current problems, beginning with the organization of industrial relations, and unemployment. This became known as the Mond–Turner Conference. Its second full meeting all but unanimously approved a report that dealt in unusually definite terms with 'the Gold Reserve and its relation to industry', trade union recognition, victimization – a burning issue after the General Strike – and the rationalization of industry that specially concerned Sir Alfred Mond. But the report also contained a proposal that both seemed to provide the necessary means of implementing its recommendations, and in practice ensured that both they and the conference itself would come to nothing. 'For the continuous improvement of industrial reorganization and industrial relations' a National Industrial Council (NIC) should be set up forthwith. It should be composed of the General Council of the TUC together with an equal number of representatives of the employers, nominated by the FBI and the NCEO. This NIC should meet regularly 'for general consultation on the widest questions concerning industry and industrial progress', and 'establish and direct machinery for continuous investigation into industrial problems.' It should also appoint Conciliation Boards to act in industrial disputes.

Evidently this proposal must now be referred to the three organizations concerned: indeed, the Mond–Turner Conference now really handed over to them. This was in July 1928. Within the month the two

employers' organizations referred it to their members. In September
the annual Trades Union Congress voted its approval by a big
majority. In the following February the FBI and NCEO were ready
with their views: in a joint letter to the TUC they said they could not
accept the proposals for a NIC, but in the interests of industrial peace
they invited the TUC to meet them to discuss how they might usefully
consult together otherwise. It was made evident that any such con-
sultations would not usually be tripartite, for emphasis was laid on the
different capacities of the two employers' bodies, 'the Confederation
dealing with labour questions and the Federation with economic and
commercial questions'. Out of discussions between the three organizations there emerged by December of that year 1929 an agreement of
Byzantine protocol. It provided that

having regard to the separate spheres and functions of the Confederation and
the FBI, and the necessity for the TUC knowing which of these two organizations will be responsible for the employers' side of any question proposed for
discussion, the Confederation and the FBI will set up an Allocation Committee, whose sole function will be to say whether any given subject proposed
by the TUC, or which the Confederation or FBI proposed to raise with the
TUC, is one which concerns the responsibility of the Confederation or the
FBI, or both. The question of allocation having been settled, the future
procedure will be carried through direct between the TUC, on the one hand,
and the Confederation or FBI, or both, on the other hand, without further
reference to the Allocation Committee.

A list of suitable subjects was attached, by way of illustration; these all,
like taxation and empire trade, concerned government policy, and the
subjects in the sphere of industrial relations which the Mond–Turner
conference had tackled were conspicuously omitted.

An obvious interpretation of this etiolated outcome of protracted
deliberation is that it marks a deliberate attempt on the part of the
employers to bring about what did in fact follow – the extinction of the
Mond–Turner impetus. But this would be to do less than justice to the
positive elements in the rigid mind of Sir Allan Smith. During the
discussions there appeared the Final Report of the Balfour Committee
on Industry and Trade, of which Committee he was a member, and
though this Report advised against the setting up of a National
Industrial Council as a permanent organization with regular meetings,
it did not disapprove of the convening of a national conference of
representatives of employers and employed, to meet say annually.
What seems at first a theologically fine distinction will have served to
avoid establishing what would look like but could not in practice
function as an institution of industrial self-government, an institution,
moreover, whose constitution must raise the question of 'spheres and
functions' between the employers' associations. If this was Sir Allan

Smith's mind, consultation at the national level was seen as useful and should be provided for. In his stiff and formal way this had now been done – the councils of the three organizations had each a standing authorization to enter into discussions at any time, and the susceptibilities of the NCEO in the matter of 'spheres and functions', like those of any craft union on an issue of demarcation, had been guarded. The new arrangements were in fact used four times in the next two years – three times for discussion between TUC and FBI, on the Macmillan Committee, the Commonwealth Conference (to which they submitted a joint memorandum on trade), and on the British film industry; and once, and only once, and then on the motion of the TUC, between TUC and NCEO on redundancy and reorganization – a sterile discussion.

One explanation that has been offered of this outcome is that the NCEO was hostile from the first to forming any settled relation with the TUC. But its policy is more probably defined by the report of the Balfour Committee, already mentioned. The immediate circumstance that prevented more from coming of the arrangements so carefully devised for consultation must have been the rapidly deepening depression, with the economic crisis and the rout of the Labour Party at the polls, in 1931. But there were also basic conditions that must have ensured the same negative outcome in any case, whatever initial steps had been taken, whether after Mond–Turner or earlier.

One of these conditions was the lack of organization on the employers' side, such as could have ensured that agreements about procedure, for instance, that were entered into at the national level, were carried down to the constituent industry and firm and made effective there. A similar lack of structure and cohesion equally limited the ability of the TUC to participate. It had enabled the Balfour Committee to impale the proposal for a standing National Industrial Council on the horns of a dilemma: either the Council must be vested with real powers of self-government, that is, with legislative powers, and that would mean a constitutional revolution; or it would only be able to engage in discussions whose lack of practical outcome would disappoint the hopes prompted by its foundation. This argument excluded the possibility, which was to be realized before long in Sweden, that the national bodies of employers and trade unions should enter into voluntary agreements which would then be passed down the line as working rules for their members: but the Report was right in saying that

it seems doubtful if the various trade organisations . . . which represent the industries of the country would be willing to delegate to a National Industrial Council the settlement, or even an advisory voice in the settlement, of the conditions of employment or other matters of domestic interest to individual industries.[29]

The other basic obstacle to the establishment of settled relations between employers' organizations and the TUC was the prevailing attitude of the employers of the time. We have seen how the proprietors of firms in the same trade did not readily combine with one another. They were preoccupied, moreover, with the affairs of their own businesses. The men at the head of the much bigger firms that were forming from the end of the nineteenth century onwards were less trammelled with the daily tasks of administration, and the fortunes or misfortunes of their concern depended more upon issues of public policy. The qualities that had brought them to their positions included the ability to see problems in general terms, and to plan. They would welcome Sir Alfred Mond's initiative, they would respond to Ernest Bevin's proposals. But there were relatively few of them; and so many of them as there were would have said that they had better ways of spending their time than by sitting in committees. They therefore did not give a lead in building or energising employers' organizations, and very likely the smaller firms (of which there had been a separate association since 1915) would have been suspicious of them if they had done so. Great or small, moreover, the employer differed from the trade union leader in that industrial relations for him were only one of his many objects of personal concern, and only exceptionally one in which he saw constructive possibilities. The employers' association remained a limited instrument, providing the protection and economy of a common floor of negotiated terms and conditions, and in some cases a grievance procedure. The number and coverage of these associations had been increased as a by-product of the extension of industry-wide negotiation, in the interests of wage control during the War, and through the setting up of Joint Industrial Councils afterwards. Thereby employers' associations took their place as part of the established 'machinery of industrial relations'. Membership fell away somewhat when the unions were in retreat after the collapse of the General Strike in 1926, but in the 1930s there were some 270 national federations of local associations known to the Ministry of Labour. These bodies had no wide purposes, and the attitude of their members denied them the impetus that would have created a presence and representation for employers at the national level equivalent to that of the General Council of the TUC.

But more than thirty years after the Mond–Turner Conference its proposals for a National Industrial Council were adopted. A new generation of employers, some of whom had had experience of planned administration of industry during the Second World War, became weary of the alternations of 'Stop' and 'Go' in government policy during the 1950s, and noted by contrast the sustained development of France under its indicative planning. The conference of the FBI in 1960 – and this marks the coming of the new generation – received from one of its committees the proposal that government policy be laid out and kept on course according to a projection of national development. The Prime Minister was now Harold Macmillan, who in 1938 had advocated the setting up of a National Economic Council made up of representatives of the government departments, the trade unions and the employers.[30] When in July 1961 the Government met a renewed crisis of sterling with familiar measures of restraint, this time it accompanied them by the creation of a National Economic Development Organization. This body was to have a staff equipped, as Mond–Turner and the Prime Minister himself had proposed, for 'continuous investigation into industrial problems'. Its Council was to contain, among others, six members nominated by the General Council of the TUC, and six employers, who attended on the personal invitation of the Chancellor of the Exchequer, and were in practice drawn from the FBI and the national council of employers, now known as the British Employers' Confederation. In 1962 the Council began to meet once a month, again in the words of Mond–Turner, 'for general consultation on the evident questions concerning industry and industrial progress'. These meetings, each lasting for only two or three hours, could not carry discussion far round the table: they came to be largely occupied in validating the work of the Commission's staff. But it was something new that the commentary of each side on papers prepared by the staff or by Government Departments should be heard, and itself commented upon, by the other side. When Reginald Maudling became Chancellor of the Exchequer, moreover, he convened a special session of the Council for two days at the weekend, in the endeavour to work out an incomes policy. Something approaching a negotiation ensued between the employers and the trade unionists, in an attempt to find conditions on which the restraint for which the Government and the employers looked could be taken by the trade unionists as acceptable to their members. The attempt failed. When later George Brown drew employers and trade unionists together in a Joint Declaration of Intent, committing them to incomes policy in the interests of his plan for more rapid economic growth, he acted outside the Council. But it was in the Council that the plan itself was – if hastily – reviewed and endorsed.

The new attitude among employers at the national level has also been manifest in the approach to pay bargaining. In 1977 the Confederation of British Industry (CBI) put forward proposals for radical changes.[31] There should be a national economic forum, in which the

CBI and the TUC would discuss their views, and that of other interested parties, on the prospects of the economy, and the resources available for allocation to various purposes. The Budget would be prepared in the light of this analysis. There would follow the annual pay round, but one much compressed in comparison with previous rounds, providing indeed for synchronization of settlements that are in practice closely linked.

What is significant in these proposals is, first and foremost, the fact that they should have been made at all. That the leaders of the national organization of employers should have felt able to invite their members to consider initiating a radical change in structure and procedure marks both the changed outlook of the businessmen typically concerned, and the pressure put upon them by cost inflation. The function proposed for the economic forum is also significant. The expectation is that it would provide a means of reaching agreement with the trade unions on an appreciation of the economic prospects, in the light of which agreement the pay bargaining would subsequently be conducted in particular negotiations. Here is an avoidance of the imposition of incomes policy by Government, through the adoption of a Swedish form of 'home rule for industry'.

9

The British people would have been more prosperous since the Second World War if employers' associations had been stronger. Full employment could have been maintained without inflation if employers' associations had held the line against the wage claims that took the flow of demand that was meant to sustain more jobs and aborted it as a merely cost-raising round of pay rises for those already employed. The object of incomes policy was to reduce that pressure at its source. Governments resorted to this policy because they believed that once the pressure was exerted, employers would not resist it effectively. At least in this country so much was taken for granted: the German employers were different.

That the British employers entered the era of full employment with so little tradition of cohesion and mutual support arises in part out of the social attitudes, temperament, and shelter from competition, that have already been noticed here. But one major consideration remains to be mentioned – the limitation of the pressure exerted directly on employers to establish and uphold associations. In their relations with unions employers are concerned with the movement of money wages in their effect on costs, and with keeping control within the works. Membership of an employers' association is a distraction and, in so far as it brings a loss of autonomy, a cost which is not to be incurred unless the costs of staying out are still higher. Most British employers did not find them so.

That remark may seem strange when one remembers the great struggles that were waged; but let us set these in perspective. Average annual earnings, which reached £50 a year in the boom of the early 1870s, were still in the low £50s in the 1890s, and had only reached £63 after the rise in prices down to 1913. Even after the rapid trade union recruitment just before the First World War, only a little more than a quarter of the working population in industry was then in membership. Since 1870 the whole population of working age had been increasing relentlessly, even after a great emigration overseas, at never less than 10 per cent a decade – the steady inflow of more and more hands seeking work ensured the authority of the foreman who could hire and fire, outside the preserves of the craft union. In the inter-war years the continued high level of unemployment, the collapse of the General Strike, and the crushing of the miners' resistance in 1926, and the break up of the Labour Government in 1931, all inhibited upward pressure. For most of the time only a quarter or less of the occupied population belonged to trade unions. Money wage earnings were no higher in 1938 than they had been in 1922. If we leave out the lift imparted to those earnings through the First World War and the ensuing boom, we find that through the remaining years from 1870 to 1938 they rose at an average annual rate of only about half of one per cent. The recurrent years of recession and depression during the eight-year cycle cut off the pressure for rises that had been exerted in the years of improving employment. Most of all, custom was a restraining as well as a stabilizing influence: if it protected the pay of unorganized labour, it limited the demands of the organized.

It may be, then, that if British employers built up no tradition of organization against the unions, they still organized as much as they needed to. In great part they were not exposed to such external pressure from competition that they were driven to break down union resistance to their innovative use of their executive discretion in the shops. Nor were they generally confronted with pressure from the unions such as they could not accommodate in the current state of the product market. When exceptions arose to those conditions, especially if the exceptions under the two heads coincided, the employers concerned showed the capacity to act together. It may be the absence of stimulus rather than the lack of capacity to respond that explains the slightness of employers' organization elsewhere.

As for representation at Westminster, it may be said that the employers' fate was sealed in 1867, when many urban workmen got the vote: henceforward workers had far more votes than employers. Still more was that so after the subsequent extensions of the franchise, in 1884, 1918, and 1928. A candidate of whatever hue and allegiance in an industrial constituency knew that any commitment on his part that was objectionable to the wage-earning voters might be ruinous to his prospects. True, employers might be foremost among the subscribers to party funds nationally and locally; they might dominate a caucus in the constituency, and control the choice of candidate. But they could not control the voters. Where the Liberal caucus refused to adopt a working man as candidate, it only expedited the replacement of the Liberal Party by independent Labour in that constituency. In the seats that remained safely Conservative, the local Conservative Party was unlikely to be under pressure from local employers. Employers generally might have been concerned to control local representation: we know that some of them were much concerned. But increasingly as the franchise widened, in matters of industrial relations the local representatives were controlled by the ballot box.

That in later years the Conservative Party became identified with restraint of the trade unions did not mark pressure from the employers or make it in this respect the agency of employers' policy. So long as the Conservatives' main struggle had been with the Liberals, they had avoided drawing the fire of Labour at the same time. After the First World War the issue that confronted and was legislated upon by Baldwin's Government was the authority of government over against 'direct action' by trade unions nationally; this was not an issue that affected employers in their industrial relations at the place of work. The initiative taken by Heath's Government in the Industrial Relations Act of 1971 arose out of a train of study and discussion within the party, especially among some of its lawyers. Employers are not known to have advocated its provisions; they certainly made little use of them. The asymmetry has remained, that the trade unions have had a political party appropriated to them in Parliament, but there has been no such relationship on the side of the employers. For the purpose of those transactions with government that have really concerned the employers, however, since the First World War they have maintained organizations which form the counterpart of the TUC.

Notes

[1] Adam Smith, *Wealth of Nations*, Bk. I, ch. VIII.

[2] Ibid., Bk. I, ch. X, pt. II.

[3] Kenneth O. Morgan, *Rebirth of a Nation: Wales 1880–1980* (Clarendon Press, Oxford, and University of Wales Press, 1981), p. 68.

[4] Royal Commission on Trade Unions, 1867–69, Parl. Papers 1867–68, C. 3980, Fifth Report, Q 10,074.

[5] First Report of the Royal Commission on Labour 1891–94, Parl. Papers 1892, vol. XXXVI, Pt. II, C. 6795, Q. 13,165.

⁶ Royal Commission on Trade Unions, 1867–69. Parl. Papers 1867, C. 3873, First Report, Qs. 3474, 3479.

⁷ Ibid., Q. 3610.

⁸ Ibid., Parl. Papers 1867–68, C. 3980, Sixth Report, Q. 12,521.

⁹ Ibid., Parl. Papers 1867–68, C. 3980, Fifth Report, Q. 10,046.

¹⁰ H. A Clegg, A. Fox, A. F. Thompson, *A History of British Trade Unions since 1889, Vol. I, 1889–1910* (Oxford, 1964), p. 201.

¹¹ R. O. Clarke, 'The Dispute in the British Engineering Industry 1897–98: an Evaluation', *Economica*, 24, 94, May 1957, 136.

¹² Eric Wigham, *The Power to Manage* (London, 1973), Appendix D, pp. 285–9.

¹³ R. O. Clarke, *Economica*, 24, 94, May 1957, 136.

¹⁴ Alfred Marshall, *Industry and Trade* (London, 1919), p. 137.

¹⁵ In letters dated 22 Oct. 97 and 5 Dec. 97 to Edward Caird, Master of Balliol, A. C. Pigou (ed.), *Memorials of Alfred Marshall* (London, 1925), pp. 398–400.

¹⁶ G. Binney Dibblee, 'The Printing Trades and the Crisis in British Industry', *Economic Journal*, 12, March 1902, 13.

¹⁷ Royal Commission on Trade Disputes and Combinations, 1906: Minutes of Evidence (Parl. Papers 1906, vol. LVI, Cd. 2826), Q. 130.

¹⁸ Royal Commission on Labour 1891–94, Fifth and Final Report (Parl. Papers 1894, vol. XXXIX, C. 7421), Pt. 1, para 81.

¹⁹ Quoted in *The Financial Times*, 24 Dec. 1979, from the CBI Members' Bulletin.

²⁰ Eric Wigham, *The Power to Manage*, pp. 68–9.

²¹ Quoted here from Rodger Charles, *The Development of Industrial Relations in Britain 1911–39* (London 1973), p. 233.

²² My account of him, and of employers' organizations at this time, is greatly indebted to Eric Wigham, *The Power to Manage*.

²³ My information concerning the British Commonwealth Union and the Industrial Group is derived from Terry Rodgers, 'Sir Allan Smith: Outsider in Politics 1918–1924' (Paper presented to the Symposium on 'Businessmen and Politics', London School of Economics, 1 May 1980).

²⁴ Cabinet minutes 31 Dec. 1920 (CAB 23/23). I owe this reference to Kenneth O. Morgan.

²⁵ Terry Rodgers, 'Sir Allan Smith', p. 30.

²⁶ Eric Wigham, *The Power to Manage*, p. 132.

²⁷ W. Citrine, *Men and Work* (London, 1964), p. 243.

²⁸ 'The Next Step in Industrial Relations', *Manchester Guardian Supplement*, 30 Nov. 1927, p. 8; reprinted in W. Milne-Bailey: *Trade Union Documents* (London, 1929), 431–8.

²⁹ Final Report of the Committee on Industry and Trade, Parl. Papers 1928–29. VII (Cmd. 3282) 413, p. 128.

³⁰ Harold Macmillan, *The Middle Way* (London, 1938), p. 290.

³¹ The separate organization of employers for the purpose of industrial relations ceased to exist in 1965 when the British Employers' Confederation, as it had then become, merged with the FBI to form the Confederation of British Industries (CBI).

VIII

TRADE UNIONISTS AT THE PLACE OF WORK

I

A major factor in moulding British industrial relations has been the continuous presence of the craftsman in the workshop from early times. In the daily conduct of the workshop he was assured of a substantial autonomy because the techniques of the trade resided in the skill of his hands: he had to be left to go about the work in his own way. But he exerted this control only within the bounds of his craft and not over the range of operations that his employer directed. In printing, for instance, though the 'chapel' is the oldest instance of the trade union branch at the place of work, and the 'father of the chapel' the prototype of the shop steward, the compositors did not extend their control over the associated processes that came in during the first half of the nineteenth century – the machine presses, stereotyping, lithography, electro-typing – and left those who worked in them to form their own unions. In the same way, in later years, the engineers were to treat the new race of electricians as outside their pale. Craft unionism was far from 'workshop organization'. Some of the aims, moreover, of the early craft unionists could not possibly be attained by action over against any one employer. They were striving to maintain the regulations that had protected the journeymen in the gilds, at a time when those regulations, and the whole system of thought that legitimized them, were fast breaking up under the impact of expanding markets, new processes, and a rapidly growing working population avid for employment. A basic issue was the regulation of apprenticeship. It would have been of little use for the craftsmen in this shop or that to prevail on their employer to limit the number of his apprentices, or refuse to take in 'turnovers' – lads who had left their indentures elsewhere before their seven years were up – if other employers were still flooding the labour market. It was the same with resistance to the employment of 'illegal' men – men who had not been apprenticed at all. The dyke must go all the way across or it would be useless. For the enforcement of rules the craftsmen looked to common action, leading to acceptance by the employers, throughout a district.

But there was an ambiguity here. On the one hand we may comment on the absence of single-employer bargaining: as bargaining grew and procedures emerged it was multi-employer bargaining and the district agreement that prevailed. But on the other hand, not only did the craftsmen preserve his sphere of autonomy in the workshop, but in negotiating at the district level the craft union might raise issues that further limited the discretion of the employer. The reaction of the employers was to distinguish between the issues on which they were and were not prepared to negotiate. That the price of labour as of any other supply should be subject to negotiation was not unthinkable, and that collective bargaining about wages should put a floor under competition even had its advantages: but for workers who should be under the employer's orders to dispute his authority was an act of insubordination that was hotly resented. In later years the distinction was made in a dissenting note drafted by Alexander Siemens on behalf of the Engineering Employers' Federation and attached to a Report of the Industrial Council on the observance of industrial agreements, in 1913. 'Industrial agreements', Siemens wrote, 'may cover two sets of questions – questions of principle and questions of fact. Questions of principle arise out of the rights and privileges of the employers and work people. . . . Questions of fact . . . are questions which are determinable by circumstances which may be rightly ascertained and which vary from day to day. A notable question of fact is the question of general alterations of wages.[1] Wages did in fact in those days go down as well as up from time to time according, as Siemens said, to the circumstances of the day, the phases of the business cycle: there might be hard bargaining, and sometimes a protracted stoppage, but the employer did not feel he was standing on principle. It was otherwise when the trade unionists put forward claims which he felt interfered with his freedom to manage. In bargaining about wages there was a clash of interests, but not of principles – not even of the principles on which wages should be changed from time to time, save in so far as the maintenance of a minimum wage through thick and thin was being demanded. But within the firm and the workshop two claims of right met head-on. The workers claimed the right to maintain practices long observed and hitherto unchallenged, and to be given the opportunity of consultation and negotiation before the unwritten terms in their individual contracts of service were varied. The employers claimed the right to implement freely managerial decisions which concerned the use of their own machines and were essential to the efficiency of their businesses in an increasingly competitive world. There was an inherent opposition of views on what was reasonable, right, and proper. The resistance of the employers to the workers' claims was correspondingly implacable.

It would still have been possible, in the nineteenth century as it was to happen often enough in the 1960s, for a strike by all the manual workers in the firm to bring the employer to terms; or even a strike by a small number of workers in one key process. But rarely did it happen. The miners apart, the workers in any one firm were commonly divided among themselves. The receipt of strike pay depended upon the accumulation of funds from a wide membership, and disbursement must be limited to struggles which concerned that membership in common. In many employments blacklegs were available to take the place of strikers, on a scale that is hard to conceive of today. Employers would offer more uncompromising resistance to the assertion of claims that seemed to them subversive. To the workers themselves that assertion would have seemed daring. For 'the ringleaders' it certainly was: they might well have paid for it with their jobs, and not been able to rely on the support of the union as they could if they had been victimized after an official strike. But beyond that calculation of the objective risk there will have been inhibition through intuitive acceptance of subordination and powerlessness.

For the engineers a greater confidence was both manifest and reinforced by the setting up of their Amalgamated Society in 1851. This became associated in the minds of employers with the pressing of objections to the working of systematic overtime, to the use of piecework, and to the employment of 'illegal' men on machines. They formed an industry-wide Association to combat those claims, and the lock-out that it enforced ended in its complete victory: the men on going back to work had to sign a 'document' repudiating their union membership.

2

The employers had won the battle but were far from having won the war. The issues would not go away. Towards the end of the century they were raised in an acute form by the introduction of new processes, mechanical and managerial. The craftsman's resistance to them was not an attempted advance into new negotiating territory, so much as an attempt to ward off the breaking up of ways of working that had always been taken for granted. The new capstan and turret lathes, the milling machines, the grinders, borers, and drills, enabled work that had depended hitherto solely upon the acquired skill of the apprenticed turner and fitter to be performed, to the highest required degree of accuracy, by men who had received only brief instruction – 'handymen' as they were called. Some craftsmen claimed that they must 'follow the work', and themselves operate the machine on which the work was now done that they had been used to do with hand tools;

others claimed that 'the rate for the job' must still be paid even though the job was now being done by unskilled labour. This was 'the machine question'.

Many of the machines were of American origin, and there came in with them methods of wage-payment that were also American. The engineers had long objected to piece-rates. These were familiar in other British contexts, but had the drawback when applied to the many and varied products of an engineering shop, when rate-fixing was in its infancy, that the prices given or times allowed for particular jobs were rough and ready, and if the time allowed was too long, the workmen made big earnings that were anomalous, and the job was expensive. The remedy, as the foreman or rate-fixer saw it, was to cut the rate. In the eyes of the workmen this was a brutally unfair return for his response to the incentive he had been offered. An escape from this dilemma was offered by the American device of the premium bonus or gain-sharing method. A time was allowed for the job: the workman was paid at his own basic time-rate for the actual time he took to do the job, and if this was less than the time allowed, the value of the time saved, again reckoned at the workman's basic rate, was divided between him and the firm. Nothing could seem simpler. Because also the formula automatically held down the total rise in earnings as the proportion of time saved rose, it was allowed the virtue of making rate-cutting unnecessary. But precisely this subtlety of the formula made it seem like a trick played on the workman – the higher he raised his output, the lower the proportionate rise in his earnings. For the craftsman accustomed to turn out a first-rate job in his own time, the straight piece-rate was bad enough: but this was far worse. The reaction came in organized resistance. Where these new methods of wage demands were being introduced, we hear of shop committees being formed to uphold the interests of the craftsmen over against the rate-setter and the foreman. In 1896 the Amalgamated Society of Engineers provided in its rules for the appointment of shop stewards. The secretary of the employers' association on the Clyde reported, also in 1896, much trouble in a number of shops through 'the newly formed vigilance committees of the ASE known as shop stewards.'[2]

Thus 'the machine question' and the new methods of wage payment see the beginning of the modern shop steward movement. By this term is intended not merely the presence of certain union delegates charged with checking cards, collecting subscriptions, or recruiting at the place of work, but the organization of the workers there for the purpose of their own direct negotiation with the management under which they are working.

We have seen how the employers' riposte to this movement came in the industry-wide association that they formed and the great lock-out that they initiated in 1897. It was a struggle in which both sides, as they saw it, had their backs to the wall. The Engineers were struggling to uphold the customary way of working of which the time-served craftsmen should be assured as of right. They saw the employers as having taken the offensive against them, to break down security in the working life and pride in craftsmanship with new machines, the intrusion of semi-skilled labour, and the premium bonus. To the employers the issue seemed utterly different. They were under pressure as never before. They must compete or collapse. In their efforts to match the advances in productivity in the shops made by their competitors overseas, they found themselves obstructed by their own workmen. Their leader, Colonel Dyer, stressed their need for 'the freedom to manage' which those competitors enjoyed.

The demand he saw the engineering employers as bound to resist was 'that the Amalgamated Society of Engineers should work machines to the exclusion of other men, and that the employers should pay whatever wages the leaders of this society decided. The employer to whom the machines belonged was not be be consulted: he had merely to do as he was told.'[3]

After six months of struggle in which the employers' unwillingness to compromise had been held to amount to a refusal of collective bargaining, they made some minor concessions, and the unionists accepted terms of settlement that appeared to give the employers all they had been contending for on the main issue. The first paragraph was headed 'General Principles of Freedom of Employers in the Management of their Works'.

The Federated Employers, [it stated] while disallowing any intention of interfering with the proper function of trade unions, will admit no interference with the management of their business, and reserve to themselves the right to introduce into any Federated workshop, at the option of the employer concerned, any condition of labour under which any member of the trade unions here represented were working at the commencement of the dispute in any of the workshops of the Federated Employers; but in the event of any trade union desiring to raise any question arising therefrom, a meeting can be arranged by application to the Secretary of the Employers' Local Association to discuss the matter.

There followed detailed provisions concerning the employers' rights to institute piece-work, require the working of overtime, take on apprentices without limit, and allocate whatever men they considered suitable to their machines. There was, however, one part of the terms which did make a first provision for industrial relations within the firm. A dispute procedure was agreed. 'With a view to avoid disputes in future', it began, 'deputations of workmen will be received by their employers, by appointment, for mutual discussion of questions, in the settlement of which both parties are directly concerned. In case of disagreement, the local Association of Employers will negotiate with the local officials of the trade unions.' There was further provision for cases being carried up to Central Conference. What is remarkable is the need to codify a procedure for negotiation – for such in effect it was – between the workers and their own management. There was no restriction of the scope of the jurisdiction except in so far as the terms of settlement would have entitled management to refuse to discuss matters which those terms had placed within its exclusive discretion.

The employers were left in possession of the national battlefield, but they were very far from having gained the control they desired in the shops. The branches of the ASE which despite the length of the stoppage had been voting by overwhelming majorities up to all but the very last against acceptance of the employers' terms, were now bewildered and outraged to find what terms had been imposed upon them. Those terms struck across deep-seated needs and basic attitudes of the craftsmen. There were tensions within their union. The impulse to organization at the place of work was strengthened. The struggle continued there on the same issues as before.

Under pressure from its districts, the union pressed the employers to renegotiate the terms of settlement, and succeeded in obtaining a reformulation in 1907, in which at a number of points the provisions were mitigated. The union had accepted in 1902 a document known as the Carlisle Memorandum laying down guidelines for employers on the use of the premium bonus system, but many branches objected to it strongly on the ground that it implicitly accepted a system that they opposed entirely – there was a notable strike against it in the Vickers Armaments Plant at Erith in 1907. The employers in 1910 'received reports that unions were systematically establishing shop committees in firms adopting the system. They opposed this on the grounds`that the function of such committees would soon extend to the negotiation of basic hours.'[4] The Union had to repudiate its acceptance of the Carlisle Memorandum. In 1914 it went on to withdraw altogether from the terms of settlement, though at the same time it adopted a revision of the dispute procedure that inserted a works conference between the first meeting between the worker or his representative and management, and the local conference.

3

So when war broke out in 1914 tensions in the workshop remained high. The War soon raised them still more. The pressure for output intensified the conflict associated with piece-rates and rate-cutting, or alternatively resentment at the working of the premium bonus system.

This was intensified when piece-rates were extended to the unskilled workers – especially women – who were brought into the shops as a war measure and who took over the simpler parts of the craftsman's former tasks. They could achieve high rates of output on this straightforward, repetitive work, and might then even earn more than the craftsmen who were left with the more demanding part. But in any case the very presence of these 'dilutees', albeit they were there only 'for the duration', raised in an acute form 'the machine question' – the employment of unapprenticed labour on machines which turned out work which the craftsmen claimed as theirs alone. In these ways the changes brought by the War represented an aggravation of long-standing grievances that the craftsman needed an exceptional degree of identification with the war effort, or trust in the promises of the Government, to transcend.

But the War had also greatly raised his power to make his resentment felt: it did so by way of full and overfull employment. Suddenly, after four decades of recurrent severity of unemployment, the shortage of labour gave the skilled men security and independence over against the foremen, and confidence in taking action without support or control by their trade union officials. These effects were described by Llewellyn Smith of the Board of Trade in June 1915, at a time when with William Beveridge he was drafting the Bill which became law the next month as the Munitions Act, in order among other things to control the employment of munition workers.

Practically any workman of any pretensions to skill at all in engineering and ship building trades [he wrote] has so little difficulty in finding work the moment he wants it that he has little economic motive left for remaining with his employer, if he is in any way dissatisfied ... On the other hand, the employers, constantly urged by the Government to increase their output, do not feel themselves really in a position to bargain with the men, and have indeed, in many cases owing to the terms of their contract, little incentive to do so. The ordinary economic control of the individual has practically broken down. The result is that to a very considerable extent the men are out of the control both of the employers and of their own leaders.[5]

So the shop stewards who spoke for these men could come forward in greater numbers and assert themselves with greater force against their immediate management. In so doing, they might throw off the restraining hand of their own officials, and sometimes form their own organization in disregard of union boundaries.

The story of the years of turmoil in the munitions industries has been told as that of the shop stewards' movement, and here in turn attention has been directed to its political coloration. It is true that some of the prominent shop stewards brought in syndicalist principles: that they came into collision with the Government through their opposition to its war measures or to the War itself; and that after the Russian Revolution a number became Communists. But perhaps these particular shop stewards owed their prominence more to their politics than to their role as stewards. The support they could command when the authorities moved against them varied greatly according to whether the issue on which they were standing was industrial or political. In any case the great majority of shop stewards were concerned only with the grievances and problems of the men around them. These grievances and problems were an extension, much magnified by the War, of those that had been seething in the shops for many years before. It was the continued preoccupation of the craftsmen with them that gave the shop stewards their agenda when labour shortage gave them their power.

Viewed in this way, the war years 1914–18 mark the rapid development of industrial relations at the place of work under the stimulus of full employment. Two landmarks may be noted. One was the embargo on overtime followed by a widespread strike on the Clyde early in 1915. The issue was simply a wage rise demanded against the rising cost of living. What made the stoppage remarkable was that it was called and led by shop stewards, not by union officials; and that these stewards came together from different factories and different engineering unions to form a Central Committee. This pattern was to be followed in other districts. In Coventry, for instance, in 1917 the Joint Committee of the engineering shop stewards were issuing the credentials of all the other shop stewards in the city, whatever their own unions. When an engineering firm in Coventry at that time refused to negotiate with shop stewards on behalf of its toolmakers, the Joint Committee was able to bring out some 50,000 members, and a Cabinet Minister summoned the parties to a conference. Out of this came the first agreement for the recognition of shop stewards within the Procedure for the avoidance of disputes in the engineering industry. This was the second landmark. The ASE itself adhered to this agreement only in 1919, when it was laid down that shop stewards 'shall be afforded facilities to deal with questions raised in the shop or portion of a shop in which they are employed'.

4

The unrest in industry during the War had risen to a menacing pitch in 1917. The Whitley Committee which was set up to investigate it found one basic cause within face-to-face relations at the place of work: men demanded respect for their manhood. Accustomed as enfranchised and literate citizens to be informed and consulted, and as voters to participate as of right in decision-taking outside the place of work, they were no longer prepared to be told once they were within it that they were not paid to think. The other side of that medal was that there lay in the work-force a fund of suggestions for the improvement of working methods, waiting to be tapped; and a readiness to respond with co-operation to an approach from management that was open, based on mutual respect, and animated by goodwill. This diagnosis led to the proposal to fill a gap in the structure of industrial relations by setting up Works Committees.

In every industry there are certain questions, such as rates of wages and hours of work, which should be settled by District or National Agreement, and with any matter so settled no Works Committee should be allowed to interfere, but there are also many questions closely affecting daily life and comfort in, and the success of, the business, and affecting in no small degree efficiency of working, which are peculiar to the individual workshop or factory. The purpose of a Works Committee is to establish and maintain a system of co-operation in all these workshop matters.[6]

The Whitley Committee was right in its diagnosis, in two respects: it seized on the clash between the subordination traditionally imposed on the worker, and his heightened personal stature; and it saw that institutions were lacking to regulate industrial relations at the place of work. But of the thousand and more Works Committees that were reported as having been set up in accordance with its recommendation, very few were still active a few years later. The difficulty was that their agenda proved narrow in practice, sometimes trifling. The hope had been that the clash of interests over the terms and conditions of employment being removed to collective bargaining, a wide field of common interests would be left open for the Works Committee to administer in 'a frank partnership of knowledge, experience, and good will.'[7] Negotiation was precluded. There must be no ground to suspect that the Committees would be used to bypass the trade unions, so no issue could be raised in them that would be of possible concern to a union. Among the issues that remained were a good many that delegates were keen to raise when a Committee first met; but when this stock of grievances and suggestions had been worked through, the agenda grew thin, and delegates began to wonder whether attendance warranted the delay in their return home. What action was taken was in any case at the discretion of management. Issues of substantial interest commonly involved negotiation, whether the process was recognized as such or not – an argument with the rate-fixer, or the shop stewards going into the superintendent's office. If the setting up of a Works Committee was regarded as a risky concession by managers – and by many it was – the slump of 1921–2 brought such a shift in the balance of power on the shop-floor that the concession could easily be withdrawn. But most Works Committees simply died of inanition.

None the less there continued to be advocacy of joint consultation. It was this term, and not the more hopeful terms co-operation and partnership, that describes the function of the Works Committees in the few firms that kept them going through the interwar-years. Yet the vitality of these Committees depended on a co-operative approach by management. The interest of their agenda depended on management's intent to use them as a means of briefing members with intelligence reports, giving advance notice of prospective developments, going through accounts, or taking soundings. The decisive factor was the acceptance of the implications of the need to gain the co-operation of the workers, the willingness of management to take them into its confidence, its readiness to change its own mind and generally to take action on the outcome of discussion. Not all the employers who kept Joint Consultative Committees going went as far as this, and some Committees subsisted on a plainer diet composed mainly of welfare questions, working conditions, and social activities. But even the more active Committees drew the line between consultation and negotiation, between matters of common interest and trade union matters. Issues that required negotiation but were not in practice covered by collective bargaining remained in a limbo.

5

The employers in engineering were exceptional in their capacity for combination and in their Federation's practice for formalizing relations. With the shift in the balance of power brought by the great depression of 1921–2 the Federation set about regaining the freedom of management on issues that concerned some of its members deeply. This might have been thought no time for the men to press claims, but the unemployment that weakened them in one way made them the more determined to make good their claim to limit overtime. Other issues continued to cause disputes – the manning of machines; the right of trade unions to negotiate on behalf of apprentices; payment by results; the union membership of foremen. From the employers' point of view the position was unsatisfactory in form as well as in substance, for since the unions had withdrawn in 1913 from the Terms of Settlement which they had accepted in 1898, they had not agreed to any alternative statement of the rights and functions of management and unions. It seemed that the time had come to obtain such a statement from them. In 1921 the Amalgamated Engineering Union (the name taken by the ASE on its absorbing some small unions in

1920) had 95,000 of its members unemployed, and paid out £2 m in benefit. The Employers' Federation took the occasion of continuing disputes to raise the general issue of managerial prerogatives, and obtain the agreement of the AEU executive to new Terms of Settlement. The first clause provided for non-interference with the exercise of managerial functions and the proper functions of the trade unions. Another clause regulated the question of the status quo, and required that 'instructions of the management shall be observed pending any question in connection therewith being discussed'. The union executive recommended acceptance to the members, warning them that the alternative was a lock-out, and the union had no resources for a fight: by a substantial majority the members voted for rejection. There follows the third great lock-out in the history of the industry – 1852, 1897, 1922: all on the prerogatives. In three months this one too broke the unions down.

The first of the terms on which work was resumed stated that 'The employers have the right to manage their establishments and the trade unions have the right to exercise their functions.' So brief a statement was possible only because the struggle for power had been decided: the employers felt no need of a detailed code to which they might appeal, or the work of any boundary commission. For the rest, the terms provided a compromise on the status quo question, by distinguishing between cases in which managers' disputed decisions should or should not be put into effect while the dispute went through the Procedure. On overtime it was said outright that 'the employers have the right to decide when overtime is necessary.' But the terms also embodied the existing agreement for the recognition of shop stewards, and provided for the appointment of Works Committees made up of not more than seven managers and seven shop stewards. The Works Committee was the first joint body before which a question might be brought in the course of the Procedure. A shop steward serving on the Works Committee might, with the consent of the management, visit any part of the establishment.

Relations at the place of work in engineering firms had therefore by no means reverted to what they had been before the War. This was true of industry generally. Trade unionism, certainly, was now subdued: membership fell in the slump of 1921–2, and again after the General Strike. Unemployment remained high. After the miners' struggle in 1926 there was no stoppage on any broad front for the rest of the inter-war years. But this was not the peace of powerlessness. The War had brought a fundamental change in the attitudes prevalent before 1914. These attitudes were so different from those of later years that an effort is needed to recapture them in the imagination. For this was a world where, for example, the bowler hat was the prerogative of the foreman, and a mere workman would be reproved for wearing one even on Sunday. The impact of the War was penetrating. The sharing of the effort and hardships that it brought, above all the loss of husbands and sons in all ranks of society, lessened the distance between classes: it was impossible for contempt, condescension, and arrogance on the one side, or deference, scorn, and bitter resentment on the other to persist at the levels of the pre-war years. For the servicemen in particular there had been lessons in leadership and understanding: officers returning from 'the democracy of the trenches' brought a new approach to management. Revulsion against the War and the ideals of patriotic unity coloured a phase of literary history and powerfully affected intellectuals whose works are read by the more intellectual of later generations; but this should not obscure the deep-going and pervasive effect of the War on attitudes and manners, and in particular its effect in heightening that 'respect for the manhood' of the working man which the Whitley Committee had called for. Before 1914 some employers had ready recourse to blacklegs in order to break strikes: they brought them in from a distance, even from abroad. There were various standing agencies for the supply of unskilled labour in this way. Even craftsmen who had been thrown out of work could sometimes be recruited to take the place of strikers in a distant part of the country. But after the War these practices disappeared. In the coal industry, it is true, 'volunteer' labour was called on in the strike of 1921 and the South Wales anthracite dispute of 1925, and South Wales again was troubled by the use of company union labour from 1927 onwards. But generally we do not hear of strike-breaking as before. This may have been because the labour force was more highly unionized; perhaps also in the changed social setting the use of blacklegs would have aroused too much disapproval.

Other events at the national level will have had their repercussion on attitudes too. During the War the trade unions had been recognized for the first time as an estate of the realm, and a place had been found for trade union leaders even in the restricted numbers of the War Cabinet. A Ministry of Labour had been set up, with a Lancashire cotton weaver as its first Permanent Secretary. After the War came the advance of the Labour Party itself through the broken ranks of the Liberals, and in 1924 the formation of the first Labour administration. The position of labour within the community had been transformed since 1914. In many unrecorded and unformalized ways this will have changed the tone of relations at the place of work, up and down the country.

There is negative evidence to indicate that the inter-war years were not a time when a head of discontent throughout industry was held down simply by men's inability to strike by reason of continuing unemployment. One such indication is the prevailing orderliness of those who were called out in the General Strike: if pent-up resentment and frustration had been widespread, would the conduct of those who now had this opportunity to demonstrate their feelings have been as careful and quiet as very generally it was? There was also the great popular vote for the National Government in the crisis of 1931. It is true that this was a vote for a coalition led by the former Labour Prime Minister, with some of his colleagues, but they were opposed root and branch by the TUC, and they had cut pensions and unemployment benefit: it is not possible to believe that the many manual workers who voted against Labour felt themselves wholly estranged from national authority by their experience at work.

But more than this: as activity rose in the mid-1930s, especially where rearmament impinged, the standing of the worker showed itself in the beginning of wage drift and an increasing number of unofficial strikes – groups of workers felt able to take action without depending on the backing of their union. Already in 1936 more than half the strikes in engineering were unofficial. The shop stewards in the aircraft section of engineering, from the various trade unions involved, formed their own national council. When war came, and from 1940 onwards brought full employment back, only in the mines did it seem to release a head of resentment pent up hitherto by the grip of unemployment. Elsewhere there came in 1941–2 a widespread creation of Joint Production Committees, and in 1943–4 a mounting number of unofficial strikes – most of them short strikes by groups of workers taking action locally on issues mainly of wages but also of working arrangements. There were many reasons why the Second World War did not bring such outbursts of industrial unrest as the First had done, but one of them was that the standing of the worker over against management at the place of work was now more assured, and management itself was less authoritarian and so less subject to revolt when the scarcity of labour brought an access of power to the worker.

6

But the War did strengthen existing tendencies. The Joint Production Committees might be used only for consultation in the narrow sense, that is, for the exchange of information and suggestions, mainly on technical problems. But some of them were used for effective negotiation of the old workshop issues of piece-rates, overtime, 'the machine question', and the like, and so as part of the disputes procedure; and it was even an open question whether the decisions that were put into effect after discussion in the Committee had been taken by management in the light of that discussion or were the act of the

Committee itself. Where the shop stewards already had the workshop issues in their hands they might let the Joint Production Committee confine itself to technical issues, and be composed simply of the technically competent; but elsewhere they seized the opportunity to open effective negotiations with management. Everywhere the wartime upheavals gave them much more to do and called for an increase in their numbers. They had to deal with all the problems arising daily in the shops through changes in methods and products, and the bringing in of green labour. Many experienced district officers of the trade unions were moved out into administrative posts; in any case there was far more work than district officers could cope with. Channels were clogged, sometimes delay was deliberate, and labour new to the procedures was impatient. Workers generally looked to their stewards to get a quick and positive answer, and were ready to support them by walking out. But management also for its own part often found the intermediacy of the shop stewards indispensable.

After the War, moreover, this time there was no slump. It is true that most of the Joint Production Committees ended with the output of munitions that they had been set up to assist, and though the Labour Government preached the common interest in raising productivity, the notion of the joint committee fell back into the ambiguity surrounding consultation. But there was no lapse of strength or numbers among the shop stewards, or in the pressures that could be exerted from the shop-floor under full employment. On the contrary, those pressures were stronger and more sustained than ever before.

One outcome was a progressive raising of unit labour costs, much of it by detailed bargaining at the place of work. For more than two years in 1948–50 the leaders of the trade unions co-operated loyally and effectively with the Labour Government to hold back pay claims at the national level: what broke down their stand in the end was the inequity created by the pushing up of the earnings of those whose jobs gave them the opportunity to get higher rates or bonus locally, while those on nationally fixed rates stayed put. When negotiations at the national level were resumed, earnings continued to rise faster than the negotiated rates, because they were being edged up by pressures exerted at the place of work. The widening margin between the formally negotiated and the actual cost of labour was called 'wage drift', a Swedish coinage. The raising of earnings at the place of work came to be seen as a source of inflation, distinct from the pull of excess demand, and termed accordingly 'cost push'.

Another outcome of the strength of groups at the place of work, their awareness of that strength and their readiness to use it, was the increase in the number of unofficial strikes. They were unofficial in that they were called without the prior authorization of the unions involved; some of them were also unconstitutional in that they took place before an agreed procedure had been exhausted. By the later 1950s their number, outside coal-mining, was rising; in 1960 it jumped abruptly; by 1964–6 it made up 95 per cent of all stoppages, and covered two-thirds of the total loss of man-days. These strikes gave employees a way of making their wishes and responses and resentments felt directly and forcibly, where often enough they had been muted before. But the effect of these interruptions to production, and not less the threat of them, was very damaging, especially in the shipbuilding and motor industries where they were endemic.

Cost push and unofficial strikes were alike manifestations of 'the shift of power to the shop-floor', which had moved the scene of greatest activity in industrial relations from the national level to the firm and from the union hierarchy to the group at the place of work. With this group the shop stewards rose in influence, prominence – and in number, for by the mid-60s there were reckoned to be 175,000 of them.

The developments thus summarized demand more detailed consideration, which we give them in the next two chapters. But first the question must be answered whether they were really new – for they might be seen as no more than a recurrence of the attitudes and behaviour that frequently prevailed whenever conditions favoured them in earlier years. Spontaneity of action on the shop-floor had welled up often enough before, and observers had recorded their sometimes alarmed awareness of readiness to strike among the unorganized, and repudiation of restraint among union members. That was how it had been with the New Unionism first signalized by the spontaneous strike of the matchgirls in 1888; and again in the summer of 1911, when the seamen and firemen of Southampton brought out the transport workers of the other ports, and the railwaymen of Liverpool started a national stoppage on the lines; and then in 'the prairie fire in the Midlands' in 1913; and once more in 1919, when strikes were begun by the rank and file, and the trade union leaders could only ratify what they were powerless to restrain. But these had been wavelike movements, which rose only to fall back. They came (we may suppose) when pent-up grievances and anxieties, and the tensions arising out of social change, could be released at a time of mounting business activity and high employment; and then, when activity fell off and unemployment returned, the initiative and indiscipline of the rank and file ebbed away too. It was not every cyclical rise that brought a surge of confidence and spontaneity on the shop-floor, but a high level of employment seemed a necessary condition for one; and when the working life of the labour force had been radically disturbed, or the predominant character and attitude of the workers had been shifting in the course of time, then the impact of the next spell of high employment would release the strain. That done, the episode seemed ended. But the changes since the Second World War were different. They were slower to take marked and widespread effect, and they were not generally linked with any programme of far-reaching change in the economic and social structure: the aims of action at the place of work were localized, and even so included little stress in practice on workers' control or self-government. Perhaps the comparative slowness to respond to the post-war situation owed something to the continued predominance of trade unionists who had learned caution in the inter-war years, and something more to loyalty to the Labour Government elected in 1945. That loyalty, and the sense of great changes long sought being made at last by Parliament, would also help to explain the absence of any political programme on the shop-floor. But the changes of recent years also differ from earlier phases of rank-and-file initiative and independence because they have proved persistent. It seems probable that the shift of power to the shop-floor during and since the Second World War is an irreversible change, because it arises not merely out of conditions of full employment which may not be sustainable, but out of the increased confidence of the worker, at a higher level of education and higher standard of living, equipped through modern media with greater information, and assured by practical experience of the power of combination. Recent developments thus appear to be differentiated by a change in the character of the labour force.

Notes

[1] Quoted here from Eric Wigham, *The Power to Manage* (London, 1973), p. 80.
[2] Ibid., p. 95.
[3] *The Times*, 7 Sept. 1897.
[4] Eric Wigham, *The Power to Manage*, p. 75.
[5] Quoted here from James Hinton, *The First Shop Stewards' Movement* (London, 1973), p. 33.
[6] Supplementary Report of the Committee of the Ministry of Reconstruction on the Relations of Employers and Employed on Works Committees, signed 18 Oct. 1917 (Cd. 9001, 1917–18).
[7] Ibid.

IX

COST PUSH

I

UNTIL the Second World War there had been little reason to depart from Marshall's finding of 1892, quoted above (chap. I), that 'the power of Unions to raise general wages by direct means . . . is never sufficient to contend successfully with the general economic forces of the age.' But under full employment the shift of power to the shop-floor was to make trade unionists themselves one of those forces.

The part they had played in the different environment of earlier years has been studied in detail for five countries – France, Germany, Sweden, the United Kingdom, the United States.[1] In all these countries the process by which a rise in money wages was accumulated down to 1914 was contained in the eight-year business cycle. This cycle was also a dominant factor in the much more various and violent movements of wages in the inter-war years.

Before 1914, the rises of wages were concentrated in the four years during which activity was rising or near its peak. In the falling phase and the trough of the cycle, what is called the ratchet effect appears: workers' resistance to cuts stopped wages falling back, at least by as much as they had recently been raised. During the years of mounting activity the rising demand for labour pulled wages up at particular points, and even unorganized workers found it fairly easy to make good their claims for a rise. But the amount of the general rise will also have depended on how far the extension of demand was met by the growth of the labour force, and this varied from time to time with the natural growth of population and with migration. There was also a third factor at work – the rise of productivity: when the product per man rose faster, the wage per man could rise faster too without any pressure on unit labour costs, and it was on these and not on the workers' money wage or his standard of living that international competition bore. Between the 1890s and 1914 money wages rose much more slowly in the UK than in Germany, Sweden and the USA, but because productivity also rose much more slowly in the UK than in those three countries, unit labour costs rose as fast in the UK as in them.

To judge how trade unions intervened in this process we must look at particular passages. In a number of instances a phase of exceptional trade union vigour was associated with a bigger rise or smaller fall in wages than we should have expected from the current course of business activity alone. In the UK, for instance, rises in wages even greater than were to be expected from the mounting business activity at the time were associated with the New Unionism of 1889, the release of the unions in 1906 from the constraint of the Taff Vale judgement, and the growth of union membership and militancy in 1911–12. In the USA the fall of wages was exceptionally small during the depression of 1884–5 when the Knights of Labour were in their heyday; and in France wages actually rose during the depression of 1909, when trade union membership had increased by more than half over the six preceding years, and the number of strikes had nearly doubled. There are instances also that suggest the effect of trade union weakness. In the UK there was the smallness of the wage rise during the increasing business activity of 1880–3, after what the Webbs called 'a general rout of the Trade Union forces' in 1879; and again the bigness of the wage cuts in 1901–2, when the cyclical recession was mild but the unions lay under the shadow of Taff Vale. In the USA the smallness of the wage rises of 1905–8 is conspicuous: union membership that had increased perhaps fourfold between 1898 and 1904 had suddenly ceased to grow, and the unions had come under organized attack by the employers, and were increasingly subjected to court injunctions. These instances all indicate a positive association between trade union strength and wage movements. But there are also negative indications. In two instances money wages rose exceptionally fast at a time of great weakness of the unions – in France, in 1874–9, when every sort of workers' organization lay crushed beneath a régime of surveillance and repression: and in Sweden, when after the defeat of the unions in the general strike of 1909 their membership fell by nearly a half, yet within three years the average earnings of men in industry rose by more than 12 per cent.[2]

In the troubled history of the inter-war years, though trade unionism initially extended more widely than ever before, there was no sustained rising trend of wages. If we except the inflations in Germany and France, the forces dominating the movement of wages appear as those of the cycle whose peaks come in 1920, 1929, and 1937, with the exceptionally deep declines that followed the first two peaks.

We may conclude that the strength of the unions was indeed a force tending to raise the general level of pay; but it was only one force among many that bore on pay, and most of the time the other forces were predominant. Occasions there were when the unions were able to add to a movement that was already going their way, or create a movement where the other forces left a zone of inertia; and sometimes their militancy reached a pitch that would not be denied advances in any but the most unfavourable conjunction of the other forces. Yet the rises they obtained, and the cuts they had to accept, generally depended on the market environment, that is, on the ease or difficulty employers expected to experience in obtaining prices that would yield adequate profit margins after the wage settlement. This in turn depended for any one employer on the force of actual and potential competition, and for employers generally on the expansiveness of sales and the course of prices in national or world markets. In the hard market environment wage rises were hard to come by, and it might be cuts that had to be staved off: but any gains would be made in real and not only in money terms, and would bring a redistribution away from profits. When the market environment was soft, unions could obtain rises more readily, but only because any consequent rise in unit labour costs could more readily be covered, with unchanged profit margins, by higher product prices – with a higher cost of living for the wage-earner.

2

The most thoroughgoing change in the market environment had been the 'cost plus' contracts of the munition makers in the First World War. It removed the employers' usual motive to resist the endeavour of workers to edge rates up, and even led them to compete for scarce labour by bidding rates up themselves. The general rise of money wages that went on during the war years was in great part negotiated by bodies newly formed for collective bargaining, but the object of public policy in setting those bodies up was to contain and moderate the impulses arising at the work-place. With the catastrophic breaking of the post-war boom, the possibility of that sort of independent local action to raise wages was sharply curtailed. While unemployment persisted through the inter-war years trade unionists continued to depend on the support of their union in wage negotiations, and the rates that were negotiated at the level of the industry or region were those that were actually paid locally.

But when rearmament began to set up certain shortages of skilled labour in the later 1930s, the possibility of edging rates up by local action returned, and then the Second World War brought back the indispensability of the individual worker as a dominant fact of the market generally, This time, moreover, there was no slump after the War. We have seen how for more than two years in 1948–50 the trade unions at the national level responded loyally to the appeal of the Labour Government to deny their members all advances in negotiated rates, but meanwhile the continuing uneven rise in earnings at the place of work created such inequalities that a near explosion of negotiations followed the abandonment of restraint by the TUC.

Through the 1950s pay continued to be raised year by year. There is agreement in describing the process by which this came about, but a basic opposition of views about whether the trade unions exerted an independent push, or only responded to the pull of demand.

The process settled into an 'annual round' of negotiations. At some stage in the round the impression would gain general acceptance that a certain rate of rise was 'the going rate' for that round. Since by definition this was the rate that most employers now expected they would have to settle for, any one of them would risk little by settling for it with his own employees when his competitors would be doing the same. Indeed, in so far as other firms who employed the same kinds of labour would be raising their pay by that prevailing amount, then even if he did himself succeed in settling for less he would only be storing up trouble for the future. 'League tables' were kept up, showing the relative standing of different industries, or different firms in a locality, according to the pay they gave to a representative grade of labour; and managers were concerned to keep their rank in the table. They must also have had it in the back of their minds that Governments were committed as never before to maintain high levels of employment, and had shown that they could do this in practice by using fiscal and monetary policy to maintain effective demand at higher levels of costs and prices. In this setting the claims presented by the unions did not need to be pressed hard.

The essentials of the new setting in the United States were seized on as early as 1952 by an experienced arbitrator, Clark Kerr. By that time, he wrote, employers had found

that concessions, particularly of wage increases, to the unions were not so burdensome as once thought. Even without industry-wide bargaining, wage increases spread quite uniformly throughout an industry: so that the first man to make a settlement is not for long, if at all, in an unfavorable position. Nor will government allow industry as a whole to be severely caught between the nether millstone of higher labour costs and the upper millstone of a fixed volume of effective demand or rigidly set price ceilings. Here is where the faith comes in; and this faith is that neither fiscal and monetary policies will be so restrictive nor price ceiling so inflexible that the added costs cannot largely be offset by higher prices with unreduced volume.[3]

A similar diagnosis was made in the United Kingdom in 1961 by the 'Three Wise Men' – the Council on Prices, Productivity and Incomes.

From one year to another [they wrote] pay and profits have very generally gone up together, and in much the same proportion. In the United Kingdom, for example, the total of wages and salaries paid out by companies was very nearly doubled in only nine years, from 1950 to 1959, but meanwhile these companies' gross profits (after allowing for stock appreciation) were likewise very nearly doubled. This constancy of proportion is the general rule: ... other western countries have experienced it too. It is highly significant for policy. Rises in pay have not been coming out of profits. When firms find that in practice they can maintain profits despite negotiating pay rises that increase their costs, and that they can maintain sales despite raising their selling prices, the restraints of the market are removed. [And again] The willingness of firms to raise rates of pay depends not on their own current or even prospective sales alone, but on their sense of the movement that is going on all around them. Many selling prices are not adjusted according to the pressure of buying orders on the available supplies day by day, but are fixed by administrative decisions, and when costs rise all round such prices readily follow a leader, or move up together although there has been no agreement that they should.[4]

The picture was of a setting in which the trade unions' claims could be met fairly readily provided that they were concerted, as in practice they came to be, informally and roughly, in the annual round. The implied diagnosis of the inflation was that it originated in the pushing up of labour costs by the trade unions. This diagnosis was implicitly accepted by Governments who in their struggle against inflation turned to Incomes Policy: when they appealed for wage restraint, laid down guidelines for permissible rises, or set up boards to examine claims, they were taking it for granted that at least within limits the rate at which pay rose was at the discretion of trade unionists.

3

But this diagnosis was challenged and is challenged still by those who hold that the trade unions have been only the vehicle and not the engine of inflation. To these observers, rates of pay appear to have been settled since the Second World War by the same market forces as settled them before it: the difference is only that the state of the labour market throughout the years of full employment after the War was what was reached before the War only rarely and briefly at the top of the boom. This was a state of the market in which a sufficient condition for a big rise in pay was provided by excess demand for labour. Though the form of proceedings in the post-war years was that trade unions entered claims and pressed them through to settlements, they were able to get what they did only because of the state of demand. Two riders may be added to this thesis. One is that if employees had not been unionized they would have obtained much the same rises: this could be supported by pointing to some unorganized workers who did in fact obtain rises equal to or even greater than those received by trade unionists. The other rider is that if Governments applied fiscal and monetary restraints, what had seemed to be the great bargaining power of the trade unions would have disappeared: at lower levels of demand, and consequently higher levels of unemployment, the trade unions though free to proceed as before would have been found to settle for less.

The basis for this view lay in the finding that British wage-rates down to 1939 appeared to have changed according to the current level of unemployment: when this was low, they rose substantially, and when it was high, they did not rise at all, or even fell a little. This relationship was set out in a paper by A. W. Phillips that appeared in 1958 and soon became widely influential.[5] What he did essentially was to divide the historical record into the periods of successive trade cycles, and show that wage-rates rose most in the more active phases of each cycle, and rose less, if at all, in the phases of lower activity – the later recession, the trough, and the early stage of recovery. But as his indicator of the cyclical movement he used the rate of unemployment, and he accepted this as showing the balance of supply and demand in the labour market, which he took to act on the wage level in the same way as the balance of buying and selling orders acts on the price in a produce market. When, moreover, he condensed the experience of a number of cycles into a single graph, in which the recorded changes in wage-rates were entered over against the levels of unemployment prevailing when those changes occurred, a curve appeared that indicated a systematic inverse relationship between unemployment and wage-rates, each rise of 1 per cent in unemployment being associated with a given reduction in the rate at which wage-rates rose. This was the celebrated Phillips curve.

It was seized on by economists who, perplexed by the persistent and seemingly self-propelled rise in wages, increasingly felt the need for an explanation of this movement that would be consistent with the general assumptions of economic theory. They were not historians, content to accept each year's wage level as emerging, like other economic developments of the year, as the outcome of a vast number of factors making for or resisting change. Nor had they been moving close to the daily affairs of labour and management. The minds they brought to the study of inflation had been trained to arrange their observations within a framework of equilibrating forces. A study of the general level of wage-rates that, on a survey of the data, ascribed its movements to the impersonal forces of supply and demand in the labour market, carried conviction with them instantly.

But the implication, that the inflationary rise of labour costs could be checked by restraining demand and increasing unemployment, by no means carried conviction with those who were following the course of negotiations in detail. The difficulty was not only that the underlying analysis failed to correspond with what these observers saw going on under their eyes – such as the way in which claims came to be formulated, the considerations that activated employers, and the influence of a key bargain on the level of settlements throughout an annual round. There was also the unmistakable ability of trade unionists to obtain rises in particular cases where the 'commercial considerations' that used to set limits to settlements would have prohibited any rise whatever. In the United States, 'in such industries as railroads and shipping, unions have bargained for and won high wages and costly manning requirements not only from unprofitable firms, but even from bankrupt ones.'[6] There was the further and fatal difficulty of accounting for the generality of the outcome. If the rise of pay was due to the pull of excess demand, why did pay rise just as much in the contracting as in the expanding industries? If the rate at which pay rose must be expected to vary with the margin of unemployment in the labour force concerned, why did pay rise just as much – or more – in the regions of the United Kingdom where considerable unemployment remained, as in those where it was slight? If rises in pay depended upon the employer's ability to pay without raising his prices, they would be limited by the advance of productivity, and there is indeed evidence from many countries that earnings have risen all along the line as fast as productivity has risen in those industries where it has grown the most rapidly. But it is the level of earnings in all industries of which that holds – all industries, including those in which productivity has risen slowly or not at all: in the countries examined there has been a far greater divergence of productivity than of earnings between industries.[7]

We can go on to call in question the significance attached by the believers in demand pull to the observed association in earlier years between the level of unemployment and the change in wages. Do we know that this association is anything but contingent? Or that the level of unemployment serves as anything more than one indicator among others of the phases of the business cycle, in the course of which wages changed systematically because of changes in the outlook of all concerned? The presence of a greater number of unemployed men could inhibit the rise of wages directly only if there were a possibility of the employer substituting some of the unemployed at a lower wage for existing employees, or using the threat of this to make those employees accept lower wages; but only in certain cases, mainly of unskilled labourers in the years before 1914, did that possibility exist. What was entirely possible, however, and did happen, was that wage rises were inhibited when unemployment was high because business was depressed; this depression was the cause both of the unemployment, and of men feeling that their jobs were at risk, and employers seeing no prospect of profit out of which to pay higher wages. But here we are brought back to attitudes and expectations, on both sides of the table.

On all these grounds we must reject the proposition implicit in the Phillips curve, that pay movements depend solely on the balance of supply and demand in the labour market, so that trade unions exert no independent push on them. We have seen this push being exerted through 'the annual round' in the 1950s. In the 1960s it was increasingly exerted through the strike.

4

A number of changes in industry had made strikes more formidable. Increased integration had gone with specialization, so that the supply of a particular component for a whole industry was concentrated in a few sources or even a single plant. Within any one firm the continuity of operation might depend from hour to hour upon the activity of certain small groups. With the aid of the computer, the holdings of stocks at intermediate stages of production were reduced, so that any interruption of the flow must soon bring work to a halt. A counterpart was the firm which avoided carrying idle money balances, and found itself in trouble with its cash flow as soon as its output was interrupted. More generally, a firm's ability to take a strike may be thought of as its ability to finance a form of investment – an investment, namely, in labour costs lower than would be given by a settlement without a strike: firms in a financially weak position have no funds for this, and may for that reason be singled out for attack by trade unions in preference to more prosperous firms. In international competition, the proven ability to keep delivery dates is a major consideration, and the threat of delaying completion of orders gives corresponding leverage in the short term to the labour force concerned – though at the price, it may well be, of pulling the house down on itself in the longer run.

But not all these circumstances are of recent origin. The tactical strength of those who command a bottleneck of production is not new – we have seen how Adam Smith observed it in the wool-combers of the eighteenth century. We have also seen how some trade unionists had acquired before 1914 the power to bring the industry of the whole country to a halt. What stood out in these latter years was the readiness of the employee to use the power of the strike new or old. This readiness may be ascribed in part to the greater availability of funds for the maintenance of the striker's household – from its own accumulated resources, at certain times from repayments of income tax, and from social security allowances. But in the growing number of short strikes these considerations hardly applied: more important was the expectation, increasingly reinforced by experience, that the strikers would not be putting their own jobs at risk, need fear no subsequent victimization, and were likely to get fairly quickly most of what they were demanding. The counterpart was the view of the employers, that resistance was costly and – again experience showed – only deferred what must be conceded in the end.

The movement was the more powerful and general because for most participants it was not aggressive in origin or feeling. Particular groups there were that were actively concerned to use every opportunity to push their own earnings up. But for most employees the pressing of claims continued to appear as a defensive action – the defence of a standard of living against the rise in prices, or of a status against the lowering of a relativity. Claims of this last kind, based on comparability, were specially hard to resist, because to deny them was to inflict a felt injustice. Trade unionists and employers were thus swept along together by the same current.

The monetary authorities were involved too, for the rise in pay and prices could not have been kept up without increasing unemployment unless the flow of spending was allowed to rise proportionally, and this generally called for an increase in the stock of money, which was in fact provided.

The process was thus one in which no priorities could be picked out in the statistical record. Trade unionists entering pay claims were largely moved by fear of being left behind, or trying to overtake rises in the cost of living that had already come about, many of them as the consequence of previous pay rises. Over the years the figures of the stock of money and of pay and prices went up together. In the late 1960s some economists could therefore still deny that trade unionists had been exerting any independent force to push up pay.

5

But now came two developments to make it appear more probable that they did this. One of these may be called the Hinge. A number of Western countries reveal in common an upturn in the rate of rise of wages about 1969, and the most probable explanation is a widespread change in attitudes among the rank and file. The second development has been called 'stagflation', the combination particularly since 1973 of stagnant production and high unemployment with inflation even faster than before. Let us consider them in turn.

Figure 1 shows the rise of hourly wage rates or earnings, mainly in

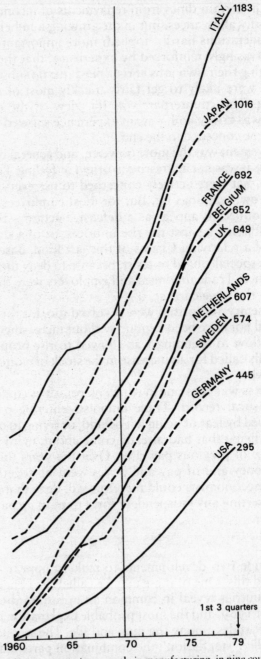

FIG. 1. Rise of hourly rates or earnings, mostly in manufacturing, in nine countries of OECD, 1960–79, showing change in rate of rise about 1969–70. (Ratio scale: number at end of each curve gives hourly rates or earnings in 1979 (average of first 3 quarters) as relative to 1960 = 100.)

manufacturing, in nine OECD countries: the ratio scale enables us to compare by eye the rate of rise in different periods. The vertical line has been drawn between 1969 and 1970. At a glance it appears that a number of the curves rise more steeply on the right of this line than on the left. In fact there are three exceptions. In the United States the rise of wages was gently accelerating throughout most of the period covered, and there is no break in the trend about 1969. In Germany the rate of rise was remarkably steady save for lower rises in 1967 and 1968. In Japan there was a marked change from a lower to a higher rate of rise, but it came earlier, in 1966, and the higher rate was held unchanged until 1973. But in the other countries as we go up the figure we find what is unmistakable first in Sweden, a hinge in the trend about 1969–70: the same upturn appears in the Netherlands, the United Kingdom, Belgium, France, and Italy. In the Netherlands the hinge may come a year later, in 1970–1; in France the new trend clearly begins in 1968. The appearance of a similar movement at much the same time in all these countries challenges explanation.

One explanation takes us back to demand. The general upsurge came, it is said, through an increase in the world's supply of money, provided by the overspill of the American inflation in the last years of President Johnson's administration. In that case we should look for signs of monetary ease, such as lower interest rates, and of excess demand, such as lower unemployment, in these countries that show the Hinge. But generally we do not find these signs. Interest rates in Europe had been eased in 1967 but were rising in 1968–9. The United States appeared as a borrower rather than a provider of dollars: it was not until 1970 that its balance of payments with European countries made substantial sums of dollars available to them. If the money supply is measured by the public's holdings of cash and current accounts, its growth was somewhat greater in the four years ending with 1968 than in the four preceding years in some of the countries concerned, but in as many others it was somewhat smaller. Unemployment did not change much in the approach to the Hinge, except in the United Kingdom, and there it doubled. It was in France that the Hinge appeared first and most dramatically, with the settlement after the general strike in the summer of 1968. Here in March of that year '84 per cent of enterprises reported that given more orders, they could produce more with existing capacities and employment levels. . . . The total number of hours worked by wage-earners declined by 1.8 per cent in the twelve months to April 1968, with an even sharper fall in manufacturing.'[8] There is nothing here to explain why within a matter of months more than two-thirds of the 15 million wage and salary earners in France would strike for three weeks or more, and the wage level would be lifted by 12 to 14 per cent. In sum, in none of the countries we have named do we find evidence of easy money and shortages of labour, such that when trade unions raised the level of their claims and settlements they can be seen to be doing no more than respond to the pull of excess demand.

We must therefore discard the explanation of the Hinge by monetary overspill. But any other explanation we adopt will equally have to rest on factors that could have taken effect at about the same time in many different countries.

It is hard to find any such objective and measurable factor. One possibility that has been put forward is that in the three years immediately before the Hinge they all experienced a slowing down of the rise in real incomes, and pay claims were pitched higher to restore the expected rate of betterment. The slowing down may have come about through a check to economic growth, but also, as happened in the United Kingdom from the mid-60s onwards, through direct taxation penetrating deeper into wages as the general level of money wages rose, and through a greater proportion of social benefits being financed by wage-earners' contributions, so that take-home pay did not rise as much as earnings. The tendency to extend social benefits by taxation was common to most OECD countries, but we are not able to compare the effects on take-home pay. If we look only at the course of real wages, as that appears on comparison of the movements of money wages and the cost of living, we find a varied outcome. In the approach to the Hinge, in 1965–8, there was a check to the rise of real wages in Western Germany (where there was an outbreak of unofficial strikes in 1969, but no Hinge), the Netherlands, and Italy. The instance of Italy seems significant: in 1962–5 the rise had been 22 per cent, but in the next three years, 1965–8, it was only half as great, at 10.5 per cent, and it is tempting to see this as building up the resentment that broke out in the 'hot autumn' of 1969. But on the other hand in Belgium, France, Sweden, and the UK there was no check to the rate of rise of real wages as measured here. In any case, even if the employees of all the countries concerned had experienced some slowing down of the rise of standards during the 1960s, we still have to explain why their reaction should have come when it did and at much the same time in different countries; and why it took the unofficial form.

An explanation that would do this has been put forward by Soskice.[9] What has been called 'the honeymoon of the Common Market' was brought to an end in 1963–6 as internally rising costs in tight labour markets came up against price ceilings imposed on international markets by the restrained level of activity in the United States, where unemployment had been high in 1960, and was being reduced only slowly. The European economies experienced difficulties in their balances of payments, and through reduced profit margins in business.

Their Governments imposed fiscal and monetary restraints and adopted incomes policies. Employers went on the counter-offensive against the advances lately made by labour in the workshop: their aim was to rationalize working practices and gain control of wage structures. The rise of real wages was checked. These measures raised the resentment of employees everywhere. When the American influence changed and the market environment became permissive that resentment exploded. After the tax remission of 1964 and the commitments to Vietnam and President Johnson's Great Society, international markets were upheld by American spending, and European profit margins widened. All that was needed then was a starter's signal, and this was provided by the near-revolution in France in May–June 1968. But the action that the workers needed could not be taken by official unionism, which was involved with governmental policies of restraint: the workers had to take it themselves.

There is much in this explanation that is instructive as an account of the economic setting, but to show why the initiative passed to the shop-floor at about the same time in so many countries it must show that the antecedent conditions on which it relies as causes were also common to all those countries in type and timing. That in all of them Governments had been applying some anti-inflationary restraint in 1965–8 may perhaps pass, though forms, timing and effects varied. It is less easy to accept that in all of them employers had been pressing a counter-offensive in the shops, so rigorously and widely as to provoke a widespread outbreak of strikes. These strikes were mostly settled, moreover, in money, not in agreements on working practices. Nor in the United Kingdom, at least, were the unions at the national level committed to government policies of restraint at the time of the outbreak: by the end of 1969 the Labour Government had virtually given up the attempt to enforce incomes policy, the Conservative Government that took office in 1970 had begun by repudiating it.

Thus though it is natural to look for economic causes as general as the wave of strikes that rose and rolled across the Western economies from 1968 onwards, we have not found any, either directly in the supply of money, or through the reactions of managers and workers to the changing phases of growth and the international market.

An alternative explanation would interpret the rising of the wave as basically the outcome of a contagious shift in the predominant attitude of wage-earners, and show how that would account for the wave rising when it did at about the same time in a number of countries. This explanation begins with the clear sense of many contemporary European observers that the strikes of 1968–70 confronted them with something quite new. It differed from earlier movements in that the initiative came from the rank and file. In France, where the function of union headquarters had been to stimulate the branches, and bring the members out for short demonstration strikes, this time the movement – after the student revolt – was spontaneous: the thrust came from 'la base'. In Italy new organizations were formed at the place of work – the Comitate Unitari di Base – and an outbreak of unofficial action in the big firms in 1968 was followed when the union organizations had regained control, by the 'hot autumn' of major engagements and big settlements the next year. There were few unofficial strikes in Sweden before that same autumn, but then came a wave of them. Even in Germany there was an outbreak of unofficial action in the iron and steel industry at this time. The trade union leadership no less than the employers were generally taken by surprise. They were conscious of a new militancy among their members, and a disregard of established procedure.

That there was in fact a change of attitude in the rank and file, an access of impatience and initiative at the place of work, we can accept as widely attested. But why should it have come about at this time, and in a number of countries at much the same time? There is one hypothesis which cannot be tested directly but fits the setting and may be entertained when explanations that rest upon more objective factors do not do so. It is that this was the time when the attitudes formed in younger employees by the experience of recent years attained a critical mass within the whole body of employees; and that these attitudes were sparked into action by the example of student revolt, beginning with the struggle in Paris in May 1968. In the first years of high employment and rising standards of living after the Second World War, the attitudes of the majority of employees would have remained as they had been formed in earlier and harder times: these employees would not have expected large advances, they would have rated security above militancy, and they would have been chary of acting without the support of their union. But the young people who are entering employment for the first time alongside them would be forming attitudes in settings of much greater security, and of alluring prospects within their reach: their experience would have taught them to expect more, and believe themselves capable of going for it and getting it. As their relative numbers grew, there came a time when, despite the hold that age and experience retain on leadership, the new attitudes must predominate. This time might well be reached at about the same number of years after the end of the War in each of several countries. A conspicuous example of spontaneous and independent action of the rank and file, such as the French students' revolt and the general strike that followed, portrayed by television, would serve as the precipitant. To many observers these events seemed the first flames from which a prairie fire of largely unofficial strikes swept across neighbouring countries in the following two years.

This explanation of the Hinge may point to some antecedents. In 1848 a wave of democratic excitement and revolutionary enthusiasm ran through much of Western Europe, at a time when the network of intelligence made far less than it does today for contagion of mood and chain reactions. The New Unionism of 1889–90 in the UK is an instance of a change in attitudes permeating trade unionists new and old, and recognized by experienced employers as having permanently changed the mood and mien of industrial relations: yet no reason can be advanced for its incidence in those particular years, save that they were years of cyclical improvement, coming after some twenty years of rising real wages, which were also the first twenty years of universal free elementary education. There is nothing inherently improbable in the hypothesis that the attitudes of employees throughout much of Western Europe underwent a substantial and lasting change at the end of the 1960s in respect of the size of pay rises they expected to get and of their reliance on their own initiative and bargaining power to get them.

The Hinge, then, on this view of it, is a mark of increased push by trade unionists as a source of inflation. But there is this to be added, that this drive was soon operating in a setting that had shed the checks on the upsurge of costs and prices in any one country that had held so long as the Bretton Woods system of exchange rates was maintained. Sterling had been devalued in 1967, and it began its 'managed float' in 1972. The US dollar was effectively devalued in 1971. Large capital movements responded to differences in interest rates. Governments found means of staving off international adjustments. An increased pushfulness was operating in a less resistant medium. We cannot therefore take the higher rate of rise as the measure of the greater pushfulness in itself.

6

None the less it is remarkable that this higher rate of rise did persist when at the same time unemployment was rising. This was stagflation – the second development that we named as indicative of the independent force exerted by trade unionists to push up pay.

For a number of reasons, the Western economies moved during the later 1960s into a new phase of their economic history. In the UK the doubling of unemployment between 1966 and 1968 seemed only to follow the cyclical pattern, and the level of 1968 was only half a million: but instead of falling from a cyclical peak the level was sustained, with only a minor betterment meanwhile, until a renewed rise went on from the end of 1969 through the next two years. Likewise unemployment rose in most of the European countries that we have been looking at, but somewhat later, in 1970 or 1971. Then in

1973 came the raising of oil prices by OPEC, and a shock to the world economy that brought a check to activity in every country. Very generally, unemployment began to be experienced such as had not been known since the War, and had not been thought possible, let alone tolerable. The recession, moreover, proved to be very different from the mild fluctuations of previous post-war years: it went deeper and it persisted. The conditions of the moment and the outlook were very different from those in which the rise in pay had gone on through the prosperous quarter century of high employment and economic growth. Yet pay went on rising: indeed it rose faster than ever. In the UK economists who still relied on the schemata of supply and demand in the labour market had to explain how the level of unemployment and the level of pay settlements could double side by side; and how it could come about in 1974–5 that with one and a half million unemployed the general level of wage earnings could be raised by 25 per cent within twelve months. As time went on the exertions of governments and the resistance of employers in a number of countries reduced the level of settlements, but these were still for substantial rises of pay in money at a time when there was no increase in real resources to be distributed. Their effect could be only to raise costs and prices. They could only prolong stagflation in both its aspects. But it was within the power of trade unionists to demand them, and it seemed not to be within the power of employers and governments to deny them.

The Hinge had marked a shift in the expectations of employees generally and their readiness to take independent action to realize them. Stagflation now showed that this readiness was not inhibited by unemployment: levels of unemployment without precedent since the War seemed to exert no restraining influence upon current claims and settlements.

7

A conquest had been snatched away. For nearly a quarter of a century after the War full employment had been maintained as never before for so many years together since industrialism took its rise; and when that spontaneous demand at last had flagged, the case seemed clear for a Keynesian policy to take its place. But stagflation could not be removed by that policy: the increased flow of spending, instead of calling forth a bigger real output at an unchanged level of unit costs and prices, would soon be absorbed by rising pay; the unbalanced budget that gave the private sector more to spend would only have given a quicker turn to the inflationary spiral. The evident remedy for this, and the necessary complement of any attempt to raise real demand by giving people more money to spend, was an incomes policy that would check the rise of unit labour costs. But incomes policy had at this time fallen into discredit as an instrument of control, except for a short time in an emergency.

This was the outcome of an experience that ran back to the years immediately after the War. It is instructive to examine some of its findings, for the light they throw on the role of trade unions and their members in cost push.

Once inflation is under way, any order or agreement to hold back from pay rises has to overcome powerful influences that operate on particular persons and groups. These influences are chiefly three. First, each of us would generally like to be better off, and many of us very much need to be so. Though we may understand and accept the proposition that a general rise in pay in excess of productivity will only raise prices and in the end put no more in anyone's shopping basket, we still can't help seeing that a rise in our own pay will not be matched by a rise in prices the next day or the next month. But there is no doubt about the rise in the cost of living since the last settlement: this has vitiated it, and brought an absolute cut in the standard of living that must be made good. Since the War there has also grown up the expectation of an annual improvement. Second, any one group may have wrongs to right. Since it last settled other groups may have made their own settlements, or edged their rates up in particular deals at the place of work, so as to upset established relativities or differentials. A strong sense of injustice now demands the raising of pay that will restore traditional relations. Third, any group asked to hold back may doubt whether, if it does so, the others will not steal a march on it.

One can envisage arrangements, drawn from Dutch and Scandinavian practice, that would contain these impulses. A national forum would arrive at agreement on the prospective increase in aggregate output, and a norm for the rise in pay – the percentage by which pay could be raised overall without raising costs and prices – would be adopted in consequence. A consortium of employers' associations and trade unions at the national level would then consider any variations from the norm to meet the special circumstances of particular sectors or industries. The settlements subsequently made would also embody retrospective adjustments to remove anomalies, such as those between time workers and piece-rate workers, that had arisen since the last settlement. Arrangements of this kind have continued to prove their usefulness in reducing cost push. They counter the first and the third of the impulses, because they are comprehensive, and are carried down to each locality: each group has the assurance that in refraining from snatching its own immediate advantage it will not be letting others get ahead of it, or losing purchasing power over the year. These arrangements also reduce the second impulse, because they do not require an indefinite halt in a disordered situation, but provide for equitable adjustments.

But implicit here are conditions on the side both of trade unions and of management very different from those obtaining in the UK. The trade unions must be capable of holding together at the national level, and this the British unions did more than once, very loyally, in support of a Labour Government – in 1948–50, and again from 1964 onwards. But much more than this, each of them must be able to make good among its own members the commitments into which it has entered: it must be able to ensure both that they accept and abide by what is now the official policy in negotiations, and that they do not evade and ultimately overturn it by edging rates up in informal dealings. This is a requirement that British trade unions have been unable to meet. The shift of power to the shop-floor has been part of a dispersive revolution by which at the same time the trade union member has achieved a greater sense of independence within his union: he has felt less need of its support, and so long as he has been acting as a militant he has been less amenable to the control of its district or national officers. Resistance to cost push at the place of work would therefore have to come from management. It has been a further implicit condition of the effectivenes of the arrangements we posited, that the employers were solidly organized, and resistant to local claims that conflicted with national principle. But this the British employers were not. We have already discussed the looseness of their associations. That they offered so little resistance to local claims requires examination as part of the explanation of cost push and the failure of incomes policy. The initial setting was one coming down from the War, in which shortages of labour over against sustained demand made rises in labour costs much less worrying at any one time than interruptions of output. Salaried managers, unlike proprietors, had no self-interest in keeping down what went to other employees: their interest was in the absence of conflict and an easy settlement, unless this would threaten the performance of the business, and the experience of some years suggested little risk of that so far. Technique was becoming more capital-intensive, so that a rise in pay bore a smaller ratio to the oncosts that continued during a strike. Local claims were negotiated, subject to local stoppages, by managers who themselves were often under the orders of higher management at a distance, and this higher management might see the immediate disruptive effects of a stoppage more clearly than the knock-on effects on the wage-structure of the concessions needed to get a particular group back to work. (Equally at the national level, when the employers in engineering had prepared to take a strike rather than concede the rise demanded in 1957, the Government in that particular conjuncture had pleaded with them to avoid a stoppage at all costs.) When the rising demand that covered the pay rises of earlier years was followed by stringency there could be a perverse effect: we have seen that firms that are financially weak and in trouble with their cash flow are liable to be picked on by unions and forced into quick settlements. The notion of the 'going rate', though it did not dictate the exact amount of each settlement, meant that there was a general movement which no firm could stay out of: even if at the cost of a struggle it held its own rates down now, it would only have to catch up later on, but by the same token if it did settle within the generally acceptable range it would not find itself at any competitive disadvantage.

Remedies were provided in incomes policy for the conditions we have been describing as leaving a gap in the firm – the lack of internal control in the trade union, the absence of employers' associations capable of administering the policy, the weakness of the resistance by management to cost push. These remedies were the setting up of a Board to which particular pay settlements could be referred for invest-igation; and price control, which also could take the form of requiring application to a Board for permission to raise prices. In both fields the hope was that the publicity given to some leading cases would ensure voluntary compliance over the great range of actual cases with which no administrative machinery could cope. In the UK the experience of the National Board for Prices and Incomes showed the that machinery could be used flexibly and pragmatically. The question of what res-training influence it exerted, in percentage points, can be answered only if we know how to project the course of pay and prices in its absence, and that is beyond the power of econometrics to do, for in the absence of the Board men's expectations would have been different. But it seems doubtful whether such a Board would be effective as a permanent institution. Resentment at its claims on the resources of those it investigated – to what purpose? – would increase. The sanc-tion it wielded – of being brought before it, of being investigated and reported on – would lose its weight as time went on, reports accumu-lated, and it all ended in words.

Nor is there a way out by providing the sanctions of a statutory policy. In the short run this can hold, as a freeze. The need for this is grasped and accepted in an emergency, and there is a superficial fairness in that everyone is treated alike, even though the standstill does not catch everyone on the same footing. But the attempt to contain cost push by legal penalties encounters this basic disability, that the arm of the law can far more readily hold men back from a forbidden action than make them perform work that is enjoined. If the law forbids men to strike for a rise, it is requiring them to get up and go to work, and do a good day's work, at their present wage: and this it cannot make them do. Penalties can be applied to trade unions that call or recognize strikes against a statutory incomes policy: their funds can be sequestered, their officers can be imprisoned. But if the members are not acting merely at the behest of the leadership of their union – and in recent years it has often been the other way round – and they choose to stay out, then their return to work has to be negotiated, and cannot be enforced by an order of the court.

A more effective prospect of closing the gap open to cost push at the place of work has been provided by the development of the works agreement. Since the Donovan Commission in 1968 drew attention to the extent of informal negotiation at the place of work, and urged that the agreements reached at this level should be drawn up systematically, there has in fact been a substantial development of this kind. It has been associated with the rise of job evaluation and the formalisation of wage structures. Within engineering at least it has brought a marked reduction in wage drift. As the structure of pay is brought under control, and changes in it are no longer made piecemeal but are negotiated for the structure as a whole, the responsibility of management for the rise of unit labour costs is engaged as it was not when wage drift could go on day by day. The possibility of cost push remains, but only to the extent that the market environment is soft, or that a union takes short-sighted advantage of a firm's inability to finance a stoppage.

If the gap at the place of work were closed, incomes policy would still encounter cost push in the determination of this or that trade union to break through a line that had been drawn at the national level. This determination might be no play for power by the leaders, but a move forced upon them by the membership. They may not dispute the need for restraint in general, but see the case for raising their own relative standing as overwhelming. So it was with the British miners in 1972. If there is then no meeting of minds between them and the Government which stands behind the incomes policy, the outcome depends on the disruption that the union can inflict by striking. Where that is great, the Government can contain cost push only if it can maintain a good understanding, and this not with the leadership alone, but with the main body of the membership – an understanding which leads the members to refrain voluntarily from using the power that is in their hands.

The upshot then, of experience of the attempt to contain cost push by incomes policy, is twofold. There has to be a structure of negotiations and agreements that will bring the pay structure at the place of work under the control of management and employees there. The ultimate safeguard against the assertion of cost push by groups who have it in their power to assert it is their understanding and free acceptance of the reasons for their not doing so.

This is in keeping with the development of cost push itself. The pressure that trade unionists can exert should no longer be given so narrowly economic an appellation as monopoly power, which implies a cool calculation of the cost of alternatives. The actual power that trade unionists now exercise over pay depends rather on the attitudes and expectations that have come to be held by them, by managers and by governments. It is the change in these, and not in the objective power of the strike, that has made the era since the War so different from the years before.

Notes

[1] E. H. Phelps Brown and M. H. Browne, *A Century of Pay* (London, 1968).

[2] The substance of this paragraph is reproduced from the author's evidence to the Royal Commission on Trade Unions and Employers' Associations, 1968: Minutes of Evidence, 38, paras 14, 15, pp. 1608–09. This evidence is reprinted in Henry Phelps Brown and Sheila V. Hopkins, *A Perspective of Wages and Prices* (London, 1981).

[3] 'Governmental Wage Restraints: their Limits and Uses in a Mobilized Economy', *American Economic Review, Papers and Proceedings*, 42, 2, May 1952.

[4] Council on Prices, Productivity and Incomes, Fourth Report, July 1961, paras. 34, 54.

[5] A. W. Phillips, 'The relation between Unemployment and the Rate of Change of Money Wage Rates in the United Kingdom, 1861–1957', *Economica*, 25, 100, Nov. 1958, 283–99.

[6] Albert Rees, 'New Policies to Fight Inflation: Sources of Skepticism', in *Brookings Papers on Economic Activity*, 2, 1978, 457–8.

[7] J. Eatwell, J. Llewellyn, and R. Tarling, 'Money Wage Inflation in Industrial Countries', *Review of Economic Studies*, 41, 1974, 515–23; T. Scitovsky, 'Market Power and Inflation', *Economica*, 45, Aug. 1978, 226.

[8] OECD, *Economic Outlook*, (OECD, July 1968), p. 53.

[9] David Soskice, 'Strike Waves and Wage Explosions, 1968–1970: an Economic Interpretation', in C. Crouch and A. Pizzorno (eds.), *The Resurgence of Class Conflict in Western Europe since 1968*, vol. 2 (London, 1978).

X

THE UNOFFICIAL STRIKE

I

THERE was extraordinarily little overt conflict in British industrial relations between the end of the miners' struggle in 1926 and the early 1950s. The system which had been established through the First World War and immediately after it proved able to take the downward thrust of the world economic depression from 1930 to 1932, and raise wages again as recovery went on, without convulsive movements or crippling stoppages. In the Second World War, even more remarkable, though strikes did multiply at one time, the system showed itself able to keep order and avoid inflation in times of more than full employment and vast changes in the deployment of labour, and to do this with little support in practice from emergency regulations. The achievement justified the trust placed in the basic principles of the system by the great trade union leader under whom it had been realized. At the end of the War many observers, and not least the experienced administrators in the Ministry of Labour, believed that here as in their unwritten constitution the British people had been able to work out a flexible and pragmatic way of managing their affairs that was an example to the world. The impression of self-control was deepened in that period of more than two years in 1948–50 when the national leaders of the trade unions maintained a complete standstill in pay negotiations at the behest of the Labour Government.

But in the 1950s the record changes rapidly. Complacency gave way to misgivings, and an urgent sense that the system must be reformed or supplemented. There was no major stoppage of a whole industry before 1957; the trouble was the increasing prevalence of the unofficial strike. We have seen how this had appeared in the course of rearmament before the War. It was necessarily the form that strikes took during the War itself. In the standstill of 1948–50 it was used to push up earnings here and there at the place of work, until the disparities between earnings raised locally and the rates of pay kept down by national agreements finally broke up the standstill. In the years of nominally unrestrained bargaining under Churchill's administration from 1951 onwards the unofficial strike extended so as to make a powerful impact on management, government, and the economy.

This was not because there was as yet any great outburst of stoppages, to judge by the tally of man-days lost. The trouble was rather that the unofficial strike exploited a gap in the established system, and that it was especially damaging to management and the economy.

It exploited a gap in the system because it was an action taken by groups for whom as such the system provided no procedure, or because they were able to disregard with impunity such procedure as it did provide. The system regarded negotiations as being conducted and agreements as being reached essentially between the officers of trade unions and associations of employers. The trade union officials would then see to it that these agreements were observed at the place of work; they would enforce them against any employer who fell short, but equally an employer whose workers claimed more than the agreement gave them, or came out on an issue that the agreement did not cover and so left to his discretion, could call on their local union officer to get them back to work. The industry-wide agreement might also prescribe a procedure accessible to the employee with a grievance, a procedure which might involve a kind of negotiation over particular cases. But subject to this there was no local procedure; and this was the gap that was to be exploited by the unofficial strike.

A strike was unofficial when it took place without the prior authorization of the strikers' union. This meant that the strikers would not receive strike pay from their union unless it granted such pay retrospectively, as some unions often did. But since most unofficial strikes were brief and would not qualify for strike pay in any case, the lack of it was of little consequence to the strikers. Not all unions issued strike pay even in official strikes. Yet alike for those who did and for those who did not there had been a presumption that particular groups at the place of work would not strike without being assured of the support of their union, for fear that without it they, and in particular their leaders, might not get their jobs back. Full employment had removed that fear. Their leaders – this meant now, their shop stewards – were able to raise claims, and enforce them directly by various forms of 'industrial action', without first assuring themselves that the whole weight of the union would be thrown against any attempt by management to penalize or discriminate against them. It followed that the union officials lost their hold over them. There was now no consequence with which the officers of the union could threaten members who struck even when that was in violation of an undertaking that the union had given, unless it was to expel them from the union: but that was a drastic step to take, especially when they had only been pursuing the improvement of terms and conditions that formed the main object of the union itself. This lack of control, moreover, widened the gap in the system, because many unofficial strikes were also unconstitutional – that is, where an agreed procedure should be followed to settle a dispute arising at the place of work, the strikers would not wait to complete it, or disregarded it from the first.

By breaking through the gap at the place of work, the unofficial strike undermined the two principles on which the established system rested. There was a principle of structure – the predominance of industry-wide negotiations. There was also a philosophic principle, namely, voluntarism: the law should not constrain the parties or be invoked by them, but their relations should be guided by custom, mutual understanding, and good faith. In respect of structure, the locus of power had been shifted, but its new exercise was still inchoate. Management at the place of work was no longer sheltered from many of the stresses of industrial relations; it found itself under the pressure of bargaining power in matters that used to be left to its discretion; it had to take up a negotiating role for which it was unprepared. On the workers' side the shop steward had been recognized by the engineering employers, and given a limited field of legitimate activity, by an agreement in 1919.[1] But elsewhere he was generally recognized, if at all, only by local practice. His position in his own union, moreover, might be uncertain; the constitution and rule book might not give him status and function, and there was sometimes a clash between the union officials and the 'unofficial' bodies of shop stewards. In any case the bargaining within the plant or company generally lacked settled procedures, and the prevalence of unofficial strikes was one mark of this. But those strikes also undermined the second principle of the established system. The philosophy of voluntarism was tenable only if agreements voluntarily entered into were voluntarily observed: but now the agreements reached at the national level gave employers no protection against subsequent demands made by members of the unions whose officials had signed those agreements, members who were prepared to enforce their claims by withdrawing their labour without the consent and it might be against the veto of their union officials.

We have said that the unofficial strike also caused concern much greater than would have arisen from the tally of man-days lost alone, because it was especially damaging to management and the economy. It was likely to upset pay structures. It could be used to obstruct changes – including the installation of new equipment and its manning – that made for greater efficiency. Investment decisions were made correspondingly hazardous, and there was a case for avoiding changes that might bring the executives who made them more blame for a consequent strike than any credit for resultant efficiency: it was said that the worst effects of unofficial strikes were those of the strikes that did not happen. The incidence of the strikes was unpredictable: they made it hard to keep to delivery dates, and contributed to British exporters' reputation for unreliability. By 1969 the experience of management as the number of unofficial strikes mounted was put by the Director-General of the Confederation of British Industries by way of analogy. 'This country', he declared, 'is being bled to death in front of us. In some ways, it's like a cow being pulled to pieces in an Amazonian river by little fishes.'[2] These effects, moreover, were a matter of public concern in an economy dedicated to growth but increasingly aware that it was growing more slowly than its neighbours. There were several ways in which its intended growth was checked by strikes. Besides the hampering of managers' decisions that we have just noted, strikes were used to maintain lines of demarcation between trades or fight out disputes between unions about 'who does what', with a consequently increasing overmanning of British equipment and processes on a comparison with counterparts in competing countries. In the four-year cycle that ran through activity, the rising phase was recurrently checked by a deficit in the balance of payments, and snuffed out by the measures that Governments took to meet a crisis of sterling: the raising of labour costs by cost push impeded exports, and the impact of a strike in a major industry contributed to more than one crisis. Governments wishing to sustain employment by injections of purchasing power saw this absorbed by rises in earnings of which one origin was the pressure exerted point by point at the place of work.

2

By the early 1960s, there was wide agreement, across party lines, that action must be taken. The once-established system was no longer established. There was much strife, which was bad in itself; and the concessions that avoided or ended it were a major source of cost inflation. The check those pressures exerted on the rise of productivity, both directly and through the balance of payments, was an obstacle to economic growth and the raising of the standard of living. The comparatively poor performance of the British economy, and the weakness of sterling which preoccupied and hampered successive Governments, came back to the troubles of our industrial relations, and these were signalized by the unofficial strike. If the parties could not restore order themselves then the public must intervene. That this country stood out among the Western democracies by reason of the small part that law played in its industrial relations had become a matter for self-question-ing instead of self-congratulation, now that it also stood out by reason of its vulnerability to the unofficial strike. The contrast with the United States was especially suggestive. The toll of man-days lost there was high in the aggregate because of some big stoppages occurring when agreements came to be renegotiated: but these stoppages could be forseen, they were constitutional, and once the agreement was signed it was a legally binding contract. Disputes about its application went to arbitration. 'Wildcat' strikes did occur, but rarely. When a great outburst of strikes followed the War, moreover, and the American economy seemed threatened with such endemic disturbance from militancy as was now troubling the United Kingdom, the Congress by its Taft–Hartley Act had done much to stabilize industrial relations and provide a code of practice enforcible in the courts. In the United Kingdom, it is true, both the Conservative Government that went out in 1964 and the Labour Government that succeeded it held that we should not think of legislation in the first place: the first appeal must be to the trade unions and employers themselves to put their house in order; but if they failed to do that then the public must do it for them. Parliament must assert the national interest.

That meant giving up the doctrine of 1906, that industrial relations should remain outside regulation by law and the concern of lawyers. A change of mind became apparent among the lawyers themselves. After the First World War the courts themselves had come to accept the doctrine to this extent, that they became unwilling to give a remedy to plaintiffs who suffered injury from the action of trade unionists whose predominant purpose was to protect their own interests. This develop-ment culminated in the case of Crofter Harris Tweed v. Veitch in 1941. Members of the Transport and General Workers' Union on the island of Lewis had refused to unload cheap yarn coming from the mainland to certain weavers on the island who were underselling the manu-facturers with whom the union was seeking a closed shop agreement. The House of Lords held that in so doing these dockers had acted in the legitimate interest of their fellow members employed by the manufac-turers, and refused relief to the boycotted competitors. Thereby the Lords extended to trade unionists a principle enunciated for trading firms in the celebrated Mogul case 51 years before. But in the 1960s the courts evidently became minded to reconsider the position of the unions before the law. Notably in Rookes v. Barnard in 1964 the Lords brought trade unions back into the toils of tort. To notify an employer that workers would be withdrawn unless a certain demand was met was, they held, to threaten a breach of contract, for the workers would be withdrawn iṅ breach of their individual contracts of employment: such a threat constituted a tort, and gave any party that suffered injury from the action taken the right to sue for damages or to seek an injunction against it. The alarm was sounded in the trade union ranks, and with reason. The judgement treated what had seemed a normal procedure as intimidation; it treated breach of contract as an illegal means, so that a strike without due notice might be deemed an unlawful conspiracy; and though the contracts to which it directly applied were only contracts of employment, it might well be extended to cover the commercial contracts between a struck firm and its suppliers and customers.

Here among the lawyers as among the politicians of the time we see the impact of what seemed the increasing lawlessness of trade unionists. The agreement of 1906 that industrial relations should be left free of legal regulation had not meant that they were to be anarchic. On the contrary, the agreement had been possible only because experience had persuaded a sufficiently influential sector of the public, including the employers, that the unions would conduct themselves voluntarily in certain well-understood ways, and exercise on the whole a stabilizing influence. It had been an unexpressed but necessary condition of the immunities of trade unionists under statute law, that they should observe certain unwritten laws, and obey the rule of custom in the wielding of their bargaining power. But now this informal code was disregarded. A formal code must be put in its place. The pressure to legislate had mounted during the Conservative administration in the early 1960s, but the Government being chary of an initiative that would of its very nature antagonize trade unionists went no farther before it lost office in 1964 than proposing to appoint a Royal Commission. When Labour took its place, it promptly brought in a Bill to reverse the decision of the Lords in Rookes v. Barnard, so that threatening breach of contract in a trade dispute should no longer be a tort. But on the self-same day as it tabled the Bill it announced the actual appointment of a Royal Commission 'to consider relations between managements and employees and the role of trade unions and employers' associations in promoting the interests of their members and in accelerating the social and economic advance of the nation, with particular reference to the Law affecting the activities of these bodies'.

The Donovan Commission thus appointed had before it a number of proposals that would expose unofficial strikers or their unions to penalties under the existing civil law. Some of these proposals would make the trade unions responsible for the actions of their members. Others would provide penalties that could be invoked directly against the strikers. Other proposals again would deny certain kinds of striker the immunities generally accorded to those acting in contemplation or pursuance of a trade dispute.

The first of these kinds of proposals attracted employers who wished to restore the old position, in which they could look to the union official to bring any deviants back into line. The trouble now was that the union leaders were either not concerned to assert their authority over unruly members, or with the best will in the world were unable to do so. If they were not concerned, it was suggested, responsibility might be forced upon them by withdrawing the vital immunities conferred by the Trade Disputes Act of 1906 from unions whose members struck in breach of an agreement. This might be done by amending the definition of the 'trade dispute' to exclude actions taken in breach of an agreement. But such actions could be specified only if there were first an agreement in form, which contained a no-strike clause, or laid down a procedure for dealing with claims and grievances; and it must be the intention of the parties to give this agreement the force of a contract. It was also necessary to have an arbiter to decide whether a breach had occurred and immunities should be withdrawn in any given case, and here stress was laid on the advantages of registration. Only registered unions, it was proposed, should enjoy the immunities conferred under the Act of 1906. A union from which those immunities were to be withdrawn because of the breach of an agreement by its members would be struck off after investigation by the Registrar, subject to appeal to the High Court. But the Registrar would have a previous and highly relevant function, for before registering a union he would have to satisfy himself that its constitution and rule book met requirements, such as defining the authority and functions of shop stewards, which were intended to ensure internal order and discipline. It was further suggested that the familiar reluctance of employers to sue their own workers for breach of contract would not extend to any reluctance to sue the workers' union, if it were made liable for its members' breach of an agreement. This indicated in turn a sanction that could be put in the hands of those union leaders who were anxious to control unruly members: for if the union itself were given the right to recover any damages of which it might be mulcted in this way from the members by whose action it was involved, it would possess a penalty to invoke against members contemplating such action.

Some proposals for direct sanctions against unofficial action took the form of penalties for action in breach of agreements, especially procedure agreements. It might be provided, for instance, that those who struck in breach of an agreement should be deemed to have voluntarily terminated their employments thereby, and forfeited all accumulated seniority for purposes of subsequent redundancy payments and entitlement to length of notice. If the definition of the 'trade dispute' were changed so as to exclude actions taken in breach of an agreement, then individuals who so acted could be sued for any damages they inflicted. Alternatively it was suggested that an Industrial Court should be set up with power to grant injunctions against action in breach of agreement; failure to obey the injunction would be dealt with as contempt of court.

The exclusion of action in breach of agreement from the definition of the 'trade dispute' for the purpose of the 1906 Act was only one of the ways in which it was suggested that the availability of the immunities under that Act, and consequently the proclivity to strike, might be reduced. In order to deter unions from allowing their members to engage in forms of strike felt to be especially vexatious, it was proposed to exclude from the definition sympathetic strikes, disputes between unions such as demarcation disputes, and even strikes called without due notice to terminate the individual contracts of service.

These proposals were all, in one way or another, for legal sanctions. But the Commission well knew that the trade unions were profoundly averse to any extension of legal regulation of their affairs, or any intrusion of the law into collective bargaining. Many trade union leaders would have been glad to find means of strengthening their hold over their activists – of being able, for instance, to discipline unofficial committees of shop stewards which involved the union in disputes but had no place in its constitution; but they did not for one moment think of seeking the power to do this by abandoning their faith that trade unions should operate outside the law. Nor, when it came to the point, had the employers any more appetite for invoking the law themselves. They found the lawlessness of the unconstitutional strike intolerable, but they saw the remedy as the restoration of the authority of the union officers and the industry-wide agreement. At present they could sue for breach of contract any worker who struck without giving due notice, but once the strike was settled that was the last thing they would think of doing.

Moreover there was represented in and before the Commission an alternative diagnosis of 'the root of the evil' that led to a completely different prescription for dealing with it, and one that respected the susceptibilities of the trade unions. As it turned to the main task in its Report, the Commission announced this theme in a Gallic paragraph: 'Britain has two systems of industrial relations. The one is the formal system embodied in the official institutions. The other is the informal system created by the actual behaviour of trade unions and employers' associations, of managers, shop stewards and workers.'[3] That was the beginning of Chapter III, and this with two of the following four chapters was given up to the theme that the great evil of the unofficial strike arose from 'the informal system' being ill-regulated, the remedy being the adoption of improved, clearly defined, and mutually agreed procedures at company and plant level.

Those resorting to unconstitutional action should not be threatened with any disadvantages imposed by law until new procedures have been put into operation, procedures which are clear where the present procedures are vague, comprehensive where the present procedures are fragmentary, speedy where the present procedures are protracted, and effective where the present procedures are fruitless.[5]

But once the new procedures had been set up, the way was open for the application of legal checks and penalties should they be needed. The Commission had no objection to them in principle. It hoped the procedures that it advocated would command the voluntary adherence of the majority, so that employers could deal with any defiant minority – most obviously, by dismissing them. But if it should prove that more backing was required it might be legal backing. The Commission thought it should be provided case by case. It went on to suggest how the Secretary of State might apply to the Industrial Court for an order making a procedure legally binding in an establishment. The enforcement of such an order would depend upon the willingness of, for example, the employer to sue employees who struck in breach of procedure: the Commission recommended this provision of sanctions despite the stress it had laid on the unwillingness of employers to sue. This part of its Report it concluded, moreover, by saying 'The possibility of the need for future legislative action should not . . . be left out of sight.'[6]

3

It was not left out of sight by some members of the Labour Government. During the three years for which the Donovan Commission had been sitting, dislocation by strikes had grown worse, and now the Commission had made no proposal to meet forthwith the urgent need to deal with it. Meanwhile strikes had dealt two major blows at the Government. The seamen's strike in May and June 1966 had done much to force the Government to reverse the engines of policy by its 'July measures' of that year, and abandon the splendid prospects of economic growth which it had been planning and proclaiming. It was the impact on international confidence of an unofficial dock strike in Liverpool in November 1967 that precipitated the devaluation of sterling. In 1968 the number of stoppages in industries other than coal-mining was nearly a third greater than in 1965, the year in which the Donovan Commission was appointed. But if 'something must be done about it' what did the Commission say should be done and who should do it? It said that higher management should promote the negotiation of factory agreements, and sizeable firms should be required to register their agreements, or explain why they had none to register. It also said that a Commission for Industrial

Relations should be set up, to endeavour by inquiry, advice, and persuasion to improve industrial relations, especially in respect of procedures within the company, and trade union structure. These measures would certainly be helpful in due course. The Commission might also be right in thinking that they would deal with the cause of the malady instead of trying, like sanctions against breaches of procedure, to repress symptoms. But when they argued that the proposed repression would in any case just not work, their case was weakened by their own willingness, noted above, to allow an eventual use of statutory powers. Much more, they seemed to have been left behind the times, and to have given much less than its due weight to the need to stem a mounting menace. Several members of the Cabinet therefore adopted a plan for early legislation, essentially to reduce the incidence of the unofficial strike.

The White Paper, 'In Place of Strife'.[7] in which this plan was set out, contained proposals designed to improve industrial relations in many ways. But the proposal specifically designed to deal with the unofficial strike was the most innovative and the most contentious, in that it provided for the fining of individual strikers, and set up a new tribunal before which they might be prosecuted. 'In unconstitutional strikes and in strikes where, because there is no agreed procedure or for other reasons, adequate joint discussions have not taken place'[8] the Secretary of State would be empowered to order strikers to return to work and desist from industrial action – that is, to order them to work normally – for a 'conciliation pause' of twenty-eight days. During this pause the employer would be required to observe specified terms and conditions, which usually would be those of the status quo ante. If the strikers did not comply with the Order, they would be proceeded against before the Industrial Board, which would be a panel of the Industrial Court. This Board would have power to fine them, and the fines would be recoverable 'by attachment of earnings and other civil remedies for the collection of debts. . . . There will be no liability to imprisonment in default of payment or on account of failure to obey an Order.'[9] When the pause was observed but agreement had not been reached by the end of the twenty-eight days the parties were free to resume industrial action.

This provision against the unofficial strike appeared to its proponents as a modest and practical measure where measures of some kind were needed urgently. It introduced statutory powers and penalties only marginally, where the Donovan Commission had already slid one foot across the line. It did not ban strikes, but only deferred the calling of them. It would be only for discretionary use, in bad cases. But those cases were of a kind that cried aloud for action if the economy were to be saved from increasing disruption.

To trade unionists these considerations counted for little against the bare fact that a tribunal was to be set up before which they might be hauled to be fined for striking. The Bill was attacked for introducing 'the taint of criminality' into industrial relations. It was felt to do this, moreover, in a one-sided way. There is a general presumption that a strike arises from a dispute in which the origin or precipitant may lie on either side, but there was no prospect of managers being hauled before any tribunal – the Industrial Board, it is true, could fine a firm which refused to resume work on the terms and conditions laid down by the Secretary of State during the conciliation pause, but the whole thrust of the provision was to check strikes and strikers. In particular, experience showed that a good many unofficial strikes occurred to prevent the implementation of decisions by management that were felt with some reason to be unacceptable, and the withdrawal of labour had to be immediate if the new arrangements were not to be irreversible. Now the return to work for the conciliation pause would be on terms and conditions laid down by the Secretary of State – generally, the assurance ran, those of the status quo ante: but suppose some Secretary of State in the future in a given case decided otherwise? He was free to do so. For the period of the pause – and this would often also mean in practice for an indefinite period thereafter – the employees would be required to work on terms and conditions not acceptable to them but externally dictated.

So the trade union leaders were opposed to the Bill root and branch. There was, moreover, a particular reason why it was unacceptable to the General Council at this time. The representatives on the Council of the two biggest unions, Jack Jones of the Transport and General Workers and Hugh Scanlon of the Engineers, were newcomers to national office, and their advent marked a change in outlook at that level. Both were closely acquainted and sympathetic with the shop-floor and the shop steward movement among their members. Both would have rejected outright the setting up of a special tribunal – the Industrial Board – before which their members could be brought and fined.

The Prime Minister tried to face out the resolute opposition of the General Council of the TUC, but was forced to drop the Bill by the intimation that it would not command enough votes among his own majority in the House. He had to be content instead with a 'Solemn and Binding Undertaking' by the TUC: in cases where it considered the strikers at fault, the TUC placed 'an obligation on trade unions to take energetic action within their rules'; but where it did not think it reasonable to order a return to work it would only offer 'considered opinion and advice'. It had itself no effective sanctions to apply to affiliated unions that neglected the obligation it imposed; and though action within the rules of particular unions meant disclipinary action, we have already noted that it was hard for unions to order their members to refrain from pursuing claims that coincided with the general aims of the union; or if they did so order them and they did not heed the order, punish them for being more militant than their officers.

So the unofficial strikes which were pouring through a gap in the established procedures were protected by the accepted rationale of strikes within those procedures. The Donovan Commission proposed to close the gap, but its proposals would take effect only gradually, as factory agreements were reached and attitudes remoulded at the place of work. Yet the need for reform remained urgent. The Conservative Government that took office in 1970 was determined to meet it, and it had ready a number of provisions that had been the subject of long study and discussion during the party's years of opposition.

4

The Industrial Relations Act of 1971 contained a vast deal more than measures to deal with the unofficial strike. It embodied, indeed, a whole philosophy of the law in relation to labour, and in Chapter XI we shall consider this, and its rejection and stultification by the trade unions even before its repeal in 1974. Here we notice the three main provisions it contained against the unofficial strike.

First, it took up what had long been a major matter of complaint and regret among employers who looked back to the old days before the spread of the unofficial strike, when agreements made with trade union officials at national or district level were honoured, and enforced by the officials on any potentially recalcitrant members, as a matter of unwritten law. Now that the unwritten law was no longer observed, many employers looked with envy on their American counterparts, whose 'plant contracts' were indeed legal contracts, respected and enforced as such by both parties to them. The Act aimed at making this the prevailing practice and attitude in this country too by providing that every written agreement should be 'conclusively presumed to be intended by the parties to it to be a legally enforceable contract'[10] unless they inserted a statement to the contrary. But the paradox appeared, that though employers deplored the unions being above the law, they were exceedingly loath to go to law themselves. What happened was that all the unions with one accord began inserting the 'statement to the contrary', and it does not appear that any employer ever seriously objected. Very likely the employers will have had it at the back of their minds that even if they had made a stand and stopped the statement going in, so that under the Act the agreement did become a legally enforceable contract, they could still not have seen themselves going to law to enforce it. So this provision was a dead letter.

One reason for these doubts of the employers was their uncertainty about being able to fix responsibility upon the union, as signatory through its officers to the agreement, for actions of shop stewards. To remove such uncertainty, the Act of 1971 required, secondly, that the rules of a union must specify who has the authority to instruct members to take industrial action, and in what circumstances they might do so.[11] This requirement was to be met by a scrutiny of the rules by the Registrar of Trade Unions when unions registered, and unions that did not register were laid under severe fiscal and legal disabilities. But in fact the great majority of unions none the less refused to register, and their rule books remained unscrutinized and unchanged.

The third and most important provision rested upon the new category of offence, the 'unfair industrial practice', which the Act of 1971 had designed together with the Industrial Court in order to lift the substantive issues of industrial relations out of the trammels of existing legal concepts and procedure. In several forms unofficial strikes were designated as unfair industrial practices subject as such to penalties to be imposed by the Industrial Court. To break a legally enforceable agreement was such a practice, or to fail to take all reasonably practicable steps to prevent the members of a union from breaching an agreement.[12] Where the parties had been unable themselves to work out an orderly procedure— it might be because of a dispute between unions – the Industrial Court might impose a settlement, on a recommendation by the Commission on Industrial Relations, and to contravene this settlement would be an unfair industrial practice.[13] The most drastic clause of all made it an unfair industrial practice for any person to induce or threaten to induce someone else to break a contract of any kind – that is, virtually in practice, for any person to lead a strike – unless that person was acting within the scope of his authority on behalf of a trade union.[14]

An unfair industrial practice would come before the Industrial Court only if an employer took it there. The unwillingness of employers to take legal action against their own employees at once negated the value of the procedure as a means of checking unofficial strikes. But some employers harassed by 'secondary picketing' – whether the original dispute was unofficial or not is irrelevant – were willing to go to the Industrial Court for an injunction against the pickets. Here came the crux, and a main cause of the collapse of the Act: for the enforcement of an injunction against persons determined to defy it requires their imprisonment, and the imprisonment of respectable trade unionists for an activity generally regarded as vital to trade unionism conferred a martyr's crown on them and a stigma on the Act and the court. A similar consideration would have applied had the relevant provisions in fact been used against unofficial strikers.

So after nearly twenty years of discussion and experiment, no effective statutory influence on the unofficial strike had been devised. The only proposals before industry and the public remained those of the Donovan Commission. But change did in fact proceed in accordance with these proposals. It is true that there were other reasons why the unofficial strike should have receded from attention. As the pace of inflation quickened the attempt to negotiate and uphold incomes policy involved government in conspicuous dealings and ultimately in struggles with unions at the national level. The rise of unemployment, and the increased hardness of the market that produced it, gradually penetrated to the outlook of the wage-earner, and weakened the hold of those shop stewards who had set up unofficial and militant organizations. But the major source of change, independent of the dramatic episodes of the time and of the current state of employment, was the development of industrial relations within the firm on the initiative of management. In part this was an effect of the current increase in the predominant size of the firm, for big firms could employ specialists in industrial relations and were more likely to value independence from employers' associations. Very widely it marked the acceptance of the shop steward not merely as the legitimate spokesman of the employees but, much more significant, as a permanent part of the institutions of industrial relations. In that capacity his relations with his own constituents changed: he became a negotiator and mediator, a channel through which the executive constraints of management were conveyed to the shop-floor as well as the needs, complaints, and aspirations of the shop-floor being made known to management. Shop stewards, foremen, and managers were sent on training courses in industrial relations. The terms and conditions of employment came to be negotiated within the company, and embodied in agreements that might cover all the plants of a multi-plant concern, or be negotiated plant by plant. Increasing use was made of job evaluation to establish wage-structures. The negotiations led to agreements of various degrees of formality, but the essentials were that they dealt systematically with many of the sources of grievance that had given rise to unofficial strikes, and that by bringing all groups into one process they prevented any one of them from exploiting its tactical strength and pushing up its pay ahead of the others.

We spoke of the unofficial strike as pouring through a gap in the established procedures. In the decade after the Donovan Commission reported, much of that gap was filled by the development of negotiating procedure within the firm. We do not know how far this development was due to the recommendations in the Report of the Commission, and how far it would have come about in any case; but the fact remains that it took the form that the Commission recommended.

5

One part of the development was an extension of the closed shop. About 1962, a survey by McCarthy[15] found that closed shop arrangements covered about one in six of all employees; a survey conducted for the Department of Employment in 1978–9 found that the proportion then was one in four. This was so although the strongholds of the closed shop had contracted: in the staples of mining, metals, engineering, shipbuilding, and printing, the labour force had fallen by more than a fifth. As a result there was actually a fall, albeit a slight one, in the proportion of TUC members covered. But the effect on the total number covered was more than offset by the extension of the closed shop into industries that had known little of it before: some of the light industries, the public utilities, the railways, and road and air transport. It made some advance, too, among the white-collared.

The old closed shop had usually rested on custom and practice. 'Before 1968 the typical closed shop agreement, if written down, occupied a single clause in a works agreement and was comprehended in a single sentence which perhaps read: "It is a condition of employment that the hourly paid employees become and remain members of the union"'[17] The new arrangements have been much more likely to be set out in detail in a union membership agreement (UMA) of several pages in length. As such they have been not only accepted but on balance welcomed by management as part of the ordering and formalization of relations within the plant or company that has been proceeding since Donovan.[18] The conclusion of these agreements was inhibited by the Act of 1971, though the underlying arrangements probably went on: at least we know that when the legal ban was removed by the Act of 1974 a spate of agreements came out, as if arrears were being overtaken.

The effects of the closed shop on trade union power are not to be assessed out of hand. The pre-entry closed shop, in which the employer can engage only those who already hold a union card, endows the union with the powers of a restrictive monopoly, but is quite exceptional. The post-entry closed shop only requires that the non-union entrant join the union on beginning to work, and though this requirement may deter some applicants, it can hardly restrict the employer's choice substantially. Where the employees' attachment to trade unionism is less than whole-hearted, the closed shop solves the problems of recruitment and maintenance of membership: a first and evident effect will be an increase in numbers. Since to be brought under discipline by the branch may be painful, the closed shop gives the local activists a greater hold on the membership as a whole: if they call a strike they can expect complete support even if a good many members would sooner not lose their pay. At the limit, the leaders have been able to threaten that if they tear up a man's card he will lose his livelihood. The conditions under which a union membership agreement will allow an employer to dismiss an employee for non-membership without the dismissal being regarded as unfair have been defined by the Employment Act, 1980. But at the last, the preponderant attitude of managers suggest that in most agreements what is at stake is not trade union power so much as the consolidation of procedures. It is the function of the closed shop to provide unified and stable representation for a group of employees within a formal system of relations at the place of work. The accession of power to the trade union, and the subordination of the individual, are the counterparts of the place accorded to the trade union in the constitution of the system.

Notes

[1] In an Agreement for Works Committees the rights of shop stewards under the Procedure for the Avoidance of Disputes were defined: they 'shall be afforded facilities to deal with questions raised in the shop or portion of a shop in which they are employed,' and those who served on Works Committees might with the consent of management visit other parts of the establishment (Eric Wigham, *The Power to Manage* (London, 1973), p. 103).

[2] *The Times*, 10 April 1969.

[3] Royal Commission on Trade Unions and Employers' Associations 1965–68: Report (Cmnd. 3623, June 1968), para. 46.

[4] Ibid., para. 1020.

[5] Ibid., para. 504.

[6] Ibid., para. 518.

[7] Cmnd. 3888, Jan. 1969.

[8] Ibid., para. 93.

[9] Ibid., para. 62.

[10] Industrial Relations Act, 1971, s. 34.

[11] Ibid., Schedule 4, para 10.

[12] Ibid., s. 36.

[13] Ibid., s. 41.

[14] Ibid., s. 96.

[15] W. E. J. McCarthy, *The Closed Shop in Britain* (Oxford, 1964).

[16] J. Gennard, S. Dunn, and M. Wright, 'The extent of closed shop arrangements in British industry, *Department of Employment Gazette*, 88, Jan. 1980, 16–22.

[17] J. Gennard, S. Dunn, and M. Wright, 'The content of British closed shop agreements', *Department of Employment Gazette*, 87, Nov. 1979, 1089.

[18] William Brown (ed.), *The Changing Contours of British Industrial Relations* (Oxford, 1981), 57–9.

XI

THE ATTEMPT TO IMPOSE ORDER: THE LEGAL CODE OF 1971

I

IN the early 1960s there was tacit agreement between the political parties that the trade unions having shown themselves unable to set their own house in order, Parliament must impose order by legislation. Even the General Council of the TUC may at this time have been resigned to the prospect. It was a Labour Government which in 1965 appointed the Donovan Commission to consider industrial relations 'with particular reference to the Law'.

But no one reading the Report of the Commission without previously consulting its terms of reference would realize that it had been so directed. Only in its Chapter VIII did it turn to the question, 'What can the law do to help to improve our industrial relations?'[1] That its answer was, in effect, 'Very little', explains why it had been so slow to raise the question. It had not overlooked it, but had become convinced that the law could not be used to impose more orderly procedures against the will of the parties. How such procedures could be established acceptably through plant and company agreements it described fully. Only when it had done that would it consider what marginal improvements might be made in the existing law. But meanwhile it had given its reasons for rejecting the attempt to order our industrial relations by a statutory code.

A main reason was that legalism in industrial relations was alien to our traditions. We should pause before we sought to transplant legal institutions from countries whose social attitudes and traditions were different from ours, and 'reverse the entire trend of our industrial history and give to the law a function it has never had in the past'.[2] In particular, employers no more than trade unionists approached their mutual relations in a legal spirit at the present time. On the contrary: when employers had the opportunity to sue for damages arising out of an industrial dispute they just would not take it. A binding contract could exist only if it was the intention of the parties that it should be such, but it was clearly the intention of the parties to British collective bargaining that their agreements should be for guidance only and observance simply by good faith. This arose also out of the way in which the bargaining was carried on, as an ongoing process of successive adjustments often made at different levels in the same industry or concern, and recorded in various ways. Neither the terms and conditions of employment nor the procedures for negotiation and handling grievances were specified in discrete documents, complete in themselves like commercial contracts: they often rested upon 'custom and practice'. This meant that legal categories and sanctions were inherently inapplicable to the processes of British industrial relations.

It meant also that the parties to those relations would resist the attempt to apply them. At a number of points the Commission argued in effect that industrial relations could not be brought under the law because the parties being long used to the absence of its restraints would now refuse to accept them. It was said, for instance, that if the closed shop were outlawed some employers would connive with trade unionists to maintain it. If unions were made responsible for the actions of their shop stewards, the result to be expected would not be any change in the communications between union officers and shop stewards, or in the behaviour of the shop steward through unwillingness to inflict losses on the union, but more probably the internal disruption of the union. To make those who struck in breach of agreements lose seniority in respect of entitlement to redundancy compensation was held to bear hardly on older workers with long service, because it was assumed that these workers would continue to take part in such strikes, rather than that the law would enable or induce them and others to refrain. Even the case of the prosecution of the miners at Betteshanger during the War was brought forward as proof of the futility of attempts to enforce penal sanctions, without comment on the determination of the accused to defy the law by refusing to pay their fines – an attitude which would prevent the enforcement of the law in any field – or any raising of the question whether this attitude was either inevitable or in the common interest. Enough that the horse had never been broken in to harness, so harness would not go on the horse.

This was realistic, but the incoming Conservative Government of 1970 brushed aside a realism that condemned Parliament to inaction while industrial relations fell into even greater disorder. The number of strikes outside coal-mining was still rising rapidly: in 1970 as a whole the total was to be nearly double that of 1968, the year in which the Donovan Commission reported. Voluntarism certainly had been the animating principle of British industrial relations, but now the country was confronted with its breakdown. It was hard not to connect the contrast between the United Kingdom and other Western countries in the type and incidence of strikes with the contrast in the immunities of the strikers before the law. Public opinion polls showed substantial support even among trade unionists themselves for measures of restraint: it was reasonable to expect that statute law, so far from having to wait upon a change of attitudes, might rest upon a public opinion that was already in being, and by affirming it extend its hold. The Solicitor-General, Sir Geoffrey Howe, who is generally regarded as the principal draftsman of the new Government's Bill, quoted with approval in November 1970 some words that the present writer had recently published:[3]

If the law were changed now it would work to change the attitudes and expectations of union members and officers . . . Law forms opinion as well as being formed by it. The British law of industrial relations has fostered habits of mind and patterns of conduct that correspond to its negativism. . . . The question then is, whether we can cease to be victims of our history.

2

The form that a statutory code should take had been long discussed, and the Industrial Relations Act of 1971 in which it was formulated contained proposals that had been put forward from various quarters; but its unifying purpose was to provide a framework within which collective bargaining might proceed under rules and arrangements which marked off the permissible from the impermissible uses of the power of combination. A main feature of this framework, and a remarkable innovation, was the creation of a new jurisdiction. The issues of the wrongful exertion of bargaining power which the courts had long struggled to deal with under the law of tort were to be removed from them. Instead, as 'unfair industrial practices', they were to be remitted to the Industrial Tribunals and the ultimate decision of the Industrial Court that was now to be set up. The concept of the 'unfair industrial practice' was adapted from the 'unfair labor practice' of the US Taft–Hartley Act of 1947. It served to define explicitly which actions such as the parties to industrial disputes resort to were ruled out, so that the aggrieved party would have an automatic remedy and not have to rely on the discretion of a court. Correspondingly the Industrial Court, where the judge would be sitting with members drawn from panels of trade unionists and employers, would be free to enter into the substance and reality of the issues before it, untrammelled by the complexities of the civil law.

The framework itself may be said to have been formed of two main structures of positive law, the one designed to protect the individual worker, the other composed of restraints on 'industrial action'. Under the former head the worker was given the right to receive further particulars of his contract of employment, including an explicit statement of his right to belong to a trade union. For the first time in British legislation he was provided with a statutory remedy for unfair dismissal. A worker claiming to have been unfairly dismissed could go to an Industrial Tribunal, and if he established his case the Tribunal could advise the employer to reinstate him, failing which the employer must pay him compensation, or it could itself order compensation. A worker who was dismissed because he was a trade union member enjoyed the same right. But the section which conferred this right also raised the issue of the closed shop, for it declared that every worker had the right not only 'to be a member of such trade union as he may choose' but also 'to be a member of no trade union . . . or to refuse to be a member of any particular trade union'.[4] To the lawyers, in the tradition of the common law, it was an intolerable invasion of the right of every man to apply his labour in whatever lawful way he chose, that a worker should be denied access to a job because he was not a member of a particular trade union. At the same time the closed shop had become widely established, and many employers accepted it as putting an end to inter-union disputes and the disturbances that splinter groups could create. A compromise was found by a distinction between the 'pre-entry closed shop' and the 'agency shop'. A pre-entry closed shop would allow access to jobs in the shop only to workers who were already members of the union: this was banned, in that the Act made it an unfair industrial practice for an employer to refuse to engage a worker on the ground that he was not a member of a trade union or of a particular trade union.[5] Where an agency shop was agreed between the employer and a trade union, a worker who did not choose for whatever reason to belong to the union had the right under the Act to be taken into and kept in employment, provided that he paid 'appropriate contributions to the trade union in lieu of membership of it'; or on grounds of conscience he might instead pay contributions to a charity.[6] But the compromise of the agency shop was still not enough to cover all the variety of actual affairs. The actors and the merchant seamen could plead that the points at which their members were hired were so numerous and scattered, and the turnover at each point so great, that they could secure the observance of the rates they negotiated nationally only if they could ensure that only union members were engaged. The Act therefore provided an escape clause, under which the Industrial Court could approve a closed shop agreement, and the safeguards of the non-member would no longer apply – save still that a specially exempted worker might pay lieu contributions to charity. Since union membership remained so important as a condition of employment, the Act provided protection for the individual against denial or loss of it, through the union infringing its own rules or departing from the guiding principles for trade unions laid down in the Act (Part IV).

Such were the main provisions to protect the individual worker. But the chief concern of the Act was with restraints on 'industrial action'. Those imposed on the unofficial strike we have discussed in the preceding section. Some of the other provisions were designed to uphold the authority of the Commission on Industrial Relations and the Industrial Court. Thus when a long wrangle about recognition had led the Industrial Court, on the recommendation of the Commission, to impose a procedure, it would be an unfair industrial practice to strike against it. But attention centred on the two clauses, s. 97 and s. 98, that dealt with sympathetic action and the secondary boycott. Section 97 made it an unfair industrial practice to strike or lock-out, or resort to 'any irregular industrial action short of a strike', in support of any action which constituted an unfair industrial practice in the first place. Section 98 made it an unfair industrial practice to cause someone not involved in a dispute to break a contract with a party to it. Evidently this meant that the other's premises must not be picketed, and his workers must not black goods coming from the party to the dispute or destined for that party; pickets lawfully posted at the place of dispute must let through lorries bringing supplies from contractors not involved in the dispute. Beyond these provisions restrictive of industrial action generally a special procedure, adapted from that set up by the Taft–Hartley Act, was instituted for dealing with disputes which because they cut off vital supplies constituted a national emergency. In the conditions of emergency, and when he had reason to believe that a settlement could be reached if industrial action were suspended or deferred, the Secretary of State could apply to the Industrial Court for an order halting all such action for up to sixty days – though the crisis, and the judgement how best to meet it, might (one would think) be essentially political, the decision was given to the Court. A further provision was made for the ordering of a ballot. If there were a strike that constituted a national emergency, or, short of that, would import serious injury to the livelihood of the workers in the industry concerned; and if there were reasons for doubting whether the workers taking part in the strike were doing so in accordance with their own wishes, and whether they had an adequate opportunity to indicate their wishes, then the Secretary of State could decide to apply to the Industrial Court for an order that a ballot be held on a specified question.[7]

These statutory provisions were supported by a Code of Industrial Relations Practice. The purpose of this Code was to hold up a pattern of good behaviour before all concerned. Its relation with the law was like that of the Highway Code: it did not have the force of law, but the

Industrial Tribunals and the Industrial Court in their adjudications would take account of whether parties had followed its precepts.

Behind all the provisions of the Act there had to be sanctions against infraction. Where the Secretary of State had obtained from the Industrial Court an order deferring a strike, in a threatened national emergency, or requiring a ballot to be held, it would naturally be for him to denounce before the Court any person defying the order, to be dealt with for contempt. Similarly if the Court on his motion imposed a procedure in a disputed case of recognition. The Registrar likewise might complain to the Court of non-compliance with a notice he had issued. But by far the most general sanction was that activated by the person who proceeded in the Industrial Court against a party charged with an unfair industrial practice. When a complaint about an unfair industrial practice was established, the Court might make an order setting out the rights of the parties; or award a sum to be paid to the complainant by the respondent, in compensation; or order the respondent to cease and desist from that action. An order of this last kind being issued, would be enforced by the sanctions generally available against contempt of court: an individual who disobeyed an injunction would be sent to prison, or a trade union that defied the Court might be fined. The intention that industrial relations should be lifted out of the existing legal system into a more appropriate jurisprudence of their own was thus disappointed in the last resort.

The Act, moreover, was lengthy: it contained 170 sections and nine Schedules. Inevitably also it was complex. Lord Donovan said in a second reading debate that 'if one takes the trouble to count up the number' of unfair industrial practices 'which the Bill creates, he will arrive at the figure of at least 179'.[8] Something depends on the method of counting – on whether, for instance, 'to induce or to threaten to induce' is counted as one or two practices: in the Act as finally adopted the number of clauses specifying practices appears to be under thirty.[9] But even in this way of reckoning the array is formidable. The understanding and use of the new Act evidently called for the work of many lawyers: so far from lifting industrial relations out of the trammels of legal procedure, the Act had devised a new branch of the law with its own convolutions. These were necessarily unexplored. The old state of the law was capable of throwing up its surprises, as Rookes v. Barnard showed, but the ground had been beaten over yard by yard down the years, and the unions mostly knew where they stood on it and were not dissatisfied. Yet now the new Act had repealed in its entirety one of the basic statutes of the old law, the Act of 1906 which gave unions immunity from action for civil conspiracy: no doubt it had made alternative provision of a sort, but of what sort, within what limits and among what pitfalls?

3

The unions were not only concerned by the contents of the Act, they were incensed by the way in which its intended provisions had been conveyed to them. The Government's Consultative Document had stated that it might not be possible to take account of views received after a date hardly more than five weeks after the document became generally available. When the Secretary of State for Employment met delegates from the TUC within that period, he told them that the Government's proposals rested upon eight 'pillars' that were not to be moved: discussion could proceed only upon details. But these pillars included such proposals as affirming the right of every worker to join or not to join a union; or limiting the immunities at present enjoyed by trade unionists in trade disputes, by narrowing the definition of such disputes. Evidently there was to be no real consultation. To be treated by a Conservative Government in this way was not only humiliating but unprecedented in the delegates' own experience. The position which the trade union leaders had held as the representatives of an estate of the realm under the Labour Governments of 1945–51 had not really been impugned in the thirteen years of Conservative government that followed. Churchill had been determined to avoid conflict with the unions. As a young man Macmillan, like Eden, had been a subaltern among the men in the trenches, and in the interwar years he had served as Member for a constituency stricken with unemployment in the North East: he too wanted an understanding. If close connection between the unions and the counsels of government naturally ceased with the coming of the Conservatives to office in 1951, the unions could continue to expect that in all matters particularly concerning themselves Conservative Governments would walk delicately and proceed only after due consultation. But now in 1970 a Conservative Government was thrusting radical changes upon them with deliberate denial of discussion.

It is true that the Government could be charged with haste rather than discrimination. It offered no effective consultation to the CBI, whose own preferences were very different from the Government's proposals. In the House of Commons the Bill was taken through its stages at such a pace that many of its clauses remained undebated.

The high-handed way in which the new measures were imposed combined with the forbidding substance of those measures themselves to harden the resistance of the trade unionists. A new and comprehensive system of regulation which ran counter to some of their basic principles could have been considered by them at all only if it had been submitted as a basis for discussion. It had been imposed inflexibly. They were determined to frustrate it.

Meanwhile the extent to which the provisions of the new law took effect upon the daily course of industrial relations depended upon the initiative of employers. But though employers wanted trade unionists to be made to keep agreements, they were as unprepared as the union leaders to receive a whole new code. Moreover, they shared the union leaders' dislike of legalism. The Director-General of the CBI was expressing more than a personal view of the Conservative proposals as those were put forward before the election of 1970, when he said in April of that year that though changes in the law were needed to 'strengthen the hands of those seeking to operate voluntary institutions in a responsible way', employers viewed with some concern the prospect of 'a legally based system with legally enforceable contracts, labour injunctions, widespread use of labour courts, legally defined bargaining units and legal obligations to bargain in good faith'. They did not want to see their industrial relations policies 'in the hands of a new profession of labour lawyers', or to find themselves 'constantly away from their businesses suing their workers and being sued by those workers in labour courts'[10] But a legally based system of that kind was exactly what had now been put upon them; and this, after the Government had given them as short a shrift as the TUC in the way of consultation.

The insistence of the trade unions on fending the law off from industrial relations had relieved employers from the need to develop what would otherwise have come to be one of the standard branches of specialized knowledge and administrative provision within management, namely, the capacity to deal with legal issues concerning industrial relations. Had that capacity existed, as it did within American management, they would have been able to make use of the Act if they chose. But it did not exist, and they were not prepared for the role which the Act assigned them. Very few of them applied to the Court for relief from an unfair industrial practice.

In one way this was a stultification of the Act. But in another, it saved the Act from a different form of derogation. For the relief the Court could give an employer was most likely be by way of an injunction against the persons engaging in the unfair practice, such as a particular form of picketing or blacking, and if those persons persisted in it none the less, they must be dealt with for contempt of court, and put in gaol. Then a great cry would go up: the Tories were taking the country back to the days of the Tolpuddle Martyrs and Botany Bay. Trade unionists had been imprisoned for what, until this Act was passed, had been accepted as a normal trade union activity. There would be the imminent threat of a widely extended strike until they were released. This was a contingency that could not be faced. After the Court had ordered two shop stewards of the London dockers to be committed to prison for violating its injunction against their picketing a container depot, the Official Solicitor applied to the Court successfully for the withdrawal of the committal order on the ground of there being insufficient evidence of the injunction having been violated. On a later occasion five London dockers actually were gaoled for violating an injunction. At that a general dock strike was threatened, and the TUC planned a one-day general strike. But the House of Lords, acting with rapidity, overturned a judgement of the Court of Appeal and found that the imprisoned men had indeed been acting as agents of their union. Within hours of that judgement being given the Official Solicitor applied successfully to the Industrial Court for the release of the prisoners on the ground that it was against their union and not them that any action should lie. Henceforward the Court avoided issuing injunctions, and endeavoured to settle such few cases of unfair industrial practices as employers brought to it by conciliation and arrangement.

So the structure of principles and procedures, delineated by the unfair industrial practices that marked departures from them, remained without effect. The employers who should have moved to bring the structure to bear did not do so in any number. Had they done so, the Court lacked an accepted jurisdiction that would give it effective powers of enforcement.

4

The Act thus hamstrung in several ways was repealed on a change of Government in 1974, though the new legislation retained provisions which had extended the rights of employees – the remedy against wrongful dismissal, and the obligation on the employer to disclose information required for bargaining. What had happened was a demonstration of the impossibility, not of modifying or extending the legal regulation of industrial relations, but of imposing a complete new system of statute law and court procedure in one quantum jump, and without real prior consultation with the parties whose conduct and whose very habits of thought would have to be changed radically. The consultation to be effective would have had to be lengthy, and no thoroughgoing system would have ever survived it in a condition its designers would recognize. But moving slowly and not very far at first was the price that had to be paid for moving at all. The incoming Government of 1970 was confronted not only with the unreasoning strength of the trade unionists' inherited and traditional aversion to the law, but with their conception of their rightful place as an estate of the realm within its unwritten constitution. This has been well put by Michael Moran:

for a generation the unions had been encouraged to believe that, whatever the outcome of elections, they would have a considerable say over policies which affected them. Now, this was being denied them over the most important piece of legislation in living memory. In a real sense the unions thought the legislation illegitimate and unconstitutional, not just because of its content but because of the way it had been prepared and passed. As a result appeals to the unions to respect the constitution and the rule of law met less response than might otherwise have been the case, precisely because of this feeling that it was the Government which had first been in breach of the constitution.[11]

Yet a Government that accepted those assumptions as genuine might not have found the implied constraints altogether crippling. Recognition that an essential part of the unwritten law of industrial relations had broken down was widespread among trade unionists as well as other people. Trade union leaders were embarrassed by their own lack of power to control the conduct of members for which they continued to be held responsible. Their traditions might have prevented them ever explicitly agreeing to, let alone welcoming, an extension of positive law in the field of industrial relations; but this was a time when such an extension, modest in scale and patiently discussed, once enacted might have come to be accepted. The effect of what actually happened was to move trade unionists' minds in the opposite direction, and deepen antipathy to the law.

Notes

[1] Royal Commission on Trade Unions and Employers' Associations 1965–1968: Report (Cmnd. 3623, June 1968), para. 458.

[2] Ibid., paras 461, 460.

[3] In a speech to the Industrial Law Society, 21 Nov. 1970. The quotation is from 'Unofficial Strikes and the Law', *Three Banks Review*, Sept. 1969, 16.

[4] Industrial Relations Act, 1971, s. 5(1).

[5] Ibid., s. 5(2.c) and s. 7.

[6] Ibid., s. 6.

[7] Ibid., ss. 141, 142.

[8] Parl. Debates, 1971, 317/44.

[9] Table II, Summary of Unfair Industrial Practices, in C. G. Heath, *A Guide to the Industrial Relations Act 1971* (London 1971).

[10] *The Financial Times*, 11 April 1970.

[11] Michael Moran, *The Politics of Industrial Relations* (1977), p. 93.

XII

COMPARATIVE STUDIES: (i) TRADE UNIONISM IN THE USA

MORE than once since the War British eyes have turned to the United States for the example of better practice in industrial relations. When the Labour Government of 1945 was leading a campaign to raise productivity at home, and narrow the wide gap between output per man in the UK and the USA, it sent out teams of managers and trade unionists to meet their opposite numbers in American industries, and the reports of those missions often laid stress on the attributes of American trade unionists and the relations prevailing in American plants. The Donovan Commission in its Report of 1968 warned against the attempt to transplant institutions from other countries, but the detailed agreements within the firm or plant that it called for as the basic means of preventing unofficial strikes had much in common with the distinctively American plant contracts. The Industrial Relations Act of 1971 followed European and not American practice when it provided access to Industrial Tribunals as a form of grievance procedure: this was quite incompatible with the standing of the trade unions in the American system of industrial relations. But others of its main provisions, notably the distinctions between fair and unfair industrial practices, and the procedure for dealing with national emergency disputes, were evidently derived from the American Taft–Hartley Act of 1947.

These approaches and borrowings imply that American industrial relations are sufficiently similar to ours for us to be able to draw on them for possible improvements of our own, but also that their development has diverged significantly. The similarities have originated from common impulses; but strongly marked differences of orientation and function have come about, and challenge explanation. In accounting for them we shall be illuminating British history by contrast, and throwing into relief aspects of British affairs that we might not have noticed so long as we kept only those affairs in view.

I

The earlier trade unions arose in much the same way, and took much the same forms in both countries. In the handicrafts, as the eighteenth century wore on, there came to be a fringe of journeymen who were sometimes self-employed or masters and sometimes reverted to the status of wage-earners, while most journeymen were having to accept that status permanently. By the end of the century most of the major trades in the bigger towns of what were now the United States had their friendly societies which embraced masters and journeymen, but already the journeymen were capable of independent action, and after the turn of the century they began to form continuous societies. When the times demanded it these societies could bring their members out on strike, but that they were of the nature of friendly societies as well as trade unions appears from the debate whether a journeyman who became a master could remain a member. In these respects these transitional societies in the USA resemble the early craft unionism of the UK. In both countries the printers were prominent.

There is resemblance also in the next phase, the rapid onrush in the 1830s in both countries of a wide and popular unionism having large, even apocalyptic social aims. Those manifestations of faith in the possibility of a vast and early change soon subsided. In both countries there then emerged to view the closely organized, centrally administered craft union as the first type of union to extend throughout the country and maintain itself through the fluctuations of trade. In the UK the landmark was the formation of the Amalgamated Society of Engineers in 1851. In the US the first national union, the National Typographical Union, was founded in 1852. In both countries this type of union was characterized by its use of the membership card as a warranty for travelling members and a means by which a local branch could deal with strangers; and above all by the control exercised by the national executive over strike action by the branches. But whereas the British 'New Model' maintained itself continuously thenceforward, its American counterpart was too often cut off by the severity of trade depressions, and did not achieve a settled existence for another thirty years.

It might seem that the strange movement which arose in the US out of the long depression of the 1870s had no British counterpart. The Knights of Labour embraced workers of all descriptions, farmers and small masters as well as wage-earners. Their doctrine discouraged militancy, and laid stress instead on raising the moral and intellectual standards of the workers. The wave of enthusiasm that in 1886 swept people by the hundred thousand into membership of the Knights seems to find its British counterpart, if any, in Robert Owen's Grand

National Consolidated Trades Union of half a century before. But there is one respect in which the Knights did resemble many of their contemporaries among British trade unionists, namely, their sense that working people in banding together to better their condition should foster high standards of conduct among themselves. Observers of British unionism at that time attached prime and practical importance to the moral uplift of their members.

But for the Knights this was not enough. As an organization they were dominated by local or city federations. These were not themselves capable of bargaining, or of lending effective support to an affiliated union when this bargained for itself. The Knights went down as rapidly as the idealistic movements of the 1830s had done. The craft unions which had their own national organization broke away and formed their own federation, which became the American Federation of Labor.

This was a body of business unions, each concerned with the practical issues of terms and conditions within its own jurisdiction. But for all the conservatism of the AFL, the quarter of a century down to the First World War saw an expansion of trade union membership much greater than that which in the UK followed the impact of the New Unionism in 1889. Between 1897 and 1914 American trade union membership rose sixfold.[1] In the UK membership rose between 1888 and 1913 rather more than fourfold.[2] But such expansion did not occur in the US and the UK alone. In about the same span of years membership was multiplied by more than 7 in France and nearly 9 in Germany, and in Sweden it rose from small beginnings to become nationwide.[3] These observations remind us of the tendency of industrial relations in Western countries to develop in remarkably similar ways at about the same time. As between the USA and the UK, how far can this be ascribed to common influence? In a letter to the author, Dr H. M. Douty has discussed the possible influences on the American side. He wrote:

In view of the judicial restraints, strong employer resistance generally, and the great wave of immigration that hit these shores (almost 9 million immigrants between 1901 and 1910), the growth of trade union membership between 1897 and 1914 is remarkable. These were generally prosperous years, and that no doubt helped. There was the closing of the geographic frontier. There was reaction to the growth and consolidation of industry, and the proliferation of social reform groups largely of middle-class composition. The trade union movement itself developed an *élan*, which I don't think it has ever had since, except possibly for a short period during the 1930s. For example, much of the organizing was done during this period by unpaid volunteers. There was much intellectual ferment within the movement, reflected in the growing influence of the Socialist Party. This influence was not negligible. In 1912 the socialist delegates to the AFL convention ran a candidate against Gompers and polled almost a third of the votes.

Some of these factors were specific to the United States; but three – the middle-class reformism, the *élan* of the trade unionists, and the socialist current – were common to the United Kingdom. It is a question in the philosophy of history why they appeared in both countries at this time. We have no reason to think that they were originally transmitted from one to the other.

But one historic link does appear at this time – the presumption of the English common law, as that was received in both countries, against the use of the power of combination. We have seen how in the UK this reasserted itself in the 1890s in the doctrine of civil conspiracy, and how the trade unions persuaded Parliament to relieve them of this onus by the Trade Disputes Act of 1906. When employers in the USA reacted from the 1890s onwards against the growing strength and activity of the trade unions, they found a ready ally in the courts. The Sherman Act of 1890 had been directed against the power of giant trusts in business, but the Supreme Court detected the same principle of monopoly in combinations of employees, and held trade unions to be covered by the declaration of the Act that every combination in restraint of trade was illegal. It was originally in reaction against the power of trade unions manifest in great railway strikes in 1877 that the courts extended the use of the injunction. They were very willing to grant injunctions against trade union activities such as picketing and the secondary boycott; or against activities of any kind whatever, in order 'to protect property'. The concept of property, moreover, included intangible business assets. The Sherman Act supported the use of the injunction. But then came the victory of the Democrats and the election of President Wilson in 1912. In the political opportunity it brought to the unions this may be compared with the Liberal victory in the UK in 1906: the Congress proceeded to pass the Clayton Act of 1914 which both purported to set trade unions free of the trammels of anti-trust law, and provided that the federal courts could not enjoin employees engaged in a trade dispute from taking part peacefully in assemblies, pickets, or boycotts. True, the former provision though sonorous in its language was actually void of content, and the latter was soon to be struck down by a decision of the Supreme Court. But at the time the Act was hailed as the unions' Magna Charta, just as the Trade Disputes Act of eight years before was seen – in this case rightly – as one of the twin pillars of the British unions' liberties.

The Treasury Agreement of 1915 has been seen as another landmark in the advance of the British unions: the affixing of the signatures of trade union leaders besides those of Ministers implied the recog-

nition of the unions as an estate of the realm. In just the same way the
First World War brought an accession of influence and of standing
within the federal administration to the American unions. Already
before the War, in 1913, President Wilson had set up a Department of
Labor, and appointed as his first Secretary of Labor the leader of the
Union of Mine Workers. (When Lloyd George formed his administration in December 1916 he appointed the leader of the Steel Smelters to
the new office of Minister of Labour.) After the US entered the War in
1917, the veteran leader of the AFL, Samuel Gompers, became one of
the seven members of the Advisory Commission to the President's
Council of National Defense. In January 1918 the President set up a
War Labor Board, which affirmed the right of employees to organize
and to receive a living wage for an eight-hour day – a declaration of
principle that was not required to be reciprocated by any renunciation
of the right to strike. But in both countries alike, within two years of
the Armistice, the power of labour had collapsed, and its standing with
Government was no more.

The AFL has not had a distinctive political philosophy. It has
approached legislature and executives with a limited list of demands.
This has enabled it to pursue a policy of bipartisanship, and play off
one party against another, even if in practice it has given most support
to, and exerted most influence upon, the Democrats. But in this sense it
has been active in politics. Over against the Federal Government it has
been concerned to ward off legislation it deems inimical to the unions,
and to promote measures such as the Clayton Act in order to protect
them. On the state legislatures it has exerted pressure likewise, through
the state federations of labour. These have engaged in lobbying and
election campaigns, for such purposes as opposing restrictions
imposed by the courts or by legislation on the right to strike, boycott,
or picket; improving labour law and its administration; or extending
public education.

One reason for the American trade unions having followed this
course of bipartisanship is that the political loyalties of their members
were already formed and divided. Those members were citizens who
entered into a long tradition of enfranchisement and of adherence to
one or other of the two parties: to try to give trade unionism a single
and exclusive political coloration would have been needlessly divisive.
But this is no less how it was, the Webbs observed, with the TUC in
1897, even though the enfranchisement of the British trade unionist
was then more recent and still incomplete.

The Trade Union Congress [they wrote] is a federation for obtaining, by
Parliamentary action, not social reform generally, but the particular
measures desired by its constituent Trade Unions. These all desire certain
measures of legal regulation confined to their own particular trades, and they

are prepared, if this limitation is observed, to back up each other's demands. On many important subjects, such as Freedom of Combination, Compensation for Accidents, Truck, Sanitation, 'the Particulars Clauses', the weekly payment of wages, and the abolition of disciplinary fines, they are united in general measures. But directly the Congress diverges from the narrow Trade Union function, and expresses any opinion, either on general social reforms or party politics, it is bound to alienate whole sections of its constituents.

It was not long after the Webbs wrote that the TUC altered course and showed that they had been mistaken – or that the outlook of trade unionists had changed. The linking of British trade unionism with a new and distinct political party was to form one of the most significant of its divergencies from American unionism. But down to 1900 it was the similarity in this matter of political connection and not any difference that was striking.

There remain similarities between the aims and actions of the individual unions in the two countries, in the pressures they exert at the place of work, their priorities in bargaining, and their sheer use of bargaining power. Our attention in the United Kingdom has been drawn repeatedly to what is distinctive in American collective bargaining, especially the negotiation of the plant contract and the procedure for its observance and application. This is rightly taken to mark a greater orderliness, an acceptance of the executive discretion of management within defined limits, and a greater understanding of the dependence of wage advances on the profitability of the firm, than have been found at all widely in the UK. Yet a major study of 'the impact of collective bargaining on management'[5] records many and varied instances of the restrictive practices enforced by American unions in the supposed interest of job security. Drivers have been prohibited from helping to unload their trucks. Electrical equipment delivered on the building site already wired has had to be rewired there. In the textile mills of the north-east limits on the number of machines a worker might operate promoted the shift of the industry to the south. Painters used to forbid the use of the spray gun. Musicians' unions required the use of an orchestra of minimum size, or the hiring of a stand-by orchestra when a visiting orchestra was engaged. Some make-work practices mark the resistance of labour to technical innovation in an old-established industry, or its attempt to hold on to employment in a declining industry; but the unions have also inserted restrictive practices in the employment contracts negotiated for the supermarkets:[6] the use of part-timers is limited, all meat preparation must be done at the store, and each warehouseman must handle only certain products. All in all, there may well be differences between American and British trade unionism in the extent of such practices, but there is no contrast in kind.

Nor, in the changed climate of the post-war years, has there been any contrast in the use of trade union power to exert a persistent upward presure on wages. We have seen how early the significance of that changed climate and the possibility of 'cost push' were seized on by one experienced observer of the American labour market.

2

In all these ways, from its earliest phase down to the present day, American trade unionism has been markedly similar to British. Yet its history has also been shot through with differences no less striking.

The early American unions, to begin with, never lasted long. None of those founded in the first half of the nineteenth century survives today: the oldest of contemporary unions, now the International Typographical Union, was founded in 1852. Though a few national unions were formed in the 1850s and more in the 1860s, most of them collapsed in the long depression of the 1870s. What distinguishes American unionism in this respect is the shortness of its continuous history: stable unionism took hold only in the 1880s.

Unionization, moreover, has never gone so far in the United States as in Great Britain, or indeed in any of the Western industrialized democracies for which we have comparable figures of the density of trade union membership – we do not know about France. At the end of the surge of recruitment through the New Deal and the Second World War, about a third of all American wage- and salary-earners were unionized, but that proportion was a peak. Through the ensuing years the most highly unionized sector of the labour force, that in manufacturing, failed to grow, but unionism made only slow and partial advances in the expanding service industries and white-collar occupations. So it came about that by 1975 trade unionists amounted to only a quarter of all American employees. About that time the corresponding proportion in Great Britain was nearly a half; in Canada it was over a third; in Australia over a half; and in Scandinavia from 60 to 87 per cent.[7]

American unionism in the present century has also been distinguished by its being business unionism. If its members have had social purposes beyond the improvement of the terms and conditions of their employment, they have not sought to advance them through a trade union movement. Nor did the unions form a labour movement or launch a Labour Party. They have found more support for their own particular concerns in the Democratic than in the Republican Party, and have endorsed Democratic candidates for the Presidency, but they have entered into no formal alliance with any party. This poses the question of why the British unions, whose relation with the political parties of the day used to be similar, should have entered subsequently on a different course.

There is a contrast also in organization for collective bargaining. We have seen how the British trade unions gained recognition and bargaining rights mainly over against associations of employers: only in recent years have agreements in substantial numbers been negotiated by single employers. In the United States also there have been some multi-employer negotiating units, in industries where excess capacity led to the formation of cartels, or where a number of highly competitive firms were operating close to one another in the same region. But by far the greater number of American negotiations take place firm by firm, and the plant contract is the typical form of the American collective agreement. In large-scale industry there will typically be a contract at company level with plant or local supplemental agreements. There may be several such agreements, each covering a given set of occupations in its own bargaining unit, which has been established or certified by the National Labor Relations Board. In each unit one and only one union can and does act as the bargaining representative. Thus though the workers in one plant may belong to different unions, there can usually be no rivalry between the unions in the representation of the workers, or instability in the arrangements for bargaining – within each bargaining unit the employer has to deal with only one union, whereas the British employer may have to deal with a dozen or more. But it is also the case in the US that where different crafts work side by side, as in construction and parts of the metal trades, their separate unions may be associated for collective bargaining.

The last salient difference between the unionisms of the two countries lies in their treatment of agreements. For British trade unionists the agreement is a note of the parties' intention to take certain steps and apply certain rules in the course of their ongoing relations. Those relations remain those of negotiation, and questions arising during the currency of an agreement, whether of interpretation, or application to new circumstances, or outright variation, will all be negotiable. They will therefore be subject to the ultimate sanction of a strike. The American unions, on the other hand, distinguish between the disputes of interest that arise when an agreement is to be negotiated, and the disputes of right that arise after the agreement has been signed and the question is how it is be interpreted and applied. What terms shall go into the agreement is a matter to be decided by bargaining and bargaining power; but the signed agreement is a contract, and most agreements provide for a dispute over application to be decided ultimately by arbitration, as the final step in a private grievance procedure which is laid down in the agreement. Employer and union alike are strictly bound by the terms of the detailed contract, thus construed legally. The 'no-strike' obligation that rests upon the union is only part of this construction.

Another consequence of the legal construction of the American contract is that it runs for a fixed term. The British agreement, by contrast, only marks a stage in a continuing process; its application is subject to subsequent negotiation; either party may at any time give notice to change it. In 1976 less than 5 per cent of American agreements covering 1,000 workers or more were for less than two years, and nearly 70 per cent, with almost the same proportion of the workers, were for three years or more.[8] This meant that American management was assured of freedom from strikes – short of 'wildcats' – for such periods: British management enjoyed no such assurance. It also meant that in the American firms the movement of pay by scheduled annual increases, improvement factors, or indexation was fixed and known in advance for those years, whereas in the British the movement was subject to the uncertainty and stresses of renegotiation from time to time.

3

In these ways the common impulses towards unionism in the two countries have been deflected. We have seen how strong and persistent those impulses were; but their workings diverged through differences of circumstance, tradition, and structure. Finding features of the setting that can be linked with what is distinctive in the American outcome will direct attention to the presence or absence of counterparts in the UK. This will throw into relief the operation of factors whose impact on British trade unionism has been overlooked because they have been taken for granted as part of the British scene. Laying rough hands on history, we can group the sources of divergence under four heads.

(1) There are first those features of the American setting that have exerted a strong influence on trade union development – actually, to check it – and that are objective *matters of circumstance*. There is the vast size of the American continent, and the difficulty of movement through the length and breadth of the settled regions even after the building of the railroads. By the 1850s, the completion of the main railway lines and the telegraph system in the UK made it possible for a union official to be summoned from his head office and reach a branch that was in trouble in an industrial district almost anywhere in the country within the day. When the TUC was founded in 1868 it was possible for delegates from all over the country to reach the place of assembly by a journey not too costly in time or money. A small island in which communications were easy and early developed facilitated

the early development of the national trade union and of a trade union movement.

In the United States that sort of consolidation was also checked by the arrival from the 1840s onwards of waves of immigrants, various in provenance and language, who soon provided the bulk of unskilled and semi-skilled industrial labour. After the Civil War the emancipated Negroes entered employment. Ethnic division promoted unionization where workers of the same national origin monopolized a particular craft in the building industry, but it inhibited the organization of the unskilled. We realize by contrast the significance of the comparative homogeneity of the British labour force.

A third circumstance inimical to trade union development in the US was the great severity of slumps there. British trade unions suffered badly enough in the depressions of 1839–42 and 1878–9 – the latter, said the Webbs, 'swept . . . many hundreds of trade societies into oblivion . . . In some districts, such as South Wales, Trade Unionism practically ceased to exist.'⁹ But this last was a depression of exceptional severity for the UK. In the US depressions were more often sharp and deep. The upturn soon followed, but by then much incipient unionism had been destroyed. The extinction of organization during a depression, whether through the breaking of strikes or simply the collapse of membership, was well known in the UK, but in the USA it was more devastating. This was not only the effect of the greater severity of the depressions: there was also a difference in the tenacity of union membership. A union gave its members a strong inducement to maintain their membership if it provided benefits as a friendly society, reduced or waived the dues of members out of work, and actually paid unemployment benefit. The American unions that took hold in the 1880s and built up funds for these purposes then were helped thereby to survive the deep depression of the 1890s. But long before that British trade unions had been meeting wage-earners' felt need for mutual insurance – indeed friendly society and trade union were sometimes fused at their origin. One reason for the difference may have lain in the individualism and willingness to chance his arm of the American worker, whereas the British worker was more concerned with security. This difference of attitudes is a basic source of divergence in development, to which we shall recur.

(2) But first we must notice a difference in *attitudes among employers*. It appears in their propensity to compete with one another in the product market, and to combine with one another against trade unions in the labour market. In a word, the American employers were highly competitive, and generally price-competitive, as sellers, but were ready to combine not for collective bargaining but for offensives against trade unions: British employers avoided competition by obser-

ving the rule of live and let live among themselves, but could seldom be
got to combine with each other for any purpose other than collective
bargaining. Salient exceptions to both these generalizations spring to
the mind: in the 1880s American industry semed dominated by a
movement towards monopoly, and there were sections of British
industry that were subject to foreign competition or the movements of
prices in international markets. But at the times when unions were
making their first pressure felt, a predominant difference appeared in
the reaction of employers in the two countries. In the land of pro-
claimed equality, the employers counter-attacked, individually and in
combination. In the land of social hierarchy, though resistance sometimes went over into counter-attack, the employers did not sustain
militant combinations, and quite widely they came to accept trade
unions and even welcome their performance of defined functions.

That the American employers took the line they did may be
explained by market forces and by attitudes. In the early stages of
industrialization, with producers and consumers scattered in small
towns over great distances, the employer who wanted to develop
output on any scale was dependent on the merchant capitalist for his
materials and his sales outlets. But it was more likely that one merchant
could draw on various suppliers, than that one supplier had access to
various merchants: a supplier generally had to take the price negotiated with, and held down by, his own merchant. As American manufacturing grew up, moreover, it had to meet the competition of imports
from the more developed European industry. It met that competition
by an expedient that intensified domestic competition: instead of
tempting the consumer by variety, it produced a plain, standardized
article capable of mass production and sold on price. These facts of the
market all meant that the selling price of the employer's product was
held down: he was not in the comfortable position of being able to
negotiate a rise in wages that he could cover by a rise in the selling price
without loss of business.

But competitiveness is also a matter of attitude – of the will to
compete and the expectation that others will be competitive. In a
spatially mobile society there was no time for settled and neighbourly
relations to grow up, such as lend themselves to tacit market-sharing.
The American historian Gary Nash has shown how already in the first
half of the eighteenth century in the north-eastern colonies, the impact
of the wars and inflation, with the profits of trade and military contracting, had broken down the traditional values of a hierarchical and
collective society, to clear the way for those of an individualist and
market economy.[10] This change of attitude took place earlier and
seems to have been far more thoroughgoing than any such in the UK.
When later the immigrants came from Europe we may expect that

many will have harmonized with it, either because they themselves were self-selected for individualism and initiative, or because these values furthered their assimilation. Employers imbued with it will have felt genuine resentment against the obstruction of their enterprise by combinations. When these tried to restrict the workers' output of effort they appeared as basically un-American. The very egalitarianism of the social creed, moreover, made it natural to deal roughly with trade unionists: the employer was not restrained by any sense of responsibility laid upon him by his own position in the community – he had no compunction about bringing his relations with employees down to 'the cash nexus', for they were not '*his*' people, he dealt with them on a business basis, and if they formed a price ring against him no obligation of benevolence inhibited his vigour in breaking it.

Reflection on these sources of American opposition to trade unionism makes the British observer realize how comparatively uncompetitive British employers have been. Here again we may distinguish facts of the market from attitudes. The British industries which took a technical lead over other countries in the Industrial Revolution gained a sheltered market – for the time being the world did indeed 'beat a path to their door', and their sales were not closely dependent on price. The final consumer at home and abroad remained accustomed to diversity in the product – standardization at that level was to be an American development – and a maker's particular design or specification attached customers to him. Manufacturers and distributors valued their independence and believed in competitition, but in competition under well-understood if unwritten rules: they disliked price-cutting. They could therefore welcome collective bargaining in so far as 'it set a floor under competition'; and they were willing to associate for that purpose. Out of this willingness came that acceptance of the trade union in Victorian society which we have already remarked. But it now appears that this acceptance did not depend solely upon factors of social cohesion: a necessary condition was the absence of external competitive pressure on the selling prices of the employers concerned. Where that pressure impinged – shipping and the exporting coal-fields were notable examples – employers were actively hostile to unionism, or arrangements for bargaining were unstable and strife was endemic. The difference between the British employers whose approach to industrial relations would generally be evaluated in later years as humane and constructive, and those who would be judged harsh and reactionary, may have lain largely in the market situations of their businesses. Certainly their personal attitudes also differed: but those attitudes were selected by the type of business that attracted them and hardened by the pressures that it exerted on them.

Competitiveness was not only a matter of shelter and exposure in the market, but also depended on the sheer pace of change. The bursts of industrial development in the US in the years after the Civil War were more rapid by far than the contemporary growth of British industry. American employers were not able to develop codes of respect for the vested interests of a labour force that they had to be able to redeploy and hire and fire from day to day as the changing setting of menace and opportunity demanded. British employers, subject for the most part to less urgent pressures and more gradual transitions, could enter into agreements with trade unions, and individually respect their men's working practices, without fear of losing their markets over-night to innovating or invading competitors.

But if British employers predominantly were not competitive, they were also not generally willing to combine in a counter-offensive against the unions. This is not paradoxical, if we regard their refraining from aggressive competition as a tacit agreement to safeguard one another's independence. We must suppose that they set a high value on this: at any rate, most of them were in fact prepared to risk some rough treatment at the hands of the unions rather than make the sacrifice of autonomy necessary if an employers' association capable of an effec-tive counter-offensive was to be formed. It is true that the engineering employers under Colonel Dyer had formed an association of that kind in 1897 and, it was alleged, used the threats of boycott to bring hesitant firms into membership. But the effort was not sustained, and the example was not followed at all widely – there was nothing here to match the American employers' reaction to the power of the unions as that was revealed by the anthracite coal strike of 1902, or the Swedish employers' reaction to the political general strike in that same year, or the German employers' use of the mass lock-out at that time. To do that meant not only contributing to common funds but conducting one's own industrial relations according to the directions of the execu-tive of the association – locking one's own work-people out, it might be, when one had no quarrel with them. For most British employers the gain from united action needed to be unmistakably great to warrant that. But another thought also held them back – they had no stomach for a fight into which they would have gone with no easy conscience.

This was so because the social norms in which they had been raised and which were generally held around them were not consonant with it. The comparison with American employers in this respect makes us aware of how gradual and incomplete the movement has been in the UK away from the values of a pre-industrial society. Political eminence and social prestige long continued to be linked with landowning. Self-made men built up businesses, but the values of the country gentleman entered the second or third generations of his family. 'The promoted workman makes a hard master', but the employer who held a superior status in a society in which recognized obligations attached to rank was also more likely to act paternally. There was a conflict between the hard bargaining required of the businessman and the benevolence required of the men of standing in the community. Under American egalitarianism the hard bargaining came about naturally between the parties negotiating a contract; but in a still hierarchical society there was a dissonance between haggling and what were felt to be the proper relations of mutual support and respect between ranks. An employer was largely relieved of this embarrassment when he joined with other employers to share the responsibility for negotiation.

What has just been written would not hold of many a small employer, or of the first generation employer, the 'self-made man', however big the business he had built up. But at the same time when trade unionism was taking hold in the United States, from the 1880s onwards, many British employers in family businesses were of the second and third generations, or if they were professional managers they controlled long-established concerns. In the early days of British trade unionism the employer had often been what many American employers remained at the end of the century, a man making a start in business. These employers of the first generation watched every penny because they needed to plough every penny back; they worked with intensity themselves, and turned fiercely on any who seemed bent on hampering them. They might form a warlike alliance to crush a union when it first tried to deny them the right to be masters in their own shops. But the British employers typified here were not under such internal and external pressure: they were not temperamentally so intolerant of those who were not willing to work unreservedly, their cash flow did not give them so much concern, and they felt assured of a market share. These characteristics were squeezed out of some employers by foreign competition, and by particular difficulties that afflicted others like the railway companies. But they persisted over a wide area, and they facilitated the acceptance of trade unionism as part of the social as well as the industrial structure.

(3) *The outlook of the American worker* was distinctive. A person's outlook comprises the categories in which he orders his observations, and the rewards and achievements that he expects of life. By the time of the Revolution the outlook of the American worker was distinguished from that of the British in two closely related ways: he saw equal citizenship as the evident and actual organizing principle of his society, and his energies and aspirations were predominantly those of an individualist in a land of opportunity.

The notion of citizenship was given actuality by the discussion and adoption of the constitutions of the states, after the Revolution, and then by the decisions of some states to give the vote to all adult men –

Pennsylvania did so in 1790, Massachusetts in 1820, New York in
1822. It seemed at first as if working men would use the vote to set up
their own party. What they wanted was to limit the working-day and
to extend free education. But these aims were taken over by existing
parties. The absence of political separation emphasized the equality of
citizenship.

We have cited one American historian for the experience that broke
down the notion of social order based on hierarchy in the north-
eastern colonies. His discussion, and perhaps the impacts he studies,
are largely confined to the one region. Another historian found a
source of the same change in a factor of wider, indeed continental
influence – the opening of vast spaces at the feet of the immigrant.
Bernard Bailyn has written:

The great social shocks that in the French and Russian Revolutions sent the
foundations of thousands of individual lives crashing into ruins had taken
place in America in the course of the previous century, slowly, silently, almost
imperceptibly, not as a sudden avalanche but as myriads of individual
changes and adjustments which had gradually transformed the order of
society. By 1763 the great landmarks of European life – the church and the
idea of orthodoxy, the state and the idea of authority: much of the array of
institutions and ideas that buttressed the society of the *ancien régime* – had
faded in their exposure to the open, wilderness environment of America.[11]

In the society that had been dissolved and reconstituted in this way
there were great objective differences in wealth and power; but in
men's self-respect and their perception of their place among their
fellows there was a felt equality. Clashes of interest occurred, and
interest groups formed for a time in particular conjunctures; but they
lacked the sense of identity, the continuity of motivation, and the
capacity for collective action, provided by class.

British wage-earners, on the other hand, continued to live in a
society whose traditional reliance upon rank for its stability was
modified as time went on in its restrictive application to the lower
orders, but was never broken down. It is a significant indication that
not until 1867 was the law changed by which breach of contract by the
employer – 'the master' – was subject only to civil proceedings,
whereas a breach by the employee – 'the servant' – rendered him liable
to prosecution and imprisonment. As Kahn-Freund observed (though
in a somewhat different context), 'if the obligation to serve arises from
a status, it is consistent to enforce it through the mechanism of the
criminal law'.[12] The wage-earners equally perceived security as struc-
tural by status. They saw that the pattern of most men's lives was
decided by their birth. That they were poorer than others was linked
with their enjoying less esteem in others' eyes and their own, and

participating less in the exercise of influence and power in public affairs. The upshot, in a word, was that they formed a class: a word that signifies far more, in cohesion and purpose, than a mere grouping of those with common characteristics. What is more, they were the *working* class: the very term, with its implied contrast with the leisured class, raised the issue of social justice. Inherently they formed a movement. Their outlook stands out by contrast with the equality of citizenship and the parity of esteem that had followed on the attrition of traditional structures in a New World, where every man had had to make his way by his own exertions.

The second distinctive characteristic of the American worker was his individualism. In the initial emigration there must have been selection of the bolder temperaments, and once on shore the newcomer had always the gleam of opportunity before him to beckon him on. But more than that, the freedom that so many had come expressly to find in America was conceived of as rooted in the rights of man: the Constitution safeguarded the freedom of the individual, and the courts would invalidate encroachments upon it, whether these were made by combinations formed for mutual protection, or legislatures thinking to promote social welfare. This did not conflict with much of the experience of the working population that spread across a continent in a rapidly developing economy: there were deserts to traverse and savage reverses of fortune to sustain, but many a life history showed that the returns from hard work and enterprise could be bountiful, and the standard of living generally attained was the highest in the world. That America was uniquely a land of opportunity for the common man became a settled belief. This belief has proved robust. It has persisted with a myth's invulnerability to fact. As the open lands filled up, and the cities grew, and an ever greater part of the working population came to be employed in large factories and offices, the paths of advancement did not open so conspicuously freely as before at the feet of the entrant to employment. Generally it has been found that the prospect of personal advancement is a great inhibitor of unionism: when it is removed people try alternatively to improve their lot by acting in combination. In the same way but even more so, widespread unemployment breaks people's faith in their ability to protect themselves, let alone advance themselves, by their own efforts. We should expect both kinds of change to promote unionization, but though they did so in the United States, it was always against the grain of the native timber. The worker's circumstances changed more than his outlook. There is a clash between the trade unionist's dependence on the support of his fellows and the self-reliant American's confidence in his ability to make his own way in a country that, he believes, more than any other gives him the chance to succeed.

That the belief is not borne out by available evidence does not make it less powerful. In recent years the collation of statistics of social mobility indicated that the rate at which the sons of fathers in the lower socio-economic levels themselves attain the upper levels is not in fact higher in the United States than in other Western countries. The finding came as a shock to American observers; was America then not 'the land of opportunity', in contrast with class-ridden Europe, after all? Two sociologists who took the question up stressed 'the persistence of ... equalitarian ideology in the face of facts which contradict it'. This ideology is an active force. 'It enables the person of humble birth to regard mobility as an attainable goal, for himself or for his children. It facilitates his acceptance as an equal, if he succeeds in rising socially and economically.' Hence an equalitarianism of manners which has worked against what the authors call 'the ideological hardening of interest-groups and status groups' – that is, their becoming a common cause, a movement. 'Surely, this has not diminished the differences themselves, but it has helped to make the representation of collective interests a thing apart from the intellectual life of the society.' [13] In practical terms, collective bargaining has been a matter of negotiating a business contract between parties not set apart by class orientation. If that is too sweeping a generalization to cover the struggles for organization and recognition in the giant corporations under the New Deal and in the South today, it seizes none the less on a distinctive aspect of American industrial relations.

For typically American unionism has been business unionism. Sumner Slichter and his associates at Harvard explained this by the individualism of both employers and workers:

The American environment has produced strongly individualistic and highly competitive employers who have been aggressively hostile to unions and who have been willing to go to great extremes in order to destroy them. In addition, the labour force in the United States is composed of strongly individualistic persons who have different racial and cultural backgrounds and who are keenly interested in getting ahead. These influences have produced business unionism – that is unionism which has little or no interest in social reforms, but which is frankly out to advance the selfish aims of its members.

The sense of equality in citizenship and the spirit of individualism formed the lens through which the American worker perceived the inequalities of wealth. The fact of these inequalities was unmistakable, as likewise of the power that wealth confers. That power might have to be opposed, but it was not necessarily illegitimate. It was not founded on privilege. Equality was believed in not as equality of condition but as equality of opportunity. Here was a society, men believed, in which the pursuit of riches was open to all. The society was so constituted that those who won its prizes generally owed their success to their personal qualities. Great inequalities were little resented.

The British observer has fresh insights into his own country to gain from these aspects of the American outlook. For one thing, when the American sociologists stress 'the persistence of ... equalitarian ideology in the face of facts which contradict it' they are dealing with the power of a myth: British trade unionism likewise has its myths. In this sense a myth is an account of past happenings that epitomizes and inculcates a certain interpretation of contemporary affairs; it reinforces and energizes a certain approach to them. The happenings may be actual: though the term 'mythical' is sometimes used in contrast with 'historical', the functions of the myth can be served perfectly well by rehearsing events that have actually occurred – indeed specially well, because it is essential that the myth be believed. That the rehearsal is dramatic and the viewpoint partisan is another matter. British trade unionism in this way has been concerned to keep alive and propagate the memory of the struggles and martyrdoms of its early years. The story can be told of many a tight-fisted employer or hard-faced magistrate, of the dragoons riding down the pickets that were striving to keep out imported blacklegs, of the judges repeatedly forging fresh shackles for humble men only seeking to protect the barest livelihoods of their wives and children. The TUC has held annual meetings at Tolpuddle to commemorate the sentencing to transportation of the farm workers convicted of taking illegal oaths when they formed a union there in 1834. 'He who forgets his history sleeps in the gutter of slavery' declared Neil Kinnock MP in the Miners' Institute at Blackwood in South Wales at an annual rally organized to commemorate the march of the working men on Newport in November 1839 to demand the release of a Chartist leader – twelve of them were killed, three were transported to Tasmania.[15] This was a political rally, commemorating a movement whose formal objects were political, but it illustrates the part purposefully assigned in the Labour movement to the myth as it has been defined here. With the force of drama it convinces the British trade unionist that he is inherently liable to oppression and exploitation, and that the working class is engaged in a continuing struggle to defend and advance itself.

The obvious requirement for that struggle was and is solidarity. The British wage-earner thought to better himself by standing shoulder to shoulder with his fellows, not by getting ahead of them. Perhaps this propensity to combine has been a characteristic of British society at all levels: so at least it seemed to Otto Kahn-Freund, who had most of a life-time's acquaintance with British legal and labour institutions but yet had the advantage as an observer of having approached them after a training in another country.

The identification of the worker with his union [he said], the intense corporate consciousness of the union members, their readiness to fight for their particular corporate body, all this too is part of a national heritage, an outstanding characteristic of British society . . . Where else in the world do you find this intensive 'we' feeling towards organized and traditional social groups, schools and colleges, clubs and trade unions, that is regarded as a matter of course in this country?[16]

It may be that this cohesivness is a characteristic distinguishing the British even from their European neighbours. But there was in any case one powerful influence at work in the nineteenth century to make British workers collectivist where Americans were individualist – the balance of population and natural resources. About 1870 the total working population of the United States had only recently overtaken that of Great Britain: both were in the region of 12 millions. Here were two working populations of very nearly the same size, that of Great Britain in an island where London was separated by only 370 miles from Edinburgh, and by 170 from Exeter, that of the United States in a continent 2,500 miles across from east to west, with 1,400 miles between the Canadian border and the Gulf of Mexico. Each year's births, moreover, were bringing many newcomers on the British scene – by the end of the century the working population would have increased by nearly a half. These newcomers could not have had a sense of opportunity opening before them, of places waiting to be taken up. Their apprehension must have been of congestion and the difficulty of finding a place: they would rate the dangers of competition above any prizes it offered; they would feel the need to defend jobs once obtained, and react passionately against the temptation to undercut.

In this difference of openings and opportunities lies the origin of a difference of attitudes on the shop-floor. Though we have pointed to restrictive practice and make-work rules as being familiar in American trade unionism, they have not attained the same extension there, nor been defended with the same tenacity as in the UK. Though cyclical unemployment in the US has been severe, and the unemployment of the great depression of the 1930s was even worse there than in the UK, American trade unionists have not given job protection the same high priority as the British. They have therefore been less resistant to innovation. Their assumption that new jobs would always be opening up has been too strongly inbuilt.

(4) *The attitude of the American worker towards the law* was formed by a distinctive characteristic of American society. Manifestations of individual lawlessness may mislead European observers, whose attention they distract from the basis of social cohesion. This is in any case unfamiliar to them. American society rests

on a basic respect for the law in a form to which there is no counterpart in more traditional societies.

This respect was linked with citizenship itself when the Union and the states set themselves up by written constitutions, and entrusted judges with the task of interpreting and upholding them. The ultimate bond of society was forged in the law. In traditional societies, on the other hand, where the trappings of sovereignty came down from antiquity, the bond of society was visible in the sway of grandeur. Working men did not ask whence the law drew its authority: sufficient that it was imposed from above, by 'the strong arm of the law'. Their obligation to obey was laid on them by the exertion of power, and the infliction of pains and penalties on the transgressor. Blackstone defined law in its most general sense as a rule of action which is 'prescribed by some superior and which the inferior is bound to obey'; and the law of the land was 'a rule of civil conduct prescribed by the supreme power in a state'. In Blackstone's scheme of things, it is true, there was room for some democratic participation in the exercise of power, but only under the checks and balances of the equal participation of aristocracy and monarchy. The essential was that in every form of government the law must issue from 'a supreme, irresistible, absolute, uncontrolled, authority'.[17] But from the Revolution onwards the enfranchised American would not have seen the legislature as set so far away from and above himself. The law arose out of the compact in which he had joined to set up the state. His obligation to obey was self-imposed. The law was part of the fabric of his democratic freedom. His acceptance of the rule of law was a corollary of his citizenship.

It must ultimately be for this reason that American trade unions have not claimed, as British trade unions have done, that they should be allowed to operate informally, outside the law. That they have not done so is to the foreign observer the more remarkable because they have suffered heavy and repeated blows from the law, and certainly they have conducted long campaigns against hostile legislation and practices of the courts. They grew up with the law against them from the first. Individualism was enshrined in the Constitution, and the legal presumption against combination was stronger even than in the tradition of the British common law, though that too was widely received. Both at Federal level and within the states the courts could and did nullify as unconstitutional legislation that had been intended to protect labour. The state courts, and the appointment of judges to them, were often neighbourhood affairs in the early days; local employers seeking injunctions against trade union activity found a ready response. The willingness of the courts to grant injunctions provided a major weapon against the rise of national unions from the 1880s onwards; the clause of the Clayton Act of 1914 that was thought to have relieved unions from the injunction was soon proved to be only sounding brass; not till the Norris–La Guardia Act of 1932 was the relief effective. These were issues that constantly engaged the AFL and the state federations of labour, in a struggle against the repressive action of legislatures and courts. To this day the unions continue to oppose the 'Right to Work' laws that some twenty states have enacted: these are laws that ban provisions in agreements making union membership a condition of employment. Yet these campaigns have never extended to a claim that industrial relations are best left unregulated. Unlike the British trade unionists, the Americans have never taken up a stance of hostility to the rule of law as such in their affairs. They have accepted the regulation of jurisdiction and bargaining units by the National Labor Relations Board based on the Wagner Act of 1935; the outlawing of 'unfair labor practices' by the Taft–Hartley Act of 1947; and the inspection of their internal administration, under the Landrum–Griffin Act of 1959.

If this acceptance has never been whole-hearted, neither has the rule of law always been observed in practice. Union leaders have defied injunctions, and made an electoral asset of their prison sentences. Strikes in the public sector are unlawful but commonplace. Clashes with the police in the course of industrial disputes have been violent. The sit-in strikes by which the CIO fought its way into industry were unlawful. Yet, by contrast with Great Britain, there still is acceptance. At least there is no repudiation of the law as of its nature an instrument of repression. This cannot be ascribed simply to the whole original purpose of the Wagner Act having been to encourage collective bargaining; or to the unions' lack of political muscle since the Second World War. It rests upon a sense of the formation of law by common consent in a society created by men born free and equal.

At the time when British trade unions were growing up most British wage-earners had no vote in the elections to Parliament where laws were made. Magistrates were men of property, and they included some employers. The legal system – both the statutes and the judicial machinery – had been intended to secure to each person what was due to him in his place in the social order; but now while the protective parts of that system had ceased to function, the coercive remained. Under the pressure of the rapid growth of population and the industrial revolution, British working people came into repeated and sometimes bloody conflict with the law. They concluded that they must gain entry to Parliament where the laws were made: hence the Chartist movement. Its essential aim, of manhood suffrage, was eventually attained by stages, the last in 1918. But the Chartists' outlook remained imprinted on the minds of their successors in the trade unions, even though they were now enfranchised: the law appeared as inherently biased against trade unionists by its origins in the legislature and the social type of those who administered it. 'Of course we ought to obey the law', one trade unionist said in all good faith about the Industrial Relations Act of 1971, 'but not a Tory law.' The forebears of British trade unionists had passed through no demolition of the hierarchical order of society as their American contemporaries had done. Whereas from the Revolution onwards the law in the United States was set over against the executive arm of government, and upheld the freedom of the citizen, the British working man must have seen the law as an instrument with which government disciplined the lower orders of society. The liberties for which British trade unionists struggled were to be won by throwing off the shackles of the law. It became an article of faith that trade unions must be allowed to operate informally, in a legal vacuum.

A price that British trade unions have paid is a lack of legal backing. In the United States it has been otherwise for the last fifty years. The National Industrial Recovery Act of 1933 laid down, as part of its code of fair competition, the right of employees to organize and bargain collectively. When this Act was declared unconstitutional, the Wagner Act of 1935 reaffirmed (Section 7) that 'employees shall have the right to self-organization, to form, join, or assist labor organizations, to bargain through representatives of their own choosing, and to engage in concerted activities, for the purpose of collective bargaining or other mutual aid or protection.' The Act laid a corresponding obligation upon employers: Section 8 declared that 'it shall be an unfair labor practice for an employer to refuse to bargain collectively with representatives of his employees'. No such positive affirmation of rights and duties was so much as sought by the British trade unions: it did not lie within their view of their relations with the law. The unions of manual workers had very generally gained recognition by their ability to strike in the works of employers who refused it, and also through the employers' increasing acceptance of it as normal procedure. But the same employers were often far from accepting the unionization of their white-collared staff after the Second World War, and refused negotiation. This led the Donovan Commission to recommend in 1968 that an Industrial Relations Commission should be charged with investigating claims to recognition; and if an employer failed to negotiate in good faith with the union that the Commission had designated as entitled to recognition, the union would be entitled to take him to arbitration, and the award would be legally enforceable against him. In drafting the Industrial Relations Act of 1971 the Conservative lawyers kept closer to the American pattern, but laid no general obligation of recognition on employers as the Wagner Act had done. The relevant provisions were in any case repealed with the Act in 1974. Instead, the Employment Protection Act of 1975 set up procedure on Donovan lines. But British trade unions have never received the backing against recalcitrant employers that the courts have given American unions since 1935. Even under the Act of 1975 the British unions continue to rely basically upon voluntarism. The successful resistance of the employer at Grunwick showed that the procedure under the Act can be stulified when the body charged with investigation of claims is denied voluntary co-operation.

There remains one outcome of American respect for the law that has been much admired in the UK. American unions treat collective agreements as legally binding contracts, and with rare exceptions honour no-strike clauses and agree to take disputes about the application of agreements to arbitration throughout the two, or more often three, years for which the agreements run. We have seen how this comes about. Because of the forces that make American unionism predominantly business unionism, and because the relations between the negotiators of the agreement are not tinged by the resentments, aspirations, insecurity, and sense of obligation associated with differences of social status, the agreement that emerges naturally presents itself as a contract. Each party values the legal sanctions against breach of contract as a means of holding the other to his undertaking. In keeping with these attitudes the Taft–Hartley Act provides, Section 301 (a), that 'suits for violation of contracts between an employer and a labor organization . . . may be brought in any district court of the United States having jurisdiction of the parties'. Employers in fact rarely sue the union local for damages. What the legal status of the contract does in practice is to license the employer to take disciplinary action – including suspension and dismissal – against particular employees who violate the terms of the contract, for example by walking out in a wildcat strike instead of following the prescribed grievance procedure. The possibility of the employer's doing this provides the national officers of the union with a threat to bring a truculent local into line.

The British negotiator, on the other hand, is dealing with a relationship in which the transition 'from status to contract' is still unfinished in men's minds. Much in the terms and conditions of employment remains unwritten. Custom and practice play a large part. The function of negotiation and of the agreement reached at any one time is to intervene in a complex and living system at one point, or impose some general inflection on its course, but not to control it in detail. The American contract is commonly lengthy and detailed; its hundreds of carefully drafted clauses cover every aspect of the working life – the wage structure, the working practices, the disciplinary procedure, the rules for promotion, redundancy, retirement, and much more. But the British collective agreement until recently has been far simpler. It has provided a note of the parties' intentions in their ongoing dealings with one another; it has dealt with only part of what, should they go to law, would be held to constitute the agreed terms and conditions of employment. It consequently does not lend itself to legal interpretation, with recourse to arbitration, as the American plant contract does. Disputes arising about its application will naturally be treated in the same way as the other issues that arise from time to time – they will be subject to the continuing process of negotiation, and if negotiation breaks down there may be a strike.

The words 'until recently' a few lines above were needed because negotiations by establishment and plant in the private sector of the British economy were greatly extended during the 1970s. It would be natural that this change in the bargaining area should increase the coverage, detail, and precision of the written agreement. This would make possible the application for the first time to British collective bargaining of the distinction between disputes of rights and disputes of interests: the agreement would be full and clear enough in its conferment of rights for trade unions to be able to submit disputes under it to arbitration without impairing the bargaining power that they must be able to wield in disputes of interests. But the existence of such an agreement is only one condition for the use of arbitration in the American way: it is also necessary that bargaining be conceived as a periodic business deal and not as a continuing social struggle.

4

In discussing the sources of divergence between American and British trade unionism we have accounted as we went along for most of the differences that we noted at the outset, but a contrast between the bargaining structures of the two countries remains to be explained. This is the contrast between the American bargaining unit consisting of a single plant or a corporation, all the manual workers being represented by a single union, and the British unit consisting of an employers' association in negotiation with a grouping of the often numerous unions representing the manual workers of the member firms. That type of American bargaining unit is by no means the only one: there is also multi-unionism where the crafts have retained their jurisdiction. In the UK, again, we have seen that the multi-employer, multi-union unit has receded in importance since 1970, its place being taken by single-employer bargaining. But the bargaining units we have described were typical of the manufacturing of their countries for the quarter century after the Second World War, and the question is how this contrast in the numbers on both sides came about.

Single-employer bargaining in the US was the outcome basically of the independent spirit of the employers. Under anti-trust legislation there was a presumption against their being seen to associate with each other, even though their associating for the purpose of collective bargaining was explicitly exempted from illegality: but the more effective inhibition would have been unwillingness to surrender autonomy to competitors. There was also the factor of distance: where a number of small firms were concentrated in one region multi-employer negotiations did arise, but the giant plant separated by hundreds of miles from the next firm of the same kind was a natural labour market and bargaining unit on its own. Lloyd Ulman has shown also that multi-employer bargaining was initiated by the employers themselves in circumstances where excess capacity and inelastic demand had led to the formation of cartels, and in this setting the employers wished to eliminate differences in labour costs, especially undercutting by non-union firms.[18] But this use of a wage agreement as an indirect form of price maintenance was exceptional; markets and temperaments alike generally worked towards fragmentation. American businessmen had been willing to associate in order to attack trade unionism when it first menaced them; but not so as to enter into arrangements that would take so sensitive a part of their competitive position as the fixing of wages out of their own control.

We have seen that British employers were the other way about – they were less ready to combine for attack, more ready to combine for negotiation. Two factors in particular had promoted the dominance of multi-employer negotiations throughout British industry for fifty years after the First World War. One was the extent of regional concentration of particular industries. To have a number of firms of much the same size in the same industry and within a few miles of one another is a situation that called out for a joint negotiation and a common settlement: a strike that started in one works would soon spread if it were on an issue of general concern, and though the employers could and sometimes did still settle separately, they might well feel that when labour was roused there could be no effective settlement except on the same terms for all. Down to the First World War it was the region that was the predominant area of multi-employer bargaining. The impact of that War is the second factor to be noted as further differentiating British development from the American. As a means of controlling the rise of earnings during the War, agencies of government promoted the extension of multi-employer bargaining, widening existing coverage and setting up new ones. At the end of the War, National Joint Industrial Councils were established to provide the same 'machinery' for industries where it had not taken shape spontaneously, and again all employers throughout the industry were to be represented in the one negotiation at national level.

What seems merely a matter of structure and form was to have profound consequences for the substance and spirit of British industrial relations. Agreements at the 'national', that is the industry-wide level, must be very simple: they can deal only with the highest common factor of the terms and conditions of employment in a great number of jobs in a great number of firms. For many years in the vastly varied engineering industry the national agreement for adult manual workers dealt with changes in only four rates – skilled, intermediate, and unskilled males; and females. At first sight that appears to leave a wide field of discretion open to the management in each particular firm: the negotiable issues have been dealt with at the national level, and for the rest the manager is free to manage. But of course he is not free at all: he has to work within an unwritten but prescriptive code of custom and practice, and precisely because no detailed agreement on working practices has been concluded, his every action is liable to be challenged. The position of the American manager with a plant contract is very different. Many of the detailed provisions of that contract limit or deny his discretion. He may feel that the limits are oppressively close, or last too long before they can be renegotiated when circumstances change. But within the bounds so set his executive function is legitimized. It is linked, moreover, with the grievance procedure specified in the contract: the union concedes to the manager freedom to initiate change in return for the freedom to protest against it through a procedure which can generally be carried in the last resort to arbitration. 'Management moves and the union grieves.'

The manual workers of American firms in some industries, including construction, railroads, and printing, belong to different unions which have traditionally been organized by craft. But those unions waged an implacable struggle against other unions within the jurisdiction that each claimed for itself. There was little tendency to live and let live, or arrive at some understanding about recruitment or demarcation: on the contrary, the vindictive pursuit of dual unionism was for many years an animating principle of the AFL. The unions of the AFL, moreover, were more likely to insist on exclusive control of their jurisdiction because they were business unions, not much affected by broader sympathies of a labour movement such as might draw them into fraternal relations with other unions organizing parts of the same labour force: they feared that in their rivalry for recognition those other unions would undercut negotiated standards. But as for workers of all grades in manufacturing, their representation by a single union in each bargaining unit is an effect of the law: for the unionization of most of them goes back to the 1930s, and when the Wagner Act set up the National Labor Relations Board in 1935 it provided that the union winning an election when collective bargaining was newly established should be granted sole bargaining rights.

The plurality of unions to be found in many though not all British bargaining units derives firstly from the factors accounting for the formation of a number of different unions among the employees of the same industry, and for the willingness of those unions to share the representation of the employees in negotiation. It is natural for a number of different unions to be formed in a work-force when the movement is spontaneous and neighbourly, and the unions often have the characteristics of friendly societies. Much of their administration is performed by voluntary and largely unpaid officers, who do not have the same interest as the full-time salaried executive in expanding membership. In so far, again, as the members of a union see it as concerned with objects of social betterment, that is, as being part of a labour movement, they look on other unions as battalions of the same army, even when they recruit in the same field. They are correspondingly able to work with them for common purposes. Conflicts of jurisdiction of course there are, and accusations of poaching. Employers willing to enter into negotiating relations with unions have found themselves caught in the crossfire between unions who refuse to negotiate jointly. The Industrial Relations Act of 1971 provided a procedure by which, in cases of disputed recognition, an orderly settlement might be imposed, and this procedure owed much to the Wagner Act; but it perished with the Act that provided it. The TUC has its own Bridlington rules to regulate frontier conflict between unions. In the course of time the patchwork pattern of British trade unionism has been greatly simplified. But this unionism is still sharply contrasted with the American by the number and variety of unions that may be found taking part in one negotiation. One reflection this prompts concerns the remarkable ability of many different kinds of union to sustain themselves in the British social setting, over many years of varying economic fortunes.

5

Running through many of the differences we have been discussing are two notions of inequality. We may call them the American and the British, though the British probably extends through most of Europe. In the American notion there is room for differences of wealth and attainment of many kinds, but not of status. The essence of status is that it attracts esteem by reason of a position held in a hierarchical society. This position may be arrived at by birth, or it may be attained by personal exertion, but in either case it is the position itself that confers the title to esteem. In the American scheme of things, the wealth or other great attainments of those who have advanced themselves in any walk of life attract the admiration that is due to personal achievement, but there is no suggestion that the millionaire or the athletic champion are in any sense the social superior of the common man. In a hierarchical society, on the other hand, those who hold a certain rank are entitled to esteem without any personal achievement whatever; and they are set apart from inferiors by a social distance.

Because of this, social mobility is in one sense irrelevant to people's perception of equality in their society. It could be that in the American society the probability of the children of poor parents themselves attaining high incomes was low, and yet because persons of high and low income were not differentiated in esteem as belonging to higher or lower orders of society, people all felt that the society was egalitarian. A hierarchical society, on the other hand, might provide many opportunities for advancement from the lower to the higher ranks, and those making their way up might be readily accepted, while the children born to parents in the higher ranks who could not meet the occupational requirements of those ranks did in fact 'come down in the world', and yet the society would still appear as very far from egalitarian, and even as oppressive, to those who saw it from below.

To the two notions of inequality there correspond two attitudes towards betterment. In the American scheme of things, society imposes no obstacle to a person getting on in the world; the way of betterment is through individual exertion. But in the British setting, failure to get on may always be attributed to social barriers, and socialism teaches that the world cannot be made a better place for most people until the structure of society itself is basically changed. The American outlook inculcates self-reliance and competitiveness. But many a child growing up in the British setting absorbs the belief that few can rise above their parents' level by their own efforts. The lesson that the British child of the working class learns is that he should be loyal to his comrades, make common cause with them, and seek betterment through solidarity.

To the two notions of inequality there also correspond two views of collective bargaining. In the egalitarian outlook this appears as a matter of business, the negotiation of a contract; and the terms once being agreed, there can be no objection to disputed questions of application being submitted to arbitration. Where the negotiators are felt to be inherently divided by class, collective bargaining is far harder to characterize. At one extreme, the communist unions of the French CGT pronounce it simply a skirmish in the class war, refuse in principle to negotiate agreements, and if for tactical reasons they enter into any understanding with the employers, justify it as a mere truce. In the American scene, by exception, that was the way with the IWW, the 'Wobblies' of the Far West, though not with the United Mine Workers. British unionists really occupy an intermediate position; they are not committed to a fight to the finish against private enterprise, but they do feel, many of them, that they are taking part in the social campaign that divides 'us' from 'them'. The negotiations may be orderly, yet they are felt to be part of a continuing struggle. The obligation to observe the agreement may be accepted, but there can be no question of giving it the force of law: that would come too near to tying down a movement that should be always stirring when it can, and in any case the law and its enforcement have been in the hands of another class. It is intelligible that disputes following failure to agree have brought more violence in egalitarian America than in the British society where conflict is restrained by the neighbourly traditions of an hierarchical society.

The difference in the two outlooks may be traced to the impact on the Americans of the opening up of the continent in which they found themselves, and the great changes, economic and political, of the eighteenth century. The early colonies of the eastern seaboard were as hierarchical as the societies from which their people had been drawn, but a number of factors combined to break that structure up and loosen the hold of the traditional social order upon men's minds. We have already noted how Gary Nash has described the impact on the eastern cities of war and inflation in the first half of the century. His work shows

how the growth and commercial development of the northern seaport towns brought about multifaceted change involving the restructuring of social groups, the redistribution of wealth, the alteration of labour relations, the emergence of states of consciousness that cut horizontally through society, and the mobilization into political life of the lower ranks of labouring people. Haltingly it was recognized by many in the cities that the ligaments of the corporate society of the past had been torn in ways that struck at their opportunities, well-being, and sense that equity prevailed.[19]

We have drawn also on the work of Bernard Bailyn, and he has noted various factors that were breaking down the hierarchical order. There was always the opening to the West – the spaces of the wilderness, in which the pioneer escaped the constraints of settled society. Then Puritanism, with the evangelicalism of the mid-century, inherently stressed the equality of every soul within God's scheme of redemption or predestination. In colonial politics, what Bailyn calls 'the constant broil of petty factions' eroded respect for authority. In the great argument that led up to the Revolution a stress was laid on equality that flowed over from political to social equality. None the less, when Bailyn surveys the publicists and controversialists of that era, he finds that

Americans of 1760 continued to assume, as had their predecessors for generations before, that a healthy society was a hierarchical society, in which it was natural for some to be rich and some poor, some honored and some obscure, some powerful and some weak. And it was believed that superiority was unitary, that the attributes of the favored – wealth, wisdom, power – had a natural affinity to each other, and hence that political leadership would naturally rest in the hands of the social leaders.[20]

It was the Revolution and the turmoil of political debate following it that set the thought of equality flowing through men's minds everywhere – equality not merely in a constitutional or political sense, but in that full social sense in which it denies the existence or need for hierarchy and order as the framework of society and guarantee of social stability. There were some so-called loyalists, conservatives who had no thought of leaving the continent for the realm of King George, but who left for Canada rather than continue to live in a society where these egalitarian notions were taking hold. But take hold they did. Not many of those who received them had a wage-earner's view of society – perhaps not more than one in ten. It was in a setting of self-employment and petty proprietorship that the working population found what was to become known as the American way of life. When trade unions arose this was to set its distinctive mark upon them.

But British manual workers at that time were undergoing a different experience. The forms of employment were entering on a course of deep-going change; but the structure of society changed relatively little. Seen from below, it still presented the tiers of rank. A freeing of the market there was to be, but this did not foster a spirit of individualism among the workers. Rather, it saw the formation of the sense of identity in a working class.

Notes

[1] The numbers were 447,000 in 1897 and 2,687,000 in 1914 (Leo Wolman, *Ebb and Flow in Trade Unionism* (New York: National Bureau of Economic Research, 1936), Table 5, p. 16).

[2] B. R. Mitchell and P. Deane, *Abstract of British Historical Statistics*, (Cambridge, 1962), ch. II, Table 1.

[3] E. H. Phelps Brown and M. H. Browne, *A Century of Pay* (London, 1968), Table 9.

[4] Sidney and Beatrice Webb, *Industrial Democracy* (London, 1897), part II, ch. IV.

[5] Sumner H. Slichter, James J. Healy, and E. Robert Livernash, *The Impact of Collective Bargaining on Management* (Brookings Institution, Washington, DC, 1960).

[6] H. R. Northrup, *Restrictive Labor Practices in the Supermarket Industry* (University of Pennsylvania Press, 1967).

[7] G. S. Bain and R. Price, *Profiles of Union Growth* (Oxford, 1980).

[8] *Characteristics of Major Collective Bargaining Agreements*, 1 July 1976 (Bureau of Labor Statistics, Bulletin 2013, Washington, DC, Govt. Printing Office, 1979).

[9] Sidney and Beatrice Webb, *The History of Trade Unionism* (London, 1920 ed.), pp. 349–50.

[10] Gary B. Nash, *The Urban Crucible* (Harvard University Press, 1979).

[11] Bernard Bailyn, *The Ideological Origins of the American Revolution* (Harvard University Press, 1967) p. 19.

[12] Sir Otto Kahn-Freund, 'Blackstone's Neglected Child: the Contract of Employment', *Law Quarterly Review*, Oct. 1977, 522.

[13] Seymour Martin Lipset and Reinherd Bendix, 'Ideological Equalitarianism and Social Mobility in the United States', Transactions of the Second World Congress of Sociology, 1954, vol. II.

[14] S. H. Slichter, J. J. Healy, and E. R. Livernash, *Impact of Collective Bargaining*, pp. 34–5.

[15] *The Times*, 3 Nov. 1980.

[16] Sir Otto Kahn-Freund, *Labour Relations: Heritage and Adjustment* (Thank-offering to Britain Fund Lectures, 1978, Oxford University Press for the British Academy), p. 34.

[17] William Blackstone, *Commentaries on the Laws of England* (1765), Introduction, section II.

[18] Lloyd Ulman, *The Rise of the National Trade Union* (Harvard University Press, 1955), ch. 16.

[19] Gary B. Nash, *Urban Crucible*, p. 383.

[20] Bernard Bailyn, *American Revolution*, p. 302.

XIII

COMPARATIVE STUDIES: (ii) CANADIAN TRADE UNIONISM

CANADIAN trade unionism is distinguished by its tardy development. It had its beginnings and fresh starts in the same periods as trade unionism in the United States, and it sprang not only from native impulses but from the leadership of British immigrants who were already steeped in trade unionism when they arrived. Yet still at the outbreak of the Second World War the unions had no settled place in economy or polity. Firm by firm, they were often struggling for recognition: they had not yet established collective bargaining at all generally. They had not set up a single united national congress. Despite many proposals, they had not yet launched a labour party. Save for some transitory passages in the West, they had been ineffective over against government, federal and provincial: there was little in statute law to support them in their struggle for recognition and status. When on the outbreak of war in 1939 the Dominion Government engaged in the thoroughgoing planning of the war economy, it left them out.

Our purpose is to find reasons for what is distinctive in the development of Canadian trade unionism, and not to trace that development in its own right, but we must begin with an outline of it; discussion will follow. The outline will generally remain within anglophone Canada: the province of Quebec has been so far set apart by language and culture that its industrial relations form a separate story.

I

Early in the nineteenth century there were unions of craftsmen in St John's, New Brunswick, and in Halifax, Nova Scotia, as there were in the cities of the eastern seaboard of the USA – unions probably of that transitional kind in which the membership contains the occasional master as well as journeymen, and the purposes are as much those of a friendly society as of a bargaining unit; though the craftsmen of St

John's certainly did try to fix wages and hours, as appears from a repressive Act of 1816 which charged them with doing so. Craft unions of the nineteenth-century form appeared in the towns of Ontario in the 1830s and 1840s; but only one of these, a printers' union, survives to this day. These early unions, moreover, were no more than local. But wider organizations came in with the British Amalgamated Society of Engineers in the 1850s and the American Molders in the 1860s; and the Molders were followed by a number of other 'internationals', as the American unions that crossed the border were called. It was natural for those unions to try to organize Canadian craftsmen: Canadian wages ruled lower than American, and Canadian workers moving south without a union card were a potential source of undercutting. There were also American union members who moved north. This advance of the internationals was accompanied by a growth of local unions that continued until economic expansion reached its peak in 1873. At this time also there arose in some cities Trades Assemblies which like the Trades Councils of British cities brought representatives of the local trade unions together for mutual support in trade questions, and joint action in political and social questions. One of these latter questions was the Nine Hours Day. The campaign for this had spread from Great Britain; in the US the National Labor Union was demanding the Eight Hour Day. The Canadian campaign brought isolated trade unions together. Just as the Manchester Trades Council had fathered the Trades Union Congress in 1868, so the Toronto Trades Assembly now set up a national congress in the form of a Canadian Labour Union to press for legislation. But the life of this body was cut short by the deep depression of the 1870s.

If Canadian trade union development was phased like the American, that was because both were responding to changes in the economy. The effect of the depression of the 1870s on trade unionism on both sides of the border was indeed devastating; only a few local unions survived. But after 1879 came economic revival, with the particular stimulus in Canada of the building of the Canadian Pacific Railway. Then the formation of local unions was renewed, and more internationals came in. Much more, in 1881 the Knights of Labour appeared. They were to exert a wide and powerful influence, that remained strong in Canada after it had ebbed away in the US. The Knights swept workers of all sorts into their Assemblies – the unskilled as well as the skilled, the white-collared as well as the manual, women as well as men. With this comprehensiveness it was natural that they should organize Trades and Labour Councils in some of the cities. In 1883 they helped to set up what became the first enduring national organization of trade unions, the Canadian Trades and Labour

Congress (TLC), and for nearly twenty years they were highly influential in it. Though trade unionism had begun to push beyond the Great Lakes with the railway in the 1880s, the TLC remained effectively an organization of unions in Ontario and Quebec.

Towards the end of the 1890s there came another phase of rapid recruitment and union formation. The prime mover this time was the American Federation of Labor. It set out to recruit, charter locals, and gain control of the TLC, of set purpose. In part, perhaps, its leader Samuel Gompers sought the satisfaction simply of seeing membership and territory extend; but he had the rational inducement of following across the border the trusts with which the AFL unions were already negotiating in the US and which were now beginning to operate in Canada. Once committed in Canada, moreover, he was bound to strengthen his hold there in order to stamp out elements to which he was implacably opposed – the Knights of Labour; 'dual unionism', that is, the existence of unions such as the Canadian Railway Brotherhoods purporting to organize the same craft or occupation as was organized by an AFL union; and the mixing of trade unionism with party politics, a propensity that many Canadian trade unionists had brought from Great Britain. Gompers appointed a full-time organizer for Canada in 1900. This organizer was vigorous: he made such progress in chartering new locals that the major unions in manufacturing became part of 'internationals' whose main membership and headquarters were in the US. By 1902 these unions had attained such strength in the TLC that they were able to drive out their rivals – chiefly the Western Federation of Miners and the remains of the Knights of Labour. These formed their own Congress, and from then until 1956 there would be no single trade union centre in Canada.

This split at the celebrated Convention of 1902 marked much more than the rounding of the forty and more AFL unions on competitors engaged in 'dual unionism'. It also consummated a major change in influences and tendencies. Until the AFL came in, trade unions had been growing up, first on the British model, and commonly under the leadership of British immigrants who arrived already steeped in unionism; and then, with broader membership, looser organization, and less capability of bargaining, under the missionary stimulus of the Knights of Labour. But a new influence now supervened. The Canadian locals were in fact to be left free to fight their own industrial battle at their own discretion; but the distinctive future of Canadian trade unionism was now decided, in two ways. First, the predominant type would be the craft union, and the existing, strongly organized unionists would not be concerned to organize the less skilled workers, still less to associate them with themselves in an industrial or general union. The divergence between the TLC and the unions of the West with their adherence to industrial unionism was marked and widened. Second, there was a move to political independence. In the 1890s the TLC had been closely associated with the Liberal Party. It now broke away and took up a stance from which it would bring pressure to bear on the Government of the day, of whatever colour, to adopt – or refrain from – particular measures. But in this it went beyond the AFL policy of 'rewarding friends and punishing enemies' from a position of detachment. The Canadian unions remained politically minded, and their leaders frequently reverted to the launching of an independent labour party, even though it was not until 1906 that they took steps to this end at the centre. We shall see that they also promoted party political action in the provinces.

Meanwhile, and for many years to come, the trade unions stood in very varied relations to employers at the place of work. Those that had power enough achieved recognition – they forced it out of the employer by striking. But how much power a union had depended on the state of the market, and a union that had achieved recognition in the boom when labour was in demand could lose it after the tide had turned. Stable arrangements for bargaining were rare. Multi-employer negotiations, which promote stability because they put a floor under competition, were hardly known outside the building industry. Struggles for recognition, moreover, inherently tended to disorder that brought government in, effectively on the employer's side. When only the unionized part of the labour went on strike and the rest tried to pass the picket line; or when the employer brought in blacklegs – and the flow of immigrants or labour force from the farms often supplied blacklegs in plenty: then fighting was always likely to break out, and the police or the militia would be called in. They might then go for 'the trouble-makers'.

The law under which the unions operated was ill-defined but generally unhelpful or adverse to them. The Constitution of 1867 had put the criminal law under federal jurisdiction, but civil law was for the provinces. Thus the law concerning industrial relations was divided between the two kinds of jurisdiction: protective legislation such as Factory Acts was within the jurisdiction of the provinces, and would have to be obtained – and enforced – in each province separately. In 1872 a Conservative administration in the Dominion Parliament had copied the two British Acts of the year before – the Trade Union Act and the Criminal Law Amendment Act – which had relieved British trade unions of the taint of criminal conspiracy and defined the law of picketing. The Acts of 1872 were held to have done the same for Canada. The immediate effect of the Trade Union Act was to secure the release of twenty-four Toronto printers who had been taken into custody for no other offence than sitting together as a strike committee. But doubts were raised about the constitutional validity of the Act, and in some provinces trade unions were still subject to the old presumption of the English common law that combinations in restraint of trade were illegal. When the criminal law was codified in 1892 the right to picket was narrowed. But in any case, beyond these uncertainties under the criminal law, the trade unions had to contend with civil liabilities as these might be interpreted in the courts and under local legislation, province by province. The Taff Vale decision continued to be followed in Canadian courts, except in British Columbia.

The dominant concern of the Federal Government was to maintain the unity of the country that had been constituted by the Act of 1867. Where that unity was threatened by industrial strife the Government sought to promote an agreed settlement. In 1900 a Conciliation Act followed the British Act of 1896 in providing procedures for conciliation and arbitration on the voluntary motion of the parties, and authorizing the Government to intervene to the extent of offering conciliation. It also went beyond the British Act, and followed American precedent, by setting up a Department of Labour. The deputy Minister of Labour who was now appointed, W. L. Mackenzie King, became active in offering his services as a conciliator under the Act. He proved highly successful. In many of the cases with which he had to deal trade unionism was making its early and as yet unorganized impact. Workers had been moved by an impulse to assert hastily formulated claims, and employers found themselves confronted by an opposition at once militant and inchoate. The great need here was for clarification. Mackenzie King showed how great a step it was towards a settlement, simply to bring out the facts and let public opinion come to bear on them. His experience was embodied in an Industrial Disputes Investigation Act of 1907. This provided that there could be no strike or lock-out in any concern employing ten or more workers in mining, transport, communication, and public utilities, until the procedure laid down by the Act had been followed; parties to disputes in other industries might invoke the procedure if they agreed to do so. The issue was to be submitted to a tripartite board; this would examine witnesses, and try to reach a settlement by conciliation: failing that it would issue a report or reports with its own recommendations for settlement. But the parties to the dispute were under no legal obligation to accept the recommendations, and were free to resort to strike or lock-out thereafter. The benefits of this procedure were held to be that the board would get the facts of the case clear, and the pause while the board was sitting would give time for cooling off and a fresh approach to negotiation, under the influence of a public opinion which would now know the facts.

These benefits seemed established by the initial successes of the procedure in Mackenzie King's hands; but it had its limitations. It was inflexible and cumbersome. The trade unionists felt that it was biased against them: while they could only lose impetus during the compulsory pause, the employer could prepare for an eventual stoppage by piling up stocks, or marshalling blacklegs, and even dismissing and replacing the discontented part of his labour force. He might also call in a detachment of police. But when the trade unionists were strong enough, they could defy the law with impunity. In the midst of the British transport strike in 1912 the British Government decided that the great conciliator G. R. Askwith must investigate the Canadian procedure. The features that he recommended for adoption in the UK did not include the compulsory pause, and he later quoted a Canadian newspaper as saying that 'strikes often occur in public utilities before investigation, though the Act forbids it . . . The prohibitory clause of the Act has been violated scores of times . . . The Act provides no machinery for enforcement, no penalty for disobedience.'[1] But the principles of the Act were generally accepted. This appeared when in 1925 the Act was successfully challenged on the constitutional ground that in applying it the Dominion Government had exceeded its jurisdiction. The consequent amendment to the Act made it apply only to disputes within that jurisdiction, but also provided that provinces could now apply the Act to disputes within their own borders if they passed enabling legislation. All the provinces save Prince Edward Island did so.

Thus trade unionism had been of sporadic and uncertain growth in the localities, and it lacked protection from above. Down to the First World War it developed only partially. In negotiation the unions were effective only here and there. At the national level they lacked unity and resources, and were unable to bring effective pressure to bear on governments for needed legislation. The TLC had been set up, like the TUC in Great Britain, to pursue a parliamentary programme: it did secure Factory Acts in four provinces, and from the Dominion Government it won a Labour Day holiday, the Conciliation Act that was modelled on the British Act of 1896, and a law against bringing in contract labour. In 1890, at a time when socialist ideas were beginning to spread among British trade unionists, the TLC had called for the public ownership of railways, telegraphs, and public utilities. The AFL unions that dominated the TLC from 1902 onwards were sufficiently responsive to the doctrines of their parent bodies to prefer 'political neutralism' to the linking of their centre with any one party. But this was quite consistent with their drawing up a list of political objectives and lobbying for them through the Parliamentary Committee of the TLC. Moreover even the AFL members of the TLC were Canadians with their own views. If the TLC did not form a party itself, in 1906 it instructed its provincial executives to form labour parties whose programme was to be based on its Platform of Principles, and such parties were in fact formed in four provinces. In 1917 again it commended to the provinces the launching of a Canadian Labour Party, which was actually founded in 1921; but two years later it withdrew its support.

In the provinces meanwhile, Trades Councils had been working for the return of labour members to the provincial and federal legislatures. The first to be so elected was the President of the Trades Council of Ottawa, who was returned to the Ontario legislature in 1872. Others followed: an independent labour party formed part of a coalition government in Ontario in 1919–23.

What stands out when the full story is told is the persistence of endeavours to secure independent labour representation; but no less prominent is the failure of a labour party to call forth a labour vote.

It seemed otherwise for a time in British Columbia. The province was distinguished both by the severity of the frequent conflicts between despotic managements and militant trade unions in its coal and hardrock mines, and by the rise of an independent labour party. In the 1890s Labour members were elected to the Legislature, and though few in number they were able to secure the passage of protective laws. American miners and lumberjacks brought in the socialism of Eugene Debs, syndicalism, and the loyalties of the Wobblies – the IWW. These movements kept their adherents in the Canadian West after they had fallen away south of the border. In 1919 many of the militant western unionists were to unite for a time in the revolutionary ideal of One Big Union.

In the same year 1919 there occurred an extraordinary general strike in Winnipeg. The advance of the railways across the prairies made Winnipeg the workshop of the west. In 1900–13 a wheat boom and a rapid immigration brought it a rapid development. Its industries became strongly unionized on British lines, under the leadership of British immigrants. In the spring of 1919 the building and engineering unions sought wage rises to restore real wages impaired by the wartime rise in prices. The claim presented by the engineers was linked with a demand for the recognition of a joint negotiating body of metal trade unions. There had been much talk of industrial unionism, and of the use of the general strike for political ends. A Western Conference of Labour in Calgary had recently decided on the setting up of One Big Union. In the claim for the recognition of the Metal Trades Council the employers must have seen the threat of syndicalism, and they rejected it resolutely. With complete unanimity the other unions joined the claimants in a general strike: ninety-four unions in all came out. This was the greatest demonstration of trade union potential yet seen in Canada. It lasted, in perfect order, for six weeks. It collapsed only after the strike leaders had been arrested, and a demonstration of ex-servicemen had clashed with the police.

These events were part of the unrest after the First World War in Canada, as in other countries. During the Winnipeg general strike there had been sympathetic strikes of some magnitude in other Canadian cities, notably Vancouver; there had also been a general strike in Seattle earlier in that year. But with the breaking of the post-war boom there followed, all unforeseen, a phase of comparative quiet that extended over two decades. The dominant factor in the West was probably the ending of the preceding phase of rapid development: the War had only suspended the impact of the change that impinged in 1913. The setting did not now favour trade union pressure; and though the failures of 1919 had not extinguished radical attitudes among wage-earners, and may even have extended them, men turned from trade unionism to political activity. In the East, the trade unions remained mostly craft unions of the AFL type, while the extension of employment was in mass production industries using inexperienced and unorganized labour. Outside the coal industry there were few strikes of consequence anywhere in 1922–9. Then came the great depression, and mounting unemployment inhibited union action.

With the beginnings of recovery, in Canada as in the US, resentment against the suffering that the depression had inflicted animated recruit-ment for a new industrial unionism of the mass production workers. But whereas in the US this expansion of unionism was supported first by the New Deal and then by the Wagner Act, in Canada it was left exposed to the opposition of employers, which remained active. In Ontario also it was opposed by the Government. While American union membership nearly doubled, the Canadian rose by little more than a third. Some Canadian unions were now formed as affiliates of American CIO unions. The TLC had no concern with the rift between the AFL and the CIO, but the AFL unions within the TLC were able to secure the expulsion of its CIO members. These formed their own national centre, the Canadian Congress of Labour (CCL).

When war came again in 1939 the trade unions still held no accepted place in industry or society. At least the Dominion Government felt able to ignore them in its planning of the war effort, for it gave the TLC seats on certain general consultative committees of little consequence, but none on the crucial Committee on Labour Co-ordination. But as the War went on the power of labour mounted with the level of industrial activity: trade union membership rose rapidly; pent-up grievances and resentment of wartime controls burst out in strikes. At the same time a powerful swing towards labour was manifest in the elections in Ontario in 1943. Ten years before, the Co-operative Commonwealth Federation (CCF) had been founded as an alliance of a farmers' movement, a Fabian-type group of intellectuals and a socialist party based on British Columbia. Many unions belonging to the TLC supported the CCF, which was particularly attractive to the new unions of the CIO type. The national centre, the CCL, set up by these unions when they were expelled from the TLC, itself affiliated with the CCF in 1943. Hence the powerful impact on public opinion and the Dominion Government when in that same year the CCF won thirty-four seats in Ontario, and nineteen of its elected members were trade unionists.

The reaction of the Dominion Government was to issue in 1944 an Order in Council modelled on the American Wagner Act of 1935. It established the workers' right to organize, prescribed procedures for defining bargaining units, and laid on employers the obligation to bargain in good faith.

This was a turning-point. The Canadian economy and industrial relations were to emerge from the War transformed. For the economy this was marked by a large-scale industrialization, achieved for the first time in and through the War. In the trade unions it was marked by numerical strength, a legal code, and participation in the Western economies' pattern of rising standards, fluctuating activity, progressive inflation, and industrial conflict increasing from the mid-1960s. The legal code was provided by an Act of 1948. This gave a permanent statutory form to the provisions of the Order in Council of 1944. It also carried forward and extended the provisions for the settlement of disputes that went back to the Act of 1907. Employers were laid under an obligation to recognize certified unions. Labour relations boards were set up to deal with unfair practices. The procedure of bargaining, conciliation, and voting on terms offered or proposed that the parties must go through was specified. If at the end of the procedure they were still not agreed, the workers could strike and the strike would be legal; but strikes and lock-outs while an agreement was in force were illegal. Equally illegal was any 'industrial action' taken before the whole appointed procedure had been exhausted, whenever a new agreement was under negotiation. The provisions of the 1948 Act were themselves applicable only within the Federal jurisdiction, but they were largely repeated by legislation within all the provinces save Prince Edward Island.

The nature of these statutes [the Task Force on Industrial Relations observed in 1968] reflects a public policy that clearly favours collective bargaining. Specifically, policy supports the formation of unions, encourages good faith negotiations, and presupposes the strike or lock-out in the event of an impasse, after the normal statutory procedures are exhausted, except during the term of a collective agreement when arbitration or the equivalent is required. In these respects the law is consistent and is relatively easily interpreted, though not always so easily enforced. Compliance problems arise most acutely on the management side when employers choose to resist unions. When they do so openly and frontally, any illegal measures they take can usually be proved and remedied. What remains are those cases where management employs more subtle tactics and abridges the spirit more than the letter of the law in ways which are difficult to detect or correct. Judging by the record of litigation in the courts, as distinct from labour board proceedings, unions violate the framework of rules and regulations established under labour relations acts more often than managements. But many of their infringements take place because of impatience over the slow-moving nature of the law.[2]

The problem of enforcement became acute. Union membership had risen by some 80 per cent through and immediately after the Second World War. After that the advance of numbers was modest, and the 1950s were a period of calm. But in the 1960s Canada in common with other Western countries experienced 'the dispersive revolution', a shift of power to the shop-floor, a seizing of the initiative by the rank and file, and a disregard of authority within the unions themselves. Indeed, it was in Canada that the change was manifest first. In Europe it showed itself in the strikes of 1968–9, but two years before that the great wave of strikes in Canada in 1966–7 had been marked by many wildcat strikes, the breaking away of Canadian 'locals' from their American parent unions, the repudiation of established authority in the unions, and the rejection of negotiated agreements. But one method of control was found effective in the last resort. On a number of occasions Provincial and Dominion Governments passed Acts requiring a return to work, and ultimately these were obeyed.

In these post-war years the paradox remained prominent, that Canadian trade unionists were distinguished from their opposite numbers within a stone's throw across the American border by their persistent proclivity to engage in politics and launch a labour party, and yet they had never succeeded in establishing a labour party that attracted wide and sustained support. There had been a time during the War when it seemed as if the alliance between the Co-operative Commonwealth Federation and the Canadian Congress of Labour – the national centre of the CIO type unions – would prove powerful. But though the CCF was to provide the Provincial Government in Saskatchewan for twenty years, and sometimes form the main opposition party in some other provinces, its representation at the national level fell away. In 1956 the union of the AFL and CIO in the USA was followed by a similar union in Canada – indeed the Canadian Labour Congress that was now formed marked a more complete integration, for the rift had never been so deep in Canada. With the blessing of the CCF the new Congress proceeded in 1961 to launch a New Democratic Party, of a social democratic tendency designed to appeal to a wide spectrum of labour voters. At long last a united trade union centre had set up an independent labour party. But it seems that most labour voters have continued to support the traditional parties.

2

There is much to account for here. How came it, first of all, that Canadian trade unionism was still so backward at the time of the Second World War? It had made its expected beginnings, from the 1850s onwards, whenever times were propitious. Its leaders were often British immigrants who arrived already steeped in trade union outlook and practice. Down to 1900 in the towns of Eastern Canada (Quebec apart) it could appeal to workmen who, whether immigrant or native-born, were little divided by national origin, language, or religion. The Irish were set apart by the kind of lowly employments they followed as well as by their religion. But the main body of workmen who were potential members of the unions of the time were not segregated from one another or from the newcomers who brought in the trade union message. Yet in 1939 the trade unions throughout Canada had not achieved recognition at all generally for the purpose of collective bargaining firm by firm. At the national level they were divided between two congresses, neither of standing over against the Dominion Government. They had been unable to maintain a labour party. The distinctive movement both trade union and political that had risen in the West, had faded out after 1920. In all Canada the trade unionists as a proportion of potential membership still amounted to only 18 per cent in 1941. True, this was higher than the corresponding proportion in the USA, which was nearer 16 per cent: but one might have expected a much higher ratio in Canada, where not only was the industrial work-force at that time still so much more homogeneous, but the atmosphere of social solidarity coming down from its conservative tradition might have been expected to let the trade unionist breathe more freely than he could south of the border. In another Dominion inheriting British traditions and largely peopled by British and Irish immigrants – in Australia – the corresponding proportion at this time was 40 per cent.[3] Why was the Canadian figure less than half that?

One basic reason lies in scale. We are led to reflect on agglomeration as a necessary condition for the development of trade unions.

The terrain and the history of its settlement conspired to deny agglomeration to the Canadian labour force. They kept it divided into penny packets and scattered over great distances. In an atlas of human geography the distinct regions of Canada might appear as a chain of islands extended over three thousand miles. The three regions of the East are separated from one another by natural barriers that shut the Maritime Provinces off from the hinterland, and divide the plain of the St Lawrence from the lowlands of the Great Lakes. Here too in the East the Province of Quebec is set apart by its history and language. The journey west of the Great Lakes from Eastern Canada could long be made readily only by traversing the United States from Detroit to Minnesota. The Prairie provinces again are separated from British Columbia by the Rocky Mountains. The insularity which nature imposed on the regions in these ways was increased by what appeared initially as a paucity of natural endowment. Outside British Columbia, the vast mineral resources of the west and north are of comparatively recent discovery. Through the nineteenth century the trade of Eastern Canada was in the furs and timber of the hinterland, and its own lands drew in neither settlers nor capital in great quantity. Only from the turn of the century did a wheat boom open up the prairie and retain a great immigration. Canada long remained a predominantly agricultural economy of small towns and small firms. In 1901 more than three-fifths of the population were still rural, and two-fifths of the labour force were occupied in agriculture. There were at that time two big cities – Montreal with over 300,000 inhabitants, and Toronto with over 200,000; but after them Quebec, Ottawa, Hamilton, and Winnipeg lay only between 70,000 and 40,000. Montreal and Quebec, moreover, were within the French-speaking province. (In Australia, Sydney reached 400,000 in 1891, and Melbourne 473,000.) No less significant is the small size of the firm. Manufacturing in Canada was on the small scale: in 1890 nearly half of all manufactures came from firms with an annual output of not more than $50,000.[4]

This was not a setting in which workers trying to form a lasting union could gain confidence from their awareness of how many of them shared a common plight and common purpose. That awareness did arise in the close-packed industrial towns and densely populated industrial districts of Great Britain, but not in the small market towns of the south of England, even though each of these commonly had its factory. It could not have arisen in the small and scattered communities of Canada in the ninteenth century: the impulses towards unionism arising out of the nature of employment or the leadership of British immigrants died away for lack of the reinforcement provided by the replication and reverberation of feelings among large numbers. But craftsmen, it is true, often formed strong unions with nation-wide coverage, without many of them ever necessarily being gathered in any one place. The bond of union of so many as were working in the same place was their fellowship in the craft and their common interest in protecting it. What enabled them then to maintain an effective union was the facility of communication – not merely that messages could pass to and fro, and delegates attend meetings, but that members themselves might find themselves working from time to time in different parts of the country, so that each had an interest in maintaining union rules everywhere. It was indeed the need to provide for the travelling brother of the craft that knit local clubs into national unions both in Great Britain and the US. But in Canada distances were vast, and even in Eastern Canada communications long remained difficult. For four months of the year, moreover, they were made more difficult still by a winter of great severity.

What was worse for trade union organization, in another way communications were easy. The lines of communications between the regions of Canada were politically obliged to run east and west: the natural lines ran north and south, across the border with the US. Ninety per cent of the Canadian population remained within fifty miles of that border. Until restrictions were applied by the US in the 1930s, the Canadian worker in quest of higher wages frequently had an immediate and practical alternative to the uncertain course of pressing for them through a trade union: he could take a job in the USA. In the matter of immigration, Canada for long provided something of a staging camp. In the hundred years from 1851 to 1951, though 7¼ million immigrants came in, 6½ million persons went out, mostly to the US.[5] Accounts also stress the extent of internal mobility. Union membership must have been correspondingly hard to maintain.

Canadian unionism was also checked by the strong opposition of employers. Some of the reasons for this were of merely local origin and significance. Thus it was, for instance, that the American trusts that came in at the turn of the century brought with them their anti-union policy. At the same time native Canadian employers found a nationalistic reason for rebuffing unions in so far as these were now locals of an American union. Employers inclined to oppose unionism are always more likely to do so actively if they can expect to break strikes, and from 1900 until the Second World War a great immigration and the annual inflow of poor labour from the farms to industry gave many Canadian employers supplies of blacklegs.

But beside these local factors were two others of more general relevance. One was the violence of the fluctuations to which the Canadian economy was exposed by its dependence on the export of a few basic commodities. The rise and fall of international markets were transmitted through the export industries to the whole economy. Employers working under these rapidly varying and often severe pressures were unwilling to commit themselves to rates that must be regarded as irreducible except after protracted negotiation. They were price-takers, not price-makers: they did not feel able to reach an amicable settlement with the union on terms which the price charged to the customer would subsequently cover. This is a factor we have already noticed in discussing the British employers, and the difference between the industrial relations of those who were and those who were not exposed to international competition. The extent to which the comparatively sheltered state of much of the British market contributed to the acceptance of trade unionism again stands out. The other factor of wider relevance is to be found in the particularly hard opposition offered to unionism by the self-made pioneering employers. Here were men who from a penurious start built up industrial empires by acumen, good fortune, and – what they themselves will have been most conscious of – unremitting hard work: they did not take kindly to the unionist who proposed, as it seemed to them, to better himself simply by extorting money under threat of blockade. As employers these men might have been paternal, but they were masters, and in any case they would not hear of an outsider – a trade union official – coming between them and 'their' men. Where a society has still to be formed out of a congeries of settlers, moreover, the hard-thrusting employer is not restrained by his neighbours' sense – as well perhaps as his own – of the conduct that is proper to his place in the social structure. There is little middle-class opinion to influence his attitude. In a developed and close-textured community, by contrast, there are gradations of outlook between capital and labour, an uncommitted element whose presence bodies forth the common bonds of society, moderates industrial relations and prevents their polarization. Much of the difference in industrial relations between East and West in Canada can be accounted for in this way. When camps are built for miners or lumber-jacks in the wilderness, even when towns rise up in a few years in a new mining area or about a railway centre, there is little community – only labour over against a management that is the agent of a remote all-powerful ownership; with at most some services that lie outside this opposition; but no web of relationships. This is the setting for syndicalism. In the same way, we see part of the reason for the greater militancy of trade unionism in those districts of Great Britain where rapid industrialization and the lie of the land created a concentration of manual workers with little local admixture of other social elements.

Governments in Canada, federal and provincial, in practice held unionism back. One reason was that they were concerned to maintain order: but in the early stages of organization, in any place and period, when an employer is resisting the unionization of his employees disturbances will break out, and then the police find themselves engaged against the strikers. Pickets obstruct the movement of materials and the entry of blacklegs; strikers resist eviction from company housing; whatever the intent of the workers' leaders, as the suffering of a lengthy strike are drawn out some men resort to violence against the property or persons of the employing concern. As in Adam Smith's day, 'The masters . . . never cease to call aloud for the assistance of the civil magistrate.'[6] The early stages of unionization can be peaceful for craftsmen, whose skill safeguards them from blacklegs. The possibility of employers carrying on with non-union labour, and of consequent fighting, might also be small in settled and homogeneous populations, where no substantial number of people were so far out of tune with their neighbours as to be willing blacklegs, and any labour brought in from a distance spoke the same language and was amenable to argument. The orderliness that Canadians noted as characterizing the British immigrant trade unionist owed something to that background. Much of the Canadian setting was very different. Where settlements were building up, where the work-force was shifting, and especially where a babel of immigrants was arriving, there was a possibility of strike-breaking. This brought disorder: the strikers were cast as the aggressors, and the Government became involved in putting down the strike.

The Governments were by no means always involved against their will. Their major concerns were with economic development and with maintaining the unity of a loose-jointed community. They made grants of rights and resources to firms to whom they looked for development and whose advance they did not wish to see obstructed by labour troubles. They did not welcome the assertion of the claims of labour when it made for social and ethnic conflict. Labour legislation, which lay within provincial jurisdiction, remained meagre. Factory laws were deficient or not enforced.

3

These things were possible because there was no labour party or labour vote to bring pressure to bear against them. For some years at the end of the nineteenth century Labour members were influential in the legislature of British Columbia, and when the CCF (the Cooperative Commonwealth Federation) came east from Winnipeg and won many seats in Ontario in 1943, for a time it seemed likely to fill the role of a labour party. But despite repeated initiatives the trade unions have never launched a party that received the sustained support of a working-class vote. This was the crux. It must have been because of the lack of that distinct and coherent support, that the independent labour members who did find their way into the legislatures did not see themselves as opening up a bridgehead, but found it politic to merge with an existing party.

The absence of a labour party cannot simply be ascribed to the same factors in Canada as in the US. Because Canada had a British parliamentary system, with disciplined parties, the Canadian unions did not have the option of avoiding commitment to any one party and 'rewarding their friends and punishing their enemies' individually in Gompers's way. Measures in the interests of the unions could generally be enacted by Canadian legislatures only on the motions of the executive and with the support of the majority party maintaining the executive in office. Labour members must either form a pressure group as members or allies of that party, or create such a party themselves.

Beyond that difference of the political system was a difference of outlook which also prevents our attributing the absence of a labour party to the same factors in the two countries. The immigrant who brought from the UK or from Europe attitudes and aspirations which at home were to express themselves in a political movement of the left did not find in Canada, as he did in the US, a way of living and thinking that disapproved of any such tendency and actively inculcated other values. On the contrary, the strong tradition of Toryism in Canada laid its stress on solidarity, and against individualism and the fissiparous impact of market forces. Here it found common ground with socialism and, implicitly, with the propensity of the worker to organize for the protection of the conditions of his working life. The difference between the Canadian and American outlooks in this respect is shown by the extent of the public sector in Canada: it comprises half of the electricity industry and the railways, most of the radio and television service, the airlines, the wheat selling agency, and the synthetic rubber industry, besides other enterprises. Whereas in the US, again, the early extension of the franchise had long made the wage-earner indistinguishable in his own eyes as a citizen from other voters, in Canada the franchise was broadened only much later and then only patchily. The varied provincial franchises usually had a property qualification, and it was these franchises that were used in the federal elections, the first of which to be based on manhood suffrage being that of 1900. Until quite a late date the wage-earner must have felt himself set apart.

We have then to seek other reasons for the absence of any broad and sustained support at the polls for a labour party in Canada. The main reason must be that too few voters felt themselves as inherently differentiated by their birth and upbringing or by the nature of their job, so that it would be natural for them to wish to be represented by someone of their own sort, someone at least who was responsive to the needs and wishes of their particular condition. Men would be more likely to see this condition as a facet of society, and something that society might change, when many of them were in it together. But in Canada the factor of scale worked against this: in a population that for long was predominantly rural, there were not enough people working in industry in any one place for them to attain the sense of identity that is imparted by sheer awareness of the number in like case. Even, moreover, had the numbers been present, a further stimulant of the labour vote was lacking. We spoke just now of voters looking to social policy to change their conditions: they will do this when they feel themselves individually boxed in and denied prospects of betterment short of a change in the whole system, but few Canadian wage-earners can have felt this. Too many of them were on the move: they were immigrants, or first generation, and still expected a change for the better; or had moved into the town from the farm, or were going to cross the border into the US; or within Canada were migrating from east to west. There was no large and settled body of persons here to form an 'us' whose members would be naturally aware of their own identity over against a 'them'. To those with such class consciousness it is self-evident that they ought to be represented in the legislature by people of their own sort. Many Canadian workers had come as immigrants from settings overseas in which class consciousness went deep; but the Canadian setting dissipated it.

There were two further constraints on the rise of a labour party. One concerns again the factor of scale. The Constitution allotted to the provinces the matters that most concerned the unions and would be the subject of the legislation they would promote: but there were nine provinces. For a labour movement that was strong in the localities this would have opened an early way to office, there would have been a 'demonstration effect'. That was indeed the effect of the health insurance scheme which the CCF introduced when it took office in Saskatchewan in the early 1940s. On a broader front the same effect would have followed if in one of the most industrialized provinces – Ontario or British Columbia – the labour movement could have gained a majority and shown what a labour government could do. But for a weak movement of scattered minorities the division into provinces raised the problem of agglomeration acutely. It imposed a task very different from that of a labour party in a state where labour legislation is within the scope of the central government. Here the party can win seats wherever in the country it has the support to win them, and if that gives it leverage enough in the national assembly, obtain legislation of general application. In Canada labour legislation had to be enacted province by province, but province by province there was no sufficient labour vote.

The other constraint was imposed by the comparative absence of a liberal middle class to provide informed support, professional guidance, and perhaps some leadership in person, for a rising labour movement. This lack appears by contrast with European movements, and more particularly with the vital support given to labour by liberal politicians and lawyers in New Zealand and Australia in the 1890s. It may be ascribed in Canada to its relatively small urban development. The nearest approaches may have been the support given to labour in Winnipeg by Methodism, and the share of a group of intellectuals in the formation of the CCF.

It is these factors of social structure that explain the absence of a sufficient labour vote. Its immediate cause was the attachment of wage-earning voters to the established parties, which had been at pains to attract and enlist them. But British experience indicates that this attachment would not have persisted if the conditions for the formation of working-class consciousness were present. In Great Britain equally, as we have seen, down to the 1880s trade unionists were largely attached to the existing parties. If they remained so in Canada as they did not in Great Britain that was because of the factors noticed here as differentiating the Canadian social structure.

4

The West presents a distinctive story for commentary. It is separate from the East in both trade unionism and politics. We have to account for the strength and militancy of the Western unions, and the intensity of the conflicts in which they engaged; the variety and persistence of labour and socialist parties, and the hold of syndicalism; the remarkable phenomenon of the Winnipeg general strike; and the no less remarkable dropping away in the 1920s of all the militancy and radicalism that had distinguished the West for the preceding thirty years.

British Columbia in particular stood out by reason of the militancy and radicalism of its trade unions, and even more, the activity of its labour and socialist parties, the support they received, and the achievements of labour in the provincial legislature. What happened here was quite distinct from the industrial relations and politics of Eastern Canada. The development of the labour movement may be likened to that of Great Britain at the time, but in some ways it went faster, for in a less complex setting its tendencies were less restrained. They built up in two phases. In the first, from the 1870s to the mid-90s, the exploitation of natural resources brought in migrants who formed unions mainly in the British tradition – miners' unions and craft unions. These engaged in struggles with the hard-driving type of employer that was opening up the territory, and as time went on these struggles increased in number and intensity. Some unity was given to these various groups of organized workers by a common interest in opposing the immigration of Chinese labour. The coming of the Knights of Labour in the

1880s, here as elsewhere, also helped to form a sense of common purpose and gave an impetus to political activity. This was stirred by the campaign for the nine-hour day, and by the 1890s was tinged with the socialism of Eugene Debs and Keir Hardie, who visited Canada twice.

Then about 1896 the second phase was brought in by the opening up of the hinterland, and the coming of American hardrock miners, bringing with them their own Western Federation of Miners, and their syndicalist faith in direct action by workers united to seize control of their own work-places. The seven stormy years that followed were outstanding in the history of Canadian labour. They were marked out not only by industrial conflicts of great severity, but also by the formation of labour and socialist parties that were vigorous and varied. The structure of a new society was at issue. There was a power struggle, and there was a labour movement, inchoate but lively, in which ideas were canvassed eagerly, and which was capable at times of exerting effective political leverage. Most notable was the Rossland strike of 1901 and its consequences. That miners' strike itself was broken by the use of imported blacklegs and the injunction. But in the next year labour was able to obtain from the provincial legislature an Act which gave trade unions protection against the injunction – as the Norris–La Guardia Act was to do in the United States only in 1932 – and which also, four years before the British Trade Disputes Act of 1906, protected the funds of trade unions from civil liability.

The seven years reached a climax in industrial conflict in 1903. For some time after that, trade union pressure was offset by the organization of employers, and transcended by the political strength of labour, especially of socialist parties. When the IWW came into the province in 1906, they found the loyalties of their potential recruits already given to socialism. In 1911–12, at a time of strife in much of the Western world, industrial conflict was renewed in struggles about the union shop; and there was talk of a general strike. But in 1913 the breaking of the long development boom of the West radically changed the setting in which the labour movement had been stimulated.

This exceptional development of radical trade unionism and independent labour and socialist parties in British Columbia may be largely attributed to three factors.

There is first the particular character of the labour force and the employers. The workers initially were men who had made their way out to the coast in order to better themselves: they were self-selected for hardihood and enterprise. Most were from Eastern Canada, but a substantial proportion came direct from Great Britain, and another group moved up from the USA. They brought with them the expectation of advancement, but this was not the sort of frontier whose natural resources enabled the individual, save exceptionally, to work up his own holding: the mine, the railroad, the lumber-camp, required massive investment, and a large body of manual workers under orders. Hence the disappointment, the sense of frustration, of many workers: they had come all that way and found no path upwards. There are some bodies of wage-earners who are themselves for the most part the children of wage-earners, and who grow up with the expectation of becoming wage-earners in their turn. It is a way of life that they may chafe under, or feel themselves pent up in, but at least it does not come upon them as a disappointment and a denial of a promise held out to them. But so it was with the employment that the far West offered to the migrants at first. These migrants, moreover, are described as mature and thoughtful men. 'Far more than the East,' said H. C. Pentland, 'the West was a great nursery of self-taught but keen and eloquent labour philosophers.'[7] This made them resolute trade unionists. But it also drew them into politics. Since they were trapped in the system, it was the system they must change, and they turned to socialism. To these men was added the influx of American hard-rock miners, younger for the most part, hardbitten, already convinced of the futility of negotiations and committed to universal workers' control.

Over against these unusual workers were unusual employers. Some were self-made men, capable of paternalism perhaps, but certainly autocratic; others were corporations, remote from the work-place, which they ruled inflexibly through a subservient local management. Both types were risk-takers pushing on development, impatient of restraint, and ruthless in the decisions they took under the pressures of their own drive to expand and markets specially prone to fluctuation. No social consideration moved them to recognize trade unions or negotiate an agreed settlement with them, so long as they could break their resistance by importing blacklegs, obtaining injunctions against picketing, and calling on the Government for the deployment of the police and even of the military.

Part of the reason for the sharpness of the consequent industrial conflict lay in the sparseness of the surrounding community. This was the second factor distinguishing British Columbia. Capital and labour were set in stark and isolated opposition to each another as they seldom are outside the covers of a Marxian text. They lacked the moral support, restraint, and guidance that a circumambient community of varied occupation will provide: in the isolated mining and lumber-camps there was no such community at all, in the company towns little enough, and in the province as a whole the occupational structure was – outstandingly for a frontier territory – weighted towards heavily capitalized industry. In 1911 agriculture contained only 12 per cent of the occupied population; only 10 per cent were recorded as professional or engaged in government service; but building manufacturers, mining, forestry, and transport contained 56 per cent.[8] The miners of Nova Scotia were to afford a contrast with the Western miners. They were to be harshly treated, by the play of economic fortune and the policy of remote management, but they were themselves an old-established community, in a province of early settlement, and the conflicts in which they were involved never made them so radical. The Western miners must have felt that they had only their own right arms with which to defend themselves – no surrounding opinion existed, and for sheer lack of persons to embody and express it none could exist, whose influence would tend to uphold standards of fair dealing between employer and employed, restrain excesses of self-seeking, and protect the weak. The employers for their part were in the presence of no standards upheld by churches or maintained in families of respected lineage or in traditional employments, that would inculcate restraint, or a duty of benevolence, on the stronger or wealthier party to a dispute. Nor were there at first established political parties with their own traditions, and their need to appeal to broad sectors of the electorate, with which the rising capitalist must come to terms. It was possible for him to proceed directly to high office – the principal coal-owner and builder of an industrial empire in British Columbia, James Dunsmuir, was Premier of the province in 1900–2, and later its Lieutenant-Governor.

One consequence of the sparseness of the community in the far West, as also of its late development, was that the traditional political parties were not established there, and did not occupy bases from which to recruit the immigrants. The field was clear for these to develop their own political ideas, which they did in some variety.

By contrast with the undeveloped community around them, the workers themselves were concentrated in substantial numbers. This was the third factor. It was the factor of scale and of agglomeration. Instead of being dispersed in small groups seeded in communities made up of varied grades and occupations, the workers in British Columbia were gathered together as the labour force of particular isolated projects, or in the cities of Vancouver and Victoria; and their view of one another as a class would not have been much blurred and diffused by the intermingling of their fellows as individuals with neighbours of other types. Over and above the high degree of unionization, this explains the existence of a labour vote. Those who are conscious of forming a distinct and large group with distinct interests in common will find it only natural to pursue those interests independently in the legislature, through representatives of their own sort.

It is this factor of scale and concentration that comes first to notice when we turn to account for the extraordinary events in Winnipeg in 1919. The brief narrative we have already offered has shown how the general strike came about as a manifestation of solidarity. But that solidarity had been created in the special circumstances of the growth of Winnipeg. As the railroads pushed out beyond the Great Lakes, and the wheat boom drew in a great immigration, Winnipeg became the workshop of the prairies. Between 1891 and 1911 its population grew more than fivefold. The builders who raised its houses, the railwaymen, the fitters and metal workers of its factories and forges, inhabited the same quarter of the expanding city, on the north side. Many of them were British immigrants. They formed trade unions of the British kind. Of the seven principal trade union leaders of the general strike, six had been born and spent their early days in Great Britain. Here, then, a labour movement was concentrated and given direction. It was concentrated physically, by the location of the workers in one section of the city, separated by the railroad tracks from more affluent residential areas. The factor of scale entered because so many were gathered together. The movement that arose out of the awareness of identity and common interest was given direction by the practice of British trade unionism with which the local leaders had been imbued before they migrated, and the current ideas of the British labour movement with which they remained in contact.

But this current was now flowing in a terrain very different from the channels of its origin. In the type of employer and the conditions of work lay another factor in the general strike. The employer was typically such – whether the individual or the corporation – as has been described in the far west. Outstanding was T. R. Deacon, a leading employer in the metal trades, and Mayor of Winnipeg. The trade unions, led by men who thought it in the natural order of things that they should be able to negotiate improvements in harsh conditions, stood over against employers who for the most part were unwilling to recognize them, and in order to break a strike were quite ready to import blacklegs and obtain injunctions against pickets. There were some hard struggles. The unions suffered defeat. The lesson they learned was that they must unite to support one another in their demands for recognition.

One other factor in this drawing up of forces for the general strike remains to be noted. A concentrated body of organized labour such as there was in Winnipeg might have been expected to go on from trade unionism to political activity – all the more so when the employers refused the unions recognition, and – as was the case here – government provided no protection through factory legislation and supported the employers in any conflict. But though a political party was launched in the 1890s, it never received sufficient support to enable the Winnipeg workers to promote measures in the provincial legislature. The reason is not clear. Perhaps it is that, here as in the East, existing parties were already too well organized. There may also be the simple consideration that though some constituencies in Winnipeg might vote solidly Labour, they would still be only a few among the constituencies of the province. Whatever the reason, the lack of a political arm led to more faith – out of necessity – being placed in the sympathetic strike.

5

When we consider the strength of the labour movement in the West, the radicalism of its unions, the persistence of labour and socialist parties, and the extent of the labour vote; and when we see the unionists of all kinds in Winnipeg sustaining a general strike in perfect order for six weeks of 1919 – how are we to account for the loss of impetus in the West thereafter? The One Big Union expanded, in 1919–20, and then its members fell away rapidly. Through the 1920s labour exerted little pressure, in industry or politics. The launching of the CCF in 1933 brought the West into action again, and the new party had a labour component. But that initiative apart, the contrast between West and East seemed at an end after 1920 because labour in the West was now restrained.

One reason that has been given for this is that the previous activity of Western labour had been a response to the long boom of development – first coastal British Columbia, next the hinterland, then the prairies. Fluctuations and minor intervening slumps there had been, but prevailingly the labour market had been a seller's market for labour. When those conditions are sustained, in any place and period, they raise expectations and intensify pressures for betterment. But in 1913 there had come a break that was to prove more than temporary. The long boom was ended. Unemployment became severe. The War, bringing back a phase of full employment to industry, deferred the impact of the great downturn. But the events of 1919 were, so to speak, an anachronism. The weakness of demand that cowed labour in the inter-war years had actually set in before the War.

This seems to be a great part of the explanation, but two other influences may have been at work at the same time. One is that as population grew, and settlement went on, the occupational and social structure became more varied. We have called attention to the stark and isolated opposition of 'capital' and 'labour' in early days, when no community of varied jobs, interests, and standing surrounded and mingled with the managers and workers of some big enterprise. But as towns and the service trades grew, and the land of the prairie provinces was taken up, the opposition of black and white gave way to the gradations of the spectrum. It became less likely that wage-earners would have a strong sense of identity and common interest setting them over against other people. The great immigration of the pre-war decade had also made the labour force more diverse ethnically and linguistically.

The second influence is, even more than the first, a matter of surmise. But employers who appear to have had the best of a costly trial of strength may still be very anxious not to renew it, and will make more changes in their policy subsequently than they would ever have conceded at the time. Canadian employers in the 1920s had the immediate task of accommodating the expectations of ex-servicemen. They also had before them the example of the American corporations of the time: these were combining an active anti-union policy with welfare programmes and employee representation plans which, albeit autocratically, did improve the conditions of employment. T. R. Deacon, the Mayor of Winnipeg who as an employer resolutely refused to recognize the Metal Trades Council, did himself some months after the defeat of the general strike introduce into his own shops a works council modelled on that of the International Harvester Company. It is possible that one reason for the quieter conduct of Western labour after 1920 was some mitigation of the bearing of Western employers.

6

The British observer of the story of Canadian trade unionism, some of whose leading features have been sketched here, will reflect afresh on certain aspects of his home affairs. He sees trade unions in Canada starting often enough in familiar ways, but lacking impetus, or encountering opposition, so that they fail to gain members, or bargaining power, or a place in the economic and political life of the country, such as the trade unions of their day were attaining in Great Britain. Similarly in politics: there were many initiatives, again along lines familiar to the British observer, but they drew out no broad or steady labour vote. If we ask what brought labour in Great Britain on where labour in Canada was held back, a great part of the answer appears at once as the factor of scale and agglomeration. It was not so much because of any innate qualities or the cultural heritage of our people, or because of the structure of society at the time, that the British labour movement gathered strength as and where it did, but simply because of the sheer concentration of large numbers of wage-earners in industrial towns and close-packed industrial regions. Mention has already been made here of the contrast between the densely populated industrial districts of Great Britain and the market towns of the South of England. Those market towns – in Wiltshire, say, Somerset, or Devon – commonly each had its own factory of some size, but how little trade unionism there was in those parts, even down to the Second World War, and how little prospect for a Labour Party candidate, if indeed there were any such! What differentiated the workers here from those of the Midlands and the North was that they were scattered in penny packets. It is by the spatial concentration of an industrialized labour force that the sense of identity and common purpose of the British labour movement has been made possible and fostered. A further condition for the political power of that movement is that those regions though compact in area contain in the aggregate a high proportion of the whole occupied population.

That it was the factor of scale that starved out many impulses towards trade unionism and labour politics in Canada prompts another reflection. In the USA the great depressant on collectivist ideas that immigrants brought with them from Europe was the moral ascendancy of individualism: the newcomers had to learn to live among neighbours who held that the principle of the responsibility of each man for his own household was not merely prudential, but lay at the basis of American society. But in Canada that was not so: the immigrants' ideas of the labour movement would not wither in the Canadian air. No tradition or doctrine inculcated an abhorrence of collectivism such as prevailed south of the border. A Tory tradition, coming down from the Loyalists who moved into Canada after 1776, stressed authority and hierarchy, but with these went solidarity and benevolence, which occupy some common ground with collectivism. We have seen how widely the public sector has extended. So it came about that for all the set-backs of the attempts to launch labour parties, Canadian trade unions have remained politically minded. At the national level they have continued to present a very different prospect, in interests and activity, from their American counterparts. The British observer will reflect on how far the progress of the labour movement in his own country depended upon the values held by the community. Collectivism and combination fell foul of the common law tradition that upheld the rights of the individual. But the conservative and traditional bearers of authority, though repressive of insubordination, understood solidarity, and valued loyalty and brotherhood. For any believer in *laissez-faire*, trade unions were plainly harmful, as obstructive of market forces; that view was expressed forcibly, but how far did it penetrate? The rise of trade unionism and of labour in politics in Great Britain was made easier because the prevailing outlook on society did make these new activities, however unwelcome at first, intelligible and ultimately acceptable.

Our account of the reaction to Canadian trade unionism stressed the character of the Canadian employer. In the early days of British industrial development many more British employers will have been like the Canadian – pioneers, hard-driven and by necessity hard-driving. We are reminded by contrast how far the typical employer had changed by the end of the nineteenth century, when the Royal Commission directed our industrial relations on the course of voluntarism that they were to follow for the next seventy years: though the professional manager was rising, the typical employer was now the owner of a family business. The severity of the fluctuations to which the Canadian economy was subject calls attention also to the comparative shelter that British manufacturers had long enjoyed – even though the eight-year cycle ran through the British economy. In respect both of the type of ownership and management, and of market pressure, the British state of affairs made for accommodation with the unions.

A last reflection concerns the part played by the middle class in the rise of a labour movement. The beginnings of the labour movement in Canada suffered from what we have called the sparseness of the surrounding community – the opposition of 'capital' and 'labour' was unrelieved; the leaders from the ranks of labour were given little support and guidance; no existing and accepted code of fair dealing between employer and employed could be carried over into the new fields of employment. In Great Britain industry grew up within a society whose existing values it never superseded, and only here and there did the new industrial population completely dominate the neighbourhood. Hence an influence on the employer, who in many cases would not be insensible to the opinion of a local society some of whose members could take a detached view of his trade. But hence also the possibility often realized, locally and at national level, of middle-class people acting as mediators, legal advisers, spokesmen, and draftsmen; or, in the party, joining and holding office themselves. Whereas a labour force set over against capital in isolation turns to a revolutionary overthrow of capitalism, one that lives as part of a wider community is more likely to accept an evolutionary and democratic socialism. Though we see it now as a condition for the rise of an independent labour party that there shall be a sufficient regional agglomeration of workers, it also appears that the labour movement as we know it has been guided and advanced by this concentration being not isolated but an integral part of a varied society.

COMPARATIVE STUDIES: (ii) CANADIAN TRADE UNIONISM 251

Notes

¹ Lord (G. R.) Askwith, *Industrial Problems and Disputes* (London, 1920), ch. XXIV.

²*Canadian Industrial Relations*: Report of the Task Force on Industrial Relations (Privy Council Office, Ottawa, Dec. 1968), paras 414–16.

³ These proportions are all drawn from Table 10.1, Total Union Density by Country, in G. S. Bain and R. Price, *Profiles of Union Growth* (Oxford, 1980).

⁴ D. J. McDiarmuid, *Commercial Policy in the Canadian Economy* (Hammond University Press, 1946), p. 190.

⁵ H. D. Woods and Sylvia Ostry, *Labour Policy and Labour Economics in Canada* (Toronto, 1962), pp. 288–9.

⁶ Adam Smith, *The Wealth of Nations*, Bk. I, ch. VIII.

⁷ 'The Western Canadian Labour Movement, 1897–1919' (Mimeographed, June 1974), section 3.

⁸ Dominion Government, Dept. of Trade and Commerce, Census and Statistics Office, Fifth Census, 1911, vol. VI: Occupation of population aged 10 years and over, 1911.

XIV

COMPARATIVE STUDIES: (iii) AUSTRALIAN TRADE UNIONISM

To those who are steeped in the history of British trade unionism, the outstanding interest of Australian trade unionism lies in a paradox. For the British worker there has seemed to be an overt opposition between compulsory arbitration and democratic freedom: to be obliged to accept whatever the award may be is to be compelled to work on terms that may be repugnant. It opens a prospect of forced labour. But in Australia, in a vigorous and even aggressively democratic society, the trade unions since the turn of the century have largely accepted and worked within a system of arbitration. They have done this not, like American unions, in disputes of rights alone, but in disputes of interests. They inherited the traditions and even followed the pattern of British unionism, from which some of their founding fathers were drawn: why then have they accepted an arbitrament of which British unionists have been so chary? Our object here is to answer this question – a narrower object than outlining the history of trade unionism or of Labour in Australia. Our inquiry may point to a difference in the setting, or the course of development, that will make the difference in attitude intelligible; or it may indicate that a turn of events at one stage was enough to set the Australian unions on their specific course, and in that case the British observer may reflect, so it might have been in his own country. Let us see what happened.

I

Australian trade unionism began with friendly societies of craftsmen. In the 1840s there were a number of these in Sydney, among the building craftsmen, the printers, the tailors, the shipwrights, and the engineers. They were small, and in a mobile community they did not last long. But as in England and Scotland, their overt purpose of providing sick and funeral benefits might overlay an agreement to maintain certain trade practices. The authorities in Sydney who maintained a flogging discipline over the convicts assigned to work for private employers would not look kindly on combinations of free workers. In the face of great shortages of labour they had tried in 1845 to tighten the employers' hold by adding to the Master and Servant Act of 1828 a provision for imprisonment of the servant for breach of contract. But many of the immigrant craftsmen were already steeped in trade unionism, and they would naturally give their trade societies the functions of the societies they had known. There actually was a strike of printers on the *Australian* newspaper in Sydney in 1829. Other strikes occurred on wage claims in 1837 and 1838; there were many in 1840, and at this time we hear of the journeymen joiners and carpenters in Port Phillip (Melbourne) striking too. Meanwhile the Sydney unionists formed something like a trades council, when the United Tradesmen of Sydney gathered delegates from the unions to campaign in public affairs, especially to oppose the proposed amendment of the Master and Servant Act. By 1850 there were twenty-five trade unions in Sydney and thirteen in Hobart, mainly of carpenters and masons.[1]

But in 1851 the Gold Rush opened a new era. Four decades of sustained expansion carried the Australian worker to what was probably the highest standard of living of working men anywhere in the world at the time. Trade unions grew in a setting distinctive in all three aspects, economic, social, and political.

2

The economy was propelled by the export of wool and gold, and the inflow of British capital. In wool and gold there were discovered two products that packed high value into small bulk, and so overcame the handicap of the long haul overland to the ports and overseas to the British market. There were fluctuations, it is true, in the inflow of capital, and in the wool market: slumps occurred, with sharp falls in prices, cuts in wages, and great suffering from unemployment in the towns. But by comparison with the depressions that were occurring in the Old World and America at the time, these breaks in Australian expansion were short, a matter of one year or two at most. Population rose rapidly. In the decade of the Gold Rush, 1851–61, the population of New South Wales doubled, and that of Victoria was multiplied sixfold; between 1861 and 1891 the whole population of Australia doubled. But ever-growing numbers found occupation at rising standards of living.

The engine of their prosperity was in the pastoral and mining industries, but most of them lived and worked not up country but in the towns. By mid-century Australia was already one of the most

urbanized countries in the world. By 1890 it held two of the world's
great cities, Sydney with 400,000 inhabitants and Melbourne
approaching the half million. The typical Australian, not in image but
in fact, was a city dweller. That was the effect of climate. Rainfall
decreases rapidly as the clouds roll inland. Only near the coast was the
rainfall sufficient for farming to thrive in family holdings of modest
acreage. Further inland, in the wheatlands and still more in the sheep
runs, ever greater acreages were needed to provide an economic unit,
and they had to be operated with great capitals. By 1890, in the vast
outback, there were only some 150 stations in Queensland and 3,000
in New South Wales. The diggers dispersing from the exhausted
alluvial goldfields; the immigrants, assisted and self-financed, still
disembarking; the increase of the native population – few of these
job-hunters could find work on the land.

The business of the bulk of the working population therefore lay in
the towns and cities. There they provided the services of the merchant,
including the financing and transporting of goods, they built their own
houses, and they manufactured some consumer's goods and productive equipment for the home market. Until the 1880s few manufacturing firms were large. In 1860–1 the leading engineering firm in Sydney
was employing 120–200 men and boys; by 1886 the biggest firm had
come to employ 1,000. But in that same year the average number
employed in the metalworking, machinery, and carriage building
establishment of Victoria was only 20.[2] The average was kept down by
the setting up of new firms, often by foremen or workmen, in prosperous times; many would go out in the next slump. Manufacturing
firms generally operated under the competition of imports from the
United Kingdom, whose industry had economies of scale and technical
advancement to offset costs of transport. The Australian manufacturers demanded preference, and they obtained a tariff in Victoria, but
in New South Wales they met with opposition from the pastoralists,
concerned to keep down the price of imports and unwilling in principle
to tamper with free markets for exports.

From the first days of the penal colony, settlement had been closely
controlled by government; or that at least is what government intended. The grim authority exercised over convicts extended to a close
regulation of the affairs of the whole community. The control was not
always effective. The thin pastures of low rainfall could be exploited
only by settlers bringing large capitals with which to finance the
stocking of vast sheep runs: these were the wealthy 'squatters', and as
they fanned out into the interior the authorities lost control of the
allocation of land. Sometimes the hand of authority was felt to be
heavy. There were diggers who in the matter of prospectors' licences
felt themselves harassed by the police, against whom they fought a

brief but epic battle at the Eureka stockade in 1854. But generally governmental control was accepted because governmental support and enterprise were indispensable. Government was responsible not only for law and order but for the laying out of the towns, the building of roads and bridges, and the equipment of ports. In a land of vast distances, when railways came only governments could build and run them, but governments also operated the railway workshops. *Laissez-faire* was not a received doctrine in Australia; the issue of public against private enterprise did not present itself there as it did in the United Kingdom. It was the less likely to have done so, because the control of public enterprise passed so early and rapidly from an authoritarian administration to democratic self-government.

The 1880s brought conflicting changes that took profound and prophetic effect upon society. A sharp if temporary recession in 1886 formed the second phase of what the UK saw as the Great Depression. In world markets it was marked by a fall in the prices of primary products, and Australians saw the prices of wool, copper, and silver fall – even the price of wool, that had been steady for ten years. After a sequence of favourable seasons there came a drought, worst in South Australia, where a bank failed. On the other hand, throughout the decade the colonial governments were raising loans in London on a generous scale, and spending them on development, especially on building and equipping railways; and the British private investor lent almost as much again to the banks. In Victoria the inflow of capital promoted a building boom and drew a great immigration of labour from other states. In Melbourne office blocks were built that may be called skyscrapers because they were taller than any in a European city at that time.[3] A speculative boom in land values and property development arose and became frenzied.

3

In this economic framework – borne along, it would be better to say, by the great expansion of the economy until 1890 – *a new society* attained a distinct identity. One simple but basic observation is to be made at the outset: whereas most of the nineteenth-century migrants into the United States and Canada had to find their place in an existing social structure, the earlier settlers in Australia created their own social structure in an open space. They built it out of traditions and attitudes they brought with them, but under the strong pressure of daily life in a new economy. From the gall of the penal settlements – and from the boldness of the voluntary immigrants – stemmed anti-authoritarian attitudes, knowing nothing of the deference due in a society of accepted rank; but the repudiation of restraints was not individualist, for among men struggling for survival in a pitiless land the basic virtue was loyalty to one's mates. These attitudes were transmitted to and typified by the bushman.[4] Some middle-class people had come out from early days, and been at pains to keep their social distance; but they were overwhelmed numerically by the Gold Rush. Many of those who came in then were Irish. Others had been Chartists. The rest, of every description, were in quest of a fortune. It is hard to believe that they absorbed all the outlook of the bushmen, but they would have had to shake down together. The imperative of loyalty within the small group or to one special chum would have imposed itself naturally upon them. The diggings must have looked like an army deployed in the field, and group loyalties are strong among men in such detachment and exposure. They would have moved on as a classless body, judging people by their capabilities and not placing them by traditional badges of rank.

Save for the clash between the squatters and poorer claimants to the land, this society remained remarkably homogeneous until the 1880s. The conditions for class consciousness were wanting. These are, that the members of a group be aware of a common interest; that they be marked off from the rest of the community by some visible distinction; and that they see the common interest as needing defence against a conflicting interest elsewhere in society. In the young Australian society the proportion of people in the middle-class occupations such as bankers, lawyers, doctors, and other professions, even merchants and shopkeepers, was very low. The units of employment were small, and relations at the place of work were necessarily familiar. The employer had often been a workman himself not long before, and a turn of the market might make him one again. There was resentment, it is true, of the immense territories that had been seized and held by a handful of squatters: land-hungry immigrants found no place left for them. But when legislation was obtained to enable settlers to carve limited holdings at will out of the vast properties, little came of it; its application was resisted with cunning and obduracy, but the ultimate obstacle was that only large acreages could be farmed efficiently in those zones of aridity. Most Australians in any case were already living in towns and cities. But many workers, it seems, at least among the better-paid workers, owned their houses. One member of the Amalgamated Society of Engineers, applying for a loan from the union to help him buy his house – though this was later on, in 1900 – wrote, 'To become one's own landlord in Australia is the ambition of 85 per cent of the workers. We could not say this of those in the United Kingdom.'[5] Over-simplifying, but so as to bring out the contrast with the UK, we may say that the actual and potential trade unionists of Australia in 1850–80 were not marked off in large groups; they had no reason to be aware of themselves as sharply differentiated in welfare and status from any social superiors, or to see the advancement of their own interests as bound up with the defeat of any adversaries.

Part of the over-simplification lies in neglect of the changes that went on in the course of growth. There was increased differentiation of function, an expansion of the learned professions, an amassing of capital by successful enterprises, a rise of individual fortunes. The 1880s, though interrupted by a depression in 1886, brought a quickening of the pace which at the end in Melbourne brought a wild boom.

This was a time in which differences of wealth and income became more assertive than before, and when alignments by affluence, and clashes of economic interest, widened the rifts within a society lately conspicuous for its solidarity. In matters of status and class it now began to assume an aspect more familiar to the observer from the UK. One such, Francis Adams, writing at the end of the 1880s, deplored 'the ever-widening and ever-deepening gulf between the rich and poor'. He went on:

Properly speaking Australia is not yet fifty years old. It has been created by sheer muscle – by the pick and the shears. The rich of today, the Anglo-Australians, have almost all of them done manual labour of some sort or other by themselves. Ten years ago it was not too much to say that town employer and employee were thoroughly in touch with one another. With what an astonishing speed and intensity must the process of the aggregation of wealth have operated to range the two great classes of capital and labour today in the bitterest hostility to one another.[6]

But such conflict was mitigated by the presence within the liberal professions of men highly educated within Australia, active in public life, and sympathetic to the claims of the working man.

4

The political setting of Australian trade unionism was even more distinctive than the economic and social settings. Many of the early immigrants had come with a hatred of oppression, some with clearly formulated programmes of democratic advancement. The demands of the Ballarat Reform League whose members fought at the Eureka stockade included the five points of the British Chartists. When the Melbourne masons secured the eight-hour day in 1856, one of their leaders was a Chartist who had taken part in the Newport rising. Surprisingly soon, the aims of the Chartists were to be realized in Australia. Manhood suffrage was enacted in the 1850s in all the colonies except Tasmania and Western Australia. To the rest of the world, it seemed a desperately daring experiment. When the Chartist petition of 1842 had been presented at Westminster, Macaulay had urged its rejection on the ground that if the majority who owned no property were given the vote, they would use it to despoil the minority who did own property. But here was 'a form of government which entrusted ultimate power to people, of whom many could not write, many owned no property, many had served long criminal sentences and most had probably voted in no previous election'.[7]

In practice the franchise was weighted towards the settled and more propertied residents of the towns, as the mobile manual workers were less fully entered on the electoral rolls. None the less, the right was established. With it, also in the 1850s, in all the self-governing colonies, came the secret ballot. Payment of members was to be added, in Victoria in 1870 and in the other colonies in the 1880s. The whole achievement as it seemed to one trade unionist was summed up in 1890 by a President of the Typographical Union and of the Sydney Trades and Labour Council. After recording the strength of trade unionism and the benefits of some protective legislation, (with) 'all these advantages', he continued, 'added to vote by ballot, manhood suffrage, equal electoral districts, payment of members and other privileges which make him the most potent factor in the political arena, the lot of the working man is one to be envied by the masses of the civilised world.'[8]

At the time those words were written 'the most potent factor in the political arena' had not organized or asserted itself as a party. It was unlikely to have done so at a time when whatever the interest, loose groupings rather than organized parties prevailed in the colonial legislatures. But when at various intervals those legislatures adopted the British Acts of 1871 and 1875, designed to place normal trade union activity beyond the reach of the criminal law, they were responding to trade union pressure. Legislation on employer's liability and safety regulations was initiated by middle-class radicals, but these were supported by a working-class vote.

There was thus a distinct labour interest. In the 1880s it became more self-conscious and determined. The increased size of the firm, the formation of large units of control, the accumulation of conspicuous wealth, were presenting capitalism in harsher aspects. The belief that opportunity lay before the foot of the pioneer was losing its hold. Many people born as the children of wage-earners saw only the prospect of a life of wage-earning before them. They began to doubt whether their egalitarian aims would be achieved by the blend of political freedom with the existing economic system. The ideas of Henry George came to be much discussed among manual workers. In 1888 an inter-colonial trade union congress endorsed the single tax on land values. Before long the ideas of socialism were discussed too. In Queensland especially, where so much of the land was held by a handful of pastoralists, or the banks as their mortgagees, the idealistic socialism of a young journalist from Bristol, William Lane, was received readily. In earlier days economic growth had made for solidarity as it offered prosperity for all, and in liberal measure provided it. Now as it raised standards higher still it divided classes and politicized relationships.

But the rising Labour Party remained distinctively Australian. The socialism that calls on wage-slaves to throw off their chains did not appeal to a people who already felt themselves masters in their own house. The objective adopted by the Labour Party in 1905 consisted of two clauses of which the second comprised 'the collective ownership of monopolies and the extension of the industrial and economic functions of the State and Municipality', but the clause to which priority was given was very different. It expressed a national self-awareness achieved only after 1890. It may owe something to the wish to attract the non-labour voter. Yet it is still indicative of the special political setting of Australian trade unionism. It ran: '(a) The cultivation of an Australian sentiment based upon the maintenance of racial purity and the development in Australia of an enlightened and self-reliant community.'

5

In the economy and society the outlines of whose development have been drawn here, down to the 1880s *trade unionism* was neither much stimulated nor resisted. The Gold Rush, it is true, gave a powerful impetus for a time to the unions that survived the exodus. It commended itself to workers who remained in the settled districts as the way to claim rises in wages commensurate with the fantastic rise in the cost of living; and in a seller's market for labour it justified itself by obtaining those advances. But after that flurry unionism settled for nearly thirty years into two types, craft unions and some unions of the semi-skilled, notably the coal-miners and the seamen. These conducted their affairs very differently.

The craft unions carried forward the market tactics of the independent master craftsman: they did not negotiate, but relied on restriction of supply, and the unwillingness of their members individually to work for less than the rate that the scarcity of their skill would enable them to set upon it. But several factors drew them into collective bargaining and conflict. In slumps the employers, cutting rates below the union's minimum, effectively imposed a lock-out. Because the craft union would only admit men of approved qualifications it could not claim the closed shop, but it tried to limit the number of apprentices, and to stop the employer using unqualified men on work it regarded as its own. It wanted shorter hours, even more as a safeguard against unemployment than as a boon in themselves, but they could not be won by individual withdrawal of labour. In practice, moreover, changes in hours much more than in wages were felt to concern all the trades of a locality in common: these trades associated to press for them, and the employers associated on the same frontage. The movement for the eight-hour day was a great unifying force. That day won by the building crafts in Melbourne in 1856 and extended to the metal trades there by 1863 was not won in Sydney until ten years later. It had then to be defended against a counter-attack by the employers. The great metal trades lock-out in that year 1874 was a landmark in two ways: it was settled by a written agreement between the associated employers and the association that the trade unions had formed, and 'thus for the first time the ironmasters formally recognized a trade union organization'.[9]

Beside the craft unions there had been from early times some unions of the semi-skilled. The great threat to the striking unionists among the miners or seamen was that their places would be filled by non-members — the term 'scab' is said to have been coined in Sydney, from a disease of the sheep. So the unionists fought for the closed shop, and its extension throughout the industry; and the employers fought back for 'free contract'. Here, too, having a fairly standardized product of coal or freight, the employers were closely competitive with one another, so that they were bound to seek a common settlement of their labour costs. A Coal Miners' Protective Association established on the Hunter River in 1854 was followed in 1861 by an employers' association that imposed a lock-out. A Seamen's Union formed in 1874 was followed in 1878 by a Steamship Owners' Association. An Operative Bootmakers' Union of 1879 was countered by a Bootmanufacturers' Association of Victoria, which became the nucleus of an association of all employers in the colony. Meanwhile in a time of boom for coal, after two strikes the miners of the Hunter River field got their hours down in 1873 from twelve to ten. The next year the gold miners of Victoria formed a union that pressed for the eight-hour shift, better ventilation of the pits, and inspection of machinery; within three years it obtained a Regulation of Mines and Machinery Act.

In the 1880s all the unions shared the quickening pace of the economy. One sign was their uniting for common purposes. Local Trades and Labour Councils, which had been formed in the 1870s or earlier in Sydney and Melbourne, were now set up in Brisbane, Hobart, and Adelaide as well. When the trade unions began to meet together in inter-colonial congresses, as they did first in 1879, they had found a common purpose in bringing pressure to bear on governments. Joint action naturally became political action. After the second Congress, in 1884, Parliamentary Committees like that of the British TUC were set up in each of the self-governing colonies. These Committees lobbied their legislatures on such issues as the copying of the British Acts of 1871 and 1875, factory legislation, the eight-hour day, tariffs, education, and immigration.

But meanwhile the unions were becoming more vigorous in their own industrial spheres, extending their membership, and supporting one another in conflict. Their solidarity, and the broad coverage of the employers' associations formed to resist them, widened the scope of conflict. In 1886 the Melbourne Wharf Labourers struck in pursuance of their claim for the eight-hour day, and the unions of Stewards and Seamen came out in their support. Their dispute was distinguished not only by this solidarity of the unions, but also because it was the first to be settled by arbitration; the tribunal awarded the wharfmen their eight-hour day. But in any case it was remarkable that workers such as the Wharf Labourers should be capable of organization. They were not alone now. The outstanding development of the times was the gathering of the gold miners and the shearers into great inter-colonial unions.

Both were the creation of one man, William Guthrie Spence, who was born in the Orkneys and had come with his parents as a child, to live and work on the goldfields around Ballarat. There he educated himself. When the earlier miners' unions had died away, and in 1878 the companies announced a sharp cut in wages, Spence formed a new union, and stopped the cut. He proved to be an organizer of skill and immense energy, and a shrewd tactician. His Amalgamated Miners' Association spread over the continent and even entered New Zealand. Then in 1886 when the pastoralists under pressure from lower wool prices and lower rainfall were going to pay less for shearing, a young shearer appealed to Spence, and all his drive went into organizing an Amalgamated Shearers' Union. The drive was needed, for the bands of shearers were spread out over the vast distances between the stations that they served in the outback. Spence's agents rode from station to station. The members of his union would lie in wait for scabs on their way to a shed, lead them off to their own camp by a waterhole, and baptize them into membership. Men used to treking, working, and messing for weeks together had a mutual loyalty, a matey ethic, to which trade unionism came naturally. Like the Miners, the Shearers organized also in New Zealand.

Here was the outstanding advance in a decade of trade union advances. Unionism that before had been so largely a matter of small local unions of the skilled had now formed big inter-colonial unions of the semi-skilled. These unions demanded the closed shop, and they were militant. They existed to raise the bargaining power of labour and make use of it. When during the strike of the Wharf Labourers, 'the Seamen's Union notified the Shipowners' Association that its members would not man vessels bringing free labour to Melbourne, "We are compelled to take this course," they wrote, "owing to the struggle having assumed a new phase, viz. Capital v. Labor."[10] The employers responded by forming their associations, the pastoralists like the mining companies. Broad fronts were aligned for bargaining, and for conflict. At the end of the 1880s the new unions were taking the offensive on these fronts with the impetus imparted by a booming economy.

They were imbued too, as were unionists generally, by a confidence born of the great material progress achieved in the previous three decades; and the knowledge that their standard of living stood high in the world. By Noel Butlin's cautious estimate, per capita consumption in Australia rose between 1863 and the end of the 1880s by about 30 per cent – a sustained if not very rapid advance. But it was an advance mounted on what, on an international comparison, was a remarkably high base.

If we convert deflated *per capita* output or consumption figures ... of Australia, Britain and the USA in the 1860s, we achieve a quite startling result. ... Australian *per capita* income and consumption appear, on a first conversion via exchange rates, to have been about 50 per cent to 100 per cent above the corresponding figures for Britain and the United States. The obvious additional allowances to be made include differences in tariff levels and transport costs. Dubious as it might be, it is improbable that the most radical allowances would succeed in reducing Australian *per capita* standards in the 1860s below those in the wealthiest and most advanced countries in the world.[11]

Labour in Australia, conscious of its strength, felt able not only to stand firm on its own feet but help its poorer brethren in the old country. Much more than half the fund raised by the London dockers in their epic strike of 1889 came from Australia – even though not all of that £30,000 will have been subscribed by the trade unionists there.

6

No one could foresee that the trade unionists who joined battle in 1890 with such self-confidence were charging over a cliff. Changes in the market had already set in, changes even in the climate were to follow, that would confound them. The boom burst in Melbourne, and bank after bank ceased payment. The panic spread to Sydney.

Demand in domestic markets contracted, as people tried to save their cash balances by cutting down their spending: unemployment rose. It rose all the more, because the loans raised in London and laid out on development were now largely cut off, even though colonial governments still raised what they could to finance what were in effect relief works. The presence of so many unemployed men without maintenance, driven by hunger to take any work offered them, made the newly formed employers' associations powerful opponents: they broke strikes with ample supplies of blacklegs. But more than this: if the trouble had been only a cyclical depression, albeit a violent one, in the industrial and financial sector, the pattern of such sequences suggests that the Australian economy would have recovered, say, in 1895 and have reached a high level of activity again by 1898. But instead there began in 1895 seven years of drought: the country's total stocks of sheep and cattle alike were to be all but halved between 1894 and 1904.[12] This fearful blow to the principal export industry held back the whole economy. There would still be no setting in which the trade unions could make good their claims.

There were four major engagements that the trade unions lost. The Maritime Strike of 1890 was the most expensive of all. It began with the Steamship Owners' Association objecting to a union of Marine Officers affiliating to the Melbourne Trades Hall Council. The militancy of trade unionism at the time is shown by the general stoppage on the waterfront that was set off when the officers struck; and Spence organized a Labor Defence Council that brought his own Shearers' Union in with three coal-miners' unions to help the five unions that were engaged on the waterfront. His Shearers had their own dispute brewing at the time with Pastoralists who were set on 'freedom of contract': instead of the existing common agreement that the union had obtained for all stations, the Pastoralists meant to make separate agreements station by station. Yet the broad front was still not broad enough, for the ship's engineers did not come out, the crews were made up with blacklegs, and the ports handled the ships with blackleg dockers. In another way the front was too broad, for when the Shearers were called out the other strikers lost their main source of funds. A minor issue raised by the extension of unionism to a group of managers had strangely set off a trial of strength between the organized ranks of semi-skilled and unskilled labour and their associated employers throughout eastern Australia; and the unions were broken.

Part of the cost of defeat was that the Shearers had to accept the Pastoralists' separate station agreements; but within a few months the Queensland Shearers came back to the fight for a common union agreement. Thus opened the second great strike, that of 1891. For six months a campaign was carried on in the outback, where the unionist fought not so much against the Pastoralists as against the armed forces of a colonial Government which the Pastoralists dominated. These armed forces protected convoys of blackleg shearers. It was again the plentiful availability of blacklegs – together this time with the conviction and imprisonment of unionists – that broke the strike.

At the great isolated mining settlement of Broken Hill, the miners had merged their local union in Spence's Australian Miners' Association, the AMA, from its earliest days. in 1889 they actually won from the Company, the great BHP, both the closed shop and the check off. When they were contributing generously to the strikers' funds in 1890, the Company locked them out, but this was an expensive gesture of employer solidarity at a time of profitable production, and the miners came back to work after only two weeks and on improved terms. But in 1892, the price of silver had fallen. The Company ended its agreement with the union. The union began a strike which in a sense never ended, for the Company drew in blacklegs under the protection of armed police, and when the strike was formally terminated it was these whom the Company engaged, rather than former unionists. Many of these went off to the newly discovered goldfields in Western Australia. BHP reported later that 'Peace reigned on the Barrier for the ensuing decade.'[13] Such was the third great strike and great defeat of the unions.

The fourth came two years later, in 1894, when the Queensland Shearers, this time with many in New South Wales, came back to the charge against station agreements. What they struck against was a new clause that made the station owner or manager the final arbiter in cases of dispute. The struggle was violent. This time both sides used firearms. A band of unionists boarded a steamer, the *Rodney*, carrying blacklegs up the Murray, expelled the occupants, and burned the vessel to the waterline. A shearing shed was burned down. But these were the marks of desperation. The blacklegs were too numerous: they broke the strike in three months. The flames of the *Rodney* flicker still over this page of history, but in fact the campaign was always doomed: in a deep and sustained depression the number of non-unionists avid for work and wages was too great to be kept out by pickets of such unionists as were left.

If the depression had been only cyclical, if the great drought had not supervened, then probably with economic revival the trade unions would have revived too, and collective bargaining would have grown up again generally in the British way, as it had promised to do at the end of the 1880s. In fact there were particular industries in which it did so. But meanwhile another procedure had taken possession of the field. The collapse of the strikes in 1890–4 provides the immediate setting for the advancement and acceptance of arbitration.

7

Proposals for arbitration had been mooted in Australia long before the conflicts of the 1890s. The British example from the 1860s onwards will have been observed: in a number of industries much harassed by strikes and lock-outs the settlement of disputes proved to be very greatly facilitated at that time in Great Britain by the setting up of joint boards of conciliation and arbitration.[14] The Australian craft unions were attracted. The weaker party to the wage bargain is likely to seek recourse to arbitration, but it may also be sought by parties who are confident of their relative strength and simply wish to avoid the costs of conflict. So it seems to have been with the craft unionists in the years when Australian society was still comparatively unified. As late as 1886 a delegate to the Inter-colonial Trade Union Congress declared

In all trade difficulties the first steps that should be taken were arbitration and conciliation. Strikes were a relic of a barbaric age, and it was time that before they ever entered upon a strike they should think of the other people who would be affected. (Hear, hear). He did not mean to say that strikes were ever rashly entered upon, but before entering upon such agitations they should have recourse to arbitration and conciliation (Hear, hear). Arbitration was growing and as it grew so would their unions become stronger and more moderate.[15]

There were trade union leaders in Great Britain who preached the virtues of moderation and good relations, and genuinely believed in them; but language such as this implies a more assured standing in the community. The approach is rather that of businessmen who take their disputes with one another to arbitration rather than incur the senseless costs of litigation.

The speaker just quoted was the secretary of the Trades Hall Council of South Australia. In that colony arbitration was being promoted by its Premier Charles Cameron Kingston. He had been born and educated there; a lawyer by training, a patrician by status (as it was said), and a radical by leaning, in later years he came to hold the governance of the colony in his hands. In 1890 he brought in a Bill that provided a pattern for subsequent legislation in New Zealand as well as Australia. The first of its stated purposes was 'to encourage the formation of industrial unions and associations', and only after that did it state its aim 'to facilitate the settlement of industrial disputes'. It provided for the registration of unions and associations by an industrial registrar, and a structure of local boards of conciliation under a State Board, whose awards would be binding for five years; any registered body engaging in strike or lock-out would be liable to a heavy fine. The Bill failed of enactment, as did another Bill for arbitration two years later. A Royal Commission reported on both Bills, and from its recommendations came a Labour Disputes Settlement Act of

1894. This armed the arbitrators with legal sanctions to require both the attendance of parties to the dispute and compliance with the award. It would have been a landmark if it had been effective: but the first time it was invoked the award went against the employers, who simply rejected it, and that was the end of the Act. So no viable arrangements had been worked out in South Australia; but the discussion there proved influential.

An early effect was in New South Wales. Proposals that the State should provide arbitration had been put forward there in the 1880s by two politicians who were each to serve the colony for several terms as Premier, Sir George Dibbs and Sir Henry Parkes, but these initiatives had met with too much opposition from employers and too little support from labour to be pressed far. The setting was changed by the great strike of 1890: the Government set up a Royal Commission 'to investigate and report upon the causes of conflicts between capital and labour known as strikes, and the best means of preventing or mitigating the disastrous consequences of such occurrences'. C. C. Kingston gave evidence before the Commission in favour of compulsory arbitration, and it may have been his Bill that the Commission drew upon for its recommendation of a Board of Conciliation and Arbitration. Meanwhile for the first time a substantial number of Labour members had been returned to the State legislature in the election of 1891, and they wanted arbitration. With their support a Conciliation and Arbitration Act was passed in 1892. But the Board that it set up proved ineffective, because no unwilling party could be brought before it, and employers often were unwilling: after two years the Board lapsed.

Thus in 1894 it seemed that the procedure that so many politicians and labour leaders in Australia still wanted had been found impracticable, by reason of the employers' ability to ignore or defy it. The advocates of arbitration did not lose their faith; various proposals were put forward; but nothing was enacted for some years. In Victoria the conclusion seemed to have been reached that the way forward was different: there the State intervened in wage-fixing to set up tripartite boards to regulate the pay of the workers who were held to need protection, in practice at first those who were the lowest paid. The small employers concerned proved amenable.

But in 1894 New Zealand had adopted an Industrial Conciliation and Arbitration Act whose working was proving so effective that it seemed to contain what was needed to improve on the first Australian models. This Act was the handiwork of a remarkable man, William Pember Reeves, born and educated in the South Island, a newspaper editor who had read widely and become an early convert to Fabian socialism. As a minister in what was virtually a Labour Government, though Liberal by title, in 1891, he initiated a vigorous programme of labour legislation. This included a bill for conciliation and arbitration, but the employers' hostility and the weight of other business caused it to be held over. Yet the Great Maritime strike of 1890 had involved New Zealand as well as Australia, and how to prevent strikes and protect trade unionists was now Reeves's chief concern. This problem he studied patiently. He consulted Judge Kettle. He came to agree with his own trade unionists of Otago that arbitration must be made compulsory; but the only case of compulsory arbitration in practice that he could find anywhere in the world was in the Territory of Wyoming. His survey comprised the voluntary boards of conciliation in Massachusetts, the Conseils de Prud'hommes in France, C. C. Kingston's proposals to the Royal Commission in New South Wales, and the subsequent Act in that State.[16]

As finally drafted his Bill provided for district boards of conciliation made up of representatives of employers and trade unions with an independent chairman. He hoped that most disputes would be settled there, but failing agreement either party or the board itself could remit the dispute to a court of arbitration. This would be presided over by a judge of the district or supreme court sitting with assessors nominated by employers and trade unions. The court was left with discretion to give its award legal force or not: if it did do so, failure to comply might be visited with a heavy fine. It had jurisdiction over all employers, but only over trade unions registered under the Trade Union Act.

The Bill when first presented was mauled by the Upper House, and it became law only after another election, in 1894. What was there in it, what new device or principle, to escape from previous failures and provide the pattern for Australia? A feature that Reeves himself stressed at the time – the discretion left to the court whether or not to make its awards binding – seems to have been of little consequence in the event. The essential difference in these new arrangements seems to have been simply that they got a grip on the employers.

Any provision for the settlement of industrial disputes faces the two problems of the enforcement of its awards on the trade unionists and on the employers concerned. In New Zealand and Australia at this time the first problem would hardly arise, for most trade unions were weak, and would look to the court to enforce better terms than they could ever hope to gain by their own bargaining power. But in any case Reeves's Act did not outlaw the strike. A union that felt strong enough to conduct its bargaining in the old way with the old sanctions had only to remain unregistered, and the employers could not take it to court. Enforcement on the employers was a different matter. So far in Australia they had been able to frustrate the operation of enactments. What made the difference in Reeves's scheme was that all employers were made liable to be brought before the court on the application of a registered union. This was a general and inescapable obligation: arbitration, though voluntary for trade unionists, was compulsory for employers. Once the employer was brought into court, the enforcement of an award as part of the terms of the individual employee's contract of service has at no time presented any great problem.

This device was now to be taken over in Australia, both by those states that adopted compulsory arbitration, and by the Commonwealth on its formation. The two landmarks were a New South Wales Act in 1901, and an Act of the new Commonwealth in 1904. These Acts were not obtained without a great struggle, for they were vigorously resisted by the employers, who saw them as means of strengthening unionism and forcing up wages. But the employers were borne down by two forces, the rising labour parties and the federalists.

We have seen how after their Congress of 1884 the trade unions set up Parliamentary Committees in each colony, and these were a first step towards the formation of labour parties; but in no legislature was there a group of Labour members capable of united and independent action by 1890. The cataclysmic strike of that year brought a great change about. When the trade unionists rallied what was left of their forces, they saw their recovery as requiring two things, the adoption of compulsory arbitration, and the control by a Labour Party of the Governments that had played a major part in their recent defeat.

The reaction was most marked in New South Wales. In June 1891 a Labour Electoral League adopted a programme of sixteen points. In the election that followed its candidates won 36 of the 136 seats in the Assembly. When the new Labour members had learned to form a disciplined and unified party, this came to hold the balance of power between the two existing parties after subsequent elections. It was thus able to secure the adoption of new arrangements for arbitration. We have seen how in 1892 it helped to secure the passing of a Conciliation and Arbitration Act, and how this failed. More attempts followed, for Labour was still intent on arbitration. What proved a decisive step was taken when a Royal Commission was sitting on the problem, and a judge was sent over to New Zealand to study the apparently successful working of Reeves's Act there. The Arbitration Act of 1901 was drafted on the recommendations of the Commission and drew many of its provisions from Reeves. Its history was chequered, and before long it was superseded. Yet it has been deemed the first effective provision for compulsory arbitration on any statute book.

As the Labour Party grew State by State, so did the pressure to legislate for compulsory arbitration, or for wages-boards as an alternative. The New South Wales Act of 1901 was the first of many measures that were to cover the six States with institutions for the prevention and settlement of disputes and the regulation of the terms of employment. Their enactment everywhere owed much to the Labour Party's commitment.

The New South Wales Act of 1901 was also the forerunner of the Act of 1904 by which the newly created Commonwealth assumed, as one of its few domestic activities, responsibility for the prevention and settlement of industrial disputes extending beyond the boundaries of one State. The movement to federate was the second of the political forces rising at this time to overcome the employers' opposition, for some of the outstanding advocates of federation were also wholehearted believers in compulsory arbitration. By no means all the makers of the new Constitution were of this mind, but in the last Convention those who were succeeded narrowly in inserting a clause empowering the Commonwealth to engage in 'conciliation and arbitration for the prevention and settlement of industrial disputes extending beyond the limits of any one State'. When the Commonwealth Parliament met, what action if any should be taken under this clause became a major issue of bitter dispute, on which two Governments fell. At length, at the end of 1904, a Commonwealth Conciliation and Arbitration Act was passed.

The fateful decision was thus taken to proceed by way of a court and not by the type of wages-board developed in Victoria. For the original purpose of the Act a court seemed the natural instrument: the procedure of the civil law for settling disputes would simply be extended over a new field, under a judge seconded from the High Court. The principle was that when the parties to a dispute within the Commonwealth jurisdiction failed to reach agreement they must not resort to strike or lock-out, but could come to the Court – either party could take the other there, willy-nilly – and be given the terms of an equitable settlement. There the functions of the Court might have ended, in occasional peacemaking and *ad hoc* settlements. But this was not how its functions were conceived by its second President, Mr Justice Higgins, nor what, thanks to him, they became. For instead of simply settling each case on its merits, he set himself to establish principles by which cases were dealt with consistently, and awards assessed uniformly. What is more, he made these principles explicit: they permeated the world of voluntary negotiations and settlements, for the parties knew what terms would be imposed if either took the other to Court. Thereby the Court was both to attract the custom of trade unions over wide sectors of the economy, and to establish itself by degrees as the major source of influential action upon the movement of the general level of wages and the proportions of the wage structure, throughout the Commonwealth.

So began a history of arbitration, in State courts and Commonwealth, that through many changes of law and practice has extended for three-quarters of a century.

8

How came it that the Australians committed themselves to compulsory arbitration at the time when, as they well knew, the British had decided that they had no more use for it? This British decision had been reached after thirty years of experience with joint boards. The constitution of these boards had often provided that if the parties could not reach agreement round the table, then the independent chairman should have the casting vote, or the issue should be remitted to an umpire whose award the parties undertook to accept. This arrangement might work well at first, but difficulties would arise as time went on. The prospect of resort to arbitration tended to stultify negotiation, because the parties became chary of making concessions that would weaken the case to be stated to the arbitrator. The role of arbitrator was hard to fill: the detachment from the industry that was a necessary condition of disinterest might also bring an embarrassing ignorance of relevant technicalities; an arbitrator who was seen to bring certain principles to bear in his awards would be unacceptable to a party that did not agree with them, but one who suppressed his own judgement and split differences would simply invite the raising of claims. In any case not all issues were amenable to arbitration. An issue of principle might arise on which no compromise was possible and neither party would accept the other's position. When the unionists were faced with a wage-cut they might be in a mood to go down fighting rather than go to arbitration meekly, even though that might reduce the cut.[17]

So it came about that an institution of which such high hopes had reasonably been entertained in the 1860s had collapsed by the 1890s. Often the trade unions had broken away from the Boards, because their members had refused to accept some award. Behind the particular difficulties that have just been set out lay a change in attitudes. The Boards had been formed in a setting of local consensus, and a basic willingness to reach agreement between trade union spokesmen and employers who were divided at that time by no gulf of residence, religious observance, or political outlook. But the ensuing years of economic development brought a divergence of attitudes. The 'two sides' drew apart; class consciousness increased among the workers; industrial relations came to be seen as a confrontation of adversaries. The established unions, moreover, felt well able to deal with the employers directly. Newly formed unions, still weak and struggling, did call for compulsory arbitration after the turn of the century because it would enable them to bring into court the employers who could refuse to recognize them as it was. But the self-reliant unions had no intention of surrendering to any arbitrator their freedom of manoeuvre in attack and defence.

What was it, then, that made Australian unions, so like the British in other respects, accept arbitration? One immediate and very evident answer we have had before us already – after their defeats in the great strikes of the 1890s and during the prolonged depression of those years, they saw arbitration as a form of protection when they were too weak to defend themselves. This is valid, and important. Those defeats gave a great impetus to the unions' advocacy of arbitration. But they believed in arbitration already. It was not that their defeats aroused them to possibilities previously neglected, still less made them change their minds. We have seen in what glowing terms a delegate to the Inter-colonial Trade Union Congress of 1886 had exalted arbitration. Two reasons may be given for this approval of arbitration, especially among craft unions whose counterparts in the UK would have none of it.

There was first the social and political setting. The adoption of manhood suffrage in most of the colonies within a decade of the battle at the Eureka stockade put the colonists far ahead of the folk at home. The secret ballot followed. The community was consciously democratic. The Australian working man was actively aware of the equality of citizenship that distinguished him from the still unenfranchised workers of the Old World. This pride of manhood became diffused into a social consensus – if not a solidarity, at least an absence down to the 1880s of a cleavage between 'us' and 'them'. The squatters stood out; but these apart, the great inequalities that did exist seemed the luck of the draw or the rewards of the pioneer. Only gradually did the field narrow that had been open to the adventurer and developer, and people's outlook change with the narrowing; only gradually did inheritance become a major source of the inequality of wealth. In this setting the trade union did not arise as a defence of the weak against the strong. For the craftsmen it was a means of upholding the value set upon their skill. The issues that concerned them were not inherently convulsive, but capable of adjustment; after the costs of a stoppage had been borne by the combatants and inflicted on the community, a settlement would have to be reached in the end: let an arbitrator give it in the first place. In agreeing to this the trade unionists did not feel that they were letting their arms be tied behind their backs, for they did not see themselves as needing those arms to ward off a superior power.

For the British trade unions, who did feel that they were confronted with a superior power, one arm of it appeared to be the law. Not so for the Australian unions: this was the second reason for their acceptance of arbitration. It is true that the law of Master and Servant, originally applied to the disciplinary purposes of penal settlements, remained on the statute book, and strikers were convicted under it for leaving work unfinished as late as the 1880s. But these were prosecutions of individuals. The trade union as an institution in Australia had not had to loose itself from legal shackles. There had been no early phase of repression of the union as a criminal conspiracy, there were no leading cases in which the right to strike was undermined. In a society of high social mobility, again, the lawyers who reached the bench were not set apart as a class; they did not seem repressive simply by virtue of their rank and office, as the judges did to British trade unionists. During the great strike of 1891 the Chief Justice of Victoria subscribed £50 to the local strike fund, and promised to renew his subscription each week so long as the employers refused to meet trade union spokesmen.

But the attitudes of trade unionists would have been very different if they had been formed only in the strikes of the 1890s, for the employers now used the full force of the law against the strikers. Especially was this true of the Pastoralists and the Queensland Government that they controlled. Trade unionists were imprisoned for conspiracy, unlawful assemblage, riot and tumult, and molestation; some were proceeded against under a British statute of 1825. W. G. Spence, the shearers' leader, told later how the employers in New South Wales began to use the injunction. 'The introduction of American employers' methods of fighting labour by injunctions placed us in a serious difficulty', he said, and he deplored 'the power of judge-made law in a new form'.[18] In one of his books he devoted a whole chapter to the biased administration of the law. 'The trade unionists of Australia', he said, 'have received far worse treatment than those of the old world. The Governments have been more cruel and unjust and judges have displayed a bias which can only be characterised as class hatred.'[19] Yet – this is instructive by its apparent inconsistency – he stood firmly for arbitration. So did W. M. Hughes, the leader of the Waterside Workers in the strike of 1891. Spence commended it in terms which implied his faith that the courts could be trusted to deal fairly between employers and unions. He would have been thinking of courts specially constituted by a democratically elected Parliament – elected in a democracy that was thoroughly social and egalitarian in sentiment, moreover, not one whose traditional hierarchy had only been modified by piecemeal extensions of the franchise. In the same way he would have felt that the courts and judges whose enmity he stigmatized were unrepresentative of the people of Australia and must yield to them. To British trade unionists the whiff of the law in arbitration brought the thought of hereditary ranks and the tilting of the scales against the lower orders of society; Australians who had grown up since 1850 had more trust in the law to do justice between man and man.

This attitude to the law depended in turn on the political setting. In democratic communities that had long enjoyed manhood suffrage, if the law oppressed working people they could reasonably expect to get it altered. Especially was this so from 1891 onwards as Labour rapidly gained seats in legislatures, and a Labour Party arose. In New South Wales and the Commonwealth the enactment of compulsory arbitration was the joint achievement of the new political force of Labour and the liberal politicians of an older school.

It was to these latter politicians that the shaping of the legislation was due. Some were men of middle-class upbringing but with genuine sympathy with the claims of labour; some had begun as manual workers themselves. For these it may have been enough that compulsory arbitration was clearly what the unionists wanted – just as, the other way about, the Liberals in the Westminster Parliament were to accept the predominant wish of the British trade unionists to be left free to strike. Other Australians again were moved by a profound conviction, deepened by the alarming conflicts of the 1890s, that orderly government itself depended upon providing a means of preventing and settling industrial disputes. This conviction was reached the more readily in societies always subject to more regulation by government than had been accepted in principle in the UK. Though the enactment of compulsory arbitration was stoutly resisted in the legislatures, particularly by the representatives of the employers, the unionists' own wish for it was thus supported by powerful political forces, including some concerned with preserving law and order.

It was also supported by the teaching of the Roman Catholic Church, to which a substantial proportion of the population – in New South Wales as much as a quarter – belonged. The Archbishop of Sydney had taken Labour's side in the great strike of 1890. He was influential in making known the teaching of *Rerum Novarum*, the Papal Encyclical of that year, which commended arbitration. Mr Justice Higgins had had a Wesleyan upbringing, but it is noteworthy that in the course of his fundamental Harvester 'Award' he referred to conditions of 'frugal comfort', which is a term that appears in the English text of *Rerum Novarum*.[20]

Here in all was a setting that was conducive to the acceptance of compulsory arbitration. But the system that was being set up in some of the States and the Commonwealth was unproven. It had to commend itself to the trade unions. They were encouraged to accept the New South Wales Act of 1901, and an Act for compulsory arbitration which Western Australia had adopted the year before, by the knowledge th t the New Zealand Court in its first award had granted union preference. The Australian courts could grant this too. It might take several forms, from an obligation to give preference to union members, other things being equal, in recruitment or redundancy, to the closed shop. The possibility of such an award was a great attraction to unions struggling to build up their membership. It added to the other great attraction of the system for them, the power to take employers to court, and so solve the problem of obtaining recognition.

These attractions took effect from the first. Only as time went on would it be seen whether the courts' wage awards were attractive. But a great impact was made by the declaration of Mr Justice Higgins in the Harvester case in 1907 that the basic wage of the unskilled labourer should be 7s. a day. The budgetary data that he cited were scanty, and did not come near filling out the figure of 7s.: how then did he arrive at it? Professor Keith Hancock has provided an answer, following studies by P. G. Macarthy.

The daily rate of 7s. had important emotional and political associations. It was a widely prevailing rate in the 1880s, but in the depression of the 1890s the wages of the unskilled fell below it. To political and industrial labour, the continued payment of less than 7s. epitomized the employers' industrial ascendancy, and the preparedness of the arbitration tribunals to enforce 7s. was a measure of their effectiveness in redressing the balance of power.[21]

Thus were the credentials of the courts established. But the Commonwealth Court extended its effective jurisdiction only gradually. From 1912 onwards the trade unions began to extend their activities and arrange their disputes so as increasingly to bring their case into the Commonwealth rather than into a State court, for it was in the Commonwealth Court that they expected to get the better terms. By the later 1920s about 60 per cent of all wage changes were being effected through it.

9

We have seen how the Australian trade unions came to commit themselves to compulsory arbitration. The special circumstances of the time played a major part. Behind them were certain characteristics of Australian society. The positive policy adopted by the Commonwealth Court was a powerful factor too. These considerations account for the initial entrance into the system. But how do we explain the continuing hold of the system over the unions down the century since? Is the persistence of the last two factors enough to account for the willingness of the unions, prevailing down the century to this day, to follow the procedures of the system and accept its constraints, even when they need no longer look to it to redress the balance of bargaining power?

The system does in fact have no effective means in the last resort of controlling the union that disregards arbitration and enforces its demands by striking. The prohibition of strike and lock-out under Commonwealth law was repealed in 1930. Only in Western Australia does an outright prohibition remain under State law. What has continued important has been the insertion in awards of a clause forbidding any strike or ban on normal working – the 'bans clause' – during the currency of the award. 'The trade union movement never accepted that compulsory arbitration took away its right to strike', a legal authority on the system has concluded. Compulsory arbitration 'merely put the right to strike further into the background',[22] that is, to be drawn on after going to arbitration and failing to secure a satisfactory award.

The main sanction against a persistently striking union used to be deregistration, with consequent loss of legal personality and union preference, and the ability to take the employer to court; but the union was usually restored to the register fairly soon. A change came in 1949, when at the climax of a time of industrial unrest in the post-war boom the Commonwealth Labour Government settled a great coal strike by emergency legislation under which several unions were fined. Employers now moved the Commonwealth and New South Wales courts to take similar action. They did so, sparingly at first, and then in the 1960s increasingly: down to the end of 1967 the unions paid their fines. One reason given is that they accepted the validity of the case against inflationary wage claims; another, that the strikes penalized were often led by communists, against whom there was at the time an organized reaction within the unions and Labour Party. But by 1969 too many fines were outstanding, and when in pursuance of the collection of one of them a trade union officer was imprisoned the outcry was threatening. Since then there has been little attempt to apply sanctions through penal proceedings. If the system had kept the unions within it, that has not been by compulsion.

Indeed it is in one sense by the very weakness of the system that their adherence may in part be explained. There has been no strait-jacket here, nor attempt to impose any uniform control. The system is one of great complexity and variety. In lively colours it has been so depicted by J. Hutson, the author of a history of wage regulation published by the Amalgamated Engineering Union, as follows:

This is the recipe. Mix together two State arbitration systems which have some similiarity, two similar State wages board systems which are different in some respects, two State systems which are crossbred betwen arbitration and wages boards systems, and a Commonwealth arbitration system which has some similarity to two of the State systems. Drop in an assortment of associated tribunals, both State and Commonwealth, such as Coal Industry Boards, a Stevedoring Industry Authority, Public Service Boards, and various other subsidiary tribunals. Season with Departments of Labour, both State and Commonwealth, a Tariff Board, State Trade Unions Acts, and special State legislation to cover such things as compensation, apprenticeship, equal pay, hours, long service leaves and adjustments to the basic wage. Throw in some common law, sprinkle with the legal fraternity, flavour with a suggestion of lunacy, and simmer the mixture well on the hotplate of employer–employee relationship.[23]

Not only is the arbitration system itself so various, but its awards mingle and interact with the settlements reached in voluntary collective bargaining. There is no obligation on the parties to enter a system which formally exists only to provide a peaceful settlement if that cannot be reached directly by the parties themselves. But parties who reach a voluntary agreement often wish to have it registered as what is called a 'consent award', for this will provide for its legal enforcement, and under State law will make it a common rule binding on employers who were not parties to it. There is interaction in the sizes of settlements. A gain made by direct action will put pressure on arbitrators to award more than they might otherwise consider. A particular award may spread out through many voluntary settlements, and those who engage in bargaining will be influenced by their expectations of what the award is likely to be if they go to arbitration.

It is natural to find in so varied and flexible a system that the type and quality of industrial relations varies greatly from industry to industry. The size of the unit, the nature of the processes, the traditions of craft, the fluctuations of the market, the impact of personalities, the sheer accidents of history, the strength of tradition – all these are free to give industrial relations their distinguishing characteristics industry by industry, as much in Australia as in other countries. They differentiate atmosphere and procedure over a wide range, from the co-operative to the combative, and from the wholly voluntary to those that rely steadily on arbitration.

Here, then, is a major reason for the willingness of the trade unions to stay with the system – its flexibility. At times when the bargaining power of the unions has been running high its restraints on them have been harassing but not overpowering; when they were weak or on the defensive it offered them the prospect of better terms than they could hope to get without it. The prolonged experience of full employment after the Second World War, with the greater bargaining power that it brought to the trade unions, did lead to a major modification of the system, through the virtual abandonment of penal proceedings: by contrast it appears that the acceptance of the system in earlier years owed much to the predominance of a depressed labour market down to the Second World War. Then when the seller's market for labour predominated, it was the system that yielded under pressure.

There remain three other considerations that help to account for the unions remaining within the system all these years. Of these the first is that they have been adapted to the system; or, it might be said, the system has proved well adapted to them. It may be that the very uneven distribution of the sizes of Australian trade unions has not been more skewed than that of British unions in the same period, but the factor of scale has been different: absolute size takes effect. Where units of employment are small, and union members are scattered in penny packets, it is difficult to organize a strike in any country, and that consideration applies to more industries and unions in Australia than in a country where unions and firms are larger. This means that more unions in Australia have very much to gain by procedures which solve the problem of recognition for the union, provide legal enforcement for rates as minima, and give a common rule. Of many unions it may be said that they cannot leave the system because they have nowhere else to go.

The second consideration is that the arbitrators have generally worked with the grain of labour: they have based their awards on principles which agree with the ways in which workers themselves think that wages should be fixed. In his historic judgement in 1907, Mr Justice Higgins in the Commonwealth Court laid it down that the basic wages should meet 'the normal needs of an average employee, regarded as a human being living in a civilised community'. This basic wage he held sacrosanct: no lack of profitability and no pressure of competition could justify reducing it by a penny. In these ways he placed the claims of humanity above the workings of the market. But on the basic wage was mounted a margin for skill, in which the rate for the fitter in engineering came to be taken as the leading case; and here there was room for adjustment to supply and demand. In considering what margins over the basic rate were appropriate in particular occupations and industries, the arbitrators would have regard to the degree of skill and responsibility, that is, to relativity taken vertically between grades, and to fair comparisons taken horizontally between one occupation and another. In considering changes in pay, they would have regard to the cost of living. These were the ways in which the workers themselves thought, and they regarded rates set in the light of these considerations as being at least potentially fair, and not imposed from on high, out of the assumption of superior wisdom. Difficulties have indeed arisen in later years when the Commonwealth arbitrators, having regard to the national interest in checking inflation, raised wages by less than the rise in the cost of living.

Third, there remains an influence which must be expected to have helped keep trade unionists in the system – namely, the belief of the community as a whole that the system should be upheld. The most consistent opposition has come from the employers. Governments have continually modified the system in detail, and twice changed the Commonwealth structure basically, but only once has a Government attempted to abolish the Commonwealth jurisdiction. This was in 1929, when the Bruce–Page administration was under convergent pressures. There was a great maritime strike. High and mounting unemployment was thought to call for wage reductions, which the arbitration system obstructed. A British economic mission had called attention to the troubles of firms entangled within both State and Commonwealth awards. Mr Bruce therefore proposed a clean cut: he would abolish the Commonwealth jurisdiction save for the maritime industry. But when he went to the country his Government was defeated; he even lost his own safe seat. The vote was taken as the people's verdict on the arbitration system, and this has stood ever since. The general opinion has been and remains that the principle is right. The present working of the system is most unsatisfactory, but a still worse thing would be to lose the system altogether. An ILO report in 1933 found that 'At almost any time there is a strong feeling against the actual system in operation, coupled with a fairly persistent faith in compulsory arbitration as a method.'[24] To adapt what Churchill said of parliamentary democracy, compulsory arbitration appears as the worst system of pay fixation except all the others. The trade unionist is enclosed by this outlook of the community, which he may well share.

Notes

[1] A. G. L. Shaw and H. D. Nicolson, *Growth and Development in Australia* (Sydney, 1966), p. 169.

[2] K. D. Buckley, *The Amalgamated Engineers in Australia, 1852–1920* (Dept. of Economic History, Research School of Social Sciences, Australian National University, Canberra, 1970), pp. 17, 19.

[3] Geoffrey Blainey, *A Land Half Won* (Melbourne, 1980), p. 215.

[4] Russell Ward, *The Australian Legend* (Melbourne, 1958).

[5] K. D. Buckley, *Amalgamated Engineers*, p. 95.

[6] Francis Adams, *The Australians, a Social Sketch* (1893). The passage quoted here was written before the great stoppages of 1890. It is taken from R. N. Ebbels, *The Australian Labour Movement 1850–1907* (Sydney, 1960), p. 42.

[7] Geoffrey Blainey, *A Land Half Won*, p. 220.

[8] E. W. O'Sullivan, in the *Centennial Magazine*, Feb. 1890; quoted here from R. N. Ebbels, *Australian Labour Movement*, pp. 46–7.

[9] K. D. Buckley, *Amalgamated Engineers*, p. 55.

[10] Brian Fitzpatrick, *Short History of the Australian Labor Movement* (Melbourne, 1968), p. 106.

[11] N. G. Butlin, 'Long-run trends in Australian *Per Capita* Consumption', ch. 1, in Keith Hancock (ed.), *The National Income and Social Welfare* (F. W. Cheshire, Melbourne, for the Australian Council of Social Service, 1965).

[12] Geoffrey Blainey, *A Land Half Won*, p. 357.

[13] Quoted here from Brian Fitzpatrick, *Short History of the Australian Labor Movement*, p. 138.

[14] See ch. VII, 3, above.

[15] W. A. Robinson, in Official Report of 1886 Congress; reproduced here from R. N. Ebbels, *Australian Labour Movement*, p. 96.

[16] Keith Sinclair, *William Pember Reeves, New Zealand Fabian* (Oxford, 1965), pp. 151–2.

[17] See E. H. Phelps Brown, *The Growth of British Industrial Relations* (London, 1965), pp. 128–32.

[18] W. G. Spence, *History of the Australian Workers' Union* (Sydney and Melbourne, 1910), p. 125.

[19] W. G. Spence, *Australia's Awakening* (Sydney and Melbourne, 1910), p. 186.

[20] I owe this observation to Professor Keith Hancock.

[21] K. J. Hancock, 'The first half-century of Australian wage-policy', *Journal of Industrial Relations* (Sydney), 21, 2 (June 1979), 131.

[22] J. H. Portus, *Australian Compulsory Arbitration 1900–1970* (Sydney, 1971), p. 90.

[23] J. Hutson, *Penal Colony to Penal Powers* (Amalgamated Engineering Union, 126 Chalmers St. Surry Hills, NSW, 1966), pp. 55–6.

[24] International Labour Office, *Conciliation and Arbitration in Industrial Disputes*, Studies and Reports, Series A, No. 34 (Geneva, 1933), p. 633, quoted here from K. F. Walker, *Australian Industrial Relations Systems* (Harvard University Press, 1970), p. 4.

XV

THE ORIGINS OF TRADE UNION POWER AND SOME INFERENCES FOR POLICY

THE practical interest of a study of the origins of trade union power lies in the guidance it may give to policy. In all Western countries there is a problem of industrial relations — a problem, in the sense of a continuing tension, and pressure to change and develop. These countries have seen cost-push change in recent years into the combination of rising labour costs and sluggish output that is called stagflation. In this common setting the United Kingdom is involved in its own predicament of constraint by the legacy of its past: it faces a task of reconstruction. The question arises what part trade unionism has to play in that task. The purpose of this chapter is to ask what guidance our understanding of the origins of trade union power gives to the shaping of policy towards trade unionism. The first step will be to review the 'critical factors and historical turning points' that have appeared in our preceding discussion. There will follow some reflections on inferences for policy.

I

If the interwoven threads of history can be separated, and its contingencies be treated as determinants, then the origins of trade union power that have come to light in the preceding discussion may be summarized under the following heads:

(a) Their *early start* gave British trade unions independence and respectability. There was no question of their being formed and controlled by an external organization such as a political party: working people had to get together of their own motion. They became accustomed to operate informally, as clubs, outside the purview of the law, and they were jealous of their independence. By the time the Royal Commission of 1867 came to consider the proper status of the trade unions, and Parliament to regulate it, the experience of informal working was so well established that by almost universal consent there was no need to bring trade unions within the process of the law, even to the extent of assimilating their position to that of friendly societies. Against any such proposal the Home Secretary in introducing the Trade Unions Bill in 1871 quoted the Minority Report of the Royal Commission:

the extreme jealousy on the part of their members of State interference, would, we are convinced, render the attempt to pass such a measure impracticable. . . . Trade unions are essentially clubs . . . the objects at which they aim, the rights which they claim, and the liabilities which they incur are for the most part . . . such as Courts of Law should neither enforce, nor modify, nor annul. They should rest entirely on consent.'[1]

Thus the early start contributed to the acceptance of the view that the trade unions should be free to exercise their functions outside the law.

But more than this. The lead in these early societies could be taken only by men of character and ability. They were recognized by their employers as good workmen, and by their neighbours as good citizens. Often they were devout men too, and local preachers. Because the craft unions were engaged in demanding the union rate for all their members, their leaders would not countenance misconduct that was incompatible with entitlement to that rate. Equally in so far as the early unions were also friendly societies, they needed members of steady habits. On all these personal counts the unionists earned the approval of other ranks of society: the early start of the unions thereby contributed to the Victorian acceptance of trade unionism.

It is significant also that part at least of the traditions of British trade unionism were formed before British manual workers had the vote. A watershed appears in 1867–75, within which the vote was first extended to many skilled manual workers, the Trades Union Congress was founded, and Parliament freed trade unions from the criminal taint. Before then, a meeting between trade unionists and employers was a confrontation between men deemed not fit to be entrusted with a vote and members of the ruling classes. The clash of interests inherent in the wage bargain was intensified by political division: the opposition of 'us' and 'them' was manifest. If the European notion of 'the social partners' has not taken hold in Great Britain, the origin of the resistance may lie here. The inference for trade unionists was the need for unity in a working-class movement. Moreover, the trade unions themselves were stronger because able men were not drawn off into politics.

(b) Some *characteristics of the British people* that appear as distinctive on an international comparison have helped to make strong trade unions. Thus it appears that the British combine their predominant individualism with a capacity for co-operation. They readily form spontaneous associations for particular purposes, devising their own forms of organization in great variety. They are conservative of established practice and dogged in defence of what they regard as their rights. Generally, then, they find it natural to join a union, and loyalty to it also comes naturally. But the trade unions have not been centralized bodies, controlled and directed by a national executive, save in so far as this was enforcing a rule book: the springs of vitality and the ultimate source of authority generally lay in the localities. Hence the difficulty of controlling the exercise of union power by such sanctions as can be effectively applied against union headquarters, be it the funds or the officers: other questions apart, there is too much local spontaneity; the headquarters may be under control but the membership is not. In one test of union power, the strike or lock-out, how often have the qualities of loyalty and doggedness enabled men and women to hold out through week after week of great hardship.

(c) The British *legal system* contributed in a negative way to trade union power, in that it was not adapted to embrace, contain and control the unions. Trade unionists saw the law as imposed by an authority in which they had no part, and which they might well have identified with classes and interests directly opposed to themselves. Their attitude would have been very different if the country had been one in which the laws had been and were being made by the people for the people: as it was, they wished only to keep out of the clutches of the law. This attitude was strengthened because of the dominance in Great Britain of the common law. The tradition of the common law was to uphold the liberties of the individual against oppression by combination: its presumptions were against the trade union. Furthermore, its content was formulated and declared by judges, and trade unionists were wary of judge-made law, both because it was uncertain, and because they suspected the judges of bias. So the possibility of the forms of exertion of union power being divided into the fair and unfair, the legal and illegal, was never realized: trade unionists became convinced, and established their conviction as of right, that trade unions must be untrammelled by the law in any way.

(d) *The employers* combined effectively on occasion, and were able to inflict defeats upon the unions; but their combinations as fighting forces were unstable, and the positive policy of their principal spokesmen came to be acceptance of the role of strong unions. The strength of the union was seen as a warrant of orderliness in industrial relations. Employers were slow to build up any body to represent them at the national level, nor did they offer organized resistance to the statutory protection of the trade unions. At the place of work, the relative importance attached by managers to maintaining good relations as against contending for control of working practices in order to raise productivity, has varied with the state of the product market. When it was open to employers to go to the courts and seek legal restraint on union pressure, they were very loath to do do.

(e) The *smallness of the country* and the early provision of *good communications* promoted the formation of strong unions. Evidently they facilitated organization and administration: national unions with central financial control were formed at an early stage. A greater sense of unity was possible where a national conference could be gathered without undue expense every one or two years. This sense was intensified by the *regional concentration of industry*: the bringing together in close proximity of many people with a common interest heightened their awareness of that interest, and strengthened their will to defend it – there was a factor of reverberation. In these ways it was possible for trade unions to cover a whole industry, and where this would enable them to withhold a vital supply or service, to confront the Government with a new and formidable exercise of trade union power.

(f) The formation of the *Labour Party* was to bring great and evident boons to the trade unions in pursuance of their requirements, in the periods when Labour was in office from 1945 onwards. But the growth of the Party passed through two critical phases. In the first, the uncertain initiative of the Labour Representation Committee became endowed with substantial trade union support only in consequence of the Taff Vale judgement of the House of Lords. In the second, a Party whose electoral prospects remained overshadowed down to 1914 by the ascendancy of the Liberal Party saw the bastions of that Party broken down from within, was able to move through, and occupied electoral ground they had enclosed. Sometimes the course of history presents itself as an ordered, even a predictable development; sometimes we speak of the accidents of history. It is more as accidents than as ordered influences that the Taff Vale judgement, and the rift between Lloyd George and Asquith, appear in their incidence upon the development of the Labour Party; yet their effect was critical upon the possibility of its developing at all.

(g) *The Liberal Governments of 1905 onwards* took a profound effect on the position of trade unions over against government. This effect was greatly enhanced by *the First World War*. In both the influence of *Lloyd George* was powerful: from the railway dispute of 1907 onwards his readiness to deal directly with the union leaders, and his predilection for their cause, gave the unions a standing with government. The Trade Disputes Act of 1906 had rested largely upon consensus, but the transition that now set in from the cap-in-hand delegation of the Parliamentary Committee to the trade unions as an estate of the realm, with Ernest Bevin of the Transport Workers arguing foreign policy with the Prime Minister – this was fostered by the Governments which Lloyd George served in or led. It will be said, rightly, that much the same development would have come about in any case: this was a time when trade unionism was growing fast in numbers and militancy in several Western countries, and the British unions would have made their increasing power felt by whatever Government was in office. But their ascent to the high places was made easier by the policy of the Liberal Government, and of Lloyd George, as sympathiser and negotiator, in particular. It was further promoted by the War. A first effect was that the agreement of the unions whose members controlled the working practices in the shops where munitions were made became indispensable at the highest level. There followed the pervasive influence of full employment, transforming relations at the place of work, and embodying in the shop steward the bargaining power of the shop-floor.

Some of the institutions and procedures developed during the War lapsed or were swept away when depression followed the post-war boom. The years of constraint and unemployment that ensued hid the magnitude of the change that had been brought about: but the raised status of the trade unions over against government had not been lost, nor did the authority of the foreman revert to what it had been before 1914. Meanwhile the War had been a leveller: it had brought a diminution of class differences, manifest in dress and manners. In this setting trade unionism was regarded with more understanding by the middle classes, and the exertion of trade union power was more likely to be tolerated even when it disrupted services.

(h) *Full employment from 1941* released some of the effects of full employment in the First World War that had been held down by the hard labour market of the inter-war years: during the Second World War the shop steward came forward again. As full employment persisted after the War the shift of power to the shop-floor went on – within the firm, a shift from junior management to the shop steward, and within the unions, from the officials to the rank and file. This shift within the union increased the power of its members to raise their pay by penetrating every opening, while the union as a body became harder than ever to contain or control, for the decisions and the initiative were dispersed among the members. The experience of full employment being maintained despite rising labour costs covered by higher prices induced an accommodating frame of mind among employers: they had reason to expect that after the pay rise was negotiated they would be able to raise prices so as to maintain profit margins, and to do that without loss of turnover. The prospect was underwritten by the commitment of Governments of both parties to regulate effective demand so as to maintain 'a high and stable level of employment'. There was no reason why the employers should be tough negotiators. The bargaining power of the trade unions was raised accordingly. Within *the nationalized industries*, subsidization from the national Exchequer removed the limit that would otherwise have been set by market forces to the combination of job security with pay rises.

In this setting the rate at which pay was raised depended largely on the pressure generated and applied by the rank and file. At the end of the 1960s their expectations and militancy took an upward turn that appears in the wage series of Great Britain and of a number of other Western countries as a change of trend characterized as *the Hinge*. It may be attributed to the attainment of preponderance by those younger trade unionists whose experience of working life had been formed wholly in the past twenty years of high employment and rising standards of living. Their outlook brought an accession of union power.

2

Though this retrospect has been arranged under eight headings, these only distinguish different aspects of a single course of historical development. The origins of trade union power lie in a process of organic growth. When we call growth organic we imply three properties. First, the parts of the growing structure are interdependent: the way in which each functions depends upon its connection with the others; unlike the bricks and beams that will be built into a house, the parts may not be capable of separate existence. Second, the effect taken by any external influence is likely to depend on what other influences are at work at the same time: in statistical parlance, there are large joint terms. And third, there is the spark of life itself – there is an element of spontaneity. This is the paradigm that we must use for the gaining of power by the trade unions. We must not think of that process as the climbing of particular steps, or the acquisition of particular weapons – steps that might be reversed, weapons that might be modified or taken away again. But, it will be objected, take the case to which so much attention has been directed recently, the conferment of immunities by the Trade Disputes Act of 1906: was not this a decisive consolidation if not accession of union power? and does it not remain a weapon in the sense just held inappropriate, perfectly capable of being modified or withdrawn? Formally that is so; but the substantial conditions go deeper. The original Act, we saw, was passed with wide concurrence: the decisive factor was not the enactment of certain provisions but the prevailing climate of opinion concerning the unions. As long as that climate persisted there could be no question of withdrawing the measure. If withdrawal or amendment have become possible, that is because of a change in the climate of opinion. This change in turn will have come about in the course of a process of historical development into which many interdependent elements have entered.

Thus it is not in the nature of our study of the origins of trade union power to reveal particular factors on which policy can operate separately. Even worse, for the purposes of those who wish to contain and control trade union power, the implication of this historical approach may seem to be forbiddingly deterministic: affairs will take their course, it seems to say, things will be what they will be, and attempts to mould them will be overborne by the ineluctable march of events. But this is to make a misunderstanding out of an insight. The misunderstanding inflates the possibility of offering any historical explanation into outright determinism: if we can trace the process by which trade unions acquired their power, and say 'You see, thus it was here, and again here', then – according to the misunderstanding – we are implying that the process is wholly determinate and predestined; and as it has gone on up to now, so it will continue, and there is nothing we can do about it but be carried on with all the rest in the great tide of the inevitable. But not so: it is the remarkable property of historical explanation that it does explain, that is, it does relate cause and effect, and yet does not yield the power to predict. History, even analytical history, is not a determinate system. Men remain free agents. Old laws can be repealed, new laws can be passed. What then is the insight? It is that if history is not determinate it is continuous. Especially in a democratic country, and in such a system of voluntary associations as industrial relations, changes to be effective must be widely accepted. Their acceptability depends upon an often tenacious climate of opinion. There may be sense in the old cant phrase, that 'the time is not yet ripe'. The essential is that desired change should be envisaged as a possible part of the process of organic growth. In the art of grafting, there are limits within which the existing stock will accept and embody new growth. There are limits also within which that stock can be cut back.

In Chapter I various ways were indicated in which we can learn from history – in which those who have followed a historical approach to a contemporary problem are likely to set about it differently from those who come to it without knowledge of its origins. The present study of the origins of trade union power suggests certain inferences for policy, and these are set out in the three following sections.

3

A major function of the trade union, and a main reason for the rise of trade unionism, is to provide protection for the worker where other forms of protection are lacking. Those other forms are chiefly law,

custom, and, in some of their phases, the forces of the market. In a free
society the law assures the worker of the same rights to go about his
business peaceably as it does all citizens. It has sometimes been the role
of custom to enjoin certain rules of fair dealing between neighbours,
and these may extend to a requirement of considerate behaviour by
employers. When the demand for labour runs high enough, the competition between employers for qualified employees ensures that each
employee has the benefit of the going rate, and few will be held down
in disagreeable posts for lack of access to an alternative. But these
safeguards taken together are still far from securing the worker from
the threat of changes in the conditions of his working life, and the loss
of earning power that in the extreme would be as devastating as the
expropriation of a peasant's land.

This is so because he is exposed to the upheavals wrought by two
collisions of forces that are basic to any Western economy. One of
these oppositions is inescapable and irreducible, the other more
prominent but more capable of mitigation. The first is between people
as producers and people as consumers. As producers, people want to
be able to work at the tasks they prefer, where they choose, in their
own way and at their own pace, for a substantial return. As consumers,
people want producers (other than themselves or brothers of their
craft) to adapt themselves to meet the demands of consumers, change
their jobs and residence as necessary to do that, and work hard for a
modest return. The pricing system purports to provide an impersonal
regulation of this joint opposition. If the response of producers lags
behind an extension of the consumers' demand, the consequent rise in
the price of the product will ration the available supplies among
consumers, and stimulate more producers to leave other forms of
output for this one; and conversely, when the demand for a product
contracts, the fall in its price will check the reduction in the quantity
sold, while by making some output unprofitable it pushes some
suppliers into other lines of production. So at least the system works in
principle. But producers dislike being pushed, squeezed, and chivvied
by it. The medieval gild was formed to resist that harrying. In later
years the same interest prompts the concern of the trade union with
working practices and job security.

This sort of opposition has been and remains more acute in Great
Britain than in some other countries, because of the greater individualism of the British worker. In an individualist culture each person is
allowed as wide as possible an enclave within which to go about his
affairs in his own way, without obligation to conform with common
rules: society obtrudes itself no more than is unavoidable upon his
self-government. But in the market economy, under the division of
labour, society does obtrude itself, by requiring anyone who has to get

a living to make not what he wants to make, but what the consumer is willing to buy. Jobs will not be tailor-made to suit the interests of workers; they may not even be maintained so as to continue to use the skill and experience of workers already in them; it is for the workers to fit themselves into what jobs are going. This opposition can only be made harder by the principles of liberal education – schooling whose object is given as the development of the child's potential and the encouragament of self-expression. What gifts can the child develop, what tastes, what interests can it discover in itself, how can it be encouraged, as the phrase goes, to do its thing? This is not the sole aim of education in practice; but in itself it intensifies the opposition between the worker's wish to work in his own way and the consumer's requirement that he meet his demand. The adjustment to the working life can bring fewer pangs in those countries where home and school make clear from the first the need to find one's subordinate place within a given structure, and adapt oneself to a prescribed role.

In this first kind of opposition the trade unionist comes into conflict with the employer only in virtue of the employer's transmitting the demands of the consumer, and the employer himself may equally be a victim of these as they shift from time to time. But of course there is another way in which the trade unionist comes in conflict with the employer, and in this the employer appears in his own capacity – he hires the worker, and directs his work. The second kind of opposition is built in here. Only rarely do the impersonal workings of the market both set rates for the job and decide the division between pay and profit in the aggregate: usually the market is imperfect, the division of the product is a matter of bargaining, and the isolated worker is at a disadvantage. When once his weakness has been remedied by collective bargaining, it is on trade union power that changes in the division of the product of industry between pay and profit depend at any one time. There is a further source of conflict in that the discipline maintained and the pressure exerted by management at the place of work conflict with the worker's desire for autonomy. How deep these differences go varies widely from firm to firm. In those with good personal relations, and established confidence, the issues that inherently oppose employer and employee may continue to be mediated by consultation and orderly negotiation. In some of these firms, especially the smaller ones, the employees may feel no need of trade unionism at all. But more generally, the trade union is correlative to this second opposition, even more than to the first. It serves both for collective bargaining over the terms and conditions of employment, and also for the upholding of custom and practice, and the protection of the worker against unreasonable or unfair treatment by management in the shop.

Because these two kinds of opposition are inherent in any market economy, trade unionism is equally natural and inherent. There may have been traditional societies in whose stable populations and narrow local markets the worker needed no more protection than was afforded him by the rigid rule of custom. There have been phases of rapid expansion in Western economies when the ratio of investment or natural resources to the labour supply stood for the time so high that the individual worker could make his own way, protected by competition for his services. There have been and are many instances of mutual trust between employer and employee such that no dispute arises between them on the terms of employment, and the employee may feel no need of trade unionism: though there is bound to be reference here to rates arrived at by bargaining in the rest of the economy. But these cases apart, the workings of the market and the organization of production compose a system of forces which, left to themselves, would often bear hard on the worker. The function of the trade unions, seen in this setting, is to protect their members from the bruising impact of forces impinging upon the working life.

They perform this function by resisting job losses and changes in working practices that threaten loss of jobs: and by removing the weakness of the isolated worker in wage-bargaining, and then using their bargaining power to resist wage-cuts. In this, it has been suggested, they have implicitly been developing the concept of 'property in the job'. Selig Perlman, of the Wisconsin School of labour economists, based on this his theory of the trade unionism of the American Federation of Labor.[2] The trade union serves a number of purposes, and no single-stranded theory can account for them all. But if we take 'property' not in the narrow sense of the ownership of transferable assets, but as meaning the enjoyment of benefits the deprivation of which carries entitlement to compensation, then the thought that trade unions exist to establish property rights *de facto* where they are lacking *de jure* is illuminating. The line between the sources of earnings that the law protects, and those equally vital that it does not, is sometimes drawn arbitrarily. In the days of the enclosure movement, the cottager whose right of access to common grazing was established in the books of the manorial court received compensation when the common land was enclosed; but his neighbour whose access, equally vital to his livelihood, rested only on long tolerance, received nothing. There is a parable here. The turner who is unable to earn his living because his tools are stolen has a remedy at law: this is theft – if possible the thief will be punished and the tools will be restored to the owner. But the turner who is unable to earn a living because a machine has been introduced that does his kind of work automatically and rapidly, so that his skill is no longer needed, has no remedy: this is progress. The economy looks to him to find some other kind of work. His union sees things otherwise. It will try to take up the shock, and at least put off the evil day of redundancy, by resisting the introduction of the new machine, that is, it will engage in restrictive practices.

Much of the history of trade unionism can be written out of this clash between the requirements that the economic system imposes impersonally on labour as a factor of production, and the welfare of workers as human beings, seeking a livelihood from the exercise of particular skills, and attached to particular neighbourhoods. That until relatively recently there was little trade unionism among white-collar workers may be attributed in great part to their being set apart from that clash by the nature of their employment. They were much less exposed to unemployment and pay changes in the cyclical fluctuations of industry. This sense of security was often increased by their being employed in smaller units, with more personal contact with management. When they had to look for another job, their skill was widely transferable across industrial boundaries. Until recently, moreover, their skill was little subject to technical change, and it was not made obsolete by the decline of particular industries. In all these respects, the contrast with manual workers brings out the weight of the pressure on these to use the trade union for income maintenance.

That also means, to use it for the obstruction of economic progress – other people's progress, that is. But the practices that are rightly called restrictive by those whose aim is national economic development are seen as protective by those whose jobs are put at risk. Often that is a short-sighted view, but it is employment in the near future that dominates the prospect. It is not then reasonable to scold trade unionists for restrictive practices, nor simply exhort them to change: those practices are of the essence of trade unionism, in the endeavour of the worker to keep his human end up against impersonal forces.

The better way is to recognize that where economic progress imposes costs on people – displacement, loss of earnings otherwise to be expected from acquired skill, worsening of 'life chances' generally – it is as reasonable for the community to compensate those costs, as for it to compensate those occupants and owners who lose income and amenity through the construction of a new and better road. Economists have developed the analysis of 'external costs' – the costs that the carrying on of a certain line of production imposes on the community but are not chargeable to the procedures themselves. But what of the external costs of progress itself? If our accounting made unemployment, loss of expected income, splitting of the family and uprooting of the home, and the like, all assessable and chargeable, how much should we have to set off against the annual rise in GNP in a progressive economy? Two developments of the past quarter-century have in fact gone far to accept the reasonableness of compensating such disturbance. One is the practice of productivity bargaining, in which firms negotiated higher hourly rates in return for the abandonment of restrictive practices; though these practices, being mostly make-work rules, were abandoned only at a time when full employment had long prevailed and was expected to continue. The other development has been that of redundancy payments, subscribed to by employers but supplemented from the public purse. These began with the Redundancy Payments Act of 1965. They constitute a measure of the first importance in principle and in practice.

The question is whether they extend far enough. They promote modernization when it cuts deep enough to throw employees out of work altogether, but they do not help to get existing employees to change their practices. On the grounds stated here, it is reasonable both that the change should be compensated, and that the community should share in the cost. There appears therefore to be a case for a national fund to assist the continual progress of productivity bargaining. In approved schemes the fund would share in lump-sum payments in return for agreed changes in working practices. These would be additional to any redundancy payments resulting from the changes, but might include compensation for accelerated retirement. A large fund would appear costly. If its resources were made available without exacting investigation it might sometimes be abused. But its cost, considered as a form of investment in modernization, would be small in comparison with that of many forms of physical equipment; and the knowledge of its availability, and experience of the effects it could produce in particular cases, might be expected to produce a cumulative effect over time on attitudes to productivity.

4

History has distorted the presentation to the British people of the relation between trade unions and the law. This is a great misfortune. The belief that trade unions, alone among the institutions of the country, are inherently entitled to immunity from parliamentary regulation has no reasonable foundation. It exerts an anomalous constraint on public policy towards industrial relations. But events have so run in the past that it is held with a conviction that is deep and even passionate. The choice that presented itself seemed to be between leaving the unions free to operate informally outside the law, and putting legal shackles on them. After the Taff Vale judgement in 1901 they ran the risk of being mulcted in crippling damages if ever they struck: they demanded to be put back where they had always been before, outside the law, where no one could sue them whatever their members did. When the choice was presented in that way, the majority of informed opinion irrespective of party held, with whatever misgivings, that they could only be put back. The presentation had been a singularly narrow one. But the same narrowness persists to the present day.

Its origins lie far back, in the tradition of law as a command imposed by an authority set above the humble working man, and the experience of the law being used to repress the early trade unionists. For these it was an unfortunate coincidence that their endeavours to protect themselves against the early stages of industrialization brought down upon them the legal pains and penalties of the reaction against Jacobinism.[3]

The manual workers getting the vote only tardily and by stages could long regard the laws only as of other men's making, and too often as a weapon in the hands of the reactionary men of property. The common law in particular, with its inherent antipathy to encroachment by combinations on the rights of individuals, was judge-made law. When trade unionists became able to make their wishes known in Parliament, what they asked was basically negative: not the affirmation of the right to form unions, but the removal of the presumption that such combinations were criminal; not the affirmation of the right to strike, but the reversal of the judicial decision that made striking subject to actions for damages.

Legislation itself thus conformed with and even strengthened the tradition of active hostility to the law. In the form at least of avoidance of the law the outlook was shared by employers. That legal proceedings and sanctions should be shunned, and our institutions rest upon informal understandings, good faith, and gentlemen's agreements, became under the name of voluntarism the accepted philosophy of British industrial relations. The economy and flexibility of voluntarism were contrasted with the time-consuming, costly, or litigious procedures of legalistic systems. There was force in this, as long as negotiations proceeded in a setting of consensus and there was underlying agreement about what issues might be raised, and what kind of settlement it was reasonable to reach. But when that agreement was dissipated, and the march of events shifted the focus and issues of bargaining, then rejection of the positive role of law did much harm to British industrial relations.

It has harmed them basically because it has prevented the adoption of a statutory code. This would state the rights and obligations of the parties, and thereby delimit them; at the same time it would provide procedures of general application. What might be envisaged in practice – what some attempt has in fact been made to approach – is not a comprehensive code, but the development by Parliament of particular rules and procedures, designed to fill gaps in existing practice, or restore order. The Industrial Relations Act of 1971 was such an attempt. Its fate shows how Parliament was denied the means of constructing institutions and providing procedures for industrial relations, because of the fixed idea that these ought to remain un-regulated by law, and that any statutory provision for them was of its nature hostile to unionism.

This was, in one way, a signal demonstration of trade union power; and because it was associated with the defence of trade union immunities, subsequent proposals for the legal regulation of trade unionism have been hailed, or condemned, as attempts to 'curb trade union power'. But this approach is unprofitable. That the aim of policy should be to maintain a balance of power has its appeal. The role of the unions, it has been said, is to provide 'countervailing power'; and as overmighty subjects they have been charged with excess of power. In both respects the aim might appear to be to secure to them the right amount of power, no more, no less: and then they might safely be left to use it as they chose. But to describe this right amount as just what is needed to offset the pressures exerted by and through employers gives no practical guidance, for there can be no measure of how big these are. An ever greater difficulty is that the quantitative conception does much less than justice to the variety of the functions of the union. It envisages only a force in equilibrium. It does not consider the problems raised for policy by the uses made of that force. Policy therefore should not be directed simply towards the strengthening or weakening of trade unions: it is the uses of the trade union power, rather than the power itself, that should form the object of policy. In order to be able to perform its functions at all the trade union does need powers that are exceptional, indeed anomalous. It needs monopoly power, in the sense that it must be recognized as the sole bargaining agent for a given group of workers; and it must be assured of the right to strike. These requirements are now widely if not universally accepted in the Western world. But meeting them is like giving a man a gun to defend himself: he may use it for more than defence. Trade unions may exploit their power in order to extort monopolistic gains for particular groups; obstruct changes that the whole economy greatly needs; discriminate against particular persons, or worsen the prospects of employment for whole categories; inflict heavy losses on firms and persons not party to the original dispute; and disrupt public services, or even hold up the whole economy. At some point the practical judgement can draw the line between actions like these which, though they may bring benefits to union members, seem on balance to be vexatious or disruptive; and those which, though they may impose costs on others, seem warranted by the benefits they bring to members. The aim of policy should then be to check action of the first kind and try to ensure that all action is of the second, reasonable kind.

How can this be done? One way that suggests itself is to distinguish between defensive and aggressive actions, or otherwise to mark off the exertions of union power that are deemed anti-social; and then provide sanctions against them. There could be no classifying of broad categories; each kind of action would have to be judged on its merits. This is in fact the path followed of late. The Taft–Hartley Act of 1947 in the USA specified and outlawed certain 'unfair labor practices'. The British Industrial Relations Act, 1971, followed suit, by outlawing certain 'unfair industrial practices'. The Employment Act 1980 checked certain forms of secondary action by making them liable to actions at tort.

But as long as the fixed idea persists that legislative regulation is incompatible with free trade unionism, the possibility of parliamentary control of the exercise of trade union power is limited. For rules whose reasonableness is not generally accepted must be enforced by pains and penalties, the infliction of which sets up a general outcry or causes a widespread stoppage. It is true that fines can be imposed that are collected by deduction from pay and do not carry the possibility of imprisonment for non-payment. But if an action such as a form of secondary picketing is made unlawful, an employer suffering from it can go to the court for an injunction against it, and a person who persists in it can only be imprisoned for contempt of court. That someone should be sent to prison for what had been thought of as a normal trade union activity is likely to call forth a spontaneous reaction of solidarity: quite genuinely the cry will be raised, are we back to the days of the Tolpuddle Martyrs? The arm of the law in any case always finds it hard to make its rules good over large numbers of persons who are united by strong bonds of mutual loyalty in resistance. In this respect there is an inherent asymmetry between trade unionists and the employers, who are so much fewer in number, and less likely to come out in support of one another. Nor can the large numbers of trade unionists be controlled by sanctions applied to their unions. In a 'dispersive revolution' the capacity for taking initiative and sustaining activity has shifted from the headquarters to the membership. With the best will in the world the national officers of a union cannot commit their members to observance of a rule that the members reject. Formidable fines may be levied on the funds of a union, but they are of indirect and uncertain effect on the conduct of individual members. In Australia in 1968 a major crisis arose when the court, seeking to distrain upon the funds of a union, committed to prison for contempt the leader of the union who would not say where those funds had been lodged: a widespread stoppage was averted only when a well-wisher appeared to pay the union's fine. This is a field, then, in which the general proposition that the rule of law depends on general acceptance takes on a special significance: the difficulty here is not just a lack of acceptance, but a tradition of rejection. There are also peculiar difficulties of enforcement.

In sum, British industrial relations have much to gain from an extension of positive law. This would give Parliament a means of improving institutions and procedures, and of defining and penalizing vexatious practices. The measures that have been and are being promoted to this end are frustrated or limited by the deep-seated tradition that sees the law as inherently inimical to trade unionism. Advance depends upon a change of attitudes.

5

The decisive role of attitudes in the last resort appears in another present problem, that of incomes policy. The difficulty, even it may be the impossibility, of maintaining a policy so necessary to the escape from stagflation, arises from the close association between wage-fixing and the adversary system. The hold which that system has on men's minds is a legacy of history.

The case for incomes policy is familiar. Its strength is shown by the way in which successive Governments, after repudiating the policy when in opposition and demolishing any existing arrangements for it when they returned to office, have found themselves obliged to come back to it, albeit under some difference of name and form. The immediate instigation has been various – to check the rise of costs and prices at a time of pressure on sterling; to stem inflation without raising unemployment; or to make it more likely that an injection of public expenditure would provide more jobs at existing rates and not simply be mopped up by higher pay for those with jobs already. In the harsh economic climate that set in from 1973, though the Thatcher Government of 1979 repudiated incomes policy in terms, its combination of cash limits in the public sector with stern injunctions in the private constituted a policy in practice; while those who still advocated an expansionary monetary and fiscal policy to bring down unemployment, when that was already acommpanied by high inflation, more clearly than ever saw incomes policy as a lynch-pin.

So incomes policy is inescapable; but it has also proved impracticable. Again and again, after a time it has broken down. Behind the circumstances of particular episodes a general cause may be discerned. A number of trade unions always have the power to breach the line that the policy is holding, and their members will continue to exercise restraint and keep within the line only in so far as they see the policy as reasonable and fair: but that policy is based on a view of how pay does and should move in the national aggregate altogether different from the way in which they are used to see their own wages as being fixed.

That way is through an age-long struggle – the adversary system, pull devil, pull baker. Rises in wages are seen as having been wrested out of profits by the exertion of the bargaining power of trade unions. It is through the unions that the advances of the workers have been obtained: by implication, had it not been for the unions the workers would still be in poverty. This division of the product between pay and profits that is decided from time to time in particular negotiations by industry or firm has had its counterpart for the last fifty years in the virtual division of the House of Commons into two opposed blocs, one linked with the trade unions, the other with the capitalists: the adversary system of fixing wages has seemed to find its political counterpart and endorsement in the national conflict between Labour and Conservative.

The strategists of incomes policy proceed from a very different view of the way in which the general level of real pay is in fact determined. They recognize that a particular group of workers fixes its money wage, and thereby its real wage, through the settlements it negotiates from time to time. These settlements decide money wages, and the whole point of incomes policy is to control the movement of labour costs. But in the aggregate they do not decide the real wages that are what matters to the worker, for after a general rise in money wages will come a general rise in prices. What gain in purchasing power, if any, will be left for workers as a whole? The record shows with surprising regularity that whatever wages in terms of money have been doing, real wages – wages in terms of purchasing power – have risen in proportion to the current rise in productivity. In their study *A Century of Pay*, Phelps Brown and Browne showed that this held for Germany, Sweden, the United Kingdom, and the United States, over wide spans of years from the later nineteenth century down to the Second World War.[4] It held whether money wages were rising rapidly at the time, or slowly, or not at all. It held whether trade unionism was expansive and militant, or weak or retreating. The National Institute of Economic and Social Research has shown that likewise in the two decades of rapid rise of money earnings in the UK from 1950, the same relationship between real earnings and productivity appears if we take five-year averages.[5] It is with this relationship in view that incomes policy is formulated. In effect it says to the employee, 'Since experience shows that by pushing your pay up above the rise in productivity you will only raise prices, and be left with no more than productivity allows you in the end, why not accept that much in the first place, and avoid inflation?'

But that is not how the employee sees the choice before him. He is dealing with his own pay, not with national aggregates. If he gets a rise in money, it will – for the time being – be equally a rise in purchasing power: prices will not have gone up the next morning, and when rises do come along, they will be extraneous to him, and only justify his next claim. It is not even clear that the rise in his own pay will necessarily raise the price of his own product: after major settlements employers rarely announce an immediate and consequential rise in prices – the nationalized industries are noticeably unwilling to allow that they ever buy peace at the expense of the consumer. These grounds for rejecting restraint are reinforced by the tradition of the adversary system. This shows wage-rises as coming out of profits. Incomes policy that would keep wage-rises down appears to be an intervention by government on the side of the employers. Or if a Labour Goverment cannot be accused of this, then it will at least be seen as asking trade unionists for sacrifices. The unionists see incomes policy – and the Government has agreed with them – as requiring them to give up rises in real wages that they could otherwise actually have enjoyed. The period for which they are willing to do this is limited, and they may in any case see themselves as entitled to bargain through the TUC for compensating benefits.

The difficulties of incomes policy have been represented here as arising out of the disparity between the movements of pay and prices in the national aggregate, on which the policy is based, and the worker's perception of the way in which his own wages are fixed; this disparity being deepened by the strength of the adversary tradition. This tradition, or its strength, we have implicitly taken to be an outstanding feature of the UK. But, it will be said, do we not find it in all countries of developed capitalism? In all of these – if we exclude the dictatorships – there are trade unions, negotiations local or national or both, and, with a few exceptions, strikes and sometimes waves of unrest. This is so; yet the countries differ significantly in their internal cleavage and their consequent ability to meet inflationary pressure. This has been brought out in an instructive study by Dr John McCallum.[6] The rise of raw material prices in 1972 and oil prices in 1973 put a strong upward pressure on the price level of OECD countries, that they varied widely in their ability to resist. What Dr McCallum shows is that this ability is closely associated with their strike record through the 1950s and 1960s: generally, the greater the strikes in a country during those years, the greater the acceleration of inflation there during the 1970s. Seven countries stand out as having the most strikes in the 1950s and 1960s and the greatest acceleration of inflation in the 1970s: Australia, Canada, France, Italy, New Zealand, the UK, and USA. Among these the UK showed the least strikes (so far as these figures are internationally comparable), and was intermediate in respect of the acceleration of inflation. At the other extreme four countries – Austria, Germany, the Netherlands, and Switzerland – had very few strikes indeed in the 1950s and 1960s, and came through the 1970s with only slight acceleration of inflation. Dr McCallum takes the figures of strikes as an inverse index of consensus: the comparative absence of strikes indicates the prevalence of attitudes, and of the institutions and procedures linked with them, that enable the parties to the pay settlement to reach a common understanding of the facts and considerations surrounding it. The countries that maintained a consensus in this way in the 1950s and 1960s proved able to absorb the check to real wages in the early 1970s with slight resort to the expedient of accelerated inflation. But countries in which the prevailing attitudes, institutions, and procedures led to frequent disputes over the division of the product – in a word, where the adversary system prevailed – proved unable to contain the shocks of 1972–3, and could only try to avoid the check to real pay through the illusion of bigger pay rises in money. The UK was one of these countries.

It is understandable that the adversary system makes trade unionists less willing to take less, each group for its own part, when there is less to be had by the community as a whole. It works as a positive encouragement to irresponsibility: each group learns from tradition and its own ongoing experience that it must press its claims lest it be left behind the rest, and since it is pressing against resistance it need take no responsibility for the size of the settlement. Let us go for a moment in imagination to the other extreme – let us suppose that Parliament granted the unions full authority to fix their members' pay, so that whatever rates they chose to name would become binding on employers as terms of the individual contracts of employment. What changes would the unions make? If they pushed rates up at once to gratifying heights, the effect on prices would be unmistakable, and so would be the effects on employment in industries exposed to foreign competition. But would it be fair to raise rates more in the sheltered industries? Again, should the rewards for skill be enhanced, or should the opportunity be taken to raise the relative earnings of the lowest paid? And so on. Questions such as these present themselves actively only to those who are given an effective voice in decisions about what pay should be. This participation in decision-taking implies partici-pation also in the formation of national economic policy, including particularly those measures that affect the allocation of economic resources.

Trade unions do not always demand active participation. Their members' attitudes may still be deferential; or their leaders may be in such basic agreement with the fiscal and monetary authorities on the imperatives of national economic policy that they accept their directives, without claiming for themselves more than a consultative voice. Such may be the explanation of the consensus obtaining in Switzerland and Germany. But in Austria and the Netherlands the origins of consensus have lain not in an initially compliant attitude of the unions, but in the arrangements made for the effective participation of the unions in the formation of policy. This holds of the Netherlands even after we have taken account of the strong effect of the link with the German economy, for we then raise the question of why the trade unions accepted that constraint. The answer may well be that the policy of which it formed part, however hard for the unions to accept, was not imposed on them from above, but in one way or another worked out with them.

This suggests that the threat to incomes policy arises when the trade unions have not too much power but too little. When the adversary system keeps them in the role of claimants, not to say assailants, they cannot identify themselves with the policy. They will accept the need for a standstill in a national emergency; and when a Labour Government imposes the policy they may accept it for a time as a sacrifice they should make for their Government's sake; but the policy is still part of the line that is habitually held against them, and sooner or later they will use their power to break through. International comparisons suggest that where they are not kept outside the walls, but take an effective part in the relevant decisions, power brings responsibility. Consensus is shown to depend not on goodwill, nor on any spontaneity of agreement, but on the willingness of the parties to accept measures for the framing of which they have been jointly responsible. It is established when the adversary system is transcended by a system of self-government.

6

The preceding discussions of policy have concluded more than once that much depends on attitudes. The OED definition of attitudes is helpful: they consist of 'settled behaviour or manner of acting, as representative of feeling or opinion'. This behaviour arises out of perceptions – how we see the world about us and the path of life before us, what we expect from them, how we expect other people to behave to us, and how we should behave to them. Attitudes do not consist of beliefs in the sense of conscious convictions or creeds: they are rather the 'feeling or opinion', the presuppositions that guide our actions because they frame and focus our view of situations, and cast both ourselves and other people in roles that we take to be inherent.

It might seem that the prevailing attitudes of a society belong among those modes of fashion or culture on which the historian may allow himself a light and diverting chapter after he has done his solid work on the political, economic, or military forces of the time. But this would be a complete misunderstanding. Because attitudes govern responses, they are among the basic determinants of the course of history. In the field of industrial relations, there are differences between countries that are explicable only by differences of attitude. Austria and Sweden on the one hand, Australia and the UK on the other, are all highly unionized: the comparative absence of stoppages in the first two, and their prevalence in the second, might be ascribed to this or that legacy of history or the working of this or that institution if we looked at each country separately, but on an international comparison can only be ascribed in the last resort to differences in the attitudes of the protagonists. The effect of a change in attitudes is also clear. The difference between German trade unionists in the 1920s and after the Second World War is a notable example. In the UK, the movement marked by the New Unionism of 1889 onwards arose from a deep-going change of attitude among wage-earners. The evidence for a shift towards greater militancy in a number of countries about 1969–70 has been set out in the account of 'the Hinge' in Chapter IX of this work.

In any free society, moreover, the ultimate safeguard against the abuse of trade union power lies in the attitude of trade unionists. Those who control a vital supply or service, and are not replaceable, can disrupt the economy by simply staying at home. Sanctions that may be applied to their union or to them personally are of doubtful effect in securing their return to work so long as claims that they consider reasonable are not met. The vital questions then are, what they consider reasonable, and in what circumstances they feel themselves justified in using their power. These are questions of attitude.

The importance of attitudes is recognized by the endeavours increasingly made to change them. The first Labour Government, after 1945, campaigned for higher productivity and wage restraint. Governments have continued to put the case for their incomes policies, in terms more or less homely. These appeals come up against the disparity we have remarked on here between the view of national aggregates on which incomes policy is based, and the employee's own immediate experience: there seems a need for an educational campaign that will make the national case widely known. But the diffusion of economic information under the auspices of government presents great difficulties. Some economic processes are remote, and many cannot really be simplified. Facts do not speak for themselves, but interpretation is controversial. The home truth, readily grasped, will as readily mislead – as witness the analogy between 'living beyond one's means' in a private household and at the Exchequer. If a note of exhortation comes through, the reaction is very likely to be negative. All this is discouraging; yet we may still be overlooking what should be a basic provision in a democratic society. The grandparents of some people still living were born at a time when the State allowed that children should not be assured of any education and might grow up illiterate; but it was a corollary of the extension of the franchise that the State should provide those who were now to decide its governance with at least an elementary education. Our own grandchildren looking back may wonder at our own shortsightedness. At a time, they might say, when the restoration of the economy depended on the understanding of every worker, what did you do to develop this, and adapt attitudes to the realities of your predicament? In 1924 Ernest Bevin wrote that 'The men and women who make up our movement will go no farther and faster than *their* appreciation of economic facts will allow them.'[7] What he wrote about the labour movement holds about change in industrial productivity or industrial relations. There are two sides to it. People will form their own appreciation. But they will form it on such economic facts as are before them.

One effective way of providing those facts has been found by the increasing number of firms that set out for their employees the breakdown of each year's 'value added'. From the year's sales (with adjustment for changes in stocks) there is deducted the cost of supplies and services bought in: the difference is the 'value added' by the joint application of labour and capital within the firm. The report shows in what proportions this 'value added' is divided between pay and profits. It also shows the allocation of profits to different heads – tax, depreciation, dividends, and reserve. This presentation deals with elements of the accounts that are readily understood. It can also be applied to the national product.

Simply to convey information in such ways as this may be the most effective way to change attitudes. These are also changed by the impact of events. But it seems that these events must be earth-shaking – like being overwhelmed in war, or seeing the currency lose its value completely in an inflation – if they are to break off the persistence of attitudes. The British explosion of 1974–5, when pay rose by 25 per cent within twelve months only for prices to rise promptly in the same proportion, had its impact at the time, but proved not to have displaced the underlying attitudes of trade unionists. Because present attitudes are largely a legacy from the past, they have been selected to resist change: those most likely to survive and be handed on have been those linked with behaviour that reinforced them. The view of society as divided between 'us' and 'them', the assumption of a dominant conflict of interest between employer and employed, and the function of bargaining power as the essential means of improving the lot of the employee, will lead to behaviour by the employee and reactions by the employer – quite apart from any militancy to which the employer's own attitudes might lead him – that will justify the combative trade union within the adversary system. In the UK this process of reinforcement by feedback has been strengthened by the remarkable continuity of the country's social history: the legacy has been transmitted without a break from generation to generation.

Changes there have been none the less – spontaneously, one might say, in the sense that they cannot be ascribed to any impact from without. Some changes are going on all the time internally – in the types of employment and kinds of work done, in pressures and prospects, health and housing; perhaps most important of all, in the way children are brought up, in the home and school. We can conceive how the cumulation of changes of these kinds engenders in time a general alteration of attitudes, which some turn of events then precipitates. To say that the use that will be made of trade union power in the future will be governed by such changes is no platitude, but the outcome of the analysis that has been attempted here of social forces. But this analysis provides us with no prescription for bringing about a desired change. The lessons of history help us to live with problems rather than to solve them. We cannot even project a likely future course of development. At the last we are left with the paradox of historical understanding, that we can trace past happenings to their causes without thereby gaining the power to predict.

Notes

[1] Parl. Debates 1871, vol. 204, 266–7.

[2] 'the ideology of the American Federation of Labor . . . was based on a consciousness of limited job opportunities, – a situation which required that the individual, both in his own interest and that of a group to which he immediately belonged, should not be permitted to occupy any job opportunity except on the condition of observing the 'common rule' laid down by his union. The safest way to ensure this group control over opportunity . . . was for the union, without displacing the employer as the owner of his business and risk taker, to become the virtual owner and administrator of the jobs. Where such an outright 'ownership' of the jobs was impossible, the union would seek, by collective bargaining with the employers, to establish 'rights' in the jobs, both for the individual and for the whole group, by incorporating on the trade agreement, regulations applying to overtime, to the "equal turn", to priority and seniority in employment, to apprenticeship, to the introduction and utilization of machinery, and so forth,' Selig Perlman, *A Theory of the Labor Movement* (New York, 1928), pp. 198–9.

[3] E. P. Thompson, *The Making of the English Working Class* (Pelican ed., 1980), pp. 194–5.

[4] E. H. Phelps Brown and M. H. Browne, *A Century of Pay* (London, 1968); see also E. H. Phelps Brown, *The Economic Consequences of Collective Bargaining*, Royal Commission on Trade Unions and Employers' Associations: Minutes of

Evidence, 38, 24 May 1966 (HMSO, 1967); reprinted in Henry Phelps Brown and Sheila V. Hopkins, *A Perspective of Wages and Prices* (London, 1981).

[5] National Institute of Economic and Social Research, *Economic Review*, Aug. 1979, 6.

[6] C. L. Barber and J. C. P. McCallum, *Controlling Inflation* (Ottawa, 1982), ch. 1.

[7] In an article in *The Record*, May 1924; quoted here from Alan Bullock, *The Life and Times of Ernest Bevin*, vol. I (London, 1960), p. 256.

NOTES ON READING

I. The Victorian Acceptance of the Trade Union

The case for the trade union put by middle-class sympathizers to the Royal Commission on Trade Unions 1867–9 is argued in the statement of Dissent by the Earl of Lichfield, Thomas Hughes, and Frederick Harrison, in the 11th and Final Report, Parl. Papers 1868–9, XXXI, C. 4123. The view to which the Royal Commission on Labour of 1891–4 came to as a whole is stated in its Fifth and Final Report, Parl. Papers 1894, XXXIX, C. 7421. The great Cambridge economist Alfred Marshall, who was a member of this latter Commission, had set out his own assessment of the contribution of the trade unions to the working of the economy and the wellbeing of the workers, in his *Elements of the Economics of Industry* (London, 1892), Bk. VI, ch. xiii. The varied attitudes and reactions of employers to the unions are dealt with under ch. VII below.

II. The Trade Union as a Combination, and the Principles of the Common Law

A clear and comprehensive account of the field of law containing the issues raised in this chapter is provided by Sir Otto Kahn-Freund's *Labour and the Law* (London, 2nd ed. 1977). The legal issues raised by the Taff Vale judgement are discussed in professional intricacy in the *Report of the Royal Commission on Trade Disputes and Trade Combinations, 1906*, Parl. Papers 1906, LVI, Cd. 2825; a guide for laymen will be found in E. H. Phelps Brown, *The Growth of British Industrial Relations* (London, 1959), ch. IV. 3. The Taff Vale judgement itself and the Trade Disputes Act, 1906, can be consulted in K. W. Wedderburn, *Cases and Materials on Labour Law* (Cambridge University Press, 1967). The endeavour of the craftsman to maintain his independence against forces of change and competition, as a source of unionism, is described in E. P. Thompson, *The Making of the English Working Class* (London, 1963; Pelican, 1968, 1980).

III. Reflections on the Settlement of 1906

The sources cited for Chapter II are also relevant here. The New Unionism is described in H. A. Clegg, A. Fox, and A. F. Thompson, *A History of British Trade Unionism since 1889*, vol. I (Oxford University Press, 1964). This work gives an account of the formation of the Miners' Federation, and the lock-out of 1893; as does R. Page Arnot, *The Miners: A History of the Miners' Federation of Great Britain*, vol. I (London, 1949). Sources for the conflict in engineering, scientific management, and the organization of employers are given under ch. VII. Sources for compulsory arbitration are given under ch. XIV.

IV. The Trade Unions and the Labour Party

Early developments may be followed in Henry Pelling, *The Origins of the Labour Party, 1880–1900* (London, 1954); Kenneth O. Morgan, *Keir Hardie* (London, 1975); Frank Beeley and Henry Pelling, *Labour and Politics, 1900–6* (London, 1958); and A. W. Humphrey, *A History of Labour Representation* (London, 1912). Much information concerning the varying relations between the TUC and Labour in Parliament is provided by Ross M. Martin, *TUC: the Growth of a Pressure Group 1868–1976* (Oxford, 1980). The relations between Liberalism and Labour are dealt with by some of the essays in K. D. Brown (ed.), *Essays in Anti-Labour History* (London, 1974), especially Roy Douglas, 'Labour in Decline, 1910–14', and Kenneth O. Morgan, 'The New Liberalism and the Challenge of Labour: the Welsh Experience, 1885–1929'. Dr Morgan's study of the special experience of Wales is developed more fully in his *Rebirth of a Nation: Wales 1880–1980* (Oxford, 1981). The work of Ramsay MacDonald in the Labour Representation Committee and Parliamentary Labour Party is described in David Marquand, *Ramsay MacDonald* (London, 1977). Recent relations between the trade unions and the Labour Party are dealt with in ch. 3 of Robert Taylor, *The Fifth Estate* (London, rev. ed. 1980).

V. The Trade Unions over against Government

The conflicts of the years 1907–18 are described in Lord (G. R.) Askwith, *Industrial Problems and Disputes* (London, 1920); see also E. H. Phelps Brown, *The Growth of British Industrial Relations* (London, 1959). H. A. Clegg, A. Fox, and A. F. Thompson, *A History of British Trade Unionism since 1889*, vol. I (Oxford University Press, 1964), come down to 1910. Alan Bullock, *The Life and Times of Ernest Bevin*, vol. I (London, 1960), is highly relevant at many points. The General Strike is studied most fully in G. A. Phillips, *The General Strike* (London, 1976). Ross M. Martin, *TUC: The Growth of a Pressure Group, 1868–1976* (Oxford University Press, 1980), describes the successive phases of the relations between the TUC and the Government.

VI. The Ban on Strike and Lock-out in the two Great Wars

For the First War, Lord (G. R.) Askwith, *Industrial Problems and Disputes* (London, 1920), and Humbert Wolfe, *Labour Supply and Regulation* (Oxford, 1923). For the Second World War, H. M. D. Parker, *Manpower* (HMSO, London, 1957), and Alan Bullock, *The Life and Times of Ernest Bevin*, vol. 2 (London, 1967). The story of Betteshanger is related by Sir Harold Emmerson in Appendix 6 of the Report of the Royal Commission on Trade Unions and Employers' Associations (Cmnd. 3623, June 1968).

VII. Employers' Organizations

There are few direct accounts of employers' associations, and information about them has to be pieced together from references in trade union histories or accounts of particular conflicts, and from histories of particular industries or firms: much of this work remains to be done. But three Royal Commissions are important sources, though the evidence was often guarded:

Royal Commission on Trade Unions 1867–9, 1st to 4th Reports, Parl. Papers 1867, C. 3873, 3893, 3910, 3952. 5th to 10th Reports, Parl. Papers 1867–8, C. 3980. 11th and Final Report, Parl. Papers 1868–9, C. 4123,

Royal Commission on Labour, 1891–94.
Parl. Papers 1892, XXXIV, C. 6708; XXXVI, Pts. 1, 2 & 3, C. 6795.
Parl. Papers 1893–94, XXXII, Pt. 1, C. 6894; XXXIII, C. 6894; XXXIV, C. 6894; XXXIX, Pt. 1, C. 7063.
Parl. Papers 1894, XXXIX, C. 7421.

Royal Commission on Trade Disputes and Combinations, 1906. Minutes of Evidence, Parl. Papers 1906, LVI, Cd. 2826.

There are references to employers' associations also in the Donovan Report – the report of the Royal Commission on Trade Unions and Employers' Associations, 1965–8 (Cmnd. 3623, June 1968); the Commission's Research Paper No. 7 contains two studies of employers' associations, by V. G. Munns and W. E. J. McCarthy. A history of the foremost employers' association, that in the engineering industry, is provided by Eric Wigham, *The Power to Manage* (London, 1973). Rodger Charles, *The Development of Industrial Relations in Britain 1911–39* (London, 1973) describes employer formations at the national level, with special reference to endeavours made to develop a joint approach with the trade unions to the problems of the interwar years. Various aspects of resistance to the labour movement are described in K. D. Brown (ed.), *Essays in Anti-Labour History* (London, 1974).

VIII. Trade Unionists at the Place of Work

The rise of the shop stewards is described in B. Pribecevic, *The Shop Stewards' Movement and Workers Control* (Oxford, 1959), and James Hinton. *The First Shop Stewards' Movement* (London, 1973). The functions of shop stewards in more recent years are surveyed in Research Paper No. 1 for the Royal Commission on Trade Unions and Employers' Associations: W. E. J. McCarthy, *The Role of Shop Stewards in British Industrial Relations* (HMSO, London, 1966); and by E. V. Batstone, I. Boraston, and K. S. J. Frenkel, *Shop Stewards in Action* (Oxford, 1977). The struggles around 'the prerogatives of management' in the engineering industry are described in Eric Wigham, *The Power to Manage* (London, 1973). Changes in management are recorded in L. Urwick and E. F. L. Breck, *The Making of Scientific Management* (London, 1945).

IX. Cost Push

The part played by trade unions in the wage movements of earlier years is discussed in *The Economic Consequences of Collective Bargaining*, Minutes of Evidence before the Royal Commission on Trade Unions and Employers' Associations, 38, 24 May 1966, reprinted in Henry Phelps Brown and Sheila

V. Hopkins, *A Perspective of Wages and Prices* (London, 1981). The controversy concerning the cause of the rise of labour costs under full employment has been carried on mostly in articles in the journals; an econometric analysis of the thrust of bargaining is in S. G. B. Henry, M. C. Sawyer, and P. Smith, 'Models of Inflation in the United Kingdom', *National Institute Economic Review*, 73, August 1976, 60–7. An earlier discussion of the part played by trade unions among other forces making for inflation in the contemporary economy is in D. Jackson, H. A. Turner and F. Wilkinson, *Do Trade Unions Cause Inflation?* (University of Cambridge, Dept. of Applied Economics, Occasional Paper 36, 1972). The accounts of incomes policy are likewise scattered, but a useful survey and discussion is provided by R. E. J. Chater, A. Dean, and R. F. Elliott, *Incomes Policy* (Oxford, 1981).

X. The Unofficial Strike

The main discussion and prescription are in the report of the Donovan Commission, the Royal Commission on Trade Unions and Employers' Associations 1965–8 (Cmnd. 3623, June 1968, HMSO, London). The following Research Papers prepared for the Commission and published by HMSO are relevant: 1. *The Role of Shop Stewards in British Industrial Relations* by W. E. J. McCarthy; 2 (Part 1), *Disputes Procedure in British Industry*, by A. I. Marsh; and 10, *Shop Stewards and Workshop Relations*, by W. E. J. McCarthy and S. R. Parker. The Labour Government's proposals of 1969 were set out in the White Paper *In Place of Strife* (Cmnd. 3888, Jan. 1969). The fate of those proposals is narrated in Peter Jenkins, *The Battle of Downing Street* (London, 1970). Changes that have taken place in industrial relations at the work-place since 1968 are described in William Brown (ed.) *The Changing Contours of British Industrial Relations* (Oxford, 1981).

XI. The Attempt to Impose Order: the Legal Code of 1971

The ideas underlying the Conservative legislation were set out in *Fair Deal at Work*, published by the Conservative Political Centre, 32 Smith Square, London, SW1 in April 1968. An account of the handling of the Bill and the reactions to the Act will be found in Michael Moran, *The Politics of Industrial Relations* (London, 1977).

XII. Comparative studies: (1) Trade Unionism in the USA

For the formation of the distinctive American outlook, the sources of stimulus were Bernard Bailyn, *The Ideological Origins of the American Revolution* (Harvard, 1967), and Gary B. Nash, *The Urban Crucible* (Harvard, 1979). The main sources for the history of American trade unionism were J. R. Commons and Associates, *History of Labour in the United States* (New York, 1918), R. F. Hoxie, *Trade Unionism in the United States* (New York and London, 1915), and Lloyd Ulman, *The Rise of the National Trade Union* (Harvard, 1955). Histories which were also consulted included Selig Perlman, *History of Trade Unionism in the United States* (New York, 1929); Foster Rhea Dulles, *Labour in America* (New York, 1949); and Henry Pelling, *American Labor* (Chicago, 1960). Various aspects of trade union development and policy, particularly in later years, were studied in

Sumner H. Slichter, J. J. Healy, and E. R. Livernash, *The Impact of Collective Bargaining on Management* (Brookings Institution, Washington, DC, 1960); Richard A. Lester, *As Unions Mature* (Princeton, 1958); Vivian Vale, *Labour in American Politics* (New York, 1971).

XIII. Comparative studies: (ii) Canadian Trade Unionism

The history of trade unionism in Canada is narrated in H. A. Logan, *Trade Unions in Canada: their development and function* (Toronto, 1948), E. A. Forsey, *The Canadian Labour Movement, 1812–1902* (Canadian Historical Association, 1974), and J. Crispo, *International Unionism: a study in Canadian—American relations* (Toronto, 1967). The development of industrial relations is described in two works by Stuart Jamieson: *Industrial Relations in Canada* (Ithaca, N.Y., 1957) and *Times of Trouble: Labour Unrest and Industrial Conflict in Canada, 1900–66* (Task Force on Labour Relations, Ottawa, 1968). A philosophic and analytic study of the industrial relations system and collective bargaining is provided by *Canadian Industrial Relations*, the Report of the Task Force on Labour Relations (Ottawa, 1968). Material on the composition and outlook of the labour force is provided by G. S. Kealey and P. Warrian, *Essays in Canadian Working Class History*, (Toronto, 1976), J. Porter, *The Vertical Mosaic* (Toronto, 1965), and G. Teeple (ed.), *Capitalism and the National Question in Canada* (Toronto, 1972). Political aspects of the labour movement are dealt with by G. Horowitz, *Canadian Labour in Politics* (Toronto 1960), M. Robin, *Radical Politics and Canadian Labour, 1880–1930* (Kingston, Ontario, 1968), and R. U. Miller, 'Organised Labour and Politics in Canada' in R. U. Miller and Fraser Isbester (eds.), *Canadian Labour in Transition* (Scarborough, Ontario, 1971); two biographies may also be consulted – R. Macgregor Dawson, *William Lyon Mackenzie King, a Political Biography*, vol. I (London, 1958), and K. M. McNaught, *A Prophet in Politics: A biography of J. C. Woodsworth* (Toronto, 1959). The history of the labour movement in the West is related in D. J. Bercusan, *Confrontation at Winnipeg* (Montreal, 1974); A. Ross McCormack, *Reformers, Rebels and Revolutionaries: the Western Canadian Radical Movement, 1889–1919* (Toronto, 1977); H. C. Pentland, 'The Western Canadian Labour Movement 1897–1919, (Mimeographed, June 1974); and P. Phillips, *No Power Greater: A century in British Columbia* (Vancouver, 1967).

XIV. Comparative studies: (iii) Australian Trade Unionism

The development of the economy is described in A. G. L. Shaw, *The Economic Development of Australia* (London, 1946), A. G. L. Shaw and H. L. Nicolson, *Growth and Development in Australia* (Sydney, 1966), and N. G. Butlin, 'Long-run trends in Australia *Per Capita* Consumption', ch. 1 in Keith Hancock (ed.), *The National Income and Social Welfare* (Melbourne, 1965). The growth of society down to 1890 is depicted in its economic, political, and social aspects by Geoffrey Blainey in *A Land Half Won* (Melbourne, 1980). Works which may be drawn on for trade union history include T. A. Coghlan, *Labour and Industry in Australia, from the first settlement in 1788 to the establishment of the Commonwealth in 1901*

(Oxford, 1918); J. T. Sutcliffe, *A History of Trade Unionism in Australia* (1921; reissued Melbourne, 1967); K. D. Buckley, *The Amalgamated Engineers in Australia, 1852–1920* (Canberra, 1970); R. A. Gollan, *The Coalminers of New South Wales: a history of the union 1860–1960* (Melbourne, 1963); D. W. Rawson, *Unions and Unionists in Australia* (Honsby, NSW, 1978). Some outstanding conflicts are described by Phillip Deery, *Labour in Conflict: the 1949 Coal Strike* (Canberra, 1978); J. Iremonger, J. Merrit, and Graeme Osborne (eds.), *Strikes: Studies in 20th century Australian Social History* (Sydney, 1973); and papers in *Labour History* (Canberra). The history of arbitration is dealt with by O. de R. Foenander, *Towards Industrial Peace in Australia* (Melbourne, 1937); H. B. Higgins,. *A New Province for Law and Order* (Sydney, 1922); J. H. Portus, *Australian Compulsory Arbitration 1900–1970* (Sydney, 1971); K. F. Walker, *Australian Industrial Relations Systems* (Harvard University Press, 1970); K. J. Hancock, 'The first half-century of Australian wage-policy', *Journal of Industrial Relations* (Sydney), 21, 1, March, and 2, June 1979.

INDEX

Aberdeen, 16
Actors, 187
Adams, Francis, 257, 278
Adelaide, 260
Agadir, 70
Agency, law of, 36
Agency shop, 187
Ahmedabad, 16
Allocation Committee, 123
AMA, *see* Miners, in Australia
Amalgamated Engineering Union
  (AEU), 140, 141
  see also Engineers, Amalgamated
  Society of (ASE)
America, American, *see* USA
American Federation of Labour (AFL):
  bipartisan policy, 198, 214, 228
  in Canada, 227, 230, 232
  and CIO, 232, 234
  and dual unionism, 219
  formed, 196
  Perlman's theory, 289
Apprentices, 20, 93, 140
Apprenticeship, 16, 131
Arbitration, 17, 75, 92, 104, 106, 221
  in Australia, 252, 261, 265–78
  compulsory, 48, 49–50, c.vi *passim*
Arbitration Act (NSW, 1901), 268–9, 273
Architects, 21
Armstrong and Whitworth, 109, 116
A.S.E., 46
Askwith, Sir George, 92, 94, 112, 230, 251
Asquith, H. H.:
  and the coal dispute 1912, 70, 71, 73, 84
  and the law after Taff Vale, 34, 35, 36, 38
  Prime Minister in War, 66, 74, 75, 283
Attorney-General, 36, 95
Australia:
  c. xiv *passim*
  arbitration, 17, 48, 49
  Labour Party, 58
  middle class, 242
  strikes, 297
  union density, 200, 235
Austria, 298–9

Bailyn, Bernard, 208, 222–3, 224
Bain, G. S., 234, 251

Baldwin, S.:
  and Act of 1927, 129
  as President of the Board of Trade 120
  as Prime Minister in 1925–6, 80, 81, 82, 84
Balfour, A. J., 42, 68, 72
Balfour Committee on Industry and Trade,
  123, 124, 130
Balfour of Burleigh, Lord, 90
Ballarat, 257, 261
Ballots, 188
Bans clause, 275
Barber, C. L., 303
Barnes, Denis, 18
Beardmore's, 91
Beckett, Sir Terence, 3
Belfast, 109
Belgium, 45, 157, 158
Bell, Richard, 34
Bendix, R., 224
Betteshanger, 94, 185
Beveridge, Wm., 137
Bevin, Ernest:
  leader of TGW, 78, 84
  negotiates with Prime Minister, 79, 83, 283
  and penal sanctions in wartime, 93, 94, 95,
  96
  proposals for employers, 125
  quoted, 301
B.H.P., 264
Biffin, John, 10
Black Friday, 78, 79, 80, 81, 83
Blacklegs:
  assaults on, 25
  brought in by employers, 103, 105, 112,
  133, 142
  in Canada, 228, 230, 237, 239, 243
  in eighteenth century, 13
Blacklist, 103, 105
Blackstone, Wm., 213, 224
Blackwood, 211
Blainey, Geoffrey, 278
Board of Trade, 89, 137
  President of, 43, 120
Boer War, 69
Bohemia, 45, 110
Bonar Law, 71, 71–2
Bookbinders, 101
Boot and shoe industry, 109